(continued from front page)

" I just wanted to thank you for helping me get a great score
on the AP U.S. History exam... Thank you for making great test preps! "
Student, Los Angeles, CA

" Your *Fundamentals of Engineering Exam* book was the absolute best
preparation I could have had for the exam, and it is one of the major
reasons I did so well and passed the FE on my first try. "
Student, Sweetwater, TN

" I used your book to prepare for the test and found that the advice and the
sample tests were highly relevant... Without using any other material, I earned
very high scores and will be going to the graduate school of my choice. "
Student, New Orleans, LA

" What I found in your book was a wealth of information sufficient to shore up
my basic skills in math and verbal... The section on analytical ability was
excellent. The practice tests were challenging and the answer explanations most
helpful. It certainly is the *Best Test Prep for the GRE!* "
Student, Pullman, WA

" I really appreciate the help from your excellent book. Please keep up
the great work. "
Student, Albuquerque, NM

" I am writing to thank you for your test preparation... your book helped me
immeasurably and I have nothing but praise for your *GRE* preparation."
Student, Benton Harbor, MI

THE BEST TEST PREPARATION FOR THE

CLEP

Western Civilization I

Robert Ziomkowski
(Cornell University, Ph.D.)

Research & Education Association
Visit our website at
www.rea.com

Research & Education Association
61 Ethel Road West
Piscataway, New Jersey 08854
E-mail: info@rea.com

The Best Test Preparation for the
CLEP WESTERN CIVILIZATION I EXAM

Published 2011

Copyright © 2006 by Research & Education Association, Inc. All rights reserved. No part of this book may be reproduced in any form without permission of the publisher.

Printed in the United States of America

Library of Congress Control Number 2005932918

ISBN-13: 978-0-7386-0110-6
ISBN-10: 0-7386-0110-1

REA® is a registered trademark of Research & Education Association, Inc.

K10

About the Author

Robert Ziomkowski, Ph.D., received a postdoctoral degree at the Pontifical Institute of Mediaeval Studies, Toronto, in 2002. He earned his doctorate in History from Cornell University in 2000. Dr. Ziomkowski's teaching repertoire includes courses in western civilization, medieval history, ancient history, science in the western tradition, Islamic civilization and Latin, as well as seminars on witchcraft and heresy, the soul in medieval culture, and paleography. His current research focuses on the medieval reception of ancient Greek science, especially as seen in commentaries on the creation narratives in the Book of Genesis and Plato's *Timaeus*. Dr. Ziomkowski's publications include a monograph on a controversial medieval thinker, *Manegold of Lautenbach: Liber contra Wolfelmum* (Louvain: Peeters Press, 2002; Dallas Medieval Texts and Translations, vol. 1), as well as articles in *The Journal of Neoplatonic Studies* and Scribner's *New Dictionary of the History of Ideas*. In 2002–2003 he curated an exhibition of Cornell University's medieval manuscripts and published an online version, *From Manuscript to Print: The Evolution of the Medieval Book* (http://rmc.library.cornell.edu/medievalbook/). He currently teaches at Ithaca College.

About Research & Education Association

Founded in 1959, Research & Education Association (REA) is dedicated to publishing the finest and most effective educational materials—including software, study guides, and test preps—for students in middle school, high school, college, graduate school, and beyond.

REA's Test Preparation series includes books and software for all academic levels in almost all disciplines. REA publishes test preps for students who have not yet entered high school, as well as high school students preparing to enter college. Students from countries around the world seeking to attend college in the United States will find the assistance they need in REA's publications. For college students seeking advanced degrees, REA publishes test preps for many major graduate school admission examinations in a wide variety of disciplines, including engineering, law, and medicine. Students at every level, in every field, with every ambition can find what they are looking for among REA's publications.

REA's series presents tests that accurately depict the official exams in both degree of difficulty and types of questions. REA's practice tests are always based upon the most recently administered exams, and include every type of question that can be expected on the actual exams.

REA's publications and educational materials are highly regarded and continually receive an unprecedented amount of praise from professionals, instructors, librarians, parents, and students. Our authors are as diverse as the subject matter represented in the books we publish. They are well known in their respective disciplines and serve on the faculties of prestigious colleges and universities throughout the United States and Canada.

We invite you to visit us at *www.rea.com* to find out how "REA is making the world smarter."

Acknowledgments

In addition to our author, we would like to thank Larry B. Kling, Vice President, Editorial, for his overall guidance, which brought this publication to completion; Pam Weston, Vice President, Publishing, for setting the quality standards for production integrity and managing the publication to completion; Diane Goldschmidt, Associate Editor, for managing content development; and Dr. Larissa Taylor, Colby College, for reviewing the manuscript. Our cover was designed by Christine Saul.

We also gratefully acknowledge the team at Publication Services for page composition, proofreading, and pre-production file mapping.

CONTENTS

About the Author..v

About Research & Education Association...v

Acknowledgments.. vi

Independent Study Schedule:
CLEP Western Civilization I xi

Passing the CLEP Western Civilization I Exam.............................. xiii

    About this Book xv
    About the Exam xv
    How to Use this Book xvii
    Format and Content of the CLEP xvii
    About Our Course Review xviii
    Scoring Your Practice Tests xviii
    Practice-Test Raw Score Conversion Table........................ xix
    Studying for the CLEP xx
    Test-Taking Tips..xx
    The Day of the Exam xxi

Chapter 1   The Ancient Near East..1

    Western and Near Eastern Civilizations................................3
    The Fertile Crescent..3
    Mesopotamia..5
    Mesopotamian Culture...7
    Egypt and the Nile..8
    Egyptian Culture...10
    The Spread of Civilization..12
    The Hittites..12
    The Sea Peoples 13

The Minoans 13
The Mycenaeans 14
The Phoenicians 15
The Assyrians..16
The Neo-Babylonians (Chaldeans) 17
The Persians 17
The Hebrews 19

Chapter 2   Ancient Greece 23

The Mycenaean Bronze Age (c. 2300–1100 B.C.E.) 25
The Dark Age (c. 1100–800 B.C.E.) 25
The Archaic Period (c. 800–500 B.C.E.) 26
Sparta 27
Athens 28
The Persian Wars...30
Periclean Athens...31
The Peloponnesian War (431–404 B.C.E.) 33
Greek Classical Culture 34
Religion..34
Literature..35
Art and Architecture..40
The Hellenistic Age..41
Hellenistic Culture 43

Chapter 3   Ancient Rome 45

The Republic..47
The Empire..52
Literature..53
Art, Architecture, and Engineering....................................55
Religion..56
The Jews in the Roman Empire 58
Christianity...59
Reorganization of the Empire 63
The Germanic Invasions 64
The Late Empire 67
The Fall of Rome 69

Chapter 4   The Middle Ages 71

The Byzantine Empire 73
Islam..74

Byzantium to 1000 B.C.E. 77
The Germanic Kingdoms 77
The Medieval Church 81
Feudalism and Manorialism 84
Population Growth 86
Trade and Towns 87
Church and State 88
The Rise of Centralized Monarchies 90
The Holy Roman Empire 91
England 92
France 94
The Hundred Years' War (1337–1453) 95
Spain 96
Eastern Europe 97
The Church in the Late Middle Ages 98
The Medieval Cultural Tradition 105
The Intellectual Tradition 106
The Vernacular Tradition 110
The Black Death 112
Architecture and Art 113

Chapter 5   Renaissance and Reformation 115

The Italian Renaissance 117
Florence 118
Italian Politics 119
Art and Architecture 120
Literature 122
Economic Innovations 122
The Northern Renaissance 123
Christian Humanism 124
The Protestant Reformation 125
Diversification of Protestantism 127
The Catholic Reformation 129
The New Monarchies 130

Chapter 6   Early Modern Europe 133

The Age of Exploration 135
The Commercial Revolution 138
Nation-States and Wars of Religion 141
France 141

Spain 142
England 142
Dutch Independence..144
The Thirty Years' War..144
A Revolution in World View 146
Modernity...149

Practice Test 1 151
Test 1 153
Answer Key...195
Detailed Explanations of Answers 196

Practice Test 2 235
Test 2 237
Answer Key...278
Detailed Explanations of Answers 279

Bibliography 315

Answer Sheets...317

Index..319

CLEP WESTERN CIVILIZATION I
Independent Study Schedule

The following study schedule allows for thorough preparation for the CLEP Western Civilization I. Although it is designed for four weeks, it can be reduced to a two-week course by collapsing each two-week period into one. Be sure to set aside enough time—at least two hours each day—to study. But no matter which study schedule works best for you, the more time you spend studying, the more prepared and relaxed you will feel on the day of the exam.

Week	Activity
1	Read and study the Introduction section of this book, which will introduce you to the CLEP Western Civilization I exam. Then take Practice Test 1 to determine your strengths and weaknesses. Assess your results by using our raw score conversion table. You can then determine the areas in which you need to strengthen your skills.
2 & 3	Carefully read and study the Western Civilization I review included in Chapters 1 through 6 of this book.
4	Take Practice Test 2 and carefully review the explanations for all incorrect answers. If there are any types of questions or particular subjects that seem difficult to you, review those subjects by studying again the appropriate sections of the Western Civilization I review.

Note: If you care to, and time allows, retake Practice Tests 1 and 2. This will help strengthen the areas in which your performance may still be lagging and build your overall confidence.

▼

INTRODUCTION

Passing the CLEP Western Civilization I Exam

Introduction

PASSING THE CLEP WESTERN CIVILIZATION I EXAM

ABOUT THIS BOOK

This book provides you with complete preparation for the CLEP Western Civilization I exam. Inside you will find a concise review of the subject matter, as well as tips and strategies for test-taking. We also give you two full-length practice tests, which are based on the official CLEP Western Civilization I exam. Our practice tests contain every type of question that you can expect to encounter on the actual exam. Following each practice test you will find an answer key with detailed explanations designed to help you more completely understand the test material.

All CLEP exams are computer-based. As you can see, the practice tests in our book are presented as paper-and-pencil exams. Even so, the content and format of the actual CLEP subject exam are faithfully mirrored. We detail the format and content of the CLEP Western Civilization I on pages xvii–xviii.

ABOUT THE EXAM

Who takes the CLEP Western Civilization I and what is it used for?

CLEP (College-Level Examination Program) examinations are typically taken by people who have acquired knowledge outside the classroom and wish to bypass certain college courses and earn college credit. The CLEP is designed to reward students for learning—no matter where or how that knowledge was acquired. The CLEP is the most widely accepted credit-by-examination program in the country, with more than 2,900 colleges and universities granting credit for satisfactory scores on CLEP exams.

Although most CLEP examinees are adults returning to college, many graduating high school seniors, enrolled college students, military personnel, and international students also take the exams to earn college credit or to demonstrate their ability to perform at the college level. There are no prerequisites, such as age or educational status, for taking CLEP examinations. However, because policies on granting credits vary among colleges, you should contact the particular institution from which you wish to receive CLEP credit.

There are two categories of CLEP examinations:

1. **CLEP General Examinations,** which are five separate tests that cover material usually taken as requirements during the first two years of college. CLEP General Examinations are available for College Composition and College Composition Modular, Humanities, Mathematics, Natural Sciences, and Social Sciences and History.

2. **CLEP Subject Examinations,** which include material usually covered in an undergraduate course with a similar title. For a complete list of the subject examinations offered, visit the College Board website.

Who administers the exam?

The CLEP tests are developed by the College Board, administered by Educational Testing Service (ETS), and involve the assistance of educators throughout the United States. The test development process is designed and implemented to ensure that the content and difficulty level of the test are appropriate.

When and where is the exam given?

The CLEP Western Civilization I is administered each month throughout the year at more than 1,400 test centers in the United States and can be arranged for candidates abroad on request. To find the test center nearest you and to register for the exam, you should obtain a copy of the free booklets *CLEP Colleges* and *CLEP Information for Candidates and Registration Form.* They are available at most colleges where CLEP credit is granted, or by contacting:

CLEP Services
P.O. Box 6600
Princeton, NJ 08541-6600
Phone: (800) 257-9558 (8 a.m. to 6 p.m. ET, Monday – Friday)
Email: clep@info.collegeboard.org
Website: *www.collegeboard.com/clep*

CLEP Options for Military Personnel and Veterans

CLEP exams are available free of charge to eligible military personnel and eligible civilian employees. All the CLEP exams are available at test centers on college campuses and military bases. In addition, the College Board has developed a paper-based version of 14 high-volume/high-pass-rate CLEP tests for DANTES Test Centers. Contact the Educational Services Officer or Navy College Education Specialist for more information. Visit the College Board website for details about CLEP opportunities for military personnel.

Eligible U.S. veterans can claim reimbursement for CLEP exams and administration fees pursuant to provisions of the Veterans Benefits Improvement Act of 2004. For details on eligibility and submitting a claim for reimbursement, visit the U.S. Department of Veterans Affairs website at *www.gibill.va.gov/pamphlets/testing.htm*.

CLEP marks a special sweet spot with reference to the new Post-9/11 GI Bill, which applies to veterans returning from the Iraq and Afghanistan theaters of operation. Because the GI Bill provides tuition for up to 36 months, racking up college credits by testing out of general introductory courses with CLEP exams expedites academic progress and degree completion within the funded timeframe.

SSD Accommodations for Students with Disabilities

Many students qualify for extra time to take the CLEP Western Civilization I exam, but you must make these arrangements in advance. For information, contact:

College Board Services for Students with Disabilities
P.O. Box 6226
Princeton, NJ 08541-6226
Phone: (609) 771-7137 Mon.–Fri. 8 A.M. to 6 P.M. (Eastern time)
TTY: (609) 882-4118
Fax: (609) 771-7944
E-mail: ssd@info.collegeboard.org

HOW TO USE THIS BOOK

What do I study first?

Read over the course review and the suggestions for test-taking, take the first practice test to determine your area(s) of weakness, and then go back and focus your study on those specific problems. Studying the reviews thoroughly will reinforce the basic skills you will need to do well on the exam. Make sure to take the practice tests to become familiar with the format and procedures involved with taking the actual exam.

To best utilize your study time, follow our Independent Study Schedule, which you'll find in the front of this book. The schedule is based on a four-week program, but can be condensed to two weeks if necessary by collapsing each two-week period into one.

When should I start studying?

It is never too early to start studying for the CLEP Western Civilization I. The earlier you begin, the more time you will have to sharpen your skills. Do not procrastinate! Cramming is *not* an effective way to study, since it does not allow you the time needed to learn the test material. The sooner you learn the format of the exam, the more time you will have to familiarize yourself with it.

FORMAT AND CONTENT OF THE CLEP

The CLEP Western Civilization I covers the material one would be taught in the first semester of a two-semester course in Western Civilization. The exam questions deal with the civilizations of Ancient Greece, Rome and the Near East; the Middle Ages; the Renaissance and Reformation; and Early Modern Europe.

The exam consists of 120 multiple-choice questions, each with five possible answer choices, to be answered within 90 minutes.

The approximate breakdown of topics is as follows:

8–10%   Ancient Near East

15–17%   Ancient Greece and Hellenistic Civilization

15–17%   Ancient Rome

23–27%   Medieval History

13–17%   Renaissance and Reformation

10–15%   Early Modern Europe, 1560–1648

ABOUT OUR COURSE REVIEW

The review in this book provides you with a complete background of all the important persons, events and developments of Western Civilization from ancient times through the first half of the seventeenth century. It will help reinforce the facts you have already learned while better shaping your

PRACTICE-TEST RAW SCORE CONVERSION TABLE *

Raw Score	Scaled Score	Course Grade	Raw Score	Scaled Score	Course Grade
100 & up	80	A	48	49	C
99	80	A	47	49	C
98	80	A	46	48	C
97	79	A	45	48	C
96	79	A	44	47	C
95	78	A	43	47	C
94	78	A	42	47	C
93	77	A	41	47	C
92	77	A	40	46	D
91	76	A	39	46	D
90	75	A	38	45	D
89	74	A	37	45	D
88	73	A	36	44	D
87	73	A	35	44	D
86	72	A	34	43	D
85	72	A	33	43	D
84	71	A	32	42	D
83	70	A	31	41	D
82	70	A	30	40	F
81	69	A	29	39	F
80	69	A	28	38	F
79	68	A	27	37	F
78	67	A	26	36	F
77	66	A	25	35	F
76	66	A	24	34	F
75	65	A	23	34	F
74	64	A	22	33	F
73	63	A	21	33	F
72	63	A	20	32	F
71	62	A	19	32	F
70	61	A	18	31	F
69	61	A	17	31	F
68	60	A	16	30	F
67	59	A	15	29	F
66	59	A	14	28	F
65	58	B	13	28	F
64	57	B	12	27	F
63	57	B	11	27	F
62	56	B	10	26	F
61	56	B	9	25	F
60	55	B	8	24	F
59	55	B	7	23	F
58	54	B	6	22	F
57	54	B	5	21	F
56	53	B	4	20	F
55	53	B	3	20	F
54	52	B	2	20	F
53	52	B	1	20	F
52	51	C			
51	51	C			
50	50	C			
49	50	C			

*This table is provided for scoring REA practice tests only. The American Council on Education recommends that colleges use a single across-the-board credit-granting score of 50 for all CLEP computer-based exams. Nonetheless, on account of the different skills being measured and the unique content requirements of each test, the actual number of correct answers needed to reach 50 will vary. A 50 is calibrated to equate with performance that would warrant the grade C in the corresponding introductory college course.

understanding of the discipline as a whole. By using the review in conjunction with the practice tests, you should be well prepared to take the CLEP Western Civilization I.

SCORING YOUR PRACTICE TESTS

How do I score my practice tests?

The CLEP Western Civilization I is scored on a scale of 20 to 80. To score your practice tests, count up the number of correct answers. This is your total raw score. Convert your raw score to a scaled score using the conversion table on the previous page. **(Note: The conversion table provides only an *estimate* of your scaled score. Scaled scores can and do vary over time, and in no case should a sample test be taken as a precise predictor of test performance. Nonetheless, our scoring table allows you to judge your level of performance within a reasonable scoring range.)**

When will I receive my score report?

The test administrator will print out a full Candidate Score Report for you immediately upon your completion of the exam (except for CLEP College Composition and College Composition Modular). Your scores are reported only to you, unless you ask to have them sent elsewhere. If you want your scores reported to a college or other institution, you must say so when you take the examination. Since your scores are kept on file for 20 years, you can also request transcripts from Educational Testing Service at a later date.

STUDYING FOR THE CLEP

It is very important for you to choose the time and place for studying that works best for you. Some students may set aside a certain number of hours every morning, while others may choose to study at night before going to sleep. Other students may study during the day, while waiting on a line, or even while eating lunch. Only you can determine when and where your study time will be most effective. But be consistent and use your time wisely. Work out a study routine and stick to it!

When you take the practice tests, try to make your testing conditions as much like the actual test as possible. Turn your television and radio off, and sit down at a quiet table free from distraction. Make sure to time yourself. Start off by setting a timer for the time that is allotted for each section, and be sure to reset the timer for the appropriate amount of time when you start a new section.

As you complete each practice test, score your test and thoroughly review the explanations to the questions you answered incorrectly; however, do not review too much at one time. Concentrate on one problem area at a time by reviewing the question and explanation, and by studying our review until you are confident that you completely understand the material.

Keep track of your scores and mark them on the Scoring Worksheet. By doing so, you will be able to gauge your progress and discover general weaknesses in particular sections. You should carefully study the reviews that cover your areas of difficulty, as this will build your skills in those areas.

TEST-TAKING TIPS

Although you may not be familiar with computer-based standardized tests such as the CLEP Western Civilization I, there are many ways to acquaint yourself with this type of examination and to help alleviate your test-taking anxieties. Listed below are ways to help you become accustomed to the CLEP, some of which may be applied to other standardized tests as well.

Know the format of the test. CLEP exams are not adaptive but rather fixed-length tests. In a sense, this makes them kin to the familiar paper-and-pencil exam in that you have the same flexibility to go back and review your work in each section. Moreover, the format isn't a great deal different from the paper-and-pencil CLEP.

Read all of the possible answers. Just because you think you have found the correct response, do not automatically assume that it is the best answer. Read through each choice to be sure that you are not making a mistake by jumping to conclusions.

Use the process of elimination. Go through each answer to a question and eliminate as many of the answer choices as possible. By eliminating just two answer choices, you give yourself a better chance of getting the item correct, since there will only be three choices left from which to make your guess. Remember, your score is based only on the number of questions you answer *correctly*.

Work quickly and steadily. You will have only 90 minutes to work on 120 questions, so work quickly and steadily to avoid focusing on any one question too long. Taking the practice tests in this book will help you learn to budget your time.

Acquaint yourself with the computer screen. Familiarize yourself with the CLEP computer screen beforehand by logging on to the College Board website. Waiting until test day to see what it looks like in the pretest tutorial risks experiencing needless anxiety into your testing experience. Also, familiarizing yourself with the directions and format of the exam will save you valuable time on the day of the actual test.

Be sure that your answer registers before you go to the next item. Look at the screen to see that your mouse-click causes the pointer to darken the proper oval. This takes less effort than darkening an oval on paper, but don't lull yourself into taking less care!

THE DAY OF THE EXAM

Preparing for the CLEP

On the day of the test, you should wake up early (hopefully after a decent night's rest) and have a good breakfast. Make sure to dress comfortably, so that you are not distracted by being too hot or too cold while taking the test. Also plan to arrive at the test center early. This will allow you to collect your thoughts and relax before the test, and will also spare you the anxiety that comes with being late. As an added incentive to make sure you arrive early, keep in mind that no one will be allowed into the test session after the test has begun.

Before you leave for the test center, make sure that you have your admission form and another form of identification, which must contain a recent photograph, your name, and signature (i.e., driver's license, student identification card, or current alien registration card). You will not be admitted to the test center if you do not have proper identification.

If you would like, you may wear a watch to the test center. However, you may not wear one that makes noise, because it may disturb the other test-takers. No dictionaries, textbooks, notebooks, briefcases, or packages will be permitted and drinking, smoking, and eating are prohibited.

Good luck on the CLEP Western Civilization I exam!

CHAPTER 1

The Ancient Near East

Chapter 1

THE ANCIENT NEAR EAST

WESTERN AND NEAR EASTERN CIVILIZATIONS

Western Civilization arose in southeastern Europe. Its earliest representatives were the ancient Greeks. Civilization itself first appeared in the ancient Near East, in a region known as the Fertile Crescent. The cultures that flourished there exerted important influences on the rise and later course of Western Civilization.

THE FERTILE CRESCENT

Valleys and Cities. The Fertile Crescent is an area of river valleys in the generally arid Near East where rainfall and drainage is sufficient to ensure the growth of crops. It stretches in a semi-circular band from the Tigris-Euphrates valley (in modern Iraq) northwest into Syria, then south along the shore of the Mediterranean sea toward the Nile river valley in Egypt. (Civilizations also appeared to the east somewhat later, in the Indus river valley in India and the Yellow river valley in China.) The favorable conditions for agriculture afforded by these river valleys encouraged population growth and enabled the people living in them to devote some of their time to pursuits other than raising food. These people became better organized than their contemporaries who lived in other parts of the world, and they began to congregate in cities, which were in essence spaces to facilitate economic interactions. With the appearance of cities, civilization was born. (The word "civilization" is related to the Latin word *civitas*, which means "city" or "community.") Since the inhabitants of a city do not produce their own food but are engaged in specialized trades, cities cannot support themselves, and thus exist only where agriculture is successful enough to produce a surplus, which the urban population purchases. Thus, cities first arose only where especially favorable conditions existed for raising food, and these conditions were first attained in river valleys at a time when the culture of human beings had risen to a certain level of sophistication.

The Old Stone Age. Cities could not have arisen without certain preceding innovations. During the earliest phase of technological progress, known as the Paleolithic Age (or Old Stone Age), human beings lived as nomads in small communities, hunting and gathering fruits for their sustenance, and using fire and crude implements fashioned principally from stone and wood to assist in the struggle for survival. The most advanced tool of the time was the bow and arrow, which may have been in use by 25,000 B.C.E.

The New Stone Age. Around 8000 B.C.E., after the most recent retreat of the glaciers that covered large portions of Europe and North America, there occurred a cultural revolution that inaugurated the Neolithic Age (or New Stone Age), during which stone tools were refined, animals were domesticated, and agriculture was developed. Many human beings abandoned nomadism in favor of a settled way of life, as necessary for the practice of farming, and organized themselves in small villages. Agriculture aided greatly in the struggle against the ever-present threat of starvation, but it required a vast commitment of labor. Until very recent times, when advances in science and technology led to labor-saving breakthroughs in agricultural techniques, the vast majority of human beings had to be engaged in agriculture, and the surpluses produced were relatively meager, so that only a small percentage of the population could live in cities.

The Bronze Age. By the time human beings began to live in cities, they had discovered how to work metals. Tools were generally no longer made from stone but from an alloy of copper and tin, known as bronze. It should be noted that "Bronze Age" is, chronologically speaking, a relative term that differs from one culture to another, since different cultures transitioned from the use of stone to bronze implements at different times. In the Fertile Crescent, the Bronze Age began with the appearance of cities, around 3000 B.C.E.

Irrigation. In addition to cities and metal-working, two key features of civilization in the Fertile Crescent were irrigation and writing. It was the discovery of irrigation that gave people living in the river valleys an advantage over people who practiced farming in the highlands. Without irrigation, a period of drought could lead to famine. Irrigation, in contrast, offered protection against drought (since water could be diverted from the river into fields nearby) and ensured a higher yield of crops (since variations in rainfall had less of an effect on growth). Since surpluses were greater and were generally maintained at a more constant level, agriculture in river valleys made cities viable in the long term.

Writing. As noted above, cities were essentially places that facilitated the exchange of goods, and were, therefore, primarily an economic development. In order to keep track of business transactions, people needed a method of keeping records. Writing developed to meet this need. Thus, although it was eventually put to many uses, its most prevalent early use was economic. Writing was also used by rulers to keep records, so cities became centers of political administration as well as economic focal points.

History and Prehistory. History itself begins with writing, which preserves details about a given culture at a certain moment in time with a fairly high degree of accuracy. All events prior to the advent of writing in a given culture are prehistoric and can only be inferred on the basis of archaeological evidence and legends (which were initially passed down by oral tradition and only later preserved in writing). Thus events during the Stone Ages are mostly hypothetical and imprecise, but events from the Bronze Age in the Fertile Crescent and later—beginning about five thousand years ago, when human beings in the region began to write—offer a much greater degree of certainty and detail. Nevertheless, the written record at this time is neither complete nor unambiguous, so it is important to supplement it with archaeology and mythology.

MESOPOTAMIA

Sumer. The earliest cities arose about 3200 B.C.E. in the Tigris-Euphrates valley, known as Mesopotamia (which means "land between the rivers"). In the southern region of Mesopotamia, called Sumer after the culture of its inhabitants, these cities became small states that governed areas about 10 miles in diameter and fought among themselves over the control of water. As the stronger Sumerian city-states conquered the weaker, larger political units were established and these fought one another on a larger scale, in an effort to unify the entire valley under their own control. Unification of the entire river-valley was desirable because it would lead to more efficient use of the river systems for agriculture, and conflict arose because one city-state was unwilling to surrender its sovereignty to another to achieve this goal.

Akkadians. A semi-nomadic people known as the Akkadians, who spoke a Semitic language, began to leave the deserts west of Mesopotamia and settle in the central region of the Tigris-Euphrates valley during the fourth millennium B.C.E. These Akkadians, led by their king Sargon (c. 2371–2316 B.C.E.), conquered the various Sumerian city-states and established an empire that unified Mesopotamia and reached beyond its boundaries, into the Iranian plateau in the east and as far west as Lebanon. Sargon's dynasty ruled Akkad and Sumer for about 200 years.

Third Dynasty of Ur. Many Sumerians resented the Akkadian attempt to dominate them, and around 2100 B.C.E. the Sumerian city of Ur attained control of Mesopotamia, after the Akkadian empire had been weakened by foreign invasions. This Third Dynasty of Ur ruled for about 100 years. Dissension led to a period of chaos during which no single dynasty controlled the entire region (c. 2000–1900 B.C.E.). By the time unity was restored, the Sumerians had lost their identity as a distinct group.

Amorites (Old Babylonian Dynasty). Mesopotamia was once again unified, this time by a people known as the Amorites. Their empire is known as the Old Babylonian, since they established their capital at Babylon, on the Euphrates. They ruled for about 300 years, from around 1900 to 1600 B.C.E. Their greatest king was Hammurabi (c. 1792–1750 B.C.E.), who is famous for his law code. Hammurabi's Code was a collection of old and new legal judgments, resulting in the most comprehensive body of law from ancient Mesopotamia. The code prescribed harsh punishments for violators, according to the principle "an eye for an eye, a tooth for a tooth." Like other Mesopotamian kings, Hammurabi claimed to be a representative of the gods, from whom he derived his authority. His code was intended to provide stability in a hierarchical society, with the king at the top of the social pyramid, the warrior aristocracy and priesthood on a level below him, freemen (such as peasants and merchants) below the nobles and priests, and slaves at the bottom. Slaves might be foreigners conquered in war or Mesopotamian citizens who could not pay off their debts. Slavery was often temporary, for freemen who fell into debt became slaves until they paid off what they owed by means of physical labor; they were also allowed to do business and own property, and they might thereby buy their freedom. Hammurabi's Code dealt principally with legislation regarding the family (regulating divorce and inheritance), the ownership of land, and commercial transactions.

Hittites, Kassites, and Hurrians. The Old Babylonian empire disintegrated around 1600 B.C.E. after it was attacked by two different groups of invaders: Hittites from Anatolia (Asia Minor) in the north and Kassites from the east (the region that is now Iran). Although the Hittites merely plundered the Old Babylonian empire and returned home with the spoils of war, the Kassites established themselves as rulers for 300 years. Another group, the Hurrians, established the kingdom of Mitanni in the upper Tigris-Euphrates valley around 1500 B.C.E.; it lasted until about 1400 B.C.E., when the Hittites conquered the Hurrians.

MESOPOTAMIAN CULTURE

Cuneiform. As noted earlier, writing was at first primarily used to keep track of goods. As early as 8000 B.C.E., tokens appear to have been used for this purpose. By about 3000 B.C.E., the Sumerians replaced these tokens with marks impressed on clay tablets, utilizing a stylus that created wedge-shaped strokes. Such script is called "cuneiform" (from the Latin *cuneus*, or "wedge"). The marks were initially pictographs, or symbols representing physical objects. These marks were later joined by ideograms, or symbols representing ideas. The symbols became even more abstract when the marks began to be used phonetically, signifying not an object or idea but the sounds of spoken words. Mesopotamian cuneiform was a combination of pictographs and ideograms that signified entire words, and phonetic symbols that represented the sounds of distinct syllables. Since the phonetic symbols represented entire syllables rather than individual sounds, Mesopotamian cuneiform did not employ an alphabet (whose components are letters) but a syllabary (whose components are syllables). Because the Mesopotamian cuneiform system required the memorization of over 600 symbols, it was difficult to learn and its use was largely restricted to a class of professional scribes. The cuneiform used by the Sumerians was later adopted by the Akkadians and eventually adapted for use with many other Near Eastern languages as well. Although cuneiform was used initially for economic and administrative documents, it later also served the needs of religion and literature.

Mathematics. Cuneiform tablets indicate that numbers were calculated on a sexagesimal, or base 60, system (which is still in use today for keeping time: hence, there are 60 minutes in an hour and 60 seconds in a minute). The year was divided into 12 months, but these months were based on the cycle of the moon's phases of approximately 30 days; consequently, a thirteenth month was inserted every few years to keep the calendar in step with the seasons.

Engineering. Mesopotamian civilization could not have arisen if it had not first acquired the ability to construct canals for irrigation and flood-control. Yet perhaps the most important of Mesopotamian achievements in engineering was the wheel, which was invented between 3500 and 3000 B.C.E. The mathematical sophistication of the Mesopotamian peoples was coupled with their practical skill in engineering to create distinctive religious structures known as ziggurats, which were multi-terraced, pyramid-like constructions crowned with a temple at the summit.

Religion. The Sumerians and their successors worshipped an anthropomorphic pantheon of gods, who were thought to behave like human beings. Since these capricious and powerful beings wielded the forces of nature, they had to be appeased, lest their wrath destroy society. This danger was sensed especially in the violent floods that washed through the Tigris-Euphrates valley at irregular intervals. Consequently, the priesthood flourished, busy not only entreating the gods for mercy, but also attempting to foretell future events by practicing divination (studying the stars and the entrails of sacrificial animals for correlations in their patterns and natural events). Mesopotamian religion was mainly concerned with life in this world, for its view of the afterlife was uncertain and gloomy: the dead were thought to wander aimlessly in a shadowy netherworld.

Literature. The Sumerian epic poem known as *Gilgamesh*, inscribed about 2000 B.C.E. on twelve cuneiform tablets, describes the ill-fated quest of the hero Gilgamesh, the king of Uruk, in search of immortality. The Mesopotamian story of creation (presented in the epic poem *Enuma Elish*) and an account of a great flood (described in *Gilgamesh*) influenced the religions of the ancient Near East, including Judaism, as suggested by parallels between the biblical and pre-biblical accounts.

EGYPT AND THE NILE

Although civilization in Mesopotamia seems to have somewhat predated civilization in the Nile valley, the Egyptians unified the Nile valley before Sargon of Akkad imposed unity on Mesopotamia. Egyptian unity was also more stable and enduring, thanks in large measure to the geography of the region. The long, narrow valley of the Nile was bounded by vast deserts which armies could not cross. Thus, the Egyptians did not suffer numerous invasions from many directions, as the Mesopotamians did. There were essentially only two strategic directions that the Egyptians needed to defend: to the north, they had to guard the delta where the Nile joins the Mediterranean sea; and to the south, the upper reaches of the river.

Egyptian Dynasties. A series of thirty-one royal families, or dynasties, ruled Egypt over the course of its first 3,000 years of history, which is divided into the following periods: Archaic (or Early Dynastic), Old Kingdom, First Intermediate Period, Middle Kingdom, Second Intermediate Period, and New Kingdom. The dynasties came to an end with Cleopatra in 30 B.C.E., when the Romans incorporated Egypt into their empire. (Since historians often disagree on the precise dates for dividing these periods, the dates given below are only approximations. Likewise, the regnal dates of the kings are also subject to debate. Throughout this review, dates following the names of leaders generally indicate the years of their reign.) The kings of Egypt had the title "pharaoh," which in ancient Egyptian meant "great house," indicating the royal palace in which the ruler lived.

Archaic or Early Dynastic Period. The first two dynasties governed Egypt from about 3100 to 2700 B.C.E., during which time they unified the Nile valley. Unlike the Tigris and Euphrates, whose flooding was both unpredictable and violent, the Nile River flooded regularly and gently. Thus, the pharoah's priests were able to predict when flooding would take place, and this made it possible to tell the peasants the best time for planting. Under centralized government, the economy was carefully planned and led to a very efficient practice of agriculture. This prosperity strengthened the political and religious aura of the pharaoh.

Old Kingdom. The Old Kingdom lasted from about 2700 to 2200 B.C.E., during the Third to the Sixth dynasties, when the power of the pharaohs was supreme. At this time, the pharaohs were regarded not merely as representatives of the gods (as in Mesopotamia), but as gods themselves. Thus, ancient Egyptian government was a theocracy. The entire country was considered to be pharaoh's personal possession and its economy completely under his control. The greatest pyramids were constructed at this time, particularly during the Fourth Dynasty (at Giza), and were enormous tombs for the pharaohs and their families. Although at later times the pharaohs' claim to divinity was still recognized, later pharaohs did not enjoy as much power in relation to the Egyptian nobles and priests as they did during the Old Kingdom. Similarly, during the Old Kingdom, only pharaohs and their household were thought to be immortal. The belief in an afterlife led to the practice of embalming (mummification), for it was believed that the departed soul would need its body in its next life.

First Intermediate Period. From about 2200 to 2050 B.C.E., the pharaohs failed to assert themselves, with the result that the nobles, or "nomarchs" (the administrators of local districts, or *nomes*), effectively controlled the government. This decentralization of power led to civil wars. As the nomarchs vied with one another for supremacy, there was a lack of coordination in agriculture, resulting in widespread famine.

Middle Kingdom. From about 2050 to 1700 B.C.E., centralized government was restored and maintained in Egypt under the Eleventh and Twelfth dynasties. This period of stability ended when foreigners, known as the Hyksos, invaded the Nile delta and overran the Egyptian army in their horse-drawn chariots. The identity of the Hyksos is not certain.

Second Intermediate Period. The Hyksos dominated Egypt from about 1700 to 1550 B.C.E. Although they were strong in the Nile delta, they were unable to assert their control over the upper reaches of the valley. The Hyksos were finally expelled by a nobleman named Ahmose, who founded the Eighteenth dynasty and inaugurated the era of the New Kingdom.

New Kingdom. From about 1550 to 1100 B.C.E., under the Eighteenth to Twentieth dynasties, the Egyptian pharaohs reasserted their power and expanded beyond the traditional frontiers, reaching southward up the Nile River into Africa and sending armies northeastward across the Sinai peninsula into the Levant and Anatolia. The Egyptians hoped to prevent future invasions of the Nile valley by dominating the eastern shoreline of the Mediterranean (Palestine and Syria)—the direction from which the Hyksos had come. There the Egyptians came into conflict with the Hittites, who claimed the same territory. These two mighty empires fought a series of wars over the course of several centuries. Among their battles was one fought at Megiddo (1457 B.C.E.)—a place where so many battles were fought over the centuries that it became immortalized in the Christian Bible as the apocalyptic battlefield of "Armageddon." Egypt's wars with the Hittites did not result in a clear victory. After a great battle at Kadesh in 1274 B.C.E. failed to resolve the outcome, the two belligerents concluded a peace treaty.

EGYPTIAN CULTURE

Religion. Like the Mesopotamians, the Egyptians were polytheists, yet their gods were less anthropomorphic: some combined human and animal features—such as Anubis, the god of the dead, who was depicted with a human body and the head of a jackal, or Ra, the sun-god, depicted with a human body and the head of a hawk. Also in contrast to the Mesopotamians, the Egyptians regarded their pharaoh as a god; some Mesopotamian rulers achieved this level of veneration, but generally they were considered merely representatives of the gods. The Egyptians also practiced syncretism, whereby over time two different gods were regarded as a single god under two different aspects. For example, Amon, an important fertility god depicted as a ram, was later identified with Ra, the sun-god, and was then sometimes called Amon-Ra and regarded as the chief of the gods and the special patron of Egypt. Perhaps the most fundamental difference between Egyptian and Mesopotamian religion was in their views of the afterlife. While the Mesopotamians had a grim view of death, the Egyptians were optimistic that the soul could attain a happy immortality. They believed that embalming, or mummification, could provide the soul with a body for its existence after death. The Egyptian view of the afterlife changed over time. During the Old Kingdom, only the pharaoh and his family and nobles were mummified.

Later on, however, immortality was extended to everyone. In addition to mummification and burial in a tomb, it was important also to furnish the deceased with texts of incantations that would protect the soul from demons on its journey to the hall of judgment. There the god Osiris would weigh the soul, and if it was found virtuous (based on the moral quality of its life on earth), it would be granted a blissful immortality, as described in the *Book of the Dead*, a collection of prayers and spells concerned with the afterlife.

The Amarna Period. Although most of the pharaohs of the New Kingdom were warrior-kings preoccupied with foreign affairs, one important pharaoh of the Eighteenth dynasty turned his attention away from the wars on the borders and into the inner world of the spirit, fostering a revolutionary religious phase known as the "Amarna period" (named after the modern city, Amarna, where historical evidence of the event was found in the nineteenth century C.E.). This remarkable leader, Amenhotep IV, adopted the name Akhenaton (c. 1375–1358 B.C.E.) in accordance with his religious vision, for he singled out Aton, the disk of the sun (distinct from Ra or Amon-Ra), as the only god he would worship ("Akhen-aton" means "devoted to Aton"). He suppressed the worship of all the other gods and moved the capital from Thebes to a new city, Akhetaton, dedicated to the worship of Aton (near the site of modern-day Amarna). In focusing attention on the sun-disk god, Akhenaton drew religious authority away from the priests who advocated the worship of an entire pantheon of gods, and especially the most influential and powerful cult led by the priests of Amon. Akhenaton thus not only changed the national god of Egypt, but also took an important step in the direction of monotheism. However, the Egyptian priests resisted the reform and, after Akhenaton's death, had it abolished; it was forgotten for millennia until ancient texts describing Akhenaton's ill-fated reform were discovered at Amarna. The spirit of the Amarna period is reflected in a dramatic change of artistic style, which altered the depiction of the human body from the traditional, stiffly formal types and gave it a more dynamic, relaxed, and naturalistic quality. However, with the suppression of the cult of Aton, Egyptian art returned to earlier forms.

Architecture, Hieroglyphics, and the Calendar. The importance of religion and concern for the afterlife are clearly reflected in Egypt's monumental architecture. The pyramids, which were tombs befitting divine royalty, are only the most conspicuous of such monuments. The Egyptians later built magnificent subterranean tombs in cliff-faces, such as the Valley of the Kings at Thebes (where the tomb of Tutankhamen, the famous "King Tut," was discovered in 1922), or within temple complexes, such as the mortuary temple of Hatshepsut at Der-el-Bahri. Massive temples to honor the gods were constructed at Karnak and Luxor. These structures were adorned with sculptures (including sphinxes), paintings, and especially hieroglyphics, or "sacred writings," which were a form of pictograph. Hieroglyphics were used not only in religious architecture, but also for official and archival purposes. The latter were not carved in stone but written on papyrus, which was formed from reeds growing along the Nile (and from which the word "paper" is derived). Such texts reveal that the Egyptians used a 12-month solar calendar consisting of 30-month days, followed by 5 days added after the twelfth month, to total a nearly-accurate span of 365 days per year. (In the second century B.C.E., the Egyptians invented the practice of leap-years in order to correct the slight inaccuracy.) Although scholars have traditionally thought hieroglyphics were inspired by Mesopotamian cuneiform, the chronology has recently been questioned, and it is now supposed that hieroglyphics may have actually predated cuneiform. The two writing systems could have developed independently. Whatever their precise relationship, both forms of writing were in use by 3000 B.C.E.

THE SPREAD OF CIVILIZATION

Around 2000 B.C.E., civilization (that is, urban culture) began to spread beyond the river-valleys into the surrounding regions where social and political organization had not progressed beyond the level of the village. This extension was due in part to trade between adjacent centers of civilization, and in part to imperialistic expansion.

THE HITTITES

At the time the Hittites invaded the Old Babylonian empire (c. 1600 B.C.E.), they had lived in Anatolia for several centuries. Unlike most of the other peoples of the ancient Near East, who spoke Semitic languages, the Hittites spoke an Indo-European language; they seem to have migrated into the region from the north. After establishing their empire in Anatolia, this warlike people raided the wealthy regions to the south, most notably bringing the Amorite dynasty of the Old Babylonian empire to ruin about 1600 B.C.E. Later the Hittites came into conflict with the Egyptians in Syria and Palestine, waging a series of wars which left both sides so weakened that they agreed to share power in the region as a border-territory and signed the first international peace treaty in history to formalize their agreement. Thus, by the thirteenth century B.C.E. in the eastern Mediterranean region, rival centers of civilization that had expanded to the point of coming into uneasy contact with one another had established an international system of coexistence.

THE SEA PEOPLES

The Near Eastern diplomatic settlement achieved by the Egyptians and Hittites lasted only a short while. The balance of power between these two great empires was upset by a series of incursions from peoples living in the less civilized lands beyond their borders. The precise origin and identity of these raiders is uncertain: the Egyptians simply called them the "Sea Peoples." They may have been motivated by famine (perhaps precipitated by changes in climate) to raid the agricultural abundance that civilization had amassed. Whatever the motives of the invaders, they overthrew the empires of the eastern Mediterranean between about 1250 and 1150 B.C.E.

THE MINOANS

An important civilization contemporary to that of the Hittites and Egyptians was located on the isle of Crete in the eastern Mediterranean. The history of this Cretan civilization is shrouded in mystery, but it has been reconstructed to a considerable degree on the basis of archaeology, with some help from mythology. It is called "Minoan" after the Greek myth of King Minos of Crete, who was said to have constructed a labyrinth to imprison his wife's monstrous son, the Minotaur. Although Minoan writings have been discovered, they have been of relatively little use to scholars. One of the scripts, a syllabary known as Linear B, is actually an early form of Greek and implies that the early Greeks invaded and occupied Crete toward the end of Minoan history. The other Minoan script, known as Linear A, has not been deciphered. It almost certainly represents the language spoken by the Minoans, but there is no way of determining what is recorded in the surviving texts.

The Minoans were flourishing on Crete by 2000 B.C.E. Relying on a powerful navy, whose ships were armed with rams for sinking enemy vessels, the Minoans forged a maritime empire by dominating the peoples living on the shores of the Aegean Sea. For centuries the fleet of the Minoans protected them from invaders so effectively that they did not feel a need to build defensive walls around their cities. The trade that the Minoans conducted between the Aegean peoples and the empires of the Hittites and Egyptians generated great wealth, and this wealth was used to build grand palaces, which often had plumbing and were decorated with frescoes depicting joyous and lively scenes, such as elegant women leading public rituals or young athletes leaping over charging bulls and participating in other sporting events. The lives of the Minoans seem to have been mostly peaceful and prosperous. However, even at their height, they sometimes suffered terrible natural disasters, including earthquakes, volcanic eruptions, and tidal waves. Although the Minoans quickly recovered from the earthquakes that destroyed their palaces around 1800 B.C.E., later disasters may have contributed to their eventual demise. An extraordinarily violent volcanic eruption around 1627 B.C.E. annihilated the Minoan colony on the island of Thera and spawned a tidal wave that slammed into Crete 70 miles away, destroying coastal settlements. Between about 1550 and 1375 B.C.E., the Cretan palaces were destroyed, probably by people from the Balkan peninsula (modern Greece) known as the Mycenaeans. Minoan civilization appears to have lingered on in isolated pockets until about 1200 B.C.E.

THE MYCENAEANS

The earliest villages on the Greek mainland appeared around 6500 B.C.E. The Cyclades islands in the Aegean sea were soon also settled, and by about 3000 B.C.E. the people living there were producing bronze implements and marble sculptures. Though the cultural background of these people is not known, they were probably not Greek, since it appears that the earliest speakers of Greek (an Indo-European language, like Hittite) migrated into the region about 2300 B.C.E. The early Greeks lived in small communities until about 1700 B.C.E., when increasing prosperity led to ambitious building projects. The greatest of the early Greek centers was Mycenae, where archaeologists have uncovered impressive royal burial sites filled with treasures. Scholars have named the mainland Greeks of this time "Mycenaeans" because the king of Mycenae appears to have exerted some measure of authority over the other Greek communities. The Mycenaeans amassed their wealth by trading with their neighbors in the eastern Mediterranean and sometimes raiding them as well. Eventually they challenged the Minoans for supremacy in the Aegean sea, invading and occupying Crete around 1550 B.C.E.

The Mycenaeans were at the height of their prosperity from about 1400 to 1200 B.C.E. Following their conquest of Crete, they adopted not only the Minoan form of writing, but also their system of economic management, which was based on the palace as an administrative center. The Mycenaeans were not united in the same way as their neighbors, the Egyptians and Hittites, but shared a common language and culture. Politically, they were divided among small kingdoms of heroic warriors who might band together from time to time for purposes of conquest under the leadership of the king of Mycenae. The legendary war against Troy seems to have been such an expedition. The vivid depiction of the legend in the Homeric epic poem, the *Iliad* (composed around 800 –750 B.C.E.), may be based on true events occurring around 1250 B.C.E. If so, the Trojan war was one of the last major undertakings of the Mycenaeans. Within a century, they fell prey to the Sea Peoples who devastated the empires of the eastern Mediterranean from about 1250 to 1150 B.C.E.

THE PHOENICIANS

After the demise of the great empires, small kingdoms flourished. This state of political fragmentation lasted until the Assyrian conquest of the Near East during the eighth and seventh centuries B.C.E. Among the many peoples who enjoyed autonomy from about 1150 to 750 B.C.E., one influential group was the Phoenicians, who were divided among a number of independent and often warring city-states (principally Tyre, Sidon, and Byblos) centered on the coast of what is now mostly Lebanon. The Phoenicians ventured out upon the Mediterranean in the wake of the Sea Peoples' raids and dominated maritime commerce for several centuries, broadcasting their cultural achievements by this means. Their influence was felt mainly in their dissemination of the alphabet, commerce, and colonization.

Alphabet. The Phoenicians were Canaanites, who spoke a Semitic language. Although they did not invent the alphabet—the first alphabet appeared by 1400 B.C.E. in nearby Ugarit, a city-state in Syria—they adapted it into a more usable form. The Ugaritic alphabet employed cuneiform script, but it differed from earlier writing systems because each symbol represented a single sound rather than an entire syllable or an entire word. It was a major advance because the whole writing system consisted of only 30 symbols that could represent any spoken word and therefore could easily be learned. The Phoenicians streamlined this alphabet by replacing the cumbersome cuneiform symbols with simpler letters that could be written more quickly (and by reducing the number of symbols to a mere 22). The Phoenicians' alphabet became the basis of later western alphabets, including the Greek, Roman, and Hebrew.

Commercial Contacts. The Phoenicians made a strong impression on the Greeks through their trading contacts. The word "Phoenician," in fact, is derived from the Greek word *phoinike*, which meant "purple" and referred to the dye that the Canaanites living along the coast manufactured from a species of shellfish and traded abroad. Furthermore, the Greek word for "book" (*biblion*) was borrowed from the name of the Phoenician city Byblos, the pre-eminent center for the production of writing materials in the ancient world. (The English word, *Bible*, is in turn derived from the Greek loanword.)

Colonization. The Phoenicians settled the island of Cyprus and then ventured out into the western Mediterranean, where they established an extensive array of colonies, beginning in the ninth century B.C.E., along the shores of North Africa, Malta, Sicily, Sardinia, the Balearic islands, and Iberia (modern Spain). The Phoenicians' trading ventures also took them beyond the Mediterranean, for they regularly visited Britain in order to acquire tin, which was needed to make bronze. According to Egyptian sources, the Phoenicians circumnavigated Africa in their explorations. The most important of the Phoenician colonies was Carthage, founded about 750 B.C.E. by Tyre. When the Phoenician homeland was overrun by the Assyrians, many colonies became independent while others accepted the authority of Carthage, which became the center of a powerful empire that threatened Rome during the third century B.C.E.

THE ASSYRIANS

Iron Age War Machine. The entire Near East was conquered from the eighth to seventh centuries B.C.E. by the Assyrians, who erupted from their homeland in northern Mesopotamia with an inexorable war machine. The Assyrians outfitted their armies with iron weapons, which were much more durable than bronze. The Hittites had first begun smelting iron, but the Assyrians more effectively ushered in the Iron Age by putting the new metal to extensive use. The Assyrians even developed engineering units to conduct siege warfare, so that no enemy could hold out for long against their armies, which conquered all of Mesopotamia, southern Anatolia, Syria, Palestine, and Egypt. By conquering Egypt in the 660s B.C.E., the Assyrians became the first power to control both the Nile and Tigris-Euphrates valleys.

Terror and Deportation. In order to hold their extensive empire together, the Assyrians applied a systematic policy of terror to discourage rebellion, becoming notorious in the ancient world for cruelty and brutal suppression of opposition. They boasted of their cruelty in their art—Assyrian relief sculptures often depict warlike scenes, such as the destruction of cities and the execution of insurrectionists. Their strategy included the deportation of rebellious populations, who would be replaced by Assyrian colonists. The purpose of deportation was to assimilate unruly subjects into Assyrian society and thereby make them lose any sense of national identity and desire for independence. The most famous example of Assyrian success with this policy was the fate of the Ten Lost Tribes of Israel, who vanished from history after their deportation.

Downfall. The Assyrians' far-flung empire did not last long. Their harsh methods were effective in the short term, but generated too much hatred among their subjects to ensure long-term stability; and by invading Egypt they had overextended themselves. When a new dynasty of the Babylonians raised a major revolt in Mesopotamia with help from the Medes (from the region of modern Iran), Assyrian terror was unable to arrest it. The Assyrians' capital at Nineveh on the Tigris river was conquered in 612 B.C.E. by these Neo-Babylonians, sometimes known as Chaldeans.

THE NEO-BABYLONIANS (CHALDEANS)

The Neo-Babylonian empire that arose late in the seventh century B.C.E. was much like the Assyrian in extent, although the Neo-Babylonians did not conquer Egypt. They were less brutal than the Assyrians but continued the policy of deporting rebellious populations. Most notable was the deportation of the Hebrew people living in the kingdom of Judah by Nebuchadnezzar II (605–562 B.C.E.), who brought them to Babylon as captives after he conquered Jerusalem. This exile is known as the Babylonian Captivity. Like the Assyrian empire, the Neo-Babylonian was short-lived. In less than a century after its founding, it was itself overthrown, falling in 539 B.C.E. to the Persian king, Cyrus the Great.

Cultural development was very important to the Neo-Babylonians, and they expressed their commitment to the arts and sciences by rebuilding Babylon on a lavish scale and by advancing the study of astronomy. While it is true that the Babylonian astronomers were also astrologers, and that divination was a central motive in their study of the heavens, nevertheless their observation of the stars and planets made an important contribution to the history of science. The restored city of Babylon surpassed its earlier greatness. King Nebuchadnezzar II built a magnificent temple as a gift for his Median wife—a ziggurat whose terraces were adorned with an assortment of trees and plants, irrigated by the Euphrates through a feat of engineering. This ancient wonder of the world was known as the Hanging Gardens. It has not survived, but an example of the building projects of Nebuchadnezzar II can be appreciated in the restoration of the Ishtar Gate (on display in Berlin). This massive rounded archway was decorated with a facade of colorful glazed bricks depicting dragons and bulls in alternating sequence, and it impressively suggests the grandeur of Nebuchadnezzar II's Babylon.

THE PERSIANS

Persia and Media. The Persian empire was founded by Cyrus the Great (559–530 B.C.E.) but is often called the Achaemenid empire after the name of the dynasty to which he belonged. When Cyrus came to power, his small kingdom on the northern shores of the Persian Gulf (in modern day Iran) was under the domination of the Median empire. Cyrus led the Persians in an uprising against the Medes and conquered them in 550 B.C.E. Cyrus proved to be an exceptional figure—he was not only a military genius, but also an enlightened ruler with an appreciation for the diversity of the cultures in the Fertile Crescent. Since the Medes were closely related to the Persians (both were Indo-European speakers who had migrated into the Near East together, perhaps around 1000 B.C.E.), Cyrus made them partners in his empire, establishing Media as his first *satrapy* (province).

Expansion. Over the next twenty years, Cyrus expanded his dominion until it dwarfed every Near Eastern empire that had gone before. In 547 B.C.E. he annexed Anatolia by defeating Croesus of Lydia, then turned east and established a defensible border against threats from central Asia. In 539 B.C.E. he conquered the Neo-Babylonians and established his control over their empire, which included Syria and Palestine. He died while campaigning on the eastern borders.

The Character of Cyrus the Great. An important factor for Cyrus' remarkable success was his moderation toward the vanquished and his toleration of the subject peoples, as well as his understanding of their psychology and his willingness to grant them vital concessions. For example, when Cyrus approached Babylon in battle array, he took advantage of an internal religious dispute among the Neo-Babylonians to achieve a bloodless victory: Cyrus identified himself as a friend of the traditional god Marduk, whose cult had been opposed by the unorthodox Neo-Babylonian king Narbonidus (556–539 B.C.E.). As a result, the people of Babylon opened their gates to him, preferring to abandon their oppressive native king in favor of a foreign ruler who would grant them religious freedom. Cyrus also reversed the Neo-Babylonian (and Assyrian) policy of destroying the identity of subject peoples through deportation. Thus, he permitted the Jews exiled in Babylon to return home to Jerusalem. Cyrus also adopted a policy of non-interference in local religious practice, allowed a limited form of local autonomy, and did not tax heavily.

Later Expansion. Cyrus' successors extended the borders of the Persian empire. Cambyses (530–522 B.C.E.) conquered Egypt and Libya. Darius (521–486 B.C.E.) added the Indus valley in the east and Thrace in the west. By conquering Thrace, the Persians crossed into Europe and came upon the borders of Greece. They intended to annex the Balkan peninsula, but the attempt led by Darius' successor, Xerxes (486–465 B.C.E.), ended in a stinging defeat that halted the westward expansion of the Persian empire. The empire lasted for two more centuries before it was conquered by a Hellenic army led by the Macedonian king, Alexander the Great (336–323 B.C.E.). The struggle between the Persians and Greeks was a defining moment in the rise of Western civilization.

Zoroastrianism. Although the Persian influence on Western civilization is not as great as it would have been had the Persians conquered the Greeks, their presence in the Near East left an important cultural legacy, mainly with regard to religion. In addition to respecting religious diversity, the Persians disseminated the ideas of their own religion, Zoroastrianism. The Persians were initially polytheists, but one of their prophets, Zoroaster (or Zarathustra), initiated a monotheistic turn in Persian theology, perhaps around 600 B.C.E. (although some scholars believe he may have lived as early as 1000 B.C.E.). Zoroaster taught that the god Ahura Mazda, who represented the forces of good and truth and light, was alone worthy of worship. Yet Zoroastrianism also posited an ethical dualism by viewing the universe as the site of a cosmic struggle between good and evil. Opposed to Ahura Mazda was Ahriman, the principle of evil, darkness, and lies. Human beings were caught up in this struggle and had to choose sides. Good would eventually triumph, and there would be a Last Judgment following a final battle, when those siding with Ahura Mazda would be rewarded with eternal bliss in heaven while those siding with Ahriman would suffer eternal torment in hell. These Zoroastrian ideas were well known in the Near East during the formative phases of both Christianity and Islam, and influenced Judaism as well.

THE HEBREWS

One of many small nations of the ancient Near East caught in the clash between empires, the Hebrews would hardly merit attention if it were not for the example of their tenacious survival in the face of daunting odds and the fact that their spiritual legacy of strict monotheism became a defining feature of Western civilization (mainly due to the spread of Christianity, which arose as a reform movement within the Hebrew tradition).

Patriarchs. The Hebrews claimed descent from a patriarch, Abraham, who lived in Mesopotamia and was instructed by Yahweh (God) to migrate to a promised land near the Mediterranean Sea. Abraham's migration is thought to have occurred between about 2000 and 1500 B.C.E. Abraham's grandson, Jacob—who was later called Israel—had twelve sons. These sons of Israel were identified by the Hebrews as the first leaders of the twelve tribes into which they were organized. During a period of economic hardship, the Hebrews entered Egypt as laborers, and there became slaves. They were liberated by the lawgiver, Moses, around 1275 B.C.E. and settled in the land where Abraham had dwelt.

Israel and Judah. The migration of the Hebrews to the land once occupied by Abraham's comparatively small household was not a simple homecoming, for the region was already occupied by Canaanites who had dwelt in the region even before the time of Abraham. Furthermore, the Hebrew migration occurred about the same time as the invasions of the Sea Peoples. One of these groups, the Philistines, settled along the coast in the region that is now known as the Gaza strip. (The word "Palestine," which was later applied to the whole area, is derived from "Philistine.") The Hebrews fought both the Canaanites and Philistines for space in which to live. In order to fight more effectively, the twelve tribes united under a single monarch, Saul (c. 1020–1004 B.C.E.). Saul's successor, David (1004–965 B.C.E.), secured the borders of the kingdom of Israel, establishing its capital at Jerusalem. In thanksgiving for the victory, David's son, Solomon (965–928 B.C.E.), built a magnificent temple to Yahweh in Jerusalem (on Mount Zion), but his extravagant rule aroused the animosity of his subjects. Soon after Solomon's death, the Hebrews became divided: ten of the tribes broke away to form the northern kingdom of Israel, while David's dynasty in Jerusalem continued to rule in the south; their state was known as the kingdom of Judah.

Monotheism. Religion had always been a vital aspect of Hebrew history and identity. Abraham's special authority derived from his relationship to Yahweh, whom the Hebrews eventually regarded as the only God. Their acceptance of this idea took centuries. Abraham first identified Yahweh as the divinity whom he would worship exclusively, pledging his loyalty through a special relationship called the Covenant. This pledge of loyalty reflects the language employed in the ancient Near East between two individuals entering into a formal agreement. Some scholars speculate that the Hebrews, who were probably living in Egypt during the reign of Akhenaton (c. 1375–1358 B.C.E.), may have acquired the concept of monotheism from the pharaoh's religious reforms. However, the Hebrews as a nation did not enter into the Covenant with Yahweh until after Moses had led them out of Egypt, while they were encamped in the desert at Mount Sinai on their way to Canaan. It was at this juncture that the Hebrews accepted the Ten Commandments, of which the first enjoined the exclusive worship of Yahweh. Both at Mount Sinai and afterwards, while living among the polytheistic Canaanites, the Hebrews found it difficult to abandon the worship of other gods completely.

Prophets. Much of the Bible recounts the unfaithfulness of the Hebrews and their resistance to special religious leaders, known as prophets, who exhorted the people to renounce polytheism once and for all. The prophets were individuals from any walk of life who felt divinely inspired to remind the people of the central importance of the Covenant. In the prophets' view of history, the welfare of the Hebrews revolved around the question of their faithfulness to Yahweh: foreign invasions and other misfortunes were considered punishments for breaking the Covenant either by worshiping other gods (especially through idolatry) or by breaking the moral code of the Ten Commandments. The Hebrew kings sometimes cooperated with the prophets in the quest for pure monotheism, but sometimes persecuted them. Yet the prophets spoke with such force and conviction that they were often able to sway the hearts even of stubborn kings. Thus, when the prophet Elijah denounced Ahab, king of Israel (871–852 B.C.E.), for executing one of his subjects on false charges so that he could seize his property, Ahab repented. By raising the question of the relationship between spiritual and political sources of authority, the prophets set a vital precedent for the later history of Western civilization. When medieval popes opposed kings and emperors, they did so with the example of the ancient Hebrew prophets in mind.

Social Justice. The prophets were instrumental in advocating social justice as an essential feature of monotheism. In the eighth century B.C.E., when many Hebrews were leaving the pastoral ways of their ancestors and settling in growing towns, their society underwent a major economic transformation. Cities by their nature generate wealth, but the wealth is never distributed evenly: some men tend to become extravagantly wealthy while others descend into dire poverty, often because the wealthy attempt to maximize profits at the expense of their fellow citizens, whom they exploit. When the prophet Amos saw this happening around 750 B.C.E., he preached against economic exploitation as a sin that would bring ruin upon the Hebrew people if they did not mend their ways.

Deportation. The divine wrath was soon recognized in the appearance of the Assyrian armies on the northern borders of Israel. In 721 B.C.E. the Assyrians deported people from the kingdom of Israel, but allowed Judah to continue its existence as a vassal state. To the Hebrews who respected the opinion of the prophets, these events seemed clear evidence that Israel had been severely punished because it continued to worship gods other than Yahweh, whereas Judah endured a lesser punishment because although it committed sins of social injustice, it had committed itself to a stricter monotheism. That the deported Israelites never returned to their homeland but vanished from history as the Ten Lost Tribes of Israel seemed to confirm this interpretation. The outcome also demonstrates a key historical truth: monotheism was not simply an extraordinary religious statement of the Hebrews, but also an effective strategy for preserving their national identity. Thus, since the deported Israelites were willing to worship many gods, they were assimilated into the polytheistic society of Assyria and ceased to exist as an identifiable national group. In contrast, when the kingdom of Judah later suffered deportation under the Neo-Babylonians in 586 B.C.E., the exiles were careful to maintain their religious integrity and thereby preserved their distinct national identity even in exile. From the time of the Babylonian Captivity, these Hebrews from Judah (later known as Judea) became known as "Jews."

Return. The Jews were not in exile for long. They were allowed to return home and rebuild the Temple in Jerusalem (destroyed by the Babylonians) when Cyrus the Great overthrew the Neo-Babylonian dynasty in 539 B.C.E. During their exile, the Jews experienced a new phase of religious awareness, and now began to see themselves as chosen by God for the sake of making known the doctrine of monotheism to all the world. Although they did not engage in missionary activity, they hoped to make the pagan (or "Gentile") world aware that Yahweh was the one true God by maintaining their distinctive way of life. Their new sense of God's plan for the good of the entire human race would eventually inspire the Christians, who arose as a Jewish sect, to preach monotheism to all the world and energetically seek to convert the pagans.

Diaspora. When Cyrus the Great allowed the Jews to return home, many chose to remain in Babylon. Thus began the Diaspora, a Greek word meaning "dispersion," which refers to Jews living outside Judea who continued to maintain their Jewish identity. Later, during the Hellenistic period, Jewish communities thrived in the Egyptian city of Alexandria, and during the Roman period, in many cities of Anatolia and Europe.

CHAPTER 2
Ancient Greece

Chapter 2

ANCIENT GREECE

THE MYCENAEAN BRONZE AGE (c. 2300–1100 B.C.E.)

The ancient Greeks were the earliest representatives of Western civilization. They first migrated into the Balkans around 2300 B.C.E. Through trade with their neighbors in the eastern Mediterranean, as well as raiding expeditions, they amassed enough wealth to undertake ambitious building projects by 1700 B.C.E. Since the most impressive of the early sites is at Mycenae, and the kings of this city seem to have exercised some influence over the other Greek towns, the early Greeks are called Mycenaeans. Other Mycenaean centers included Tiryns, Pylos, and Athens. Mycenae is renowned for its royal tombs whose interiors are shaped like beehives, its massive "Cyclopean" walls (named after the mythical race of one-eyed giants), and its sculpted entryway known as the Lion's Gate. The Mycenaeans owed much of their cultural advancement to the Minoans who lived on the isle of Crete and dominated the eastern Mediterranean, learning from them the art of writing and the method of administration that centered on the royal palace.

The Mycenaeans were at the height of their power from about 1400 to 1200 B.C.E., when they conquered the Minoans on Crete and sacked the city of Troy in Anatolia. Yet around 1100 B.C.E. the maritime empire of the Mycenaeans was destroyed during the raids of the Sea Peoples, and the mainland centers were overrun by the Dorians, a people who spoke a dialect of Greek that differed from the one spoken by the Mycenaeans.

THE DARK AGE (c. 1100–800 B.C.E.)

The Dorian Greeks were culturally less advanced than the people they displaced, many of whom fled across the Aegean Sea to Anatolia, where they established Greek culture along the coast in a region called Ionia. At this time the art of writing was lost, as was the administrative skill that writing made possible. Since the cultural level of the Greeks declined and little is known of their history from about 1100 to 800 B.C.E., the era is known as the Dark Age of ancient Greece.

THE ARCHAIC PERIOD (c. 800–500 B.C.E.)

Geography and the Polis. As Greek culture revived between about 800 and 750 B.C.E., the basic unit of social, economic, and political organization that emerged was the *polis*, or city-state (plural, *poleis*). The word "politics" is derived from *polis*, for it was in the context of the *polis* that the Greeks first developed the theory and practice of the various forms of government that have been prominent in Western civilization. The *polis* was a force for unity on the local level, but loyalty to one's *polis* encouraged fierce regionalism that led to endemic warfare between neighboring *poleis* and prevented the unification of the Greeks as a whole. Greek disunity was also due in part to the geography of the Balkan peninsula, a mountainous region where the terrain hampers overland travel and communication. Since travel by sea was more efficient than travel by land, sea-faring became an important aspect of Greek life, and the Aegean Sea, located between the Balkan peninsula and Anatolia, became the geographical center of Greek civilization.

Colonization. The revival of Greek culture after the Dark Age was accompanied by rapid population growth and economic change that destabilized society. Since farmers tilling the limited area of the rugged Balkan soil could not supply enough food for an expanding population, the economic crisis was partially resolved by establishing colonies outside Greece, from about 750 to 500 B.C.E. Thus the Greeks transplanted the *polis* to the Black Sea and the further shores of the Mediterranean Sea, including Iberia (modern Spain), southern Gaul (the Mediterranean coast of France), Corsica, Sicily, southern Italy, Libya, and even the Egyptian Delta (at the port of Naucratis). The most intensively settled region was southern Italy, which was home to so many Greeks that it became known to the Romans as *Magna Graecia*—"Great Greece." Like the Phoenician colonies, those of the Greeks tended to be independent of their mother city-states, although cultural ties were maintained.

Revolution. Colonization alone could not resolve the social dislocation caused by increasing population and a rising volume of trade. At issue was not only the ability of farmers to feed the people, but also the relationship between social classes, for as trade increased while farming stagnated, the wealthy became wealthier, the middle-class became poor, and the poor became so overwhelmed by debt that they were sold into slavery. In order to avoid bloody anarchy between the classes, the *poleis* experimented with two basic measures: the extension of political power to the lower classes and the guidance of a dictator who mediated between the classes.

Hoplites and the Phalanx. The first of these two measures depended on a revolution in military technique. In ancient Greece, soldiers were responsible for their own equipment. During the Dark Age, the military was dominated by relatively small units of wealthy nobles who could afford to fight on horseback. With the growth of population around 800 B.C.E., the focal point of the military shifted from small, elite units of cavalry to massed infantry. The citizen-soldiers who could afford spear and armor were known as *hoplites* and were organized into massive units called *phalanxes*, which could defy cavalry charges. As the *phalanx* became the decisive factor in winning battles, *hoplites* demanded more political rights from the nobles who dominated the *polis*. By granting concessions, the nobles prevented anarchy and extended political power to a broader base.

Tyrants. When social tensions could not be resolved by mutual agreement, a *polis* might resort to the mediation of a tyrant. The term "tyrant" did not originally carry a negative connotation; it referred to an individual who received absolute power to restore order to a *polis*. Tyrants were usually nobles who sought to enhance their standing at the cost of rival aristocratic families by posing as the friends and guardians of the common people. Although commoners generally appreciated the help of tyrants, they remained suspicious of their motives. Thus, tyranny was inherently unstable and served as a temporary measure until a more stable form of government could be achieved. It was, nevertheless, a common phase in the evolution of the Greek city-states between 700 and 500 B.C.E.

SPARTA

Spartan Society. Located in the Peloponnesus, Sparta came to dominate the peninsula after fighting two wars against its neighbor, Messenia (c. 735–715 B.C.E. and 650–620 B.C.E.), whose inhabitants it enslaved. These conflicts nearly destroyed Sparta, and the Spartan response was to put its entire society on a permanent war-footing, becoming highly regimented in order to improve its ability to win wars. Thus all male citizens became part of a standing army, the freedom of the individual was completely subordinated to the needs of the state, and the Spartans abandoned the arts. The laws that regulated the new Spartan society were attributed to a legendary lawgiver named Lycurgus. Under the Lycurgan code, all males from the age of 7 to 30 lived in barracks and received military training. Women also received physical education and were hardened to a lifestyle without comforts in order to promote a militaristic mind-set. The citizens of Sparta were known as *Spartiates*, while the subject people they ruled were known as *helots*. Since *Spartiates* were not allowed to conduct business (which was seen as a corrupting influence), the services of merchants were provided by a third, marginalized class known as *perioikoi*, who were not citizens and had no political authority.

Spartan Government. Sparta was ruled by two kings of limited authority who shared power with a Council of Elders and an Assembly that consisted of all male citizens over the age of 30, who voted by acclamation (shouting "yes" or "no" on a proposal rather than taking a precise count). The Council of Elders consisted of twenty-eight men who were at least 60 years old. The elders were elected for life and served as judges; since they also decided what proposals would be presented to the Assembly (thereby setting the agenda of the *polis*), they wielded the greatest power of any branch of the government. The Assembly did have a certain check on the Council of Elders inasmuch as it annually elected a board of *ephors*—five men who conducted foreign policy and made sure that the kings and generals did not overstep their authority during military campaigns.

The Peloponnesian League. Since the *helots* outnumbered the *Spartiates* about 10 to 1, the ruling class had to spend almost all its energy in vigilance against revolt. In order to defend itself from outside threats, Sparta spearheaded a system of alliances known as the Peloponnesian League. Almost all the city-states in the Peloponnesus joined this league for mutual defense under the leadership of Sparta, and in this way achieved a rudimentary level of unity that overcame to some extent the Greek tendency toward political fragmentation.

ATHENS

Origins and Early Evolution. Located in the region of Greece known as Attica, Athens was the only Mycenaean center to survive the Dorian migrations, receiving refugees from other parts of the mainland. By the end of the Dark Age, its people were divided into four major tribes and subdivided into clans and brotherhoods called *phratries*, which were controlled by wealthy aristocrats who belonged to a council known as the Areopagus, or "Hill of Ares," named after the god of war. The Areopagus annually elected 9 *archons*, or magistrates, who guided the administration of the Athenian *polis*, becoming members of the Areopagus when their term was over.

Draco. The Athenian nobles were often at odds among themselves and were ill-suited to deal with the socio-economic turmoil of the seventh century B.C.E. In 632, a noble named Cylon tried to create order by establishing himself tyrant of Athens, but was defeated by his aristocratic rivals. Yet in 621, as the crisis continued, the nobles set aside their differences and temporarily granted tyrant-like status to a certain Draco for the purpose of establishing a law code. Until this time there was no written body of laws. Since Draco had to deal with revolutionary violence, the punishments he prescribed were harsh—hence, "Draconian" acquired the connotation of great severity. Nevertheless, Draco's code of laws was a first step toward curbing the power of the nobility, since it bound all Athenians to its prescriptions, regardless of social class.

Solon. The Draconian law code did not adequately address the agrarian crisis at the root of Athenian instability. As small farmers struggled to raise crops from overworked land, they often had to borrow from the wealthy nobles, who charged high rates of interest. In time many debtors could no longer pay the interest and either lost their farms or were sold into slavery. Those who were dispossessed or at risk began to threaten violence and demand that the debts be canceled and the land redistributed. In 594 B.C.E., Solon was elected *archon* and given extraordinary powers (like Draco) to deal with the crisis. He instituted laws which canceled debts and restored freedom to citizens who had been forced into slavery, but he stopped short of redistributing the land.

Constitutional Reforms. Solon's greatest legacy was the constitution he imposed on Athens, an achievement which he described in poetry. He established a Council made up of 400 members (the *boule*), a general Assembly (the *ekklesia*), and public courts of law. These new organs of government assumed most of the traditional powers of the Areopagus, which now assumed the status of a supreme court. Participation in the various branches of government, as well as military service, depended on wealth. Solon divided Athenian citizens into four classes based on how many units of agricultural produce their land yielded annually. Only the wealthiest class (which produced 500 or more units) could be elected as *archons* and belong to the Areopagus. The top three classes could be elected to the Council of 400. The lowest class, known as *thetes* (who owned little or no land), could not serve in public office, but they had the right to participate in the general Assembly and serve in the lower courts. While the upper classes provided cavalry and the middle class provided infantry, the *thetes*, who could not afford arms or armor, served as rowers in the navy.

The Tyranny of Peisistratus. Solon's reforms checked the crisis but were too moderate to satisfy the radicals on either side of the warring factions. A nobleman named Peisistratus seized power in the name of imposing order on the chaos that continued to plague Athens. He ruled securely from 546 B.C.E. until his peaceful death in 527. A benevolent dictator, Peisistratus strove to win popular support by funding public works and instituting new religious celebrations, most notably the festival dedicated to Dionysos, the god of wine and reproduction. He also enlarged the *agora* (marketplace) where the Council of 400 met. Peisistratus left Solon's constitutional reforms intact, but staffed public offices with his supporters while exiling his enemies. His sons ruled after his death until Athenian aristocrats assassinated one of them in 514 B.C.E. and deposed the other, with the help of the Spartans, in 510 B.C.E.

The Democratic Reforms of Cleisthenes. The tyranny was followed by a revolution, from which progressive democratic forces led by the nobleman Cleisthenes emerged triumphant. In 508 B.C.E. Cleisthenes went far beyond Solon's limited reforms by altering the very units of civic identity. Thus, he replaced the *phratries* (brotherhoods), which were dominated by aristocratic families, with the *demes* (townships of the people), an altogether new political district that had no long-standing traditional loyalties. He also transformed the four traditional tribes of Athens, which had ties to aristocratic families, into ten new tribes that were made up of the *demes*. He replaced the Council of 400, which had been made up of 100 members from each of the four traditional tribes, with a Council of 500, which was made up of fifty elected officials chosen by lot from each of the ten new tribes. This new Council received additional powers to deal with financial and foreign affairs. Yet Cleisthenes gave ultimate political authority to the Assembly itself, made up of all adult male citizens, who discussed and decided policy by vote.

Ostracism. To ensure that no politician amassed too much power, the Athenians adopted the practice of ostracism, whereby an individual would be sent into exile for ten years if a vote decided that he was a potential threat to democracy. The voting was done by writing the name of the individual on a piece of broken pottery (*ostraka* in Greek).

THE PERSIAN WARS

Origins. Not long after the democratic reforms in Athens, the very existence of the various Greek city-states was threatened when the Persian Empire embarked upon the conquest of the Balkan peninsula. The Persians had been neighbors of the Greeks since 546 B.C.E., when Cyrus the Great conquered King Croesus of Lydia in Anatolia and made the Ionian Greeks living there his subjects. In 499 B.C.E., the Ionians rebelled against Persian rule and sought military aid from the Greek mainland. Athens sent ships and raided the Persian-controlled city of Sardis. Satisfied that they had done their part, the Athenians returned home. However, by 494 B.C.E., the Persians regained control of Ionia and decided to invade Greece in retaliation.

Greek Victories. A Persian army entered Greece in 490 B.C.E. at the command of the emperor Darius I, yet the vastly outnumbered Athenians managed to defeat it at Marathon in Attica, some 26 miles from Athens. (A herald ran this distance to report the astounding victory, which inspired the endurance race known as the "marathon.") Ten years later the next Persian emperor, Xerxes, invaded with a much larger army and a massive accompanying fleet. Most of the Greek city-states were cowed and decided to remain neutral, but the Athenians managed to assemble a few allies, most notably the Spartans, who brought with them the armies of the Peloponnesian League. Unfortunately, a detachment of Spartans, making a daring stand at the strategic pass of Thermopylae in central Greece, were killed to a man, and the Athenians had to abandon their city, evacuating their population by ship to nearby islands for safety. After the Persians sacked Athens, they located and attacked the Greek fleet. Yet they were lured into a narrow strait near the isle of Salamis where they could not bring their numerical superiority to bear. Thus the smaller Greek fleet, led by the Athenians, crushed the Persian fleet. Without ships for supply, the Persian army was isolated, and the Spartans led the Greek armies to victory on land at Plataea in 479 B.C.E. With the Persians humbled, the Ionian cities were able to reassert their independence.

PERICLEAN ATHENS

The Delian League. The victories against the Persians preserved the autonomy of the Greek city-states, but the Greeks expected the Persians would strike again. An Athenian leader, Themistocles, persuaded his fellow citizens to build walls around the city and its port, the Piraeus, for defense against future invasions. The Athenians also saw wisdom in forging an alliance system, like Sparta's Peloponnesian League, and organized the Delian League. This was a naval alliance, founded in 478 B.C.E. on the isle of Delos, where the league's treasury was established. At its height it included well over a hundred *poleis*, located all along the shores of the Aegean Sea, including all but the southernmost of the Aegean islands, and parts of the northern Peloponnesus. Athenians provided most of the ships while the smaller members mainly provided funds to maintain this fleet, which patrolled the Aegean Sea and raided Persian cities in Anatolia.

The Athenian Empire. The Delian League became increasingly vital to Athens, for the Athenians became dependent on the income it provided not only to maintain their fleet, but also to pay their public servants and fund their artistic endeavors and building programs. However, after a particularly successful raid against the Persians was staged in 467 B.C.E., some members thought the Delian League had served its purpose and should be disbanded, for they no longer wanted to pay the annual tribute that membership required. Yet when the *polis* of Thasos decided to leave the Delian League in 465 B.C.E., the Athenians overthrew its government and prevented its secession. Other cities that attempted to secede met the same fate. Thus, the Delian League was transformed into the Athenian Empire. In 454 B.C.E. this transformation became plain for all to see when the treasury was moved from Delos to Athens.

Pericles. The transformation of the Delian League into the Athenian Empire occurred under the leadership of the Athenian general Pericles, whose imperialistic ambitions were matched by his commitment to democracy. Democratic reforms did not end with the age of Cleisthenes, but continued according to the implied rule that those who provide indispensable service in wartime should acquire a share of political power. Since the Athenian fleet was victorious at the crucial Battle of Salamis (480 B.C.E.) thanks to the efforts of the *thetes*—the poorest Athenian citizens, who served as rowers in the *triremes* (warships with three banks of oars)—they agitated for more political rights and found their champion in a young statesman named Pericles (c. 495–429 B.C.E.). In 461 B.C.E. he helped initiate new reforms that further reduced the powers of the Areopagus by transferring some of its judicial functions to the peoples' courts. The most important innovation of Pericles, however, came in the 450s, when office-holders began to be paid for their service. This measure made it possible for poor citizens to participate in government—a privilege that had been theirs more in theory than practice when it lacked payment. Although Pericles himself was an aristocrat, his actions made Athens a full-fledged democracy and won such favor from the people that they frequently elected him general (an annual office) and heeded his proposals. During the leadership of Pericles, Athens was rebuilt on a grand scale and enjoyed a golden age. Among the programs initiated by Pericles was the construction of the Parthenon (a temple to Athena) set on the hill known as the Acropolis, which has defined the image of the city for millennia.

Limitations of Athenian Democracy. Athens in the age of Pericles is a study in contradictions. On the one hand, no government in history had been as direct a democracy as Athens under the leadership of Pericles, inasmuch as all male citizens, regardless of rank or wealth, regularly served in the government. However, the money that made it possible for poor citizens to serve their turn in public office was drawn from the imperial tribute that Athens forced out of the city-states that it dominated. Thus democracy and aggressive imperialism were linked in Athenian practice. Furthermore, those who enjoyed political privileges were still a minority of the population. Female citizens could not participate in government. Resident aliens, called *metics*, who were required to pay taxes and perform military service, were also excluded from government, and they could not become citizens through a process of naturalization, since the requirement for citizenship was that both parents be Athenian citizens. Finally, slavery was widespread, and thus much of the Athenian labor force was excluded from the decision-making process. Only about a quarter of the inhabitants of Athens actually participated in the democracy.

THE PELOPONNESIAN WAR (431–404 B.C.E.)

Outbreak. The aggressive imperialistic stance taken by the Athenians destabilized the Greek world. Greece was now organized into two armed camps, the land-based Peloponnesian League led by Sparta, and the sea-based Delian League led by Athens. Fearing that its rival would eventually try to take over all of Greece, Sparta took the opportunity presented by a dispute between some colonies in western Greece to launch a pre-emptive invasion of Attica in 431 B.C.E., hoping to break the power of the Athenians by defeating them in a decisive battle. Yet the Athenians adopted a defensive policy advocated by Pericles, who recognized that the Spartans were superior to the Athenians on land but could not challenge them on the sea, the vital link of the empire. Thus, the Athenians retreated behind their walls and used their fleet to import food while the frustrated Spartans destroyed the farms outside. Pericles hoped the Spartans would abandon their siege before too long, but the standoff continued for several years, and the cramped conditions inside the city led to an epidemic that killed at least one-fourth of the population, including Pericles.

Athenian Defeat. The fighting continued in fits and starts for almost thirty years. Without Pericles to guide the Athenians, they vacillated between one strategy and another, depending on the ability of rival politicians to sway the people's vote. The most notorious of the Athenian leaders was Alcibiades (c. 450–404 B.C.E.), Pericles' nephew, who in 415 B.C.E. convinced the Athenians to invade Syracuse (in Sicily), an ally of the Spartans. The invasion failed, in part because Alcibiades ended up colluding with the Spartans in order to escape a plot hatched by his political rivals. Athens never recovered from its defeat at Syracuse in 413 B.C.E. When the subject city-states that made up the Athenian empire learned of the disaster, many of them rebelled. A short-lived oligarchy took control of Athens in 411 B.C.E. during the upheaval. Although democracy was soon restored, the humbled Athenian fleet could no longer effectively prosecute the war, for the Spartans now had an effective fleet of their own, paid for by the Persians, who took advantage of the war in Greece to play their former enemies against one another. Finally, in 404 B.C.E., the Athenians surrendered. The terms of peace required them to tear down their city's defensive walls and forbade them from building a fleet or attempting to revive their empire. An oligarchy known as the Thirty Tyrants, friendly to Sparta, took control of the city. With the defeat of Athens, the Classical culture of the Greeks declined.

GREEK CLASSICAL CULTURE

The Greeks made major contributions to viritually every aspect of culture. Not only did they lay the foundations of Western civilization, but also served as models for later westerners to imitate or emulate in various fields of endeavor. The culture established by the Greeks in the fifth and fourth centuries B.C.E. is called "Classical," for later generations regarded it as the standard by which they measured their own achievements. Thus, the Romans were entranced by Greek art and architecture, and they admired their poetry and rhetoric so much that Roman aristocrats adopted Greek as a second language. Medieval churchmen looked to Greek philosophy for inspiration in their formulation of theological problems. The Renaissance celebrated classical civilization and rediscovered Greek culture. Finally, in the modern age, Enlightenment thinkers drew much inspiration from the rationalism of the Greeks and their political innovations. The ancient Greeks themselves were so complacent about the superiority of their civilization that they considered all non-Greeks to be barbarians, regardless of their cultural achievements.

RELIGION

Greek religion was polytheistic. It lacked a large professional priesthood that could dominate religious observance. Ordinary citizens performed the sacred rites in their own households, and holders of public office fulfilled the role of priest in the civic rituals of the *polis*. A concept of separation of religion and politics did not exist. Each city-state had a special patron: the Athenians worshipped Athena above all other deities; the Spartans looked primarily to Zeus; the city of Delphi had a special shrine to Apollo; yet all members of the pantheon were respected in all the city-states. Various social events could also be offered to the gods. For example, athletic contests, such as the Olympics, which were first held in 776 B.C.E. at Olympia, honored the gods of Mt. Olympus. Other events that the Greeks offered to the gods included drama, recitations of poetry, dances, and singing. The ancient Greeks did not have a fully developed theology that answered the central questions of life and death. For insights into these matters they looked to their poets, whom they considered divinely inspired. In time, philosophers sought more precise answers by applying logic in their speculations.

Cults. The principal Greek gods were the twelve Olympians (Zeus, Hera, Apollo, Artemis, Poseidon, Ares, Aphrodite, Hephaestus, etc.). The Greeks also worshiped fertility cults, especially those of Dionysos, the god of wine, and the Olympian goddess of the harvest, Demeter. There were also mystery cults which required special rites of initiation, such as the Eleusinian Mysteries, associated with the worship of Demeter at Eleusis, whose members performed secretive rituals through which they apparently hoped to acquire immortality.

LITERATURE

The Greeks were renowned for their mastery of language. They made major contributions in virtually all forms of writing, including poetry, drama, history, and philosophy.

Poetry and Literacy. Early Greek poetry was oral rather than written, for it originated during the illiterate period of the Dark Age. Such poetry was preserved by bards who memorized thousands of lines of verse. When the Greeks reacquired literacy through trading contacts with the Phoenicians, this early poetry was recorded in writing to give it a fixed form. While Greek writing after the Dark Age was based on the Phoenician alphabet, the letter-forms were simplified and the phonetic values of several letters were changed to represent vowels as well as the distinctive sounds of the Greek language. (Phoenician letters represented only consonants.)

Homer. The Greeks attributed their greatest epic poems, the *Iliad* and *Odyssey*, to a blind poet named Homer, who is believed to have lived sometime between about 850 and 700 B.C.E. (although some scholars have wondered whether Homer might not actually be a legendary figure who represents the accumulated efforts of several generations of bards). The *Iliad* describes the Mycenaean siege of Troy (which was also called Ilion), and the *Odyssey* describes the subsequent return home by one of the Mycenaean heroes, Odysseus, king of Ithaca (an island off the western shore of the Greek mainland). The values Homer emphasized can be summarized in the Greek word *arete*, which means "virtue" in the sense of "manliness," the ideal behavior of warlike aristocrats who glorified bravery, physical strength, honorable reputation, and loyalty to family and friends.

Later Poets. After Homer, the most important of the Greek poets was Hesiod (c. 700 B.C.E.), who wrote *Works and Days*, which describes the hard life of the small farmer, and the *Theogony*, which describes the birth of the gods and their legends. In addition to epics, the Greeks wrote lyrics—short poems on selected themes that focused on some aspect of the human experience. The most famous of the lyricists were Archilochus (seventh century B.C.E.), who pioneered the new poetic form, Pindar (518–438), who wrote odes of victory for athletic contests, and the woman Sappho of Lesbos (seventh century B.C.E.), who in her love poetry described her own feelings of attraction for other women (hence the word "lesbian" to describe female homosexuality).

Drama. Of the many cultural legacies of the Greeks, one of the most prominent is drama, which was essentially the performance of a narrative by a group of interlocutors rather than by a single bard. Beginning initially as a recital of verse by a *chorus* (or group of singers) alternating with a single leader, the art form eventually developed into a dialogue between an increasing number of principal actors. Drama was one of the many ways that the Greeks honored their gods. Indeed, it had its origins in religious festivals, specifically those of the Athenians in honor of the god Dionysos. Greek drama developed in two main categories—tragedy and comedy.

Tragedy. The Athenians engaged in competitions for drama as they did in athletics. The first competition for tragedy was instituted by the tyrant Peisistratus in 534 B.C.E. The three greatest tragedians were Aeschylus, Sophocles, and Euripides.

Aeschylus. The plays of Aeschylus (c. 525–456 B.C.E.) are profoundly moral and religious, focusing on the vice of *hubris*, or overweening pride, by which headstrong individuals call down *nemesis*, or divine punishment, upon themselves. He portrayed this theme in *The Persians*, *Prometheus Bound*, and the *Oresteia* trilogy.

Sophocles. Like Aeschylus, Sophocles (496–406 B.C.E.) was motivated by religious and moral concerns, expressing deep sorrow at the plight of human beings, who are born into a world of suffering and ignorance. He wrote two plays describing the misfortunes of *Oedipus*, king of Thebes, and one about Oedipus' daughter, *Antigone*, among other surviving works.

Euripides. The plays of Euripides (c. 480–406 B.C.E.) depart from the moral and religious certainties of Aeschylus and Sophocles while demonstrating greater psychological sophistication in the portrayal of characters. Euripides' play *Medea*, named after a sorceress who murdered her children in a fit of rage upon learning of her husband's adultery, unconventionally ends with the escape of the sorceress rather than her punishment at the hands of the gods. Euripides won fewer awards than Aeschylus and Sophocles, in part because Athenian audiences seldom appreciated unconventional treatments of traditional themes.

Comedy. Like tragedy, comedy was performed at the festival of Dionysos. Comedies were intended as light-hearted, often slapstick, performances following the tragedies, but might also use humor to make serious, satirical critiques. The pre-eminent writer of comedies was Aristophanes (c. 450–385 B.C.E.), who used the medium to ridicule his fellow Athenians. Living during the Peloponnesian War, he wrote several plays (such as *The Acharnians* and *Lysistrata*) to demonstrate the stupidity of the fighting. Sparing no one, Aristophanes poked fun at the tragedian Euripides in *The Frogs*, and he depicted the philosopher Socrates as an absent-minded crackpot in *The Clouds*.

Prose. Athenian drama was written in verse. Prose literature appeared in the fifth century B.C.E. as a new form of writing that an author could employ when primarily interested in scientific analysis of a subject rather than artistic presentation. Prose was used mostly in the study of history and philosophy.

History. The two greatest historians were Herodotus and Thucydides. Herodotus (c. 484–425 B.C.E.), an Ionian Greek who is known as the "Father of History," wrote an account of the Persian Wars. He was the first to divide civilization between East and West, and to identify the Greeks as representatives of a distinctive Western civilization. Thucydides (c. 460–400 B.C.E.) was the most prominent historian of the following generation and wrote an account of the Peloponnesian War. An Athenian general who lost his command early in the conflict after failing to fulfill a mission, Thucydides spent the rest of his life interviewing participants of either side. He established a remarkably impartial account of events (up to the year 411 B.C.E.) that methodically resolved contradictions in eyewitness reports. He reconstructed the speeches given by the leaders in order to summarize their political positions. The most famous of these speeches is the funeral oration of Pericles, given in 430 B.C.E. to honor the Athenian soldiers who had died in the first season of campaigning.

Philosophy. The earliest philosophers, who were primarily interested in physics, are known as "Pre-Socratics" because they came before Socrates, who gave philosophy a new orientation by focusing on ethics. Socrates' successors as leading Athenian philosophers were Plato and Aristotle.

The Pre-Socratics. The inquisitive nature of the ancient Greeks is demonstrated in their thinking about the physical world. Like modern scientists, they attempted to explain natural phenomena without reference to religion, yet they did not establish a distinctive scientific method. The earliest of the Pre-Socratics, who originated in Ionia, was Thales of Miletus (c. 600 B.C.E.). He established a long-running debate in physics by trying to identify the most basic substance that constituted all physical objects. Heraclitus (c. 500 B.C.E.) believed the prime substance to be fire; he was preoccupied with the problem of change and permanence and is best remembered for his famous statement that one cannot step into the same river twice. Eventually a theory of four elements (earth, water, air, and fire) was put forward by Empedocles (c. 450 B.C.E.) which remained the basic orthodoxy of western science until modern times. Some Greeks, such as Democritus (c. 400 B.C.E.), theorized that physical objects were made up of atoms (*atoma* in Greek means "indivisible"). The philosopher Pythagoras (c. 530 B.C.E.) believed that all reality could be described in terms of mathematical relationships. Thus, the ancient Greeks established the foundations of western science by developing basic theories of elements and atoms and by using mathematics to describe relationships between physical objects.

Medicine. Hippocrates of Cos (c. 460–377 B.C.E.), known as the "Father of Medicine," inspired the code of medical ethics known as the Hippocratic Oath. He stressed observation and experimentation, described diseases in reports which detailed symptoms, and emphasized the importance of hygiene, diet, and the environment to maintain good health.

Sophists. The term "philosopher" is believed to have been coined by Pythagoras, who, when asked whether he was a wise man (*sophos*), denied it, saying he was merely a "lover of wisdom" (*philos*, friend; *sophia*, wisdom); thus, the philosopher was one who strove to acquire wisdom without presuming that he had attained it. By the fifth century B.C.E., however, there appeared itinerant teachers, calling themselves "Sophists," or wise men, who for a price promised to make their pupils well-informed and skillful public speakers, and thereby successful politicians.

Socrates. Although Socrates (469–399 B.C.E.) was mistaken for a Sophist, he differed from them in several ways. Most importantly, he did not charge tuition and he considered himself less a teacher than one who merely helped others learn the truth for themselves. He also called himself a "gadfly" because he found that few of his interlocutors cared to be questioned in the rigorous method that he devised (later known as the Socratic method). He focused on ethics because he thought his *polis* needed moral citizens more than anything else. Socrates served with distinction in the Athenian military, yet he felt he could best serve the interests of Athens by persuading his fellow citizens to care for their souls rather than military and economic success. He did not write books, so we are dependent primarily on the *Dialogues* of his student, Plato (c. 428–347 B.C.E.), for details of his philosophical doctrines. During the chaos in Athens after the Peloponnesian War, Socrates was accused of corrupting the morals of the youth with his subversive questioning. He was found guilty and executed by drinking hemlock. Plato wrote the *Dialogues* to refute the charges that had been leveled against his beloved teacher.

Plato. In order to preserve Socrates' legacy, Plato not only wrote the *Dialogues* but also founded a school in Athens called the Academy. The core of Plato's philosophy was his Theory of Ideas (or Forms). Plato argued there is a spiritual world that exists beyond the material world of sense-perception and gives it its existence. The Ideas are abstract principles that exist in the spiritual world in a perfect, unchanging state, while particular physical objects in the material world are merely imperfect copies of these Ideas. For example, a wheel with its circular form is an imperfect copy of the Idea of a circle, which exists in a perfect, unchanging state on a plane of reality that can only be perceived by the mind. While Plato used geometrical examples to illustrate his theory, he believed the most important of the Ideas was the Good, which he compared to an intellectual sun since the mind that could perceive the Good could use it as a source of illumination for making accurate moral judgments. Thus, Plato believed that Socrates was put to death by the Athenians because they did not truly know the Idea of the Good; instead, their mistaken opinions about good and evil led them into the error of thinking that executing Socrates was for the good of Athens. Politically, Plato was not a believer in democracy, largely because Athenian democracy wrongfully put Socrates to death. The most famous of Plato's *Dialogues* is the *Republic*, which describes an ideal city made up of three classes arranged in a hierarchy: workers at the bottom, guardians (who serve as warriors and police) in the middle, and enlightened philosopher-kings at the top. In the opinion of ancient and medieval readers, however, Plato's most important dialogue was the *Timaeus*, because it describes the creation of the universe and the place of human beings in the cosmos.

Aristotle. Plato's most gifted pupil was Aristotle (384–322 B.C.E.), who founded his own school in Athens, called the Lyceum. Aristotle taught every subject, including biology, astronomy, and literary criticism, as well as metaphysics, politics, and ethics, all of which he organized into a comprehensive system of knowledge. Most importantly, he formulated rules of logic that could be applied to any subject of study. Aristotle's metaphysical approach was very different from Plato's. Emphasizing the primacy of individual objects rather than abstract principles, he rejected the Platonic theory of Ideas and postulated that all objects are made of matter and form, existing in a single universe set in motion by a Prime Mover. In ethics, Aristotle taught that the good life can be achieved by following the doctrine of the golden mean, whereby moderation in all things is preferable to extreme behavior of any sort. Aristotle's political theory was influenced by his ethics, for he believed that the good life could only be attained by people living in a *polis*, which educates its citizens by providing laws to guide their behavior. He divided governments into three types: rule by one man, which he called "monarchy" when the ruler was just and "tyranny" when the ruler was unjust; rule by a few men, which he called "aristocracy" when the rulers were just and "oligarchy" when the rulers were unjust; and rule by the majority, which he called "polity" (that is, the ideal government of the *polis*) when the majority ruled for the good of all, but "democracy"—which he equated with mob rule—when the majority oppressed innocent minorities or individuals (for example, like Socrates). Thus, Aristotle agreed with Plato that democracy was a bad form of government.

ART AND ARCHITECTURE

Pottery. Greek art from the Archaic age survives mainly in the form of paintings on pottery vases (which were used in the transportation of agricultural produce) and other vessels. The style evolved from the geometric patterns of the Mycenaeans to representational art using black figures on red backgrounds and vice versa. The subject-matter ranged from famous mythological events to scenes of daily life.

Statues. The Greeks excelled in three-dimensional representations of the human form, sculpted especially from marble or bronze, and occasionally from gold or ivory. Early Greek statues were influenced by Egyptian models and had a stiff, formal appearance, often presenting a bland smile. Sculpture evolved to a refined level of realism around 480 B.C.E., which marks the beginning of the Classical Age. While the Greeks produced life-like imitations of famous individuals such as Pericles and Socrates, their statues often served religious purposes. Statues of patron deities were placed within temples, which were themselves a form of art.

Temples. Greek temples were simple yet elegant, epitomizing the classical ideals of harmony and proportion. They were typically rectangular, with angled roofs terminating at either end in gables (enclosing triangular spaces known as "pediments") that overhung columned porches. The pediments and friezes (horizontal bands below the roofs) were usually adorned with sculptures depicting mythological scenes. The temples were often surrounded on all sides with columns, forming colonnades. The columns were typically fluted (adorned with vertical grooves) and conformed to three basic designs, or "orders," which were distinguished by their capitals: the Doric order had a plain capital; Ionic capitals were adorned with a pair of volutes, or scroll-like spirals; and Corinthian capitals were the most ornate, adorned with intricate acanthus leaves.

The Parthenon. The characteristics of the Greek temple are illustrated in the architecture and art on the Acropolis of Athens. The Parthenon, or temple to Athena, was built during the 440s and 430s B.C.E. as the apex of Pericles' building program during the golden age of Athens, and still stands today, even after it was badly damaged in the seventeenth century. The sculptures that once adorned the pediments with depictions of battle-scenes, known as the Elgin Marbles, were removed in the nineteenth century to the British Museum. The immense statue of Athena that once stood inside the temple (long since destroyed) was designed by the sculptor Phidias (c. 490–430 B.C.E.), who was hired by Pericles. Phidias was famous for excelling in a stately naturalism and for fashioning an immense statue of Zeus. A smaller temple on the Acropolis, the Erechtheum, was adorned with *caryatids*, or columns sculpted in the form of draped maidens holding up the roof with their heads.

THE HELLENISTIC AGE

The Classical Age of Greece drew to a close with the rise of the Macedonian empire established by Philip II (359–336 B.C.E.) and his son, Alexander the Great (336–323 B.C.E.), who extended that empire to the Near East. The culture that resulted from the blending of eastern and western civilization is called Hellenistic, or "Greek-like," to distinguish it from the Hellenic, or simply "Greek," culture. It should be noted that the Greeks actually called themselves "Hellenes," and they called Greece "Hellas," after the legendary hero, Hellen, from whom they claimed descent. The "Greeks" were actually just one of the Hellenic tribes (like the Dorians and Ionians). However, since they colonized southern Italy and thus were the first to come into contact with the Romans, the Romans misnamed all the Hellenes "Greeks" and handed down this form to later history. Hellenistic culture lasted from Alexander's death in 323 B.C.E. to Rome's conquest of Egypt, the last of the Hellenistic kingdoms, in 30 B.C.E.

Philip of Macedon. Sparta won the Peloponnesian War at great cost and was too exhausted to win the peace. The Athenians overthrew the Thirty Tyrants in 403 B.C.E. and restored their democracy, which lasted a century and a half (before the Roman Empire finally suppressed it). Sparta soon found it was not strong enough to dominate all of Greece. It could not prevent Athens from challenging its authority, nor other city-states, such as Thebes, which took advantage of the power vacuum left by the Peloponnesian War to make its own bid for supremacy. The disunified Greek city-states continued their squabbling until Philip II of Macedon, king of a semi-Greek state in the northern part of the Balkan peninsula, invaded Greece in 338 B.C.E. and established unity after winning the battle of Chaeronea. He organized the city-states into an alliance known as the League of Corinth, whose members nominally enjoyed self-rule but had to follow Macedon's lead in foreign affairs.

Alexander the Great. Philip's great ambition was to lead the Greeks in a war of revenge against the Persian Empire, but he was assassinated in 336 B.C.E. and the undertaking was left to his son, Alexander the Great. This youthful and energetic king overthrew the Persians, unified the eastern Mediterranean and the Near East, and created the largest empire the world had yet seen before he reached the age of 33. Starting out with only 35,000 men in 334 B.C.E., Alexander outwitted and defeated forces of superior numbers in three great battles (Granicus River, Issus, and Gaugamela) until finally he assumed the title of king of Persia in 328 B.C.E. He pressed on and added to his empire Asian territories that Persia had not controlled, until his war-weary men mutinied on the borders of India. Returning to Persia, Alexander adopted many Near Eastern customs and ruled like a Near Eastern despot. He died suddenly, of uncertain causes, in 323 B.C.E.

The Hellenistic Kingdoms. Alexander's sudden death left a power vacuum that resulted in a struggle among his generals. After some forty years of warfare, the territory of Alexander's short-lived empire was divided between three kingdoms, each named after the general who founded a new dynasty: the Antigonid kingdom (in the Macedonian homeland and Greece), the Seleucid kingdom (from Anatolia and Syria in the west to Mesopotamia and Persia in the east), and the Ptolemaic kingdom (in Egypt and Palestine). Many of the Greek city-states were able to reassert their independence, banding together in either of two alliances: the Aeolian League in the north and the Achaean League in the south. The borders between states shifted constantly as a series of wars kept Greece and the Near East politically fragmented. This situation persisted until the Romans established their empire and forced unity upon the divided peoples of the Mediterranean. Many Greeks and Macedonians migrated to the Near East, colonizing the new cities founded by Alexander and his generals. Urban culture flourished as new trade routes linking Europe and Asia stimulated the accumulation of wealth, mostly by a minority of Greeks and Macedonians who formed the upper class. The city of Alexandria in Egypt boasted one million inhabitants, as well as two harbors, a huge lighthouse, a museum, and a world-famous library that served the leading thinkers of the day.

HELLENISTIC CULTURE

Science and Technology. Although the literary works of the Hellenistic period pale in comparison to the texts of the Classical Age, the study of the physical world reached new heights. Hellenistic natural philosophy is characterized by the development of rigorous methodologies based upon experimentation. This nascent experimental method also stimulated the development of technology and resulted in increasing specialization and professionalism as individuals concentrated on understanding one area thoroughly rather than trying to develop comprehensive systems of knowledge. Greek thinkers of the Classical period had already accepted the idea that the earth is round. Now Eratosthenes (c. 276–196 B.C.E.) accurately calculated the circumference of the earth. Aristarchus (c. 310–250 B.C.E.) postulated a heliocentric theory, arguing that the earth revolves around the sun and causes the succession of day and night by its rotation, but his theory was rejected in favor of the geocentric, or earth-centered, theory preferred by Aristotle. Hipparchus (c. 190–120 B.C.E.) developed the astrolabe, a device for making accurate observations of celestial bodies. In mathematics, Euclid (c. 300 B.C.E.) established a collection of geometrical theorems in a book called the *Elements*, while Archimedes of Syracuse (287–212 B.C.E.) calculated the value of *pi*. Archimedes also made major advances in the study of mechanics, developing a hand-cranked pump known as "Archimedes' screw," as well as more efficient configurations of pulleys and levers (which were used in catapult technology). He is famed for having said, "Give me a lever long enough and a place to stand, and I will move the world."

Architecture and Sculpture. During the Hellenistic period, colonists transplanted Greek architecture to the Near East and the Levant, and inspired the Romans, who were politically on the rise, into adopting their forms. Theaters in the round became a standard feature of urban centers throughout the Mediterranean and the colonized cities, and Corinithian capitals became the favored order of columns. The Greek predilection for naturalistic statues also spread throughout these regions. Artistic virtuosity reached a new level as sculptors depicted not only gods and famous men, but also non-idealized images of the lower classes in scenes of daily life. Figures tended to be depicted in very dynamic, theatrical poses, as demonstrated by a sculpture known as the Laocoön group, which portrays a Trojan priest and his sons attacked by sea-serpents. Other famous Hellenistic statues include the Venus de Milo and the Winged Victory of Samothrace.

Religion. The decline of the *polis* brought on a crisis of faith in traditional religion, to which many responded by joining mystery cults that Hellenistic armies brought home from the Near East. Much of their popularity was due to their promise of life after death. The most prominent of these was the Persian cult known as Mithraism, which involved the ritual sacrifice of a bull in honor of the god of light.

Philosophy. Educated people tended to seek guidance from new schools of philosophy, most prominently Epicureanism and Stoicism, both of which were founded in Athens. These philosophies turned away from the traditional emphasis on public life to a new emphasis on the inner perfection of the individual. Epicurus (c. 341–270 B.C.E.) taught that the good life consists in the pursuit of pleasure, although he recommended the pleasures of the mind and friendship over the pleasures of the body. Stoicism was founded by Zeno of Citium (c. 335–263 B.C.E.), who urged the complete suppression of desire, so that a state of enlightened apathy would blunt the psychological impact of misfortunes. His school of thought, which was named after the building (*Stoa*) where he taught, took inspiration from the idea that the cosmos is governed by divine providence. It urged people to respect one another as members of a universal brotherhood and recommended a world-state characterized by tolerance. A third philosophical school that became prominent in Hellenistic culture was Skepticism, which questioned the very possibility of philosophical certainty; but since it had little to offer by way of psychological comfort, it did not become a dominant movement. Stoicism was perhaps the most successful of the Hellenistic schools of philosophy. It became dominant in the Roman Empire and exerted an influence on Christianity.

CHAPTER 3
Ancient Rome

Chapter 3

ANCIENT ROME

Geography. Rome was founded in the eighth century B.C.E. (traditionally 753) near the mouth of the Tiber River by speakers of the Latin language, who lived in a region called Latium. The location of Rome about halfway down the west side of the Italian peninsula favored its rise to power. Far from the powerful centers of advanced civilization in the Near East, Italy was protected from land invasions by the waters surrounding it on three sides and by the Alps, which provided a barrier that was infrequently crossed by invaders. The Italian peninsula itself is not very mountainous: the range of the Apennines running down the center does not greatly inhibit overland travel. Thus a single state could conquer and control the various peoples of Italy. Rome's central location within Italy gave it an advantage, since its armies did not have to travel far to get to any point on the peninsula, and its situation on seven hills helped them defend the city from attackers. Once the Romans unified Italy, they found that their position in the center of the Mediterranean gave them an advantage in controlling the entire sea. The Romans were also helped by the mild climate of Italy and its good farmland, which spared them the economic troubles that afflicted Greece.

The Etruscans. The early Romans were governed by a neighboring group called the Etruscans, who lived to the north in Etruria. Etruscan kings governed Rome until the Romans rebelled and drove them out in 509 B.C.E. Nevertheless, the Romans were indebted to the Etruscans for many things, including engineering techniques (draining marshes and constructing sewers), the use of the arch in architecture, the alphabet (which the Etruscans had acquired from the Greeks), and many religious rituals, especially techniques of divination by observing omens such as the entrails of sacrificial animals and the flight of birds.

THE REPUBLIC

Having expelled the Etruscan kings, the Romans rejected the institution of kingship, since they believed government belongs to the people, not an individual. They called their new government the "public thing" (*res publica*), or Republic, which functioned by electing magistrates to hold public office. However, the right to hold office was initially limited to the wealthy, land-owning families of nobles, known as *patricians*, who comprised about ten percent of the population. They controlled policy mainly through the Senate, which was made up of approximately 300 members. In theory the patricians represented the rest of the citizens, known as *plebeians* (or *plebes*), but in practice the two classes were usually at odds. Over the course of centuries, the plebeians managed to expand their political rights, partly by threatening to withhold military service unless they received concessions. Among the earliest concessions was a written code of laws known as the Twelve Tables, published about 450 B.C.E. They were also granted a People's Tribune (a magistrate who could veto the Senate) and the right to hold an assembly, which in 287 B.C.E. no longer needed the approval of the Senate to pass legislation. The plebeians were eventually allowed to hold public office and work their way up the political ranks as the patricians did. Between the patricians and plebeians were the equestrians, a knightly class who initially served as cavalry, but later on assumed financial roles as tax collectors and contractors for the government.

Public Office. Advancement in public office required military service and began with low-ranking positions, such as the *quaestor*, who kept finanicial accounts, and the *aedile*, who organized public works. Higher positions included *praetor*, who presided at legal trials, and *censor*, whose principal task was to maintain census records (in order to determine who was eligible for military conscription and public office), but who also enforced morals. Censors were highly respected, for they were drawn from a select pool of officials who had once served as *consuls*, or chief magistrates. Two consuls were elected each year by the assembly and had a range of administrative, judicial, and military functions; since they enjoyed king-like powers (known as *imperium*), each consul had the right to veto the other in order to prevent abuses. In times of crisis, the Senate could appoint a *dictator* who for six months held supreme power that was not subject to veto. Romans who sought election as praetors or consuls wore a special garment called the *toga candidata*, or "whitened toga"; the English word *candidate* is derived from this Latin expression.

Expansion. As Roman population increased, the supply of land became insufficient, and the Romans began to look beyond their borders to settle colonists. They also adopted conquest as a defensive strategy after Rome was sacked in 390 B.C.E. by the Gauls, a Celtic people living in the Po river valley to the north. Early Roman armies, like those of the Greeks, were organized into *phalanxes* of about 8,000 men, but the Romans later devised a more flexible form of organization, the *legion*, which was made up of about 5,000 men organized into small units called *maniples* that could act independently and take on larger forces by outmaneuvering them. Using this innovation, the Romans steadily conquered their neighbors.

Conquest of Italy. By 265 B.C.E., the Romans united the entire Italian peninsula as far as the Po River. They demonstrated their determination in the 270s B.C.E. when they kept fighting against the defender of the Greeks in southern Italy, King Pyrrhus of Epirus (307–272 B.C.E.), even after suffering several defeats. Dismayed by Roman tenacity, Pyrrhus is said to have remarked, "If we win another battle against the Romans, we shall be utterly ruined," thereby originating the concept of the Pyrrhic victory (a victory so costly that the victor cannot afford to go on fighting).

The Punic Wars. The Romans soon became embroiled with the Carthaginians over Sicily as the two growing empires collided. Carthage, founded as a Phoenician colony in North Africa (modern Tunisia) around 800 B.C.E., had expanded into an empire that dominated maritime trade. The rivals engaged in three terrible conflicts known as the Punic Wars (*Punicus* in Latin means "Phoenician") to decide who would control the Mediterranean. The First Punic War (264–241 B.C.E.), which consisted principally of naval engagements, gave Sicily to Rome. The Second Punic War (218–201 B.C.E.) began in Spain and spread to Italy as the Carthaginian general, Hannibal, daringly crossed the Alps with his war elephants. Although Hannibal raided Italy for 15 years, he was unable to conquer the Romans, who changed tactics after the disastrous Battle of Cannae (216 B.C.E.). Their general Fabian refused to fight Hannibal in a pitched battle, but harrassed his supply lines. These "Fabian tactics" prevented Hannibal's occupation from breaking the Roman state. The Second Punic War ended when the Romans opened a new front by invading North Africa under the leadership of Scipio the Elder and defeated the Carthaginians at the Battle of Zama (202 B.C.E.). Over half a century of uneasy peace followed until the conclusive Third Punic War (149–146 B.C.E.), which was instigated by the Roman statesman, Cato the Elder, who ended all his speeches with the phrase, "Carthage must be destroyed." Carthage was soon reduced to ruins by Scipio the Younger.

Conquest of the Mediterranean. Without a rival to oppose them, the Romans methodically conquered all the shores of the Mediterranean Sea. After fighting four wars with Macedon, in which the Romans demonstrated the superiority of the legion over the phalanx (especially at the Battle of Cynocephale in 197 B.C.E.), they subjugated Greece and moved through Anatolia into the Near East. The Romans did not have to fight for all their acquisitions. The heirless king of Pergamum in western Anatolia willed his kingdom to the Romans in 133 B.C.E., and the kingdom of Bithynia (in northern

Anatolia) was granted to Rome by a similar arrangement in 74 B.C.E. The last major state to resist the Romans was Egypt, which fell in 30 B.C.E.

Unrest. The influx of wealth from the conquered territories, as well as the devastation suffered in Italy during the Second Punic War, altered the character of the Republic. The wealthy profited from new overseas markets that had been opened by conquest, whereas small farmers were ruined. Their farms were bought up by large landowners to form immense estates called *latifundia*. These estates were devoted to raising cattle and were worked by prisoners of war whom the wealthy owners imported as slaves. Harsh treatment of these slaves led to sporadic revolts on a massive scale, most famously the one led by the gladiator Spartacus in 73–71 B.C.E. Yet the greater threat for the Republic came from the dislocation of citizens as class struggle escalated.

The Gracchi. The brothers Tiberius and Gaius Gracchus, reform-minded members of the aristocracy who opposed the self-interest and conservatism of the senators, championed the dispossessed plebeians as People's Tribunes. However, their drastic attempts at reform led to their assassination in riots (in 133 and 121 B.C.E., respectively). They tried to redistribute the land, extend Roman citizenship to the Italian allies, and curb the power of the senators over the courts by transferring judicial duties to the equestrian class. Their only lasting measure was to ease the plight of the impoverished by means of a state subsidy for the purchase of bread.

Marius. Constitutional shortcomings which indicated that the Roman Republic was ill-equipped to run an empire became evident when Numidia, a client state in North Africa led by Jugurtha, rebelled and German barbarians (the Teutones and Cimbri) threatened Italy from the north. Both of these threats were overcome by the brilliant general Marius, who won the Jugurthine War in 111–106 B.C.E. and defeated the Germans in southern Gaul in 102–101 B.C.E. However, the extended fighting required him to be elected consul for several years consecutively, which was a major breach of precedent. Marius also found it necessary to reform the Roman army. Since recruits were drawn from among the owners of small farms, the decline of these farms led to a serious shortage of manpower. To deal with this problem, Marius waived the property requirement, paid his troops wages, and provided them with land when they retired. This policy set a dangerous precedent, for soldiers now became loyal to their general, who provided the necessities of life, rather than to the state, which had failed to help them in their need.

Clientage. As order broke down, power shifted from the machinery of government to the client system, whereby a patrician would use his personal wealth to support poor men, who would in return support him politically. As wealthy patricians accumulated private armies, they used their power to oppose the Senate, and the Republic descended into a series of civil wars. The Senate itself became divided between two groups: the *optimates*, who represented the entrenched interests, and the *populares*, who demanded reform.

Extension of Roman Citizenship. Another constitutional challenge arising from tensions imposed by the empire occurred in the Social War (90–88 B.C.E.), named after Rome's allies (*socii* in Latin) who seceded because the Senate refused to grant their demands for status as full citizens. The Senate finally conceded when threatened by a massive uprising in the eastern provinces led by Mithridates, King of Pontus in Anatolia.

Civil War. The Romans became divided over which general to send against Mithridates: Sulla, favored by the *optimates*, or Marius, favored by the *populares*. When Sulla finally left for the front, Marius used his private army to march on Rome and kill his opponents. Marius died in 86 B.C.E., and when Sulla returned to Italy, he executed Marius's supporters and broke Roman precedent by serving as *dictator* for more than the maximum of six months. Although he relinquished power in 80 B.C.E., rival generals continued to jockey for position.

The First Triumvirate. The most ambitious men at this time, whose power rested in their private armies, were Pompey, Crassus, and Julius Caesar. Although they were rivals, they established a three-way alliance known as a triumvirate in order to oppose the Senate, which thwarted their designs for personal aggrandizement. This delicate balance was upset in 53 B.C.E. when Crassus died and the two remaining triumvirs could not agree on redrawing their spheres of influence, in part because of Caesar's stunning conquest of the Celts in Gaul (modern France) during the 50s B.C.E. The situation exploded into civil war (49–45 B.C.E.) when Caesar, returning from Gaul, crossed the Rubicon River on the border of Italy without disbanding his army, as demanded by Pompey and the Senate. Pompey was defeated by Caesar at Pharsalus in Greece (48 B.C.E.) and died a fugitive in Egypt. Although Caesar showed magnanimity to his vanquished opponents, alarmed senators led by conservatives Brutus and Cassius feared he would try to proclaim himself king. In the hope of saving the Republic, they organized a conspiracy that assassinated Caesar on the Ides of March (March 15), 44 B.C.E. Caesar's supporters were outraged and Rome suffered another round of civil war (44–42 B.C.E.), which ended in the defeat of the assassins. Among Caesar's achievements, his most far-reaching was the reform of the calendar by adding leap years. This Julian calendar, with minor adjustments, is still in use.

The Second Triumvirate. Caesar's supporters were led by three men who formed a second triumvirate to dominate affairs in Rome: Marc Antony, Lepidus, and Octavian, who was Julius Caesar's grandnephew. Eventually, Marc Antony and Octavian squeezed Lepidus out, then fought one another for supremacy. Octavian, a shrewd propagandist, undercut support for Marc Antony by drawing attention to his love affair with Cleopatra, the Ptolemaic queen of Egypt, and raising fears that Marc Antony would try to rule Rome as an oriental despot. In 31 B.C.E. he defeated Marc Antony and Cleopatra in a naval battle at Actium, off the western coast of Greece. With Cleopatra gone, the last of the Hellenistic kingdoms came to an end and the Romans added Egypt to their territorial possessions.

Augustus Caesar. After almost a century of strife, the war-weary Romans looked to Octavian to restore order. A cunning politician, Octavian assured the Romans that his only intention was to restore the Republic, and he maintained the outward forms of traditional government even as he worked behind the scenes to replace it with a political system that served his will alone. In 27 B.C.E., the Senate bestowed on Octavian the title *Augustus* ("revered one"), but he said he preferred the title *princeps*, the traditional republican term which meant "first citizen." He also used the title *imperator* (indicating one who held the power of *imperium*), from which the term "emperor" is derived. For all his deception and cunning, Augustus did institute much-needed reform, for the government of the Republic had been intended for a small agricultural community and was unable to administer an immense empire. Many of his measures were also better for the Roman people than the policies of the Senate had been. He established a civil service that was open to men of talent rather than birth, gave Rome its first police and fire departments, improved the roads, and sponsored a civic building program. In his published memoirs, Augustus boasted, "I found Rome a city of brick and left it a city of marble." Although Augustus tried to reform Roman morals through laws that were intended to revive the sanctity of marriage and the centrality of the family, this effort was not successful.

THE EMPIRE

The Emperors. The Republic's death and the Empire's birth were never openly proclaimed. One can argue that the conquest of the Mediterranean had killed the Republic about a hundred years before the age of Augustus, since their rise to supremacy brought the Romans more power than their political machinery could handle; in that sense, the Republic was a victim of its own success. The Senate continued to exert some influence and consuls were still elected, but power now resided in the hands of one man. In order to legitimate the idea of a single prominent man governing the empire, the Romans instituted the cult of the emperor, who was worshiped as a god. As a god, he was above the law; his power to create law thus legitimated his authority. The early emperors were deified only after their death and were worshiped retrospectively, but later emperors were worshiped during their lifetimes. It is a testament to the viability of the new system that it survived even when the holder of power was unstable, like Nero (54–68 C.E.), or even insane, like Caligula (37–41 C.E.). For the most part, however, the early Roman emperors were effective rulers, and the sprawling region under the control of Rome benefited from the ability of a single ruler to make decisions for the entire empire.

Pax Romana. For a period of about 200 years, from the reign of Augustus (27 B.C.E.–14 C.E.) to the death of Marcus Aurelius (161–180 C.E.), Rome enjoyed a period of stability and prosperity known as the *Pax Romana*, or "Roman peace." Foreign wars of conquest continued on the borders, but Rome was free of civil wars (with the exception of the year 68 C.E., when four rivals claimed the imperial throne upon Nero's death). Augustus managed to unite the Mediterranean, but his invasion of Germany failed in 9 C.E. The Empire continued to expand elsewhere for over a hundred years, most notably into Britain (43 C.E.) and Dacia in the Balkan peninsula (106 C.E.). It was at its greatest extent in 117 C.E., when Roman legions briefly occupied Mesopotamia.

Bread and Circuses. As the Empire expanded, citizenship was gradually extended to the subject peoples until 212 C.E., when the emperor Caracalla declared all inhabitants of the empire full citizens. The population of the city of Rome expanded to about a million as uprooted farmers drifted to the capital in search of work. Poverty and unemployment consequently rose. Despite the measures instituted by Augustus, the Empire failed to solve these severe problems. The best it could do was to address the symptoms of social dysfunction by providing free grain and entertainment (in the form of gladiatorial games and chariot races) according to a social welfare policy known as "bread and circuses."

LITERATURE

Early Poetry and Drama. The earliest Roman poet was Ennius (239–169 B.C.E.), who presented the history of Rome in an epic called the *Annales*.

Exceptional poets of the late Republic included Catullus (85–54 B.C.E.), who wrote passionate love lyrics about his unfaithful mistress, and Lucretius (96–55 B.C.E.), who described the Epicurean world view in his philosophical poem *On the Nature of Things*. The early Romans were generally not deep thinkers; they had little interest in tragedy, but greatly enjoyed comedy, which was mastered by Plautus (254–184 B.C.E.) and Terence (c. 190–159 B.C.E.). Their works influenced generations of later playwrights, including Shakespeare.

Prose. The earliest known prose work is Cato the Elder's manual *On Agriculture*, which gives advice on running a country estate (c. 160 B.C.E.). The most accomplished writer of Latin prose was Marcus Tullius Cicero (106–43 B.C.E.), a senator and lawyer whose massive output included speeches given in the Senate and the courts, letters to friends, and philosophical works, which he wrote during his enforced retirement by Julius Caesar (who was also an accomplished writer, publishing his memoirs on the conquest of Gaul). Cicero popularized Greek philosophy and espoused Stoicism. As a defender of the Republic, he wrote diatribes against Marc Antony known as the *Philippics*, but he was executed for his outspoken opposition.

Golden Age (43 B.C.E.–14 C.E.). Augustus Caesar patronized three poets whose celebrated works represent the golden age of Roman literature. The most famous of them was Virgil (70–19 B.C.E.), whose *Aeneid* (modeled on Homer's epics) describes the legendary foundation of the Roman state by the fugitive Trojan prince, Aeneas. It was written at the request of Augustus, and in a "prophecy" celebrates his glorious reign. Virgil's contemporaries were Horace (65–8 B.C.E.), who wrote lyrics on various themes, and Ovid (43 B.C.E.–17 C.E.), who wrote the *Metamorphoses*, which portrays myths of transformation in Greco-Roman mythology, and a long poem *On the Art of Love*, a manual for seduction. Ovid was later exiled by Augustus for his connection to a scandal involving a member of the imperial family. The greatest prose author of the golden age was the historian Livy (59 B.C.E.–17 C.E.).

Silver Age (14–c. 138 C.E.). During the first century of the Roman empire, writers found that they could not afford to offend emperors who ruled with absolute power. This limit on freedom of expression coincided with a general decline in Roman virtues, which led to a pervading sense of pessimism in literature from the reign of Tiberius (14–37 C.E.) to Hadrian (117–138 C.E.). In the *Germania*, the historian Tacitus (c. 55–117 C.E.) deplores the decline of Roman character while ironically praising the heroic simplicity of the barbarians. The Stoic philosopher Seneca (c. 4–65 C.E.) wrote tragedies and was executed by Nero, as was his nephew, Lucan (39–65 C.E.), who wrote the epic *Pharsalia*, which depicts the civil war between

Caesar and Pompey. Satirists vented their frustration at the general decline in morals, most notably Persius (34–62 C.E.), Petronius (d. 66), and Juvenal (c. 65–128 C.E.).

Later Works. The first Latin novel, *The Golden Ass*, was written by Apuleius (c. 125–200 C.E.), a philosopher who had to defend himself in court against an accusation of sorcery. The Emperor Marcus Aurelius (161–180 C.E.) wrote an influential work of Stoic philosophy known as the *Meditations*. Two highly influential scientific authorities appeared during the second century: Galen (c. 129–199) provided a systematic theory of medicine, and Ptolemy (c. 100–170) wrote a book of astromony known as the *Almagest*, which offered mathematical proofs to support the geocentric theory. In the later period, however, creativity began to wane, and many authors devoted themselves to preserving the literary and intellectual heritage in encyclopedic works. Two influential encyclopedic writers were Macrobius (fourth century) and Martianus Capella (fifth century).

Law. Perhaps the most important contribution of the Romans was their sophisticated body of written law. They constantly added to the original code of the Twelve Tables (c. 450 B.C.E.) as need arose, on the basis of decrees by the Senate, assemblies, judges, and emperors. The later development of Roman law was motivated by the need of the emperors to govern diverse peoples according to a universal code, and it received inspiration from the Stoic concept of natural law. By the second century C.E., the emperors were the only source of law and, beginning with Hadrian, ordered compilations that conveniently formulated existing decisions. Trained legal scholars became vital in this endeavor from the second to the early third century, and produced authoritative textbooks. These formed the basis for the final codification ordered by the Emperor Justinian (527–565) known as the *Corpus Juris Civilis*, or Body of Civil Law. In the interim, the Emperor Theodosius II (408–450) codified imperial legislation in a collection known as the *Codex Theodosianus*, or Theodosian Code (438).

ART, ARCHITECTURE, AND ENGINEERING

The Romans combined elements of Etruscan, Classical, and Hellenistic art. Their art and architecture was often designed to make a political statement, especially in monumental structures that reflected the power of the emperors. Roman engineering was an essential ingredient for maintaining the vast empire.

Etruscan Art. The Etruscans painted frescoes and made sculptures in terra-cotta, most notably to adorn their sarcophagi (tombs), which commonly depicted a reclining husband and wife in a cheerful attitude. The style is reminiscent of Greek art from the Archaic period (seventh century B.C.E.), particularly with regard to the stiffness of the figures, their formal smiles, and their almond-shaped eyes.

Roman Art. In addition to naturalistic sculpture, carved reliefs, and frescoes, the Romans excelled in mosaics—colored tiles arranged to represent images, commonly of human figures or scenes of marine animals. Romans also sculpted equestrian statues, most famously one representing Marcus Aurelius (c. 175).

Roman Architecture. The Romans made extensive use of concrete (a mixture of cement and stone fragments). From the Etruscans they took the arch and the barrel vault (a curved ceiling made up of a series of arches). By arranging arches in a circle, they constructed domes—an architectural feature that the Greeks did not use. The most impressive example of a domed building is the Pantheon, a temple to all the gods (built in Rome between 118 and 128 C.E.). Roman public buildings were arranged around a *forum*, or square. Their law courts were housed inside large buildings known as *basilicas*, which later became the model for Christian churches. They also constructed massive edifices to celebrate their victories, such as the Arch of Titus, constructed by the emperor Domitian (81–96 C.E.) to commemorate his brother's conquest of Judea, or the Arch of Constantine (built 312–315). Similarly, a pillar carved with figures in relief, known as Trajan's Column, was erected around 106–113 C.E. to commemorate the conquest of Dacia. The Romans used columns as supporting elements in their structures, but, unlike the Greeks, frequently embedded the columns within the walls, as in the Colosseum, an amphitheater built between 72 to 80 C.E. for gladiatorial games. No Roman city was complete without bathhouses.

Engineering. Municipal bathhouses would not have been possible without the extensive use of aqueducts, which supplied fresh water and made sewers possible; Roman sanitation was unequaled until the nineteenth century. One of the most impressive Roman aqueducts is the Pont du Gard, near Nîmes in southern France, which was built around 1 C.E. At one location along its 31-mile course, the aqueduct crosses the Gard River on a bridge some 160 feet high supported by massive rounded arches. The Romans connected their cities with straight roads designed to expedite the movement of armies.

RELIGION

Polytheism and Syncretism. The Romans were polytheists and worshiped many of the same gods as the Greeks, though they often gave them alternate names (Jupiter for Zeus, Juno for Hera, Minerva for Athena, etc.). The Romans were also very eclectic and practiced syncretism, like the Egyptians. Their techniques of divination reflect Etruscan influence.

Ancestor Worship and State Religion. A central feature of Roman religion was the worship of deceased ancestors and "household spirits" (minor gods who guarded the home), which were commonly represented by idols. The goddess Vesta protected the hearth and was served by twelve Vestal Virgins, whose primary task was to keep her sacred fire burning. The Romans linked religion with politics; priesthoods were, in fact, public offices. The office of chief priest, or *Pontifex Maximus*, was held at one time by Julius Caesar and was later adopted by the emperors. The cult of the emperor arose as an expression of patriotism.

Mystery Cults. State religion, with its emphasis on the here and now, eventually ceased to offer meaningful spiritual satisfaction. While many Romans of the imperial period looked to philosophy (especially Stoicism) for their spiritual needs, others turned to mystery cults, which offered the promise of eternal life. At first the Romans adopted the Greek cults of Dionysos (Bacchus) and Cybele (a mother goddess from Anatolia). Later they accepted the Egyptian cult of Isis and Osiris (popular among women) and the Persian cult of Mithras (popular among soldiers).

Gnosticism and Manichaeism. There were also religions that combined philosophy with elements of the mystery cults, such as Gnosticism and Manichaeism, both of which competed with Christianity for followers. The Gnostics, who were influential during the second and third centuries C.E., claimed that they possessed a secret form of revealed knowledge (*gnosis*). Their elaborate mythological theology and writings known as Gnostic Gospels reflected a dualistic world-view in which spirit was regarded as good while matter was despised as evil. The Manichaeans, followers of a Persian mystic named Mani (c. 216–275 C.E.), were also dualists and believed the world was caught in a struggle between the forces of light and darkness (which were associated with spirit and matter, respectively). In the third century C.E. there was also a very influential revival of Platonic philosophy known as Neoplatonism.

Neoplatonism. Although Neoplatonism was founded by Plotinus (c. 205–270 C.E.) as a school of philosophy, it included a mystical dimension. Later Neoplatonists, such as Porphyry (c. 233–305), Iamblichus (c. 250–300), and Proclus, (c. 410–485), added magical rituals. There were important parallels between later Neoplatonism and Christianity, and the two influenced one another considerably, even though they generally condemned one another's teachings. Although the Roman Empire finally accepted Christianity in the fourth century, its attitude toward the Judeo-Christian tradition until then was one of hostility.

THE JEWS IN THE ROMAN EMPIRE

Roman Rule. Relations between Romans and Jews began on a positive note. Led by the Hasmonean dynasty (the Maccabees), the Jews of Palestine rebelled against the Hellenistic rule of the Seleucids in 175–164 B.C.E. and allied themselves with Rome in 161 and 134 B.C.E. After winning their independence, they began to fight among themselves. When Pompey the Great visited the region in 63 B.C.E., he found two brothers struggling for the throne and intervened to stop the civil war by imposing Roman rule. At first the Romans tried to rule Judea indirectly, through local kings such as Herod (37–4 B.C.E.), but when this approach proved ineffective, they transformed the region from a client state to a province ruled directly by a Roman governor. Jewish society under Roman occupation was deeply divided. There were four major groups. The *Zealots* were violently opposed to the occupation. The *Sadducees* collaborated with the Roman occupation. The *Pharisees* resisted assimilation into Greco-Roman culture by adhering carefully to Mosaic Law. The *Essenes* fled to the wilderness and lived a kind of isolated monastic lifestyle. To maintain peace with the Jews, the Romans granted them certain concessions, such as exemption from honoring the cult of the emperor or performing military service. Yet even such favored treatment was not enough to conciliate the occupied people.

Rebellions. In 66 C.E. Judea erupted in a revolt that was bloodily suppressed after years of fighting; the last isolated Jewish fortress, Masada, was taken in 73 C.E. The Romans destroyed the Temple of Jerusalem in 70 C.E. and deported many. Later, the emperor Hadrian's attempt to Romanize Judea—particularly his decision to build a pagan temple in the holy city—triggered a revolt under the Messianic leader Bar-Kochba (132–135 C.E.). Many died in the ruthless suppression of the rebellion, and survivors had to flee the devastated area.

Diaspora. The suppression of Bar-Kochba's rebellion marked the end of Jerusalem as the effective focal point of Jewish life. Synagogues replaced the Temple as the center of worship, and Jewish culture endured in the Diaspora. Its theological development continued in the rabbinic schools, which established a comprehensive body of Jewish civil and religious law, known as the Mishnah, around 200 C.E. Over the following centuries until about 600 C.E., the Mishnah received commentary known as the Gemara, of which there are two versions: one compiled in Palestine, the other in Babylonia.

The Babylonian version became authoritative. Together the Mishnah and Gemara are known as the Talmud. This transformation of Judaism after the destruction of the Temple was also partly a reaction to an attempt to reform Judaism by a sect known as the Christians.

CHRISTIANITY

Jesus of Nazareth. Christianity began as a reform movement within Judaism led by Jesus of Nazareth, who was born around 4 B.C.E. and died around 30 C.E. (The modern reckoning of years began to be used in the sixth century C.E., but was based on a miscalculation of the year of Jesus' birth.) Jesus was alive during a time when the Jews eagerly awaited the appearance of a leader specially chosen by God to liberate them from oppression. This individual was called the "anointed one" (*Messiah* in Hebrew, *Christos* in Greek). The followers of Jesus believed he was the Messiah, though his teaching lacked overt political content and instead focused on an enlightened moral code summed up in two commands: first, love God; and secondly, love thy neighbor. Jesus promised that his followers would receive salvation and immortality when he returned at the end of the world to judge all human beings, and he chose twelve disciples called Apostles to spread the Gospel ("Good News") of salvation. He also instructed his disciples to remember him by sharing a special meal of bread and wine which he said were his body and blood, the sign of a new Covenant. Jesus was critical of the Pharisees for failing to live up to the ancient prophets' ideals of social justice. He became seen as a dangerous radical, and around 30 C.E., during the reign of Tiberius (14–37 C.E.), Jesus was arrested, brought before the Roman governor Pontius Pilate, and crucified.

Early Preaching. After their leader's death, the followers of Jesus began to proclaim that he had risen from the dead and would soon return. They now believed that the Messiah, or Christ, was not a king who would free the Jews from political oppression but one who would free all people from the oppression of sin and death. Thus they began to preach the Gospel and convert not only Jews, but also Gentiles (non-Jews), having made the crucial decision to remove the requirement of adherence to Mosaic Law. Gentiles who converted to Christianity had to accept only a few simple practices, including baptism and the Eucharist (meaning "thanksgiving"—the ritual meal in memory of Jesus), and to live up to the Christian moral code. The most instrumental missionary was Saul of Tarsus, better known as St. Paul, who regularly traveled the eastern Mediterranean as far as Rome preaching, converting, and guiding the fledgling Christian communities through his letters of advice and reprimand.

The New Testament. The first Christians expected Jesus' imminent return within their own lifetime. Yet as it became clear this would not happen, they began to write down Jesus' oral teaching. Thus the four Gospels, named after the disciples Matthew, Mark, Luke, and John, were composed around 70–100 C.E. The Gospels became the core of the New Testament, which was regarded as a fulfillment of the prophecies of the Hebrew Bible (renamed the Old Testament). The New Testament also includes letters, known as Epistles, written by early Christian leaders such as St. Paul, who is regarded as the first Christian theologian. The new Scriptures were written in *koine*, a form of Greek that represented everyday speech rather than the literary models of the Classical period.

The Appeal of Christianity. Christianity began as a religion of the oppressed and marginalized. The earliest converts were the poor and slaves. Women found the new faith attractive because it valued the salvation of their souls equally with that of men, unlike the mystery cult known as Mithraism, which was popular among Roman soldiers but excluded women. For three centuries Christianity competed with the mystery cults before it became the official religion of the Roman Empire. During most of this time, it was an underground movement that suffered periodic persecutions.

Persecutions. The earliest communities of the nascent religion blended Jewish and Christian practices. They were persecuted by some Jewish leaders who opposed their religious reforms. Saul of Tarsus initially hunted Christians before he himself became one after a dramatic conversion experience. He then endured the torments that other Christians suffered; according to tradition, he died in Rome in 64 C.E., a victim of the emperor Nero, who blamed a disastrous fire in Rome on the young sect. Nero's persecution was the first official action by a Roman emperor against Christians. Although angry mobs sometimes perpetrated acts of violence against them, it was not until the third century that energetic attempts were made to eradicate their religion. The Empire suffered a series of crises at this time, and Christians were seen as a threat to political order because they refused to worship the emperor—an act that was as much a statement of patriotism as a form of religious observance. Furthermore Christian rituals were misunderstood (the Eucharist was viewed as cannibalism), and Christians were resented for their non-conformism: for example, they opposed violent entertainment such as gladiatorial combats. The most serious official persecution was organized by Diocletian (284–305). Earlier attempts were also made by Marcus Aurelius (161–180) and Decius (249–251), among others. Christians who died in the persecutions were revered as martyrs, or "witnesses," of the faith and were accorded the status of saints ("holy ones").

Toleration and Official Status. The emperor Constantine (306–337), who succeeded Diocletian, reversed the policy of persecution by issuing the Edict of Milan (313), which granted toleration to Christians. Although Constantine's motivations are debatable, he is reported to have had a vision on the eve of the Battle of the Milvian Bridge in 312 (near Rome) which promised him victory against a rival emperor if he accepted the Christian religion. After the Edict of Milan, the Church received legal rights and soon became wealthy from donations. It was not until later, however, that paganism was forbidden, making Christianity the sole religion of the Empire. The emperor Julian (361–363) tried to revive paganism (using Neoplatonism as its theology), but otherwise all Roman emperors beginning with Constantine were Christians.

Monasticism. The transformation of Christianity from an oppressed faith to the official religion of the empire ensured its survival but also changed its quality. Many people became Christians in order to ingratiate themselves with the imperial family or to take advantage of the wealth that now belonged to the Church. Some devout Christians reacted by fleeing to the wilderness and living lives of prayer in seclusion. These became the first Christian monks, known as the "Desert Fathers." Although many of them were hermits who practiced a harsh ascetic regimen, such as St. Anthony of Egypt (c. 250–350), or St. Simon Stylites (c. 390–459) who lived on top of a pillar in Syria, others began to live in communities, such as the one organized by St. Pachomius (c. 290–346). All three of these prominent Desert Fathers lived in the Near East; from there monasticism was spread to western Europe by men like John Cassian (c. 360–433).

Heresy and Orthodoxy. Another effect of Christianity's rise to dominance in the Roman Empire was the politicization of its theological disputes. Differences of opinion over doctrine, always a matter of controversy, now became an occasion for persecution by one Christian group against another. Doctrines that were sanctioned by the imperial government were labeled "orthodoxy" (right teaching), whereas doctrines without such support were called "heresy" (sectarianism). Heresy was regarded not merely as religious non-conformism, but a crime against the state. Orthodoxy generally corresponded to the majority view, as determined by bishops in council, but often emperors pushed their own views against the judgment of bishops, or entire provinces might oppose the official teaching, as a political statement of regionalism. These disagreements sometimes erupted into riots and undermined the unity of the empire. Since Constantine had intended Christianity to be a unifying force within the empire, he was the first to take measures to resolve the theological disputes. The principal mechanism for establishing correct teaching was the general, or "ecumenical," church council. These conferences of bishops were initially convened by emperors. The early controversies focused on the Trinity, that is, the three persons of God (Father, Son, and Holy Spirit), and generated three main heresies.

Council of Nicaea (325): Against Arianism. Constantine convened the Council of Nicaea in 325 in order to settle the dispute over the nature of the relationship between Jesus Christ and the Father. This council established the Nicene Creed, a series of dogmatic statements which assert that Jesus, as the Son of God, is equal to the Father (these two persons are "consubstantial" and "coeternal"). The Council of Nicaea therefore condemned Arianism, the teaching of the theologian Arius that the Son is subordinate. The next council, at Constantinople (381), reaffirmed the Council of Nicaea and added that the Holy Spirit is also equal to the Father and the Son.

Council of Ephesus (431): Against Nestorianism. The third general council focused on the person of Christ and condemned the teachings of the theologian Nestorius, who taught that the two natures of Jesus (human and divine) require that he should be regarded as two persons. The Council of Ephesus defined the orthodox position as follows: Jesus has two natures (human and divine) which are joined in a single person (the second person of the Trinity). Despite persecution, Nestorian Christians continued to exist in Syria.

Council of Chalcedon (451): Against Monophysitism. The fourth general council also focused on the person of Christ. It condemned the teaching, known as Monophysitism, which holds that Jesus has only one nature (*mono-*, one; *physis*, nature). Monophysites claimed that Jesus is divine, but not human. Orthodox thinkers condemned this teaching because it opposed the position defined at Ephesus and seemed to deny the possibility of salvation (which was thought to depend on Christ's role as mediator between divinity and humanity). Although persecuted, Monophysitism persisted in Egypt and in Syria (where it was known as the Jacobite Church).

Leadership of the Church. During the late Roman Empire, there was tension over the question of ecclesiastical leadership. By the second century, Rome had become the center of Christianity. The bishops of Rome claimed to be the successors of St. Peter, the Apostle designated by Jesus as leader of the Church, who according to tradition was the first bishop of Rome, martyred during the persecutions of Nero in 64 C.E. This concept of *apostolic succession* served as the basis of the claim by the bishops of Rome to spiritual authority over the whole Church. They adopted the title of "pope" (*papa* in Latin, which means "father") to designate their special status. However, Christians did not agree on the supremacy of Rome. When the capital of the empire was moved to Constantinople, the bishops (patriarchs) of that city claimed leadership in the east. The patriarchs of other ancient Christian centers—Jerusalem, Antioch, and Alexandria—also claimed a certain status of regional leadership. The situation was complicated by the emperors, who often intervened in religious affairs (their claim to church leadership is called "Caesaropapism"). The various conflicting claims to leadership were never resolved but became the cause of later divisions within the Church.

REORGANIZATION OF THE EMPIRE

Crisis of the Third Century. After the reign of Marcus Aurelius (161–180), the Roman Empire faced a series of threats that nearly destroyed it. The barbarians breached the borders in the north while a new Persian dynasty, the Sassanians, launched aggressive campaigns in the east. Military expenditures increased while a period of economic decline set in. Manpower shortages hampered both defense and economics, and they were aggravated by waves of disease that swept through the Empire. To make matters worse, as the military became more prominent, power fell into the hands of the generals, who recklessly fought one another for control of the empire, ruling through puppet emperors who were frequently murdered in coups d'etat.

Diocletian's Reforms. The turmoil was finally checked by the rise of Diocletian (284–305), who initiated a comprehensive series of reforms that saved the Empire. To prevent future civil wars over imperial succession, and to deal more effectively with invasions on the far-flung borders, Diocletian instituted the Tetrarchy, or rule by four emperors, consisting of two seniors named Augusti and two juniors named Caesars. Each of them was in charge of a quarter of the empire known as a prefecture. Furthermore, to prevent provincial governors from amassing too much power, Diocletian reorganized imperial administration. He broke large provinces up into small ones, thereby limiting the resources that an overly-ambitious governor could use to stage a coup d'etat. The many provinces were organized into twelve units called dioceses (three in each prefecture), and each diocese was managed by a vicar who answered to a Caesar or an Augustus. The new imperial administration improved the centralization of power by streamlining the chain of command. A larger bureaucracy, which was needed to collect increased taxes, likewise diluted the power of individual governors.

Social and Economic Policies. Diocletian took drastic measures to deal with the shortage of manpower and revenue. He required that farmers remain tied to the land (thereby setting the foundation for serfdom in the

Middle Ages) and that sons carry on their father's trade (which foreshadowed the guild system). He tried to stop inflation by fixing prices and wages, but this measure was impossible to enforce and was a complete failure. In order to enforce obedience to his imperial authority, which he structured on the model of oriental despotism, Diocletian severely punished dissent. Frustrated by the refusal of Christians to show their patriotism by worshiping the cult of the emperor, he tried to stamp out Christianity.

Constantine the Great. Diocletian's administrative reforms were successful, but his solution for the imperial succession was not. As long as he governed as the senior Augustus, the other three emperors did as he intended. After he retired in 305, however, the emperors came into conflict. By 312, two remained standing: Constantine in the west and Licinius in the east. They ruled their halves of the empire until 324, when Constantine defeated his rival and became the sole emperor.

New Rome. In 330, Constantine (306–337) abandoned Rome, which had become a strategic and financial backwater, and founded a new capital called Constantinople at a defensible position in the northeast of the Empire, upon the site of the ancient city of Byzantium at the entrance to the Black Sea. He chose this location because it would facilitate the defense of the unstable northern and eastern borders and set the capital in the more prosperous eastern provinces, where revenue could be raised more effectively. The transfer of the capital was nothing new—Diocletian had made the nearby city of Nicomedia in Anatolia his capital for similar reasons, and emperors before them had transferred the capital to Milan in northern Italy. What was new was the decision to transfer the capital permanently to the east. Although this measure was intended to strengthen the empire, it foreshadowed the decline of the city of Rome and the western empire in the following century.

THE GERMANIC INVASIONS

Early Contact. The Romans first encountered Germanic tribes when the Teutones and Cimbri tried to invade Italy but were defeated by Marius in 102–101 B.C.E. Around 50 B.C.E. Julius Caesar challenged the Germans across the Rhine during his conquest of Celtic Gaul. Augustus Caesar later sent three legions to subdue the Germans and add their territory to the growing empire, but the Roman forces were annihilated in 9 C.E. by the German general Arminius (Hermann) in the Teutoburger Forest, ending Roman attempts to subjugate Germany.

Border Wars. Relations between Romans and Germans consisted largely of peaceful trade, but toward the end of the second century c.e. Germanic tribes began to raid the provinces, forcing Marcus Aurelius (161–180) to spend long years campaigning to protect the northern borders. Faced with shortages of manpower, he established a dangerous precedent by conducting alliances with some of the German tribes, known as *foederati* ("federates"), who were allowed to settle within the borders of the empire in exchange for defending it against other Germanic tribes. Over time, more and more tribes became *foederati*, and an increasing percentage of Roman legions were manned by German recruits, eventually with German generals commanding them. Entrusting the empire's defense to allied barbarians was effective in the short term, but ultimately contributed to the decline of the empire.

The Great Migrations. In the third century Germanic groups seized the Roman province of Dacia and invaded the Balkans, plundering Greece and Anatolia. German pirates even raided Mediterranean shipping for a time, but eventually the invaders were expelled and the borders stabilized. In the fourth and fifth centuries, however, the northern borders effectively disintegrated. German tribes entered the empire at will, and Roman emperors could not force them back. Most of the barbarians were not intent on destruction. They were impressed by Roman civilization and attracted by its wealth, which they hoped to control. The invasions beginning in the fourth century are often described as "migrations" because they involved the movement of entire tribes, including women and children, who wandered through the empire like nomads. They typically would settle in one place for years until supplies were exhausted, then move on to another location. Violence against the Roman population was not continuous, although it did flare up at times. While the number of barbarians wandering through the empire was always a small fraction of the imperial population, their presence strained the economy and weakened imperial administration, even in the absence of violence.

Visigoths. The migrations began with the Visigoths ("West Goths"), who received permission from the Emperor Valens to enter the Balkans in 376 in order to escape the Huns, an Asiatic group of marauding nomads. Abused by Roman administrators, however, the Visigoths revolted and Valens was killed in 378 at the Battle of Adrianople (in the Balkans). The Visigoths then made peace with the Romans and remained in the northern Balkans until 395, when a new leader, Alaric, guided them into the wealthier provinces of Greece and Italy. They plundered Rome in 410—the first time the city was seized by outsiders in 800 years (since the Gauls in 390 b.c.e.). However, the Visigoths did not conduct a general massacre of the inhabitants. They had already been converted to Christianity by Ulfilas (c. 311–382), an Arian who translated the Bible into Gothic, so they did not destroy churches or harm anyone who sought sanctuary in them. Soon Alaric died, and the Visigoths were led by Alaric's successor into southern Gaul and Spain, where they settled.

Vandals. In 406 a number of tribes, including the Suevi, Vandals, and Alans (a non-Germanic group), crossed the Rhine into Gaul, beginning migrations that brought some of them into North Africa. The movement was led by the Vandals, who passed through Visigoth-occupied Spain and reached North Africa in 429 under their king, Gaiseric (428–477). In 455 they mounted a raid into Italy across the Mediterranean and sacked Rome; the modern term "vandalism" is derived from them. The Vandals, like the Visigoths, were Arian Christians and were therefore despised as heretics. They in turn persecuted Orthodox (Catholic) Christians.

Angles, Saxons, and Jutes. By 410 the Romans had pulled all their legions from Britain in order to defend the provinces on the Continent. For protection against the Picts (ancient inhabitants of Scotland), the Britons asked for help from Germanic tribes, who then turned against the Britons, forcing them into Wales and occupying most of the island. The three principal tribes were the Angles, Saxons, and Jutes, who over time became one people. The region of Britain occupied by the invaders was named England after the Angles, who predominated. Unlike the Visigoths and Vandals, the Germanic invaders of Britain were pagan, not Christian.

Burgundians. Around the 440s, a group known as the Burgundians established themselves in southeastern Gaul, which was renamed Burgundy after them. Among their achievements was an early Germanic law code that extended to the Roman subjects within their newly-formed domain.

Huns. A pagan group from central Asia known as the Huns had established an empire over several German tribes in Europe. Under their leader Attila (433–453), known as the "Scourge of God," they invaded Gaul in 451 but were stopped near Châlons by an alliance of Romans and Visigoths. In 452 Attila threatened to sack Rome, but Pope Leo I (440–461) persuaded him to spare the city. The following year Attila died and his empire disintegrated.

The Last Roman Emperor in the West. When the Visigoths approached Italy early in the fifth century, the western emperor withdrew to the more defensible city of Ravenna on the Adriatic coast. In 476, however, a Gothic general in the Roman army named Odoacer (Odovacar) staged a coup d'etat with his German troops, seized Ravenna, and deposed the youthful emperor, Romulus Augustulus (475–476). This emperor was not replaced by a successor. Instead, Odoacer made himself king of Italy with the acquiescence of the eastern Roman emperor, Zeno (474–491), who was momentarily powerless to affect events in the west. Thus ended the western line of Roman emperors.

Ostrogoths. In 488 Zeno sent his ally Theodoric, king of the Ostrogoths (474–526), to overthrow Odoacer in Ravenna. Theodoric thus became king of Italy in 493. Although the Ostrogoths ("East Goths") initially ruled with the approval of the emperors in Constantinople, Justinian the Great (527–565) launched a war against them and reclaimed Italy in a long and terrible struggle lasting from 535 to 555.

Lombards. Justinian's reconquest of Italy did not endure. In 568, the pagan Lombards invaded Italy and by 572 established a kingdom in the Po valley, which became Lombardy. Constantinople was able to retain only southern Italy and a few coastal cities in the north, including Ravenna. Rome was claimed by the eastern emperors but not effectively defended by them. The Lombards finally converted to Christianity, but they often threatened the popes, who eventually turned to the Franks for protection. The Lombard kingdom lasted until 774, when it was overthrown by the Frankish king, Charlemagne.

Franks. The most successful of the barbarian groups were the Franks, from whom France gets its name. They were pagan when they entered Gaul, but converted to Catholicism rather than Arian Christianity around 500 under their king Clovis (481–511), thereby winning the goodwill and support of the clergy. The Frankish kingdom was ruled by two dynasties—the Merovingian and Carolingian—whose policies shaped the early Middle Ages in western Europe.

THE LATE EMPIRE

Augustine of Hippo. The period of the Germanic migrations corresponded with a decline in secular learning, but there was a flowering of literature and theology among the Christians, who were enjoying a period of favor after three centuries of oppression. The sack of Rome in 410, prompted pagans to blame Christianity for the disaster, but their criticisms were refuted by the North African bishop, St. Augustine of Hippo (354–430). His response was a theological interpretation of world history entitled *The City of God*, which presents a linear conception of time and a sense of history guided by providence. Augustine argued that disasters like the fall of governments were unimportant compared to the rise of Christianity, for the former were concerned only with the fate of the body, whereas the latter was also concerned with the fate of the soul. This thesis led Augustine to posit two cities—the city of God, consisting of faithful believers, and the city of Satan, consisting of those who do works of evil (these included hypocritical Christians as well as pagans). Augustine did not condemn all secular philosophy; he urged instead that Christians "despoil the Egyptians"—that is, take what is useful from pagan philosophy and put it at the service of Christian theology. He himself was well versed in Neoplatonism (having also dallied with Manichaeism) and wrestled with all manner of philosophical problems. He revealed the inner struggle that preceded his conversion in his autobiography, *The Confessions*.

Jerome and Ambrose. Two other leading Christian scholars were St. Jerome (c. 347–420), who translated the Bible from Hebrew and Greek into Latin (called the Vulgate), and St. Ambrose of Milan (c. 339–397) who served as an imperial administrator before he became a bishop. Ambrose challenged the power of the state by forcing the emperor Theodosius (379–395) to do public penance under pain of excommunication (denial of church services) when he had executed a number of citizens for participating in a riot. Thus Ambrose demonstrated the psychological power of the Church and at the same time established that Christian statesmen are not free to ignore the moral injunctions of Christianity for the sake of political expediency.

Doctors of the Church. The vital service rendered by these men in the foundation of the Church was acknowledged during the Middle Ages by identifying them as "Doctors" (teachers) of the Church, of which there are four Latin and four Greek. The Latin doctors include Augustine, Ambrose, Jerome, and Pope Gregory the Great (590–604). The Greek doctors include Athanasius (c. 293–373), Basil the Great (c. 329–379), John Chrysostom (c. 354–407), and Gregory of Nazianzus (c. 329–389).

Imitation and Preservation of the Classics. While churchmen explored uncharted intellectual territory and laid down principles for a new society, the educational institutions of the empire disintegrated. Apart from theology, little that was written was new. Most literary productions either imitated earlier models or summarized previous learning, and the emphasis was on preservation rather than creation. Yet there were certain innovations. For example, in preserving ancient texts, there was a transition from the use of the papyrus scroll to the *codex*—a book with pages—which is still in use today.

Architecture. Ecclesiastical culture showed vitality in the realm of architecture. For the first three hundred years, when Christianity was an underground religion, it was practiced either in catacombs or private houses. When it became legalized, there was an explosion of church-building. The characteristic design of Latin churches was established at this time on the model of the Roman court of law (*basilica*). Apart from ecclesiastical structures, however, the Late Empire had relatively little to offer by way of monumental architecture. The best example is the Arch of Constantine, but this structure demonstrates that craftsmanship had declined since the era of the *Pax Romana*.

THE FALL OF ROME

Much has been argued about the reasons for the "fall of Rome" which was actually a gradual process of disintegration. Essentially, the empire in the west disintegrated because the resources needed to defend the entire empire could no longer be raised, and the emperors in the new eastern capital sacrificed it as the less defensible region. It is important to distinguish between the fate of the city of Rome and the fate of the Roman Empire, for the fall of the city did not result in the immediate disintegration of the Empire. Most importantly, the emperors in Constantinople persisted until the end of the Middle Ages, and justifiably called themselves "Romans," since the Empire they governed was really a continuation of the evolving institution founded by Augustus Caesar. Furthermore, even in the west, the Roman Empire did not come to an end in any clearly identifiable year—the end of the western imperial line in 476 C.E. merely recognized the fact that the office of the western emperor had become a meaningless position some time before it was finally abandoned. The cultural tradition of the Roman Empire continued to exert its influence and blended with the cultural tradition of the Germanic barbarians, resulting in the creation of a distinct, medieval culture.

CHAPTER 4
The Middle Ages

Chapter 4

THE MIDDLE AGES

THE BYZANTINE EMPIRE

Characteristics. The eastern half of the Roman Empire which survived the Germanic migrations is known to modern historians as the "Byzantine Empire," since the new capital was built on the site of the ancient city of Byzantium at the entrance to the Black Sea. The "Byzantines" continued to call themselves "Romans," but Greek replaced Latin as the common language. The Byzantine Empire, based in the wealthy commercial cities of the east, was better able to afford armies for its defense than the rural west, and thus remained intact.

Beginnings. Constantinople was founded in 330, when the Roman Empire was united under a single emperor, Constantine the Great (306–337). In 395, however, it was divided into two halves to ease administration. In 476 the last of the western emperors was deposed. Attempts by the eastern emperors to control the western provinces through barbarian allies were ineffective. A dramatic effort to reclaim the west was made by Justinian the Great (527–565), whose armies retook North Africa, part of Spain, and Italy. Most of these reacquisitions were lost, however, within a few years of Justinian's death. The Byzantines were able to hold only southern Italy and a few northern coastal cities, most notably Ravenna. Although they claimed Rome, they were not able to exercize control over it.

Justinian and Theodora. Early Byzantine history is dominated by a great leader, Justinian I. Much of Justinian's success was due to his wife, the Empress Theodora, who had been a dancing girl in her youth. Early in Justinian's reign (532) a fight between political factions erupted at the chariot races and became a protest against the government known as the Nika riots. Justinian considered fleeing, but Theodora urged him to stay and risk his life suppressing the rebellion. Her courageous intervention thus made possible all the later achievements of Justinian's reign.

Religion. Theodora's influence was particularly important in religion. She sympathized with the heretical Monophysites and was able to secure toleration for them, thereby improving the obedience of the southeastern provinces, where the sect predominated.

Architecture and the Arts. Justinian and Theodora embarked on a lavish building program of public works. Their greatest monument in Constantinople was the cathedral of Holy Wisdom, known by its Greek name, *Hagia Sophia*. This structure boasts a massive dome atop a rectangular base, and its interior is decorated by colorful mosaics which use an iconic, otherworldly style to emphasize the power and majesty of the empire in its role as defender of the Christian faith.

Military Policy. While Justinian committed his armed forces to the reconquest of the west, he secured the eastern borders against attacks by the Sassanian dynasty of Persia through a combination of war, diplomacy, and the payment of tribute.

Law. Perhaps Justinian's greatest achievement was the codification of Roman Law, which he entrusted to a team of legal experts led by the jurist Tribonian in the 530s. Justinian's Code, a collection of volumes written in Latin and known by the title *Corpus Juris Civilis* ("Body of Civil Law"), put many centuries of Roman legal precepts and judicial decisions into an orderly system. It served as the law code for the Byzantine Empire until the ninth century, when a condensed version known as the *Basilica* was issued in Greek. Later, Justinian's Code served as a textbook during the revival of legal studies in western Europe.

Aftermath of Justinian's Reign. The deeds of Justinian and Theodora were described by the Byzantine historian Procopius, whose official texts praised them, but whose *Secret History* depicted them as bloodthirsty tyrants and demon-worshipers. Justinian's achievements came at a high price. His successors had to deal with the bankruptcy incurred by his spending, as well as rebellion in the far-flung corners of the empire. They gave up the west for lost and turned their attention eastward, where they had to fight seemingly endless wars against the aggressive Sassanians. Heraclius (610–641) finally achieved victory in 628, but his empire was so weakened by war and internal dissension that the southeastern provinces soon afterwards fell to a new eastern power—the armies of Islam that erupted from the Arabian peninsula in 634.

ISLAM

A New Religion. Islam was founded by Muhammad (570–632), who is considered the final Prophet by the Muslims. The Arabic word *islam* means "submission" to the will of God (*Allah*) as set forth by the Prophet Muhammad, and *muslim* means "one who submits." The religion is a monotheistic faith within the Judeo-Christian tradition whose basic tenets, or practices, are summed up in five "pillars": (1) the profession of faith ("There is no God but God and Muhammad is his Prophet"), (2) daily prayers at specified times, (3) almsgiving, (4) fasting during the month of Ramadan, and (5) a pilgrimage to the holy city of Mecca known as the *hajj*. The Islamic holy book is the Quran, which means "recitation," and refers to the oral revelation that Muhammad gave to his followers. The Quran urges believers to spread the faith by any means, including military, although it requires that respect be shown to Jews and Christians ("People of the Book"), who could not be forcibly converted but were required to pay a special tax if they refused to become Muslim.

Muhammad. Arabia during Muhammad's youth was a polytheistic society that was acquainted with monotheism through Jewish and Christian contacts. Muhammad's revelations began in 610. His early attempts to convert fellow Arabs in the holy city of Mecca, which contained the shrine known as the Ka'ba, met with little success. In 622 Muhammad was invited to Medina as a peacemaker and became the leader of the city. This event is known as the *Hegira*, or "migration," and marks the first year of the Muslim calendar (which is lunar rather than solar). After fighting several battles with the Meccans, Muhammad became the first ruler to unite all of Arabia.

Conquest. Soon after the death of Muhammad in 632, the Arabs began a dramatic series of conquests that established an Islamic Arab empire stretching from India in the east to Spain in the west, which they achieved within the span of a mere hundred years. Reasons for their success are several. The new faith inspired zeal for action and urged spreading the faith through conquest. The Arabs also struck at an opportune moment: the long wars between the Byzantines and Sassanians had weakened both of these empires and prevented them from mounting effective resistance. The Byzantines were also divided by religious controversies: the Monophysites of Syria and Egypt had suffered persecution from the emperors in Constantinople and preferred Arab masters who granted them religious freedom to Christian masters who did not. The Arab migrations also relieved population pressure in their desert homeland, which could not support an expanding population and depended on imports of food. By 656 the Arabs had conquered Persia, Mesopotamia, Syria, Palestine, and Egypt.

Succession: Division between Sunnites and Shiites. Arab expansion was then momentarily checked by the outbreak of a civil war over the question of succession. When Muhammad died, he had no male heir and had not designated a successor. The Muslim community, or *Umma*, elected an early convert to Islam named Abu Bakr to serve as Muhammad's "successor," or *caliph*. This theocratic office combined religious and political power. The brief caliphate of Abu Bakr (632–634) was spent putting down revolts in order to maintain the unity of the Muslims. The next caliph, Umar (634–644), initiated the conquests. His successor, Uthman (644–656), alienated many Muslims by his practice of giving important positions to members of the old Meccan elite. Uthman was assassinated and the Muslims became divided over the next successor. The Shiites (sectarians) believed the caliph should be a descendant of Muhammad and chose his son-in-law Ali; the Sunnites (traditionalists) sided with Muawiyah, who was a kinsman of Uthman and demanded vengeance for his death. The civil war ended in 661 with Ali's murder, and another flared up in 680 at the next succession, which ended with the death of Ali's son, Hussein. The split between Sunnites and Shiites generated long-lasting animosity and instability within the Muslim world.

The Umayyads (661–750). The two civil wars established Muawiyah's dynasty, the Umayyads, and enabled the Muslims to continue their conquests. The Umayyads transferred the capital from Mecca to Damascus in order to direct the conquests more effectively. There they received the help of skilled Christian administrators and adopted many Byzantine techniques of government. Since non-Muslims could be taxed heavily, the Umayyads did not encourage mass conversions to Islam.

The Abbasids (750–1258). The luxury and worldliness of the Umayyads antagonized many devout Muslims. In 750 they were overthrown by Abul Abbas, who founded the Abbasid dynasty. He moved the capital from Damascus to the newly-built city of Baghdad beside the Tigris River, which became an advanced center of learning as the Abbasids patronized scholars who translated the philosophy, science, and medicine of the ancient world into Arabic. Most of the Near East and North Africa converted to Islam during their reign.

Division of the Muslim World. One of the Umayyads escaped the purge and set up a rival caliphate in Spain, with Cordoba as its capital. Under the Umayyads, Cordoba became a magnificent cultural center, boasting libraries and a mosque that combined Roman architectural features, such as rounded arches and domes, with geometric designs characteristic of Arabic art (which shunned the use of representational images in public places). Over the centuries, both the Abbasid and Umayyad caliphates became politically fragmented. A third caliphate, that of the Fatimids, established itself in North Africa during the tenth century and challenged the Abbasids, who eventually became puppets of their Turkish soldiers. They were finally overthrown by the Mongols in 1258.

BYZANTIUM TO 1000 C.E.

The division of the Muslims saved the Byzantine Empire, which had been nearly destroyed by the Arab invaders. Constantinople itself was attacked several times beginning in 672, and most seriously in 717–718, but it survived thanks to its strong defenses, including a secret weapon known as "Greek fire," which burned even on water and could devastate enemy forces that came near the walls. The Byzantines were attacked by many groups in addition to the Muslim Arabs. Their provinces in the Balkans were harassed by Avars (a Turkic group from central Asia), as well as Slavic groups such as the Bulgarians, and even by Vikings (known as Varangians). All these groups at one time or another assailed Constantinople itself. The Byzantines remained on the defensive until the ninth century, but in the tenth century were able to reconquer Anatolia from the Muslims and much of the Balkans from the Slavs. By the year 1000, their empire had expanded once again to include much of the Balkans, Anatolia, southern Italy (which they held since the wars of Justinian), and the islands of Crete and Cyprus.

THE GERMANIC KINGDOMS

During the age of Islam's rapid conquests and Byzantium's struggle for survival, the Germanic peoples established kingdoms in the west. Those in Gaul and Britain established the foundations for the modern European states of France and England.

Visigothic Spain. After sacking Rome in 410, the Visigoths settled in Spain and southern Gaul, but were driven from the latter by the Franks in 507. Confined to Spain, the Visigoths lost some territory to the Byzantine Empire during Justinian's wars. The kingdom was finally overthrown by Muslims from North Africa in 711.

The Franks under the Early Merovingians. The Roman province of Gaul came under the control of the Franks in the fifth century, and a dynasty founded by Merovech (448–458) united the two main groups, Salian and Ripuarian, from the lower and upper reaches of the Rhine River. The most important of the Merovingian kings was Clovis (481–511). Unlike the Visigoths and Vandals, who entered the Empire as heretical Arian Christians, the Franks arrived as pagans and were converted to Roman Catholic Christianity during the reign of Clovis, around the year 500. With the blessings of

Catholic churchmen, Clovis attacked his Arian neighbors and established a large and powerful kingdom. The events of this age are described by Bishop Gregory of Tours (538–594), whose flawed writing style indicates the low quality of literacy among the Franks at this time.

The Late Merovingians. The Frankish practice of dividing up the kingdom among all the surviving sons when a monarch died led to periodic phases of civil war as brothers fought one another to re-establish a strong monarchy. In such endemic warfare, the nobles on whom the kings relied tended to become strong. In time, the nobles were able to manipulate the Merovingians, who became mere figureheads known as the "do-nothing" kings.

The Carolingians. The most powerful of the Frankish nobles were the members of the Carolingian dynasty, named after its founder, Charles Martel (whose name in Latin is *Carolus*). This dynasty held the office of Mayor of the Palace and used it to control the Merovingian kingdom. In 732 Charles Martel (c. 688–741) led the Frankish defense against Muslim raiders and defeated them at the Battle of Tours. This event prevented Islam from establishing itself beyond Spain.

The First Carolingian King: Pepin the Short. Charles Martel's son, Pepin (or Pippin) the Short (c. 714–768), was not satisfied to rule the Franks as Mayor of the Palace. In 751 he deposed the last Merovingian king and asked the pope to legitimize his seizure of power. Pope Stephen II (752–757) needed help against the Lombards, so in 754 he crowned Pepin king of the Franks. In gratitude, Pepin defeated the Lombards and in 755 gave part of their territory to the pope. This land grant, known as the Donation of Pepin, founded the Papal States. The alliance of the Carolingians and the papacy enhanced the authority of each: while the Carolingians became the legitimate kings of the Franks, the popes received a sizable state in central Italy and became recognized as kingmakers.

Charlemagne. Pepin's son, Charlemagne (768–814)—whose name means "Charles the Great" (*Carolus Magnus* in Latin)—inherited the largest territory in the west since the days of the Roman Empire and greatly expanded it during his long reign. He took northern Italy from the last Lombard king (774), seized a strip of territory from the Muslims in Spain (778), subjugated the Avars on the Danube (795–796), and forcibly converted the pagan Saxons to Christianity after campaigns spanning 32 years (772–804). In upholding his alliance with the papacy, Charlemagne suppressed an uprising in Italy, and on Christmas Day of the year 800 Pope Leo III (795–816) crowned him Roman Emperor. According to Charlemagne's biographer, Einhard, the Frankish king was surprised and not pleased by the event, which implied that the emperor's authority came from the pope. Nevertheless, Charlemagne refused neither the title nor the coronation. The event certainly displeased the Byzantines, who governed southern Italy, but eventually they recognized Charlemagne as the legitimate ruler in the north.

The Carolingian Renaissance. Charlemagne's achievements were not limited to conquest. In administration, Charlemagne regularly met with his counts and bishops, and he sent special agents, called *missi dominici*, throughout his realm to check up on them. He also took great care to ensure the spiritual and intellectual well-being of his realm. He founded schools to train the clergy, regulated monastic practice by promoting the use of the Benedictine Rule, and gathered together the finest scholars from all over western Europe to his court at Aachen, which became an international center of learning. Charlemagne was concerned to make available accurate copies of the Vulgate Bible and encouraged the development of a more legible script to keep errors from creeping into the text. The script, which is known as Carolingian minuscule, was developed at the monastery of Tours under the guidance of Alcuin of York. Charlemagne favored the use of Latin as the common language so that men from various parts of his diverse empire could easily communicate with one another; to facilitate its study he encouraged the preservation of the Latin classics by careful copying of manuscripts.

The Later Carolingian Kings. Charlemagne was able to hold his empire together through personal energy and charisma, but toward the end of his life it began to disintegrate. His son, Louis the Pious (814–840), was unable to keep it intact. The sons of Louis fought over their shares of the realm but eventually came to an agreement known as the Treaty of Verdun (843), which divided the realm into three parts: the western part went to Charles the Bald, the central part (along with the imperial title) went to Lothair, and the eastern part went to Louis the German. By 870, the northern parts of the middle kingdom had been swallowed up by its neighbors, and the new boundaries were then formalized in the Treaty of Mersen. These divisions were to have long-lasting effects inasmuch as they roughly established the borders of the modern European states of France and Germany. Disagreements over the division of the middle kingdom—particularly the regions of Alsace and Lorraine (which is named after Lothair)—were a cause of friction between France and Germany as late as the twentieth century.

The Conversion of Britain. While the Franks were busy on the Continent, important changes were taking place in the former Roman province of Britain. In the fifth century, the Celts at the northern end of Britain and the Germanic invaders who occupied the southern and central parts of the island were pagan. In the sixth century, both groups were converted to Catholicism by monastic missionaries, one group from Ireland (which St. Patrick converted around 430), the other from Rome. Irish monks led by St. Columba began converting the Picts (in Scotland) in 563, and Roman monks sent by Pope Gregory the Great and led by Augustine of Canterbury began to convert the Anglo-Saxons in 597. The Irish monks made vital contributions to the preservation of ancient texts and produced lavishly illuminated manuscripts of religious texts. Their art influenced the Anglo-Saxons. By the mid-seventh century the foundations of Christianity in Britain were laid, but the two groups of missionaries—Celtic and Roman—came into conflict over discrepancies in religious practice, such as the calculation of the date of Easter and questions of ritual. The conflict was resolved at the Synod of Whitby in 664 when the Celtic church accepted Latin practices.

Anglo-Saxon England. The Germanic invaders of Britain established seven kingdoms (known as the Heptarchy). They fought among themselves until the tenth century, when the Kingdom of Wessex united all the others. An important source for the early history of the Anglo-Saxons in Britain was written by the Northumbrian monk the Venerable Bede (c. 673–735), whose *History of the English Church and People* testifies to the high quality of education in the English monasteries. Charlemagne drew upon this talent when he invited Alcuin of York (735–804) to head the educational reforms of his own realm.

Vikings. Around the year 800, England, Ireland, and the northern coasts of the Continent began to suffer raids from Scandinavian pagans known as the Vikings. These Northmen used their longships to conduct hit-and-run tactics along the coasts and up rivers. Since the Vikings initially avoided pitched battles and struck isolated targets of opportunity, they were very difficult to deal with.

Invasions of the Ninth and Tenth Centuries: Vikings, Saracens, and Magyars. Eventually the Vikings began to settle in Ireland, Normandy (which was named after these "Northmen" or Normans), and England (in the region known as the Danelaw, named after Vikings from Denmark). As the Vikings struck in the north, two other groups assailed Europe from the south and east. In the south, the Muslims (whom medieval Christians generally called "Saracens") gained control of the Mediterranean, established several bases outside Spain, and conducted piratical raids along the southern coasts of Europe. In 843 they even attacked Rome. In the east, a nomadic group known as the Magyars entered Europe around the year 900 and raided the crumbling remnants of the Carolingian empire. However, the victory of the German ruler Otto the Great over the Magyars at the Battle of Lechfeld in 955 ended their depredations, and the defeated people settled in

Hungary. By the year 1000, the devastating raids finally ended and Europe was poised for a period of peace and prosperity that was to transform medieval civilization.

THE MEDIEVAL CHURCH

Diocesan Structure. The Christian religion was the major civilizing influence in Europe during the Middle Ages. The Church was modeled after the structure of imperial Roman administration, which was organized into regional units known as *dioceses*. When Roman government completely broke down, the parallel ecclesiastical structure remained intact, and amid the chaos of political fragmentation it continued to provide a framework for unity at least on the spiritual level. In many cases the bishops who ran the ecclesiastical dioceses assumed some of the political functions that Roman governors had previously performed. Nowhere is this more obvious than in the case of the papacy.

Rise of the Papacy. The bishops of Rome used the title "pope" (in Latin, *papa*, "father") to assert their claim to spiritual leadership of the Church. They based this claim on the concept of apostolic succession—the idea that they were successors to an Apostle—and the belief that St. Peter, whom Jesus chose as the leader of the Apostles, was also the first bishop of Rome. As the Empire disintegrated, the papacy began to assume an important political dimension. For example, when the western emperor was hiding from Attila the Hun at Ravenna, Pope Leo I (440–461) spoke with the barbarian warlord and persuaded him not to sack Rome. The weakness of the western emperors, and later their complete absence, was a major reason for the rise of the papacy to a position of leadership. By contrast, the patriarchs of Constantinople did not achieve a similar eminence because they were overshadowed by the eastern emperors, who often interfered in the governance of the Greek Church. But although the papacy enjoyed spiritual freedom, it also had to endure political instability.

Gregory the Great. The pontificate of St. Gregory I (590–604), known as the Great, demonstrates how the papacy was threatened by the chaos of the age and responded by assuming a political role. Rome was threatened at the time by the Lombards. To counter the threat, Gregory negotiated with the barbarians and paid them tribute, which he raised from the papal estates. He also used this source of wealth to feed the poor of Rome and to maintain public works—functions that had once been performed by the imperial civil service. All this activity was in addition to the role of spiritual leadership that Gregory brilliantly promoted. He maintained papal primacy over the patriarch of Constantinople in his regular communications with the eastern empire and wrote voluminous theological works for the education of the Christian people, earning the title "Doctor of the Church." His works include a massive commentary on the Book of Job known as the *Moralia*, and his *Dialogues* recount the life of St. Benedict of Nursia, who founded the dominant monastic order in the Latin west. Gregory himself was a monk, and his promotion of Benedictine monasticism contributed to its preeminence in medieval Europe.

Donation of Constantine. As noted earlier, Gregory's successors established an alliance with the Carolingians against the Lombards and in 755 received a temporal state, carved from Lombard lands, through the Donation of Pepin. Hoping to justify this new temporal power, the papal chancery forged a document later in the eighth century that purported to be a grant of sovereignty to the papacy from Constantine the Great (306–337). This so-called Donation of Constantine was proven to be a forgery by the Renaissance humanist Lorenzo Valla (1407–1457), but until the fifteenth century it was used to justify papal claims to temporal power.

Conflicts with the Greeks. The popes used their new political prestige to reassert the claim to primacy in matters of doctrine and ecclesiastical administration. They assumed the power to convene church councils (which once belonged to the emperors)—a move which caused tension with the eastern empire and church.

Iconoclasm. The popes intervened in the Iconoclastic Controversy that shook the Greek Church in the eighth and ninth centuries. The controversy arose in 726 when the Byzantine Emperor Leo III (717–741) forbade the veneration of *icons* (paintings of saints), which he condemned as idolatry. The papacy supported the use of icons in devotions and condemned the imperial decrees, which were finally reversed in 843 by the Byzantine Empress Theodora II.

The Filioque Controversy. Tensions flared again when the popes added a clause to the Nicene Creed in order to clarify the Church's teaching on the Trinity. This *filioque* clause asserted that the Holy Spirit proceeds not only from the Father but also "from the Son," thereby giving the Son a greater role than the original Nicene Creed stated. This theological difference, coupled with centuries of antagonism over the question of papal supremacy, resulted in a schism during the ninth century between the Greek church led by the Patriarch Photius and the Latin church led by Pope Nicholas I (858–867). This temporary schism became permanent in 1054 when Pope Leo IX (1048–1054) attempted to extend papal jurisdiction over the Byzantine churches in southern Italy and was rebuffed by the Patriarch of

Constantinople, Michael Caerularius. The two churches declared one another heretical, using the *filioque* clause to justify their action.

Monasticism. In the age of the late empire and during its disintegration, many devout Christians became monks in order to leave the corrupting influence of the world and to focus on the spiritual life. Inspired by their example, Christian society often turned to the monks for guidance. Thus, the isolation of the monasteries was tempered by the service that monks performed, much of which consisted in converting pagans. Monasticism was a self-regulating institution—it was not imposed by the papacy or church hierarchy, but arose independent of the diocesan structure as a kind of grass-roots movement. In the fifth and sixth centuries, there were many independent groups of monks following different visions of what the monastic life should entail, as reflected in written guides called "rules." An Italian monk, St. Benedict of Nursia (c. 480–547), revised one of these rules and added important innovations that made his monastic order superior to others. The Benedictine order, which began at Monte Cassino in Italy, became the dominant form of monasticism in western Europe until the twelfth century.

The Benedictine *Rule*. St. Benedict's *Rule* rose to preeminence partly because its inherent qualities made it successful and popular, and partly because it was promoted by popes like Gregory the Great and by the Carolingians. The Benedictine *Rule* differed from other monastic rules not so much in requiring its adherents to renounce private property, sex, and free will (the standard vows of poverty, chastity, and obedience), but because it struck an ideal balance between three important requirements of monasticism: work (which was needed to make the monastery economically self-sufficient), study (which was needed to ensure the community's orthodoxy), and prayer (which was the central goal of the whole enterprise). Benedict's *Rule* also differed from other monastic rules in focusing on the life of the community. Its aim was to put the spiritual life within the reach of any devoted soul, not just the advanced individual. While many other rules demanded difficult and painful acts of austerity, Benedict wanted his monks to receive enough food and sleep so that they could concentrate on prayer, and he did not encourage physical pain (such as flagellation) as a form of devotion. Benedict did, however, allow corporal punishment, but only for the purpose of disciplining unruly monks who would not respond to more lenient forms of correction.

Benedictine Monasticism. A Benedictine monastery was governed by an abbot ("father") who was chosen by the monks of the community. The abbot had absolute power over the community and appointed the lower offices, of which the most important was the prior. Nevertheless, he was sworn to uphold the Benedictine *Rule* and he conferred with his monks when important decisions had to be made. St. Benedict's monasteries were designed to be independent of the outside world, producing their own food, tools, and books. To produce the books they needed for prayer and study, monasteries had a special room called the *scriptorium*, where monks copied texts onto parchment made from animal-skins (paper was unknown). While most of the books in the monasteries served religious purposes, the monks also preserved much classical pagan literature because these works offered models of good Latin, which the monks tried to imitate in their own writing. Monasteries were islands of literacy in a sea of ignorance.

Peace Movements. The central message of Christianity was at odds with the tenor of early medieval society, which was dominated by violence—not only from invaders, but also between neighboring lords, who frequently fought one another. In order to minimize the disruptive impact of war among Christian lords, the Church promoted two movements, known as the Peace of God and Truce of God. The Peace of God began in northwestern Europe during the tenth century as an effort to protect non-combatants, such as priests and peasants. The move was at first resisted by the nobles, but by the eleventh century they tended to promote it in an effort to stop fighting between their henchmen. The Truce of God was an attempt begun in the eleventh century to limit the number of days on which combat could take place. It tried to keep Sundays and major holidays such as Easter and Christmas free of fighting, and punished violators with excommunication (denial of the sacraments and exclusion from the Christian community).

FEUDALISM AND MANORIALISM

Origins of Feudalism. The barbarian kings who took control of the crumbling Roman Empire tended to treat the territories of the western provinces as their personal possessions. They rewarded their retainers with grants of land which supplied wealth, mainly in the form of agricultural produce. These land grants were not initially hereditary. The Carolingians granted estates called *benefices* to support troops as long as the troops remained in their service. It was not until about the year 1000 that the grants of land became hereditary and began to be called *fiefs*. The fief gave rise to a new form of political organization called "feudalism."

Limitations of the Terminology. The term "feudalism" is derived from the word "fief" (*feudum* in Latin), not from "feuds" or dynastic struggles. One should be aware that the entire concept of feudalism has been criticized by some historians, who object that it was not actually a well-defined system and did not exist in all parts of Europe throughout the Middle Ages. Indeed, what historians call feudalism did not appear until the eleventh century, and mainly in the region of northern France, the Low Countries, and England, where it was most fully developed during the twelfth and thirteenth centuries. Yet even within this limited time and place, there was considerable variation from one region to another. Feudalism is closely associated with the Normans. Since this adventurous group conquered southern Italy, Sicily, and the Holy Land, feudal practices were exported to these regions as well.

Classical Feudalism. The abstract concept of "classical" feudalism designates a form of political and military organization. At its heart was the *fief*, a land grant made by a *lord* to a lower member of the nobility called a *vassal*. Lord and vassal entered into a personal relationship that involved contractual obligations on both sides. In addition to the land grant, which provided an income, the lord promised to protect his vassal from enemies. In exchange, the vassal swore oaths of *homage* (respect) and *fealty* (loyalty); he thereby agreed to use the wealth produced by the fief to arm himself and his retainers in order to provide military service for his lord (in addition to fulfilling his other duties, such as serving in his lord's court of law). Fiefs were hereditary as long as the vassal's heir paid an inheritance tax and swore homage and fealty to the lord or the lord's heir. If the lord granted a large enough fief, the vassal could parcel it out to yet lower members of the nobility, in which case the vassal became a lord to his own vassals. This process is known as *subinfeudation*, whereby a social pyramid of nobles was erected with knights at the bottom and the king at the top. Although in theory the king was supreme and owned all the land, feudalism was characterized by weak central authority, for in an age of poor long-distance communication, the fief rather than the nation was the effective foundation of political power.

Manorialism. The economic form of organization associated with feudalism is known as manorialism. While feudalism describes the relationship between a lord and his vassal, manorialism describes the relationship between the owner of a fief and his laborers. The manor (which was the same as the fief, but from an economic point of view) was derived from the large agricultural estates of the Roman Empire. In the tumultuous third century, the emperors decreed that agricultural laborers (whether slave or tenant) could not leave the land. Likewise in the Middle Ages these laborers, called serfs, were unfree. Nevertheless, they had certain rights: since they could not be separated from the land which they worked, they could not be sold as slaves.

Organization of the Manor. The best portion of the manor was reserved for the lord as his *demesne*. The serfs were required to work the *demesne* in addition to the strips assigned to them for their own support. Strips assigned to the serfs were scattered in several fields in order to ensure that all had a share of the best and worst land. Much of the manor was not cultivated, but was left wild as the lord's hunting preserve. When more cultivated fields were needed, however, some of the woodland would be cleared; these newly-cleared regions were called *assarts*. The manor was essentially a self-sufficient economic unit, as it needed to be in an age of poor transportation when there was little trade.

POPULATION GROWTH

Stability. Around the year 1000, the invasions that had plagued Europe for centuries finally stopped. The Vikings and Magyars converted to Christianity and became part of European society. Although Europe remained politically fragmented, a period of relative stability ensued.

Agricultural Improvements. After centuries of decline, European population experienced an explosion that was aided by improvements in agricultural technique and technology. A three-field system replaced the old two-field system of agriculture, allowing one-third of the land to lie fallow (unused) every three years while crops were rotated in the other two fields. In this way nutrients in the soil were replenished and crop yields were boosted. The development of the horse-collar replaced oxen with horses as draft animals and allowed the use of a heavier plow, which was fitted with a moldboard that could turn over the dense soils of northern Europe more efficiently. Climate also favored agriculture at this time, for a long spell of warmer weather extended the growing season.

Changes on the Manor. The increased quantities of produce could now be processed more efficiently through another widespread technological innovation: mills. Both water mills and windmills were in use by the twelfth century. These, along with communal ovens for baking bread, were owned by the lord of the manor, who charged a fee for their use. As coinage came into increased circulation, lords increasingly preferred payment of manorial dues from their peasants in the form of a fixed money rent rather than service or a share of produce.

Social Opportunities. The lot of the peasants generally improved. In exchange for clearing forests, they might receive a reduction of manorial obligations. They might also win their freedom by escaping to one of the new towns that were rising all over Europe; if they stayed there for a certain length of time, they became burghers (citizens of the town) and could engage in any of the specialized trades that were plied there. The situation was summed up in a medieval proverb: "town air makes one free."

TRADE AND TOWNS

The Rise of Towns. A consequence of political stability and the population explosion of the eleventh century was the revival of trade and the rise of towns. Since travel was now safer, trade began to revive and towns, which are focal points for the exchange of goods, began to appear at intersections along the paths of commerce.

The Threefold Model of Medieval Society. The agricultural society of the early Middle Ages conceived of itself as three classes, or orders, characterized by the function each performed: "those who fight, those who pray, those who work." The three classes depended on one another. The warriors protected men of prayer and laborers; the men of prayer cared for the needs of the soul; and the laborers provided food. When trade and towns arose, so did a new social class, that of the merchants. The merchants lived in towns rather than on the manor and were therefore called burghers, or bourgeois, after the medieval words for "town" (*burg*, *bourg*). Since they did not fit into the three traditional orders but defied convention by seeking to acquire wealth and privilege, they were at first frowned upon. The Church in particular distrusted their interest in making money, which was denounced as the sin of avarice, and tried to regulate their activity by forbidding profits from the charging of interest (which was called usury) and by recommending the "just price," which urged the earning of a modest profit rather than charging as high a price as the market would bear. Eventually, however, the merchant came to be accepted as a vital member of medieval society. Kings allied themselves with merchants in order to increase their own power and came to rely on them for loans.

Merchant Guilds. Although travel had become safer by the eleventh century, there were still dangers. Merchants banded together in caravans for protection against highway robbery, and this cooperation was the origin of the merchant guilds (corporations), which tended to dominate the economic life of the towns. By joining forces through a guild, merchants were able to set prices, ensure quality control, and help one another in legal disputes, thus preventing unwanted competition from outsiders and presenting a united front against attempts to weaken their position. Entry into a guild had to be approved by the existing members.

Fairs. Trade benefited the regions where it occurred. In order to draw merchants into a given region, rulers or towns would organize fairs, which facilitated trade by bringing merchants and their goods from distant parts into close contact. The most famous of the medieval fairs were those of Champagne in France.

Maritime Trade. While fairs were good for stimulating trade inland, it flourished most of all along the coasts, since ships could move goods more quickly and efficiently than wagons and carts. By the twelfth century, the Muslims had lost control of the Mediterranean and trade became dominated by Italian cities, most notably Venice and Genoa, who fought one another in naval battles as an extension of their commerical rivalry. Trade was also robust along the shores of the Baltic and North Seas, where the cities of the Netherlands and the coastal German cities dominated commerce.

Trade Organizations. Sometimes merchants from neighboring towns joined forces. The most notable example of such an association was the Hanseatic League, or Hansa, which began among German towns such as Lübeck, Hamburg, and Bremen, for protection against piracy. It dominated trade between the North Sea and the Baltic Sea. The Hansa arose in the twelfth century, was at its height in the fourteenth, and was rendered obsolete by the commercial ventures of nation-states during the sixteenth century.

Craft Guilds. The craftsmen who bought raw materials from traveling merchants also began to organize themselves into guilds, and by the end of the twelfth century were able to challenge the merchants for domination of economic life in the towns. These craft guilds were organized around specific trades (e.g., shoemakers, weavers, butchers); members of the same guild would all live in the same quarter of town. A craft guild dominated all aspects of a given trade, from quality control to setting limits on production and prices. The guilds strove to curb competition, so that no one who had met the requirements for membership would be driven out of business. Candidates for membership were carefully trained. They began as apprentices who learned a trade by assisting a master and were eventually promoted to the rank of journeyman, at which point they received a fixed wage. Finally they might be inducted into the guild as masters when they met the requirements imposed on them. The craft guilds were eventually overshadowed by the rise of capitalism during the early modern age.

CHURCH AND STATE

At the time that trade and towns were beginning to revive, the Church also began a process of renewal. Reformers intended to establish a purer form of worship, and one that was free of control by laymen. Since the functions of the Church were to an extent political, this reform movement was perceived by some rulers as a challenge to their authority and resulted in a conflict between church and state.

The Cluniacs. Over time, monasteries tended to become wealthy from endowments given by secular rulers who wanted the monks to pray for their souls. The lords often used their generosity as an excuse for interfering with the operations of the monasteries, and the monasteries often strayed from a strict interpretation of the Benedictine *Rule*. An attempt to free monasticism from lay control and to revive a strict use of the Benedictine *Rule* began at the monastery of Cluny (eastern France), founded in 910. By the year 1200, about 1,500 monasteries had joined the movement and formed an international association that spanned western Europe. The Cluniacs used their influence to reform the Church in general, including the papacy, which had sunk to a low point during the tenth century.

Reform of the Papacy. The temporal power that came to the bishops of Rome from their alliance with the Carolingians solved some problems, but also created new ones. The Roman nobles, hoping to expand their own power against rivals, began to treat the papacy as a secular office that could be used to dominate local politics, so they fought one another in the attempt to get their sons elected pope. The situation deteriorated severely in the tenth century with a series of worldly popes, most notoriously John XII (955–964), who became pontiff at the age of 18 and was infamous for his sinful behavior. John XII called upon the German ruler, Otto I, for aid against his enemies in Italy, and in gratitude for the help revived the imperial title, crowning Otto the Holy Roman Emperor in 962. However, Otto I (962–973) later replaced the profligate John XII with a worthier pope (Leo VIII), and German emperors thereafter regularly intervened in papal elections. This was often to good effect. For example, Otto III (996–1002) appointed his former tutor and the foremost scholar in western Europe, Gerbert of Aurillac, as Pope Sylvester II (999–1003), who was committed to reform. However, since he was the first Frenchman to receive the office, he was viewed with enmity by some as an outsider, and his intellectual abilities led to malicious gossip that he was a magician in league with the devil.

College of Cardinals. Many churchmen, including the Cluniacs, in principle disapproved of imperial interference in the affairs of the Church, even when it was beneficial. In 1059 the reformers established the College of Cardinals, whose purpose was to elect the pope. Only the highest-ranking members of the church hierarchy, known as cardinals, belonged to this electoral college, which thus excluded emperors.

The Gregorian Reforms. The College of Cardinals immediately began to elect popes from among the reformers. The most extreme was an Italian named Hildebrand, who took the papal name Gregory VII (1073–1085). The reform movement was named after him. The main goals of the Gregorian reform were to enforce the ideal of clerical celibacy (priests often had wives or concubines until this time), to end the sale of church offices (known as simony), and to end lay interference in ecclesiastical appointments.

Canons Regular. In order to institute clerical celibacy, the reformers promoted the foundation of the canons regular, a semi-monastic order following the *Rule* of St. Augustine, which recommended that diocesan priests live together in a community rather than in private homes, where they were more susceptible to temptations.

The Investiture Controversy. The appointment of bishops was a major problem in the German church. The Holy Roman Emperors, who could not depend on their rebellious nobles, relied on churchmen to perform political functions for them, and they regularly appointed bishops to key offices. Gregory VII's demand that they stop this practice faced the Emperor Henry IV (1056–1106) with a crisis. He responded in 1076 by convening a council at Worms to depose Gregory VII, who answered with excommunication. Henry IV's nobles required him to seek absolution or abdicate, which led the humiliated emperor in 1077 to go to the pope's winter retreat at Canossa, where he stood outside in the snow for three days before Gregory VII absolved him. In 1084, however, when Henry's position in Germany was more secure, he challenged Gregory VII once more and captured Rome with an army, driving the pope into exile. The controversy over the appointment of bishops raged until 1122, when a compromise solution was finally reached with the Concordat of Worms. This agreement allowed churchmen to elect bishops and invest them with the symbols of spiritual authority, but required the approval of the emperor, who invested the bishops of the Empire with their political authority. Nevertheless, tension on this issue remained throughout the later Middle Ages.

THE RISE OF CENTRALIZED MONARCHIES

Beginning in the late eleventh century, a movement began toward the centralization of power in the hands of monarchs. Theoretically, the king was supreme in his realm, but in reality, due to the fragmentation caused by the invasions and the feudal system of government, his nobles were often stronger than he was. The centralization of power was best achieved in England and France. Spain did not become a strong centralized state until the fifteenth century. Germany and Italy remained politically divided well into the nineteenth century.

THE HOLY ROMAN EMPIRE

Germany and Italy. The Investiture Controversy weakened the Holy Roman Empire by aggravating the divisions within the realm. The emperor, in fact, constitutionally owed his position to the nobles who elected him. Although the nobles generally respected dynastic continuity, they insisted on strong privileges within their own domains, thereby preventing emperors from imposing centralized power on the vast territories of the Empire. Even after the Concordat of Worms, antagonism between emperors and popes continued, mainly because of imperial claims to Italy. While the Holy Roman Empire was essentially a German state, it theoretically included Rome and the northern half of Italy. The Italian city-states, however, like the German nobles, were fiercely independent, and they often rallied around the pope to oppose imperial attempts to control their lands.

The Hohenstaufens. Vigorous efforts were put forth by the Hohenstaufen dynasty to control the lands south of the Alps, but an alliance of northern Italian cities known as the Lombard League defeated Frederick I Barbarossa (1152–1190) at Legnano in 1176 and forced him to abandon his political ambitions there. Frederick II (1215–1250) was more successful in subduing his Italian subjects, but when he died the nobles would not accept his infant son as emperor. The result was the Great Interregnum (1254–1273), a period when there was no emperor. As rivals fought for the title, nobles strengthened their hold over their own territories.

Guelfs and Ghibellines. In Italy, politics were polarized over the question of whether to oppose the emperor and acknowledge the pope's political leadership, or vice versa. Those who supported the pope against the emperor were called Guelfs, and their opponents were called Ghibellines. The names of both these political parties, which dominated events from the twelfth to the fourteenth centuries, were Italian adaptations of German family names—Welf and Waiblingen (better known as Hohenstaufen)—who had contended for the imperial throne. In Italy, however, the labels became separated from their original context, so that after the emperors gave up their Italian ambitions, the labels were used to indicate support of or opposition to the claims of temporal power made by the popes.

The Hapsburgs. The Great Interregnum was finally ended when the German nobles elected Rudolf I Hapsburg (1273–1291) of Austria. The medieval Hapsburgs were usually elected emperors. They did not try to impose their authority over Germany or Italy, but were content with the imperial title and based their real power strictly on their own dynastic possessions. Their attempt to make Swiss territories part of their hereditary lands precipitated a revolt in 1291, when a group of local governments, known as cantons, banded together in a loose confederation for defense. Over time neighboring states joined the Swiss Cantons, forming the core of Switzerland.

The Golden Bull. To streamline the often difficult process of imperial succession, the Emperor Charles IV of Luxemburg (1347–1378) issued the Golden Bull (1356), which fixed an electoral college at seven members: the archbishops of Cologne, Mainz, and Trier; and the secular rulers of Bohemia, Brandenburg, Saxony, and the Rhineland-Palatinate. A majority of these electors was needed to choose an emperor. By formalizing the electoral college, Charles IV hoped to prevent popes from meddling in imperial elections.

ENGLAND

The Anglo-Saxon Kingdom. The seven kingdoms of the Anglo-Saxons in England were unified in the tenth century by Wessex, whose most illustrious ruler was Alfred the Great (871–899). Alfred led the resistance against the Danish Vikings who settled the region of England that became known as the Danelaw, which was later conquered by his successors. This English kingdom was the most advanced state in Europe, boasting a remarkably efficient system of taxation and balanced government at the local and national level. The kingdom was divided into shires, each of which was governed by an officer of the king known as a *shire-reeve*, or sheriff, who linked local government with the centralized monarchy of the entire nation.

Conquests. In the eleventh century, the Anglo-Saxons lost control of England to two separate groups who were descended from the Vikings: the Danes and the Normans, both of whom were now members of the Christian community. King Canute (1016–1035) made England part of his North Sea empire, which included Norway as well as Denmark. This empire disintegrated after Canute's death, and an Anglo-Saxon king, Edward the Confessor (1042–1066), once again ruled England. When Edward died without an heir in 1066, three men struggled for control of the kingdom: Harold Godwinson, Earl of Wessex; Harald Hardrada, King of Norway; and William, Duke of Normandy. Although Harold Godwinson defeated Harald Hardrada at Stamford Bridge in September, he was defeated in October at Hastings by William, who was thereafter known as the Conqueror (1066–1087).

Norman Rule in England. William was both an outstanding warrior and administrator. He combined the English system of shires with the feudal system of government in Normandy to create a powerful, centrally organized realm. In 1086 he conducted a systematic inventory of all property in England known as the *Domesday Book* in order to determine taxes accurately.

The Angevin Empire. After a period of chaos (1135–1154), England became the centerpiece of an empire with holdings in France. This occurred during the reign of Henry II, a member of the Angevin (or Plantagenet) dynasty. Henry II (1154–1189) inherited the County of Anjou and the Duchy of Normandy from his father. He acquired territories in southwestern France through marriage to Eleanor of Aquitaine, and he claimed the Kingdom of England through his mother Matilda (Maud). Henry later invaded Ireland, and he forced Wales and Scotland to recognize his authority. Unlike the empire of Canute, Henry's survived for centuries. Its rise illustrates how marriage and dynastic ties could be used in medieval Europe to forge a large state rapidly. It also demonstrates how the feudal system tended toward the decentralization of power, for although Henry II was king of England (and therefore the supreme lord within that realm), he was a vassal of the king of France in his capacity as Count of Anjou and Duke of Normandy and Aquitaine. Nevertheless he controlled far more of France than the French monarch did.

Henry II's Reign. Henry II built on the foundations of his predecessors to strengthen the centralized monarchy of England. His most important achievement was the promotion of common law through his system of justice, which was available to all freemen, made use of juries, and was administered by judges who traveled around the country on a regular basis. Henry's courts thus applied a common body of legal rules throughout his realm, which took business away from the courts of his feudal lords. However, Henry was unable to do away with separate ecclesiastical courts. His attempt to try churchmen accused of wrongdoing in the royal courts rather than in the church courts was opposed by the Archbishop of Canterbury, Thomas à Becket. After years of bitter conflict, the quarrel ended in 1170 when Becket was murdered by four of Henry's knights. Henry professed ignorance of the plot, but since Becket was widely regarded as a martyr and soon declared a saint, he had to accept the continued existence of the ecclesiastical courts. Henry's last years were saddened also by the rebellion of his sons, who were incited by his wife Eleanor.

Magna Carta. Richard I (1189–1199), known as "the Lion-Hearted," was an adventurer who spent nearly his entire reign outside England. His younger brother, John (1199–1216), was an inept ruler whose attempt to raise new taxes for a war against France without first consulting his barons (as he was required by feudal law) sparked a rebellion. In the end John had to make a concession known as the Magna Carta (1215). This "Great Charter" guaranteed the protection of feudal privileges traditionally held by the English barons against royal attempts to expand the powers of the monarchy.

Parliament. Relations between the English kings and their barons were often troubled. In 1263–1267, Simon de Montfort led the barons in a revolt against Henry III (1216–1272), who refused to recognize some amendments to the Magna Carta known as the Provisions of Oxford (1258). In 1264 the barons took Henry III prisoner, and in 1265 Montfort summoned an assembly with representatives from the towns—the first Parliament. This assembly did not meet regularly but was called on special occasions when the king wished to institute some innovation (such as a new tax); it did not at first pass legislation, but served as a body of council, as well as a court of justice. As Parliament was called into session with increasing frequency, it evolved to acquire a broader range of powers. In the fourteenth century it was divided into two parts—the House of Commons and the House of Lords—and was empowered to assume responsibilities concerning laws, taxation, and impeachment.

FRANCE

The Carolingians continued to rule the western Frankish kingdom until 987, when the title of king was seized by one of the powerful nobles, Hugh Capet (987–996), Count of Paris. His Capetian dynasty held the royal title until 1328, during which time West Francia was transformed into France, and the Franks became the French. The transformation of the realm from a feudal state to a national monarchy was very gradual, since the nobles of the realm were often stronger than the kings and were unwilling to give up their power and privileges. As late as the twelfth century, the kings had direct control over only a small region in the northeast centered on Paris and Orleans, known as the Ile de France ("Isle of France").

Philip II Augustus. The Capetians focused on consolidating their power around Paris until the reign of Philip II Augustus (1180–1223). Philip, finally, was able to challenge his most powerful and menacing vassals, the Angevins (Plantagenets), who possessed many French lands and also ruled England. He seized many territories from King John, including Normandy. After his victory at the Flemish town of Bouvines in 1214, Philip threatened to invade England itself until he was forbidden by Pope Innocent III.

Yet Philip succeeded in his objective of making the Capetians the dominant family in France.

Louis IX. During the long reign of Louis IX (1226–1270), the monarch's authority in the lands of his vassals was strengthened and the royal bureaucracy was built up. Louis was a very active king, committed to regularizing the system of justice in his realm, and he participated in the Crusades. Because of his deep personal piety, which motivated his service to the French people, he was recognized as a saint after his death.

Philip IV the Fair. St. Louis' grandson, Philip IV (1285–1314), known as the Fair, also strengthened the French monarchy, but he was very different in temperament. He used his enhanced royal power to crush his enemies, including Pope Boniface VIII (1294–1303), who died soon after some of Philip's henchmen manhandled him during a dispute over the taxation of the clergy. Philip's reign was preoccupied with measures to raise money, which he needed for his wars against England and Flanders. He destroyed the Knights Templar, a military monastic order founded during the Crusades, in order to seize their assets. He likewise expelled the Jews from France and seized their property. (The Jews in England had been expelled in 1290.) He also debased the currency. Philip's more legitimate means of raising revenue was to use his bureaucracy of lawyers to negotiate tax agreements with the provinces by reinterpreting and manipulating feudal law. Despite all this, Philip was a popular king. During his quarrel with the pope, he called the first meeting of the Estates-General, which was composed of the three orders (clergy, nobles, and burghers), and received their support.

THE HUNDRED YEARS' WAR (1337–1453)

The growing power of the centralized monarchies in France and England set off a long series of conflicts which are known collectively as the Hundred Years' War.

The Opening Phase. At the time the war began, England had lost most of its French possessions. The most important region still under English control was Gascony in the southwest. The Angevins hoped to revive their once-proud empire by claiming the French throne according to the rules of succession. Their opportunity arose in 1328 when the last Capetian king died without a male heir. The Angevin claim was based on the fact that the English king, Edward III (1327–1377), was the son of the French princess Isabella, daughter of Philip IV; Edward believed this entitled him to receive the French crown. The French, however, refused to recognize the English claim and cited early Frankish law which forbade women from inheriting the crown or transmitting it to their sons. They chose a new dynasty, the Valois, to receive the crown. Fighting commenced in Flanders, which favored the English cause because of the close commerical ties between the two regions due to the wool trade. The opening phase, which lasted until 1360, was a resounding English success. At the Battle of Crécy (1346), English longbowmen repeatedly halted charges by mounted French knights, proving the superiority of ranged weapons against cavalry and sounding the beginning of the end of chivalric warfare. At the Battle of Poitiers (1356), Edward the Black Prince (son of Edward III) captured the French king of the new Valois dynasty, John II (1350–1364), and took him to England as his prisoner. Although Edward III's claim to the French throne was still not recognized, the French gave him the province of Aquitaine (about a third of the country) in the Peace of Brétigny (1360).

Reversal. The fighting was revived in 1369 by the next French king, Charles V (1364–1380), who was able to reverse the losses and push the English back to the coastlands. His sudden death, however, resulted in a truce that took effect in 1389. Since both France and England then experienced a period of instability as each country fell into internal conflict, the fighting did not resume until 1415. It was revived by Henry V of England (1413–1422), who invaded northern France and quickly won the Battle of Agincourt (1415). With help from Philip the Good, Duke of Burgundy, the English were able to seize Normandy and parts of northwest France. The French struck back in 1429 under the leadership of the charismatic peasant girl, Joan of Arc, who convinced her king, Charles VII (1422–1461), to go on the offensive. Although Joan was captured by the Burgundians in 1430 and executed the following year when she was handed over to the English, the French rallied. In 1435 Philip the Good ended his feud with France and abandoned the English, who were now overextended. After some desperate fighting, the English capitulated and retained only the coastal city of Calais. The last few battles were decided by the use of a new weapon, artillery.

SPAIN

The Reconquista. Like Germany and Italy, Spain was too divided to foster a centralized monarchy, but the foundations for one were laid during the *Reconquista*, or "reconquest" of the Iberian peninsula from the Muslims. Although most of Spain had been quickly overrun by the Muslims in the invasion that began in 711, the Visigothic Christians were able to hold out in a small northern region known as the kingdom of Asturias. Over the course of eight centuries, the successors of these Christian warriors gradually pushed the Muslims back. The reconquest was not a continuous or unified effort. There were long periods of peace when Muslims and Christians, who were both highly fragmented politically, cooperated and shared in a beneficial cultural exchange. While many of the early fighters were adventurers like El Cid (Rodrigo Diaz de Vivar, 1043–1099), the reconquest eventually took on strong religious overtones, and was eventually declared part of the crusading movement. Several Christian kingdoms emerged, most notably Navarre, Castile, Leon, and Aragon. While some of these political units combined, they also often fragmented. Most notably, Portugal declared its independence from the combined kingdom of Castile–Leon in 1139 and was recognized by the pope in 1179.

EASTERN EUROPE

Conversion to Christianity. Eastern Europe did not enter recorded history until its conversion to Christianity, when missionaries brought literacy to the pagan peoples. The effort was begun by the Byzantine Church in the ninth century, when the monks Cyril and Methodius converted the Czechs and Slovaks to Greek Orthodoxy and gave them the Cyrillic alphabet (which is based on Greek). The Slavs of Ukraine, centered at Kiev under their Varangian (Viking) rulers, adopted Greek Christianity late in the tenth century. By that time, however, the Czechs and Slovaks had transferred their allegiance to Roman Catholicism as Latin missionaries converted their Polish neighbors. Poland remained the easternmost Catholic region until the fourteenth century, when the pagan Lithuanians—faced by Latin Christians in the west and Greek Christians in the east—decided to accepted Catholicism. Their ruler, the grand duke Jagiello, was motivated to do so by the proposed union of his people with the Poles, on condition of accepting Catholicism. The two peoples were united by the marriage of Jagiello (1386–1434) with the Polish queen Jadwiga. (An earlier Lithuanian ruler, Mindaugas, had actually converted to Catholicism in 1251, but when he was assassinated in 1263, the Lithuanians remained pagan.)

Teutonic Knights. One of several military religious orders founded during the Crusades, the Teutonic Knights transferred operations from the Holy Land to Europe and in 1226 received Prussia on the Baltic Sea as a fief from the Holy Roman Emperor Frederick II (1215–1250), who charged them with the task of converting the pagans who lived there. In 1234 Pope Gregory IX (1227–1241) gave the Teutonic Knights permission to expand their state through additional conquests of pagans. By 1300 the Knights became the most powerful state in the Baltic region, invited German settlers to colonize the lands which they conquered, and made an alliance with the Hanseatic League. When the Lithuanians, the last European pagans, converted to

Christianity in 1386, the Teutonic Knights faced a crisis of purpose. In the end they fought with Poland-Lithuania, and were defeated in 1410 at the Battle of Tannenberg. In 1525 the grand master of the order, Albrecht of Hohenzollern, converted to Lutheranism and established a Prussian duchy on the basis of the lands that the Teutonic Knights held. His Hohenzollern dynasty would unify Germany in the nineteenth century.

Russia. The Vikings who founded colonies in eastern Europe during the ninth century were known as Varangians or Rus, and the lands where they lived became known as Russia ("lands of the Rus"). In 862 one of the Russian chieftains, a legendary figure named Rurik, became ruler of Novgorod, and in 882 this northern city-state became part of the state of Kiev, which had been taken over by Varangians in 860. The combined state is known as Kievan Rus. It reached its zenith in the eleventh century under Jaroslav the Wise, but after his death in 1054 it became fragmented into about a dozen rival principalities that were often at war with one another. Novgorod became dominant by the thirteenth century, especially under the rule of Alexander Nevsky (1236–1263), who halted the eastward expansion of the Teutonic Knights at the Battle of Lake Peipus in 1242.

The Mongols. At that time Europe was struck by the last wave of invasions from the east. The Mongols, a nomadic people led by Genghis Khan (c. 1167–1227), formed an immense empire across Asia in the thirteenth century that reached east into China and west into Europe. A group of Mongols seized Russia in 1237 and founded a state known as the Golden Horde (which included Tatars). Alexander Nevsky cooperated with them, and they appointed him their lieutenant in Kiev. The key to survival and success at this time was a willingness to collaborate with the Mongols by paying tribute. The rulers of Muscovy (Moscow) did so and were thus able to maneuver into a dominant position among the other subjugated Russian states. When Ivan III the Great (1462–1505) finally overthrew the Golden Horde in the fifteenth century, the Muscovites were poised to assume control of the other Russian principalities.

THE CHURCH IN THE LATE MIDDLE AGES

Papal Monarchy. While the Holy Roman Empire was weakened by the Investiture Controversy, the papacy benefited from it, and used the prestige it acquired by challenging the emperors to adopt the Gregorian reforms. The popes then put forth an ambitious program of reshaping Christian society that gave them a considerable measure of political power extending far beyond the boundaries of the Papal States, as exemplified by the series of invasions that they initiated known as the Crusades.

Council of Clermont. Pope Urban II (1088–1099) began the crusading movement at the Council of Clermont in France (1095), when he urged Christian warriors to stop fighting one another and devote their energy to a worthier task, namely, recapturing Jerusalem from the Seljuk Turks, a group of Muslims who hindered Christian pilgrims from visiting the Holy Land. The Turks, a group from central Asia, had accepted Islam in the tenth century and invaded the eastern Mediterranean region in the eleventh. In 1071 they defeated the Byzantine armies at Manzikert in Anatolia. Desperate for help, the Byzantine emperor Alexius I Comnenus (1081–1118) asked the pope to organize military support (despite the unresolved schism between the Latin and Greek churches). The First Crusade was the result of this request.

The First Crusade. In 1096, several groups led by lesser Frankish nobles or demagogues set out for Jerusalem. They captured it in 1099 and massacred the inhabitants. Four feudal states, known collectively as Outremer ("Beyond the Sea"), were carved out by their conquests: the Latin Kingdom of Jerusalem, the Principality of Antioch, the County of Tripoli, and the County of Edessa. The first three of these were located on the coast; the last was inland, on the upper reaches of the Euphrates River. The First Crusade succeeded partly because the Muslims were divided against one another.

The Second Crusade. In 1144 the Muslims staged a counterattack and overthrew the County of Edessa. A new crusade was proclaimed to win back Edessa, preached by the Cistercian monk Bernard of Clairvaux (1090–1153). Although led by the Holy Roman Emperor Conrad III (1138–1152) and the French King Louis VII (1137–1180), the Second Crusade was a failure.

The Third Crusade. In 1187 the Muslim warrior Saladin, Prince of Egypt, dealt a crushing blow to the crusading armies at the Battle of Hattin and captured Jerusalem. The crusade to win back Jerusalem attracted three kings: Richard I the Lion-Hearted of England (1189–1199), Philip II Augustus of France (1180–1223), and Frederick I Barbarossa of the Holy Roman Empire (1152–1190). This crusade, like the one before it, was a failure. Frederick died on the way to the Holy Land, while Philip found it impossible to cooperate with his rival, Richard, and soon returned to France. Richard stayed on to fight Saladin, but was unable to do more than win back a few coastal cities, most notably Acre, where he slew over two thousand Muslim prisoners of war. Jerusalem remained under Muslim control when Richard finally returned to England.

The Fourth Crusade. Relations between the Byzantines and the Crusaders, who mistrusted each other, had been strained from the very start, but during the Fourth Crusade they reached an irreconcilable low. The crusaders found themselves unable to pay the Venetians for passage to the Holy Land and were persuaded by them in 1203 to acquire the money first by raiding the Christian city of Zara (a rival of the Venetians) on the Adriatic Sea, and then to sack Constantinople itself, which they did in 1204. The Byzantine imperial dynasty set up a government in exile, and the crusaders set up a Latin Empire in the Balkans in which the Venetians had special trading privileges. Diverted by the wealth of Byzantium, the crusaders never reached Muslim lands. Pope Innocent III was initially displeased by this turn of events, but he eventually accepted it, since the new Latin patriarch of Constantinople was cooperative, unlike the old Greek patriarchs. The Latin Empire lasted until 1261, when the Byzantines were able to regain control of Constantinople.

Later Crusades. The crusading movement never regained its initial momentum. The emperor Frederick II (1215–1250) took an army to the Holy Land in 1228, but this Fifth Crusade relied on diplomacy rather than fighting; Frederick negotiated a treaty by which the Egyptians, who controlled the Holy Land, gave Christians access to Jerusalem. In 1249 Saint Louis IX of France (1226–1270) organized the Sixth Crusade which struck Egypt and took the coastal city of Damietta, but he was forced to surrender the following year and pay a huge ransom. He organized the last major effort, the Seventh Crusade, in 1270. This crusade tried to conquer Tunisia, but it was called off when Louis died during the campaign. In 1291 the last outpost in the Holy Land, the city of Acre, fell to the Muslims, ending the crusader states. Although there was talk of reviving the Crusades for several centuries, no significant action against the Holy Land was taken. The military action that did continue under the name of the Crusades shifted to other theaters: the reconquest of Spain, the suppression of a heretical movement in southern France (known as the Albigensian Crusade), and the conquest of the pagans in the Baltic region.

Military Religious Orders. One curious development of the Crusades was the rise of military religious orders. These were made up of men who took the monastic vows of poverty, chastity, and obedience, but who also provided military service. The three main orders arose in the Holy Land: the Templars, the Hospitallers, and the Teutonic Knights. The Templars devised an innovative method of banking to fund their military activities and became very wealthy and powerful, with chapters all over Europe. Their immense wealth aroused the envy of the French king Philip IV, who exploited rumors that the Templars were engaged in immoral behavior and devil worship to have the order suppressed in 1312; he then confiscated their money. The Teutonic Knights, as noted earlier, transferred their operations to the Baltic region of Europe, where they waged crusades against pagans. The Hospitallers got their name from the fact that they initially provided charitable services for pilgrims and only later acquired military functions, such as providing escort.

New Religious Orders. The new military religious orders were part of a larger movement of Church reform, which saw the rise of several new monastic orders. Although the Cluniac movement had arisen as a reform in the tenth century, in time the Cluniacs themselves had become too worldly, and new reformers set about founding orders to live a simpler Christian life. Foremost among them were the Cistercians, who were founded at Cîteaux (France) by Robert of Molesmes in 1098 with the intention of following an even stricter interpretation of the Benedictine *Rule*. The new order's most prominent spokesman was Bernard of Clairvaux (1090–1153). Other orders (all originating in the twelfth century) included: the Carmelites, founded at Mt. Carmel (Palestine); the Carthusians, founded in the Chartreuse valley (France); and the Premonstratensians, or Norbertines, founded at Prémontré (France).

Heretical Movements. The popular religious ferment of the twelfth century did not always produce results that were favorable to the Church. Heretical movements arose as devout Christians who were scandalized by the luxurious lifestyle of some Catholic bishops openly denounced the clerical hierarchy. Although many of these radical reformers worked in isolation, some banded together and became highly organized, such as the Cathars and the Waldensians. The Cathars ("pure ones") were a dualist sect akin to the ancient Manichees and believed that the material world was created by an evil god who opposed the creator of the spiritual world. They rejected the Old Testament and organized themselves into a rival church in southern France centered at the town of Albi; they were, therefore, sometimes called Albigensians. The Waldensians took their name from Waldo of Lyons, a rich merchant whose reading of the New Testament inspired him to give away his property to the poor and embrace a life of poverty. His followers traveled throughout Europe preaching against the luxurious lifestyles of many Catholic bishops and winning converts on the strength of their own simple, impoverished lifestyle and their strict interpretation of the social message of the Gospel.

Albigensian Crusade. The ecclesiastical hierarchy responded to the challenges of the Cathars and Waldensians by declaring them heretics, but excommunication did not deter their growth. Alarmed at the Cathars' highly organized challenge to the Church's authority, which included the slaying of a papal envoy, Pope Innocent III declared a crusade against the Cathars which was known as the Albigensian Crusade (1208–1229). The northern French nobility eagerly participated in the campaign out of worldly motives, for they hoped thereby to seize the lands of the heretics. The fighting was brutal and indiscriminate. Entire towns were razed if they were suspected of harboring heretics, without regard for killing innocent Catholics. A Cistercian abbot named Arnaud Amaury, who served as papal legate, is said to have recommended killing all 20,000 citizens of Béziers so that some 200 heretics who were thought to be hiding there would not escape, exclaiming, "Kill them all—God will know his own!"

Inquisition. Pope Gregory IX (1227–1241) established the Inquisition in 1231 to ferret out Cathars who had escaped the Albigensian Crusade and gone into hiding. The effort was entrusted to a new monastic order, the Dominicans. The Inquisition also persecuted the Waldensians and all who opposed the authority of the Catholic Church.

The Height of Papal Monarchy: Innocent III. The persecution of Cathars and Waldensians was an expression of the new temporal powers that the papacy had acquired over the course of the twelfth century. The most prominent representative of this politically forceful "papal monarchy" was Innocent III (1198–1216). It was Innocent who declared the Albigensian Crusade. In looking after the interests of the Church, Innocent frequently intervened in the affairs of kings. He refused to allow Philip II Augustus to divorce his wife and forbade him from invading England. He also put England under interdict (a suspension of celebrating the sacraments) when he excommunicated King John for resisting his choice for the office of Archbishop of Canterbury. To end the controversy, King John was forced to submit the kingdom of England as a papal fief.

Fourth Lateran Council. Innocent III's most significant achievement was the Fourth Lateran Council in 1215. This church council was the largest in the Middle Ages, consisting of some 400 bishops and 800 monastic leaders, as well as secular rulers or their representatives. It was attended by the Latin patriarchs of Constantinople and Jerusalem. As a canon lawyer, Innocent sought to define in detail the requirements of membership in the Roman Catholic Church. The Fourth Lateran Council required that all adult Catholics receive the sacraments of confession and communion (the Eucharist) at least once a year and accept the doctrine of transubstantiation (that the bread and water used in the Mass actually become the body and blood of Jesus Christ). The council formally condemned the Cathars and Waldensians as heretics and forbade the foundation of new monastic orders in an effort to regulate religious fervor.

Mendicant Orders. The ban on new religious rules followed Innocent III's approval of two new "mendicant" orders of friars, which he wanted to promote. The friars (from Latin *frater*, "brother") differed from traditional monks in that they did not take vows of residence at a specific monastery, but lived in the secular world as itinerant preachers. Their mission was to bring the Gospel to the people. Since the friars owned no property, they could not support themselves except by donations from the faithful who appreciated their service. For this reason they are called "mendicants," derived from a Latin word which means "beggers." The friars were so greatly appreciated that they quickly became quite wealthy, despite their vows of poverty, and soon constructed churches as well as friaries where they slept after the day's preaching. Unlike monasteries, which raised their own food and manufactured their own goods, friaries were not economically self-sufficient; they were essentially just dormitories. St. Francis of Assisi (1181–1226) founded the first mendicant order, known as Franciscans. St. Dominic Guzman (c. 1170–1221) later founded the Dominicans.

Decline of the Papacy. Popes after Innocent III were not as successful in controlling the rulers of Europe. As kings consolidated their power, they became unwilling to obey the will of the pope. Even the threat of excommunication ceased to have much of an effect. A low point came during the pontificate of Boniface VIII (1294–1303), whose attempt to reassert papal supremacy over kings and emperors, as formulated in the papal bull known as *Unam Sanctam* (1302), was met with hostility. He was at that time in the midst of a dispute with Philip IV of France over the king's right to tax the clergy. During the controversy, a band of French soldiers raided the papal residence and took Boniface prisoner. He escaped, but was so weakened by the ordeal that he soon died.

Avignon Papacy. The next pope, Clement V (1305–1314), was a Frenchman who was persuaded by Philip IV and the French cardinals to move the papal residence from Rome to Avignon on the Rhone River, where the papacy came under the influence of the French monarchy. The papal residence remained in Avignon from 1309 to 1377, a period which is known as the "Babylonian Captivity." All the popes elected during this time were French.

The Great Schism. Many Christians were scandalized by the self-imposed exile of the papacy and demanded it return to Rome. The last pope at Avignon, Gregory XI (1370–1378), finally yielded to pressure. When he died, the College of Cardinals elected an Italian successor, Urban VI

(1378–1389). Not long afterwards, however, when Urban VI refused to make compromises with the cardinals, they protested that they had voted under duress—in fact, a Roman mob had demanded they elect an Italian. The disgruntled cardinals therefore declared the election invalid and chose an antipope, Clement VII (1378–1394), who established himself in Avignon. Urban VI, however, refused to abdicate and created his own College of Cardinals. Europeans were unsure who was the true pope, and became divided along political lines: France, the Spanish kingdoms, the Kingdom of Naples, and Scotland supported Clement VII in Avignon while the Italian city-states, England, Ireland, Scandinavia, Hungary, and Poland-Lithuania supported Urban VI in Rome. The Holy Roman Empire was divided. The Schism continued beyond the deaths of Urban VI and Clement VII when the two rival groups of cardinals elected rival successors. The situation became even more complicated in 1409 when the two colleges finally tried to end the Schism. They cooperated to elect a new antipope, John XXIII, but the other two popes refused to resign, resulting in three men claiming the papal office.

The Conciliar Movement. In order to resolve the deadlock, John XXIII was persuaded to call a general council. This measure envisioned a new theory of the Church, which reasoned that ultimate authority does not reside in the papacy but in the body of all believers, so that a representative assembly consisting of church leaders could make decisions in emergencies. The result was the Council of Constance (1414–1418), which deposed the other popes and elected Martin V (1417–1431) as the true pope. This time the Christian community was in agreement, and the confusion of the Great Schism (1378–1417) was finally over. The papacy emerged from the Schism a much humbled office. It could no longer exert significant political influence outside Italy.

Wycliffe and Huss. The Council of Constance also took measures to curb heresy, which had not been controlled during the Schism. They consequently condemned a Bohemian (Czech) reformer, John Huss (or Jan Hus, c. 1370–1415), who was influenced by the writings of John Wycliffe (c. 1330–1384). Wycliffe was an English reformer whose theology had been condemned because he was critical of the church hierarchy and emphasized the primacy of the Bible over the teachings of councils. Wycliffe rejected the doctrine of transubstantiation and translated the Vulgate (Latin Bible) into English, which was used by his followers (called Lollards) to interpret Scripture as they saw fit. Huss attended the Council of Constance in the hope of defending his beliefs, but was instead seized and burned at the stake. His death touched off a patriotic conflict in Bohemia known as the

Hussite Wars (1419–1436), which ended in a compromise between the Hussites (followers of Huss) and the Catholic Church.

End of the Conciliar Movement. After the successful Council of Constance, there was momentum for regular meetings of councils in cooperation with the pope for the governance of the Church. Yet this momentum soon dissipated. Pope Martin V called the Council of Basel in 1431 to continue a general reform of the Church, but this council later ran afoul of Martin's successor, Eugene IV (1431–1447), whom it tried to depose in 1437 by electing a new pope. Eugene IV reasserted papal superiority over church councils by convening the Council of Ferrara–Florence (1438–1445), which coincided with the Council of Basel (1431–1449). The Council that met in Ferrara and Florence tried to end the schism between the Eastern and Western churches, but the draft that was worked out with the Byzantines in 1439 was rejected by the Eastern Church in 1472. It had ceased to be effective, however, in 1453, when the Ottoman Turks conquered Constantinople and forbade the Eastern Christians from maintaining relations with the Western church.

THE MEDIEVAL CULTURAL TRADITION

Medieval thought depended largely on the study of the ancient classics of Greece and Rome but used these pagan texts in novel ways for the benefit of Christian society. At the heart of medieval education was the tradition of the liberal arts, which was used in combination with the Bible and the writings of the Church Fathers in the study of theology.

The Liberal Arts in Antiquity. The ancients distinguished between practical and liberal arts. The former were used in technical vocations while the latter were disciplines worthy of "free" men (*liberalis* in Latin means "free"). They identified seven liberal arts organized into two groups: the three disciplines of the *trivium* were linguistic (grammar, rhetoric, and logic or "dialectic") and the four mathematical disciplines of the *quadrivium* (arithmetic, geometry, astronomy, and music). The word "trivial" comes from *trivium*, since the linguistic disciplines were considered basic prerequisites for the more advanced mathematical studies.

The Liberal Arts in the Early Middle Ages. Each liberal art had a set of classical textbooks that were used to teach it. The most prominent of the liberal arts in the Middle Ages was logic, which relied on the writings of Aristotle. The Roman scholar Boethius (480–525), who devoted himself to the study of Plato and Aristotle and is most famous for his Neoplatonic text *The Consolation of Philosophy*, prepared a translation of Aristotelian logical texts known as the *Organon* ("Tool"). The liberal arts were also summarized in encyclopedias which preserved ancient learning in a simplified form. The most important preservers of ancient learning were Martianus Capella (c. 400), Cassiodorus (c. 490–585), and Isidore of Seville (c. 560–636), who were commonly read in the medieval schools.

THE INTELLECTUAL TRADITION

Translations from Spain and Sicily. Toward the year 1000, medieval scholars became acutely aware that they had lost much of the ancient tradition. They also discovered that the Muslims in Spain and Sicily had preserved most of this tradition in Arabic translations of the Greek classics. Christian scholars, such as Gerbert of Aurillac, who later became Pope Sylvester II (999–1003), traveled to Spain and met with Arab and Jewish scholars in order to acquire this learning; the Jews, who traveled between the Muslims and Christians as merchants, were often trilingual and made excellent interpreters. Throughout the twelfth century, Christian scholars traveled to Spain and Sicily where they translated the works of Aristotle from Arabic into Latin. These imperfect translations greatly increased interest in Aristotle, so that later, in the thirteenth century, a new effort was made to translate Aristotle directly from Greek into Latin, using texts acquired from the Byzantines.

Plato and Aristotle in the Middle Ages. Until the twelfth century, the most respected ancient philosopher was Plato, whose description of the creation of the world in the *Timaeus* was avidly read and compared to the biblical account in Genesis. The *Timaeus* was in fact the only work of Plato's to be translated into Latin during the period of the late empire and therefore available in the west. In the twelfth century, only two more Platonic dialogues were translated into Latin (*Meno* and *Phaedo*). Plato lost favor because he wrote dialogues on a few select topics rather than systematic treatises, and Aristotle gained favor because he had taught every subject in a comprehensive system of knowledge. Thus, even when medieval scholars disagreed with Aristotle's conclusions (for example, they rejected his doctrine of the eternity of the world), they appreciated the framework he provided. By the thirteenth century he was so greatly favored that he was called simply "the Philosopher."

Arabic and Jewish Influences on European Philosophy. Aristotle was often read in conjunction with a commentary on his works by the Muslim Arab scholar, Averroes (1126–1198). Other Arab philosophers who influenced medieval scholarship were Alfarabi (c. 870–950) and Avicenna (980–1037). The most influential Jewish thinker was Maimonides (1135–

1204), who is best known for his attempt to harmonize reason and revelation in his *Guide for the Perplexed*.

Cathedral Schools and the Renaissance of the Twelfth Century. The new translations of Greek philosophy were studied primarily in the cathedral schools that arose during the cultural flowering known as the "Twelfth-Century Renaissance." Like the Carolingian Renaissance before it and the Italian Renaissance after it, the Twelfth-Century Renaissance focused on reviving the study of the ancient classics. The cathedral schools were a counterpart to the monastic schools; they were attached to the church of a bishop for the education of the secular clergy. ("Secular" clergy were churchmen who did not follow a monastic rule but served as diocesan priests; "regular" clergy were churchmen who belonged to a monastic order and therefore followed a rule.) The most famous cathedral schools of northern France were Paris, Chartres, Orleans, and Laon.

Universities. The medieval universities arose in the towns of the twelfth and thirteenth centuries. Teachers and students organized themselves as guilds in order to set the curriculum, set fair prices for instruction, and negotiate with townsmen, on whom they depended for food and accommodation. In fact, the Latin word *universitas*, from which "university" is derived, originally meant simply "guild" or "corporation," and could be applied to describe any formal association of individuals, such as the guilds of merchants or craftsmen. Since the early universities were associations of scholars who banded together for economic and legal protection, they did not have a permanent location; classes were held in rented halls or perhaps a teacher's house. This situation was useful in early instances of "town and gown" fights, for when a group of scholars wished to protest high costs of room and board, they could leave town as a group and thereby weaken the local economy until the townsfolk relented. Kings often became patrons of universities, relying on them for skilled men to staff their growing bureaucracies. The earliest universities grew out of the schools in Bologna and Paris; Oxford was soon founded by scholars who had studied in Paris. The universities began the practice of granting degrees in order to provide evidence that a student had passed all the rigorous requirements for becoming a master in the guild of scholars and was qualified to teach others.

Colleges. The universities began to acquire a permanent physical identity when wealthy benefactors founded colleges in the thirteenth century, such as the one built by Robert de Sorbon in 1257. The colleges were originally residence halls for the support of students who could not afford to pay living expenses. Since these buildings were a convenient place to conduct classes, they eventually became associated with instruction.

Curriculum and Specialized Studies. The universities recognized four faculties: liberal arts, law, medicine, and theology. The last three were advanced studies, and universities initially specialized in only one or two of them. There were two kinds of law: civil law (Roman law), and canon law (church law). Instruction in each of the faculties was based on the intensive study of established textbooks, which the teacher would read publicly and explain by way of commentary. Eventually the comments (known as "glosses") of important teachers would be written into the margins of a text as a special edition for study. The textbook for Roman law was Justinian's *Corpus Juris Civilis*, whereas canon law, which was based mainly on the decrees of church councils and papal decrees, was studied with the help of the *Decretum* of Gratian (c. 1140). Medicine was largely based on the works of the ancient physician Galen (c. 129–199). Theology used the *Sentences* of Peter Lombard (c. 1100–1160), a twelfth-century theologian who provided a thorough outline of topics that every theologian should cover. Although theology was the most prestigious and regarded as the "queen of the faculties," it was actually the least studied. Most advanced degrees were granted in law or medicine, which were financially more lucrative fields than theology.

Peter Abelard. The rise of Paris as a center for the study of theology is associated with the career of Peter Abelard (1079–1142), a charismatic teacher who promoted the use of logic in his *Sic et Non* ("Yes and No"). While Anselm of Canterbury (c. 1033–1109) had recently demonstrated how logic could be used to prove the existence of God, Abelard demonstrated how logic could be used to resolve seeming contradictions in Scripture and the Church Fathers. Abelard made many enemies among conservative thinkers who resisted the use of logic in theology, and they condemned his doctrines without a fair trial. Abelard also became notorious for his seduction of a young woman named Heloise, whom he was hired to tutor. They married secretly, but when Heloise's family learned of their liaison, they had Abelard castrated. In disgrace, Abelard became a monk and Heloise a nun.

Scholasticism. Even though Abelard's teachings were condemned, his method of resolving contradictions in religious texts by the application of logic was retained and became a standard feature of "scholasticism." The scholastic method treated philosophy as the "handmaiden" of theology.

St. Thomas Aquinas. The preeminent example of scholastic philosophy is the *Summa Theologiae* (Summary of Theology) by the Dominican friar St. Thomas Aquinas (1225–1274). This text, which proposed to reconcile faith and reason, became the favored theological work of the Catholic Church. It used the Aristotelian concepts of "substance" and "accident" to give a philosophical explanation of the doctrine of *transubstantiation*. Aquinas reasoned that the bread and wine used during the Mass become the actual *substance* of the body and blood of Jesus Christ even though they do not change their appearance, which is an *accidental* quality. Thus, Aquinas demonstrated how ancient Greek philosophy could be used to discuss the mysteries of religion.

Nominalism. A long-lasting debate that generated interest in the twelfth century concerned the relationship between words and reality. One school of thought, influenced by the Platonic doctrine of Forms and known as *realism*, maintained that universal concepts substantially exist in an intelligible world. The contrary school of thought, known as *nominalism*, objected that universals are merely words (*nomina*) that are used to describe abstractions and therefore do not correspond to any substantial reality. In the fourteenth century a prominent nominalist named William of Ockham (c. 1285–c. 1349) formulated a principle of logical economy which would later be used in the scientific method. This principle, known as "Ockham's razor," requires a logical explanation for the existence of any presumed entity and thus reduces any given system to the smallest possible number of elements. Ockham did not use this "razor" against central Christian doctrines, but against elaborate scholastic systems of theology. His teaching was condemned for its rejection of Thomism (the philosophy of Thomas Aquinas, which became the standard teaching of the Catholic Church).

Political Theory. The principal political thinkers of the Middle Ages were John of Salisbury (c. 1115–1180), who described medieval society as an organic unity in the form of a human body whose head is the king, and Marsilius of Padua (c. 1275–1343), whose *Defender of the Peace* (1324) argued that all political authority is derived from the people. Marsilius opposed papal claims to political power, and he argued that popes could not even justify their claim to the spiritual leadership of the Church; he favored councils organized by laymen to govern the Church.

Science and Technology. Europeans owed a debt to the Muslims for much of their scientific knowledge. Gerbert of Aurillac (Pope Sylvester II) opened the way by visiting Spain and introducing Arabic numerals into Christian Europe. His example inspired later generations of Latin scholars to visit Spain or Sicily in order to translate ancient scientific texts into Latin. Although by the year 1100 westerners thus acquired treatises on astrology of dubious value, they also received devices for measuring the position of celestial bodies known as astrolabes, which were useful for legitimate astronomy. Magnetic compasses for navigation came into use around 1100 or after. The scientific thinker Roger Bacon (c. 1214–1294) knew the formula for gunpowder, which had been discovered by the Chinese and was later used during the Hundred Years' War. Roger Bacon and another English thinker, Robert Grosseteste (c. 1175–1253), began to develop a theory of experimental science. A tradition of making careful observations of nature began to take root, as demonstrated by Albert the Great (c. 1200–1280). Significant advances were made in the study of optics: lenses began to be used to correct vision during the thirteenth century. Most natural philosophy, however, was conducted by "thought-experiments," which led two French thinkers, Jean Buridan (c. 1297–1358) and Nicole Oresme (c. 1330–1382) to challenge Aristotle's theory of motion with a theory of "impetus," which came fairly close to the correct theory of momentum. There were improvements in mechanical devices. Gerbert of Aurillac was credited with the invention of the pendulum clock in the tenth century; by the fourteenth century, fairly sophisticated mechanical clocks were being constructed. Paper also came into use during the fourteenth century, acquired from the Muslims (who had acquired it from the Chinese). Paper was relatively inexpensive to manufacture compared to parchment and would become the standard writing surface when the printing press was invented in the fifteenth century (c. 1450).

THE VERNACULAR TRADITION

While Latin was the common language spoken by educated men throughout Europe (all university instruction was in Latin), national literary traditions based on the vernacular languages came into prominence during the Middle Ages.

English Literature. The Anglo-Saxons translated the Bible into their own language, known as Old English, soon after their conversion and developed religious poetry of high quality. Their major epic, *Beowulf*, was not written down until about the year 1000, but was based on an earlier tradition. The story describes a hero's quest to vanquish terrible monsters. After the Norman Conquest of 1066, the language was transformed through the absorption of many French words and became Middle English. The most famous Middle English author was Geoffrey Chaucer (c. 1343–1400), whose most popular work, *The Canterbury Tales*, is a collection of short stories in verse told by pilgrims on their way to visit the shrine of St. Thomas à Becket. These tales offer a cross-section of English society.

French Literature. Among the earliest works in Old French is *The Song of Roland*, written around the year 1100, which describes the heroic defense of Charlemagne's rearguard during his campaign against the Muslims in Spain. The French developed a tradition of courtly literature, which described the ideals of chivalry (the culture of mounted knights) in ballads known as *chansons de geste* (songs of deeds). A key element of chivalry was a complex form of romantic love, inspired by the troubadors of southern France, which drew parallels between feudal law and the feelings between the sexes. A favorite theme of the chivalric poets was the cycle of Arthurian legends, based on the exploits of a legendary leader of the Britons who fought the invading Anglo-Saxons, which inspired the twelfth-century poets Chrétien de Troyes and Marie de France. The most popular of French literary works was a long allegorical poem called *The Romance of the Rose*, a thirteenth-century epic begun by Guillaume de Lorris and later expanded by Jean de Meun, whose characters are abstract personifications that depict the virtues and vices of the time.

Spanish Literature. The Christians in Spain hosted a tradition of troubadors and courtly love poets, who wrote about the *Reconquista*. The legends of El Cid are a prominent example of their work.

German Literature. German courtly love poets were also inspired by the Arthurian cycle, as seen in *Parzifal* by Wolfram von Eschenbach. Another legend of Celtic inspiration was the tragic love-story of *Tristan and Isolt* by Gottfried von Strassburg. The Germans also recorded their own pre-Christian heritage in the *Nibelungenlied* (Songs of the Nibelungs), which drew upon material in the Scandinavian saga of the Volsungs.

Icelandic Literature. The oral traditions of the Vikings were not recorded until after the conversion of the Scandinavians. The tales were preserved in Old Norse by Snorri Sturluson (1179–1241), whose *Younger Edda* is a prose work composed as a complement to the *Elder Edda*, a collection of poems. This Eddic literature preserves the pre-Christian mythology of the Northmen.

Italian Literature. The most impressive example of vernacular literature was the *Divine Comedy* of Dante Alighieri (1265–1321), who wrote in the Tuscan dialect of his native city, Florence. Dante also wrote love poems idealizing a young woman named Beatrice. He was involved in Italian politics and eventually suffered exile, at which time he wrote the *Divine Comedy*. This epic is written in three parts—*Inferno*, *Purgatorio*, *Paradiso*—and depicts a mystical journey through hell, purgatory (the region where the saved are purified from their sins), and heaven. Dante's work summarizes the history of Western Civilization while it explores the nature of virtue and vice. The *Divine Comedy* reveals the influence of the classical tradition in a way that the other vernacular traditions do not (for example, Dante's guide through hell is the Latin poet Virgil) and thus points to the Renaissance, which was essentially a revival of classical culture. Two other prominent

Italian poets who ushered in the Renaissance were the Florentine authors Giovanni Boccaccio (1313–1375) and especially Francesco Petrarch (1304–1374). Petrarch championed the revival of a pure form of Latin (which had become corrupted, from his point of view, during the Middle Ages), but his most popular works were vernacular love poems (sonnets) which idealized his love for a woman named Laura. Boccaccio's most famous work is the *Decameron*, a collection of bawdy stories told by a group of men and women staying in the countryside in order to escape the effects of the Black Death.

THE BLACK DEATH

Spread of the Plague along Trade Routes. During the Hundred Years' War, most of Europe was struck with bubonic plague (or perhaps a collection of epidemics) which became known as the "Black Death." After the initial wave (1347–1351), the plague recurred at intervals in parts of Europe until the eighteenth century. The disease was spread by fleas living in the fur of rats. It was introduced into Europe from Asia by Italian merchant ships that plied the Black Sea. The course which the plague took reveals that it followed the trade routes, and the speed with which it spread reflects the fact that commerce by the fourteenth century was vigorous and connected Europe with China (where the plague may have originated). The Italian merchant and explorer, Marco Polo (1254–1324), had pioneered these overland routes through central Asia known as the "Silk Road," as he describes in his *Travels*. The plague first struck Constantinople, then Italy (a center of commerce), after which it spread through France to Spain, England, and Germany. Poland and other parts of east central Europe were minimally affected, due to the low volume of trade there.

Demographic Effects. In the space of just a few years, the plague reduced the population of Europe by about one-third—some regions suffered the loss of about half their population. The plague was all the more terrible because of ignorance about its communicable nature. The inability of doctors to explain the disease, coupled with its terrifying effects, created mass hysteria. There was a widespread belief that the plague was a punishment sent by God, which prompted processions of flagellants—people who beat themselves publicly with whips in a show of repentance.

Famine. The plague was not the first instance of declining population. Earlier in the fourteenth century there were a series of crop failures (reflecting a shift in climate as the weather became colder and wetter and the growing season became shorter), which resulted in widespread famines.

The most serious occurred between 1315 and 1317; tax records indicate that the number of households in some places decreased at that time, reflecting at least a regional decline in population. Thus, after three centuries of rapid growth beginning around the year 1000, Europe had reached the limits of population that its agriculture could sustain. The malnutrition that Europeans suffered as a result of food shortages weakened people's immune systems and made them more susceptible to the plague.

Economic and Social Consequences. The high mortality of the plague caused businesses and banking institutions to collapse. The long-term effects were actually beneficial to laborers but hurt the employers. Before the plague there was high unemployment in Europe, but afterwards labor was in high demand and low supply, which resulted in greatly increased wages. In contrast, the price of food decreased as the supply was suddenly able to meet the decreased demand. Yet employers and governments initially resisted granting concessions to laborers, which prompted a series of peasant rebellions (aggravated in England and France by the Hundred Years' War), such as the Jacquerie in France (1358) and the Peasants' Revolt led by Wat Tyler in England (1381). There was also a revolt of the wool-workers in Florence in 1378.

ARCHITECTURE AND ART

The revival of European economic life and culture around the year 1000 inspired a phase of church-building that evolved through architectural styles known as Romanesque and Gothic. While the Romanesque structures of the eleventh and twelfth centuries were mostly established by monastic houses, the Gothic structures that arose between the twelfth and fifteenth centuries were often funded by the rising merchant class.

Romanesque. Although there is considerable variety in examples of Romanesque ("Roman-like") architecture, common characteristics include the use of the rounded arch, the barrel vault, and the introduction of the tower as a prominent feature. In order to support the high ceilings, the walls had to be very thick and windows had to be small, resulting in a rather dark interior. Sculpture was also used to adorn the building. Romanesque sculptures have an elongated, unreal quality to them and depict religious themes, often involving demonic figures and scenes of the Last Judgment. Representations of beasts and floral patterns are also typical.

Gothic. The earliest Gothic church was built at the Abbey Church of St. Denis outside Paris by the Abbot Suger in the 1140s. The great cathedrals were mostly built in the thirteenth century, predominantly in northern

Europe. Gothic architecture is more homogeneous than Romanesque and its features include the pointed arch (possibly inspired by Muslim architecture), the use of larger windows and stained glass to create a luminous interior effect, and flying buttresses to support the walls so that large windows could be used. A favorite device was the rose or wheel window. In comparison to the heavy quality of Romanesque architecture, the Gothic style has a "skeletal" quality. Church-towers became more ornate, with angular design motifs, like the *fleur-de-lis*. Sculptures included fantastic creatures, such as gargoyles.

Script. By the twelfth century medieval handwriting also changed from the simplicity of Carolingian minuscule (on which modern typography is based) to the more elaborate and ornate Gothic minuscule, which inspired black-letter typography. The original letter-forms used by Johannes Gutenberg (c. 1400–1468) were based on Gothic script, but they were replaced later by Italian humanists who preferred the clearer Carolingian script, which they erroneously believed had been the letter-forms used by the ancient Romans. "Gothic" art and script received this name as a pejorative by humanists of the Renaissance, who thought the styles were inspired by the barbarians who had invaded the classical world.

Painting. Although frescoes (watercolor paintings on plaster) were used in the walls of medieval churches, most painting appeared in books, where they were called "illuminations" (illustrations) or "miniatures" (not because they were small but because they used lead oxide, called *minium*, as a pigment). The early Celtic style consisted of very intricate, abstract designs. The much later Gothic style was a lively departure from the flat Byzantine models that dominated Romanesque art. Gothic manuscript art tended to adorn the margins with fantastic creatures (dragons, birds with human heads, etc.) known as "grotesques" or "drolleries." A favorite device was the "historiated initial"—figures painted within an oversized letter of the first word of a chapter to provide a visual accompaniment that symbolically summarizes the text.

Giotto. The preeminent fresco painter of the medieval period was Giotto (c. 1267–1337), who transformed the two-dimensional quality of Gothic painting by adding the illusion of depth, introducing a move toward naturalism, and emphasizing the human rather than divine. His innovations inspired the art of the Italian Renaissance.

CHAPTER 5

Renaissance and Reformation

Chapter 5

RENAISSANCE AND REFORMATION

The Renaissance, or "rebirth," was a general revival of European society marking the transition from the medieval to the modern age. In its most specific sense, it was the revival of classical culture advocated by Petrarch, especially with regard to literary production. This classical revival soon spread to architecture and sculpture; classicism also influenced painting in terms of subject matter, but in terms of technique, Renaissance painting was a new departure rather than a return to an earlier model. In its broadest sense, the Renaissance was a time of recovery from the effects of the Black Death that led to new developments in various aspects of culture. Although humanists expressed a new confidence in the ability of human beings to endure in the face of adversity and establish a flourishing culture, the humanism of the age was not a complete break with the medieval tradition, for Christianity still remained the focal point of European civilization and the most important factor in most people's lives. Especially north of the Alps, humanists combined the new interest in pagan Greece and Rome with a desire to refine Christian practice, resulting in a vibrant new Christian humanism that set the foundations for the Reformation.

THE ITALIAN RENAISSANCE

Humanism. Francesco Petrarch (1304–1374) is known as the Father of Renaissance Humanism. He advocated both imitating the Latin style of the ancients (above all Cicero) and the attitudes that the ancient authors expressed. Thus, Petrarch opposed the scholastic theologians and canon lawyers, and the intellectual culture of the universities in general, because he thought they marginalized the human experience by analyzing it in cold, abstract terms and without sensitivity to rhetorical sophistication. He rebelled against medieval culture in general, calling it a "dark age" of barbarism, and thus introduced the historiographical tradition that divides Western civilization into ancient, medieval, and modern phases. Petrarch was not opposed to Christianity, but wanted a more emotional, psychologically nuanced approach to religion. In his introspective work, *The Secret*, he converses with St. Augustine of Hippo, author of the soul-searching autobiography, *The Confessions*. Although Petrarch's most popular works were his vernacular sonnets of unrequited love for a woman named Laura, he hoped to acquire literary immortality for his Latin epic, the *Africa*, which depicts the Punic Wars. Petrarch was elected poet laureate by the Roman Senate in 1341.

Classical Scholarship. In advocating a return to the classical literary tradition, Petrarch inspired a movement to recover works of the ancient authors from neglect in the monasteries and study them intensively. Boccaccio (1313–1375) was among the scholars whom Petrarch inspired to collect ancient manuscripts. The intensive study of Latin texts established the modern discipline of philology (historical linguistics). On the basis of Latin style, the humanist Lorenzo Valla (1407–1457) was able to prove that the so-called Donation of Constantine was actually an eighth-century forgery. Because of its hostility to university culture, humanism developed outside that tradition. Humanists were often supported financially by wealthy patrons who appreciated their talent and wished to enhance their own prestige through their association with cultivated men of letters. They studied Greek in addition to Latin, and thus revived the ancient Roman tradition of the upper classes (who were fluent in Greek). Humanists founded secondary schools that stressed the study of the classics, bringing about a revolution in education that was to last until the early twentieth century.

Civic Humanism. Unlike Dante, Petrarch was not a political figure. Averse to the idea of a legal career (which his father wanted him to pursue), he shunned politics and sought the solitude that was conducive to a career as a writer. Petrarch thus advocated the contemplative life over the active life. Many of the humanists he inspired, however, did not share this attitude. Men like Coluccio Salutati (1331–1406) and Leonardo Bruni (1369–1444) advocated "civic humanism," which maintained that the most virtuous kind of life was one that used humanistic study for public service.

FLORENCE

The Medici. Salutati and Bruni both served the city-state of Florence, which was the preeminent center of culture in Renaissance Italy. Florentine politics in the fifteenth century was dominated by the wealthy Medici family, who arose in the thirteenth century as merchants and bankers. They were the effective rulers of Florence during the leadership of Cosimo (1389–1464) and Lorenzo the Magnificent (1449–1492). In time their influence extended far beyond Florence. Three members of the family became popes (Leo X, Clement VII, Leo XI) and two became queens of France (Catherine and Marie). The Medici were great patrons of the arts, funding the projects of artists like Botticelli and Michelangelo. They also patronized humanists, such as Marsilio Ficino (1433–1499), who translated the complete works of Plato from Greek into Latin for the first time. Ficino also translated the works of Neoplatonists such as Plotinus and wrote his own works of philosophy and theology. Although the Medici suffered exile twice after Lorenzo died, they were able to return to power each time with help from Spain.

Savonarola. The first exile of the Medici occurred in 1494 when the French invaded Italy and seized Florentine territory, prompting the people to depose the Medici despots and restore the republic. Florence then came under the influence of a Dominican preacher, Girolamo Savonarola (1452–1498), who railed against the luxury and corruption of the Medici age. He convinced the Florentines to destroy works of art in repentance (the "bonfire of the vanities"), but he lost popular support and was burned at the stake after Pope Alexander VI (1492–1503) excommunicated him as a dangerous fanatic.

ITALIAN POLITICS

Wars between the City-States. The Italian city-states arose from the medieval communes (towns holding charters from a feudal lord) and became self-governing after their successful resistance against the Holy Roman Emperors. Although many of the city-states were republics, they were often ruled by despots (either behind-the-scenes or overtly). Italian politics was chaotic and tumultuous as the city-states vied for supremacy within the peninsula while trying, at the same time, to maintain stability within their own domains, which were usually riven by factionalism. Such an environment was ideal for *condottieri* (mercenary generals) like the successful Gattamelata and Bartolommeo Colleoni, both of whom were commemorated in equestrian statues modeled on the ancient effigy of Marcus Aurelius. The most successful *condottiere*, however, was Francesco Sforza (1401–1466), who seized Milan in 1450 and established a dynasty there.

Treaty of Lodi. A measure of order was achieved in 1454 by the Treaty of Lodi when three of the five major Italian powers—the northern city-states of Florence, Milan, and Venice—organized an alliance against the other two: the centrally located Papal States and the Kingdom of Naples in the south. The Papal States had nearly vanished during the Avignon papacy, when local rulers seized much of the territory. After returning to Italy, the popes fought their neighbors to recover these domains. The Kingdom of Naples, which included Sicily (and was sometimes called the Kingdom of the Two Sicilies) had changed hands many times during the Middle Ages—Byzantines, Muslims, Normans, Hohenstaufens, French, and Spanish rulers all claimed it at one time or another. In the fifteenth century it was ruled by the Spanish house of Aragon.

Invasions. In 1494 the French king Charles VIII (1483–1498) lay claim to the throne of Naples and invaded Italy. Although he seized the kingdom from its Spanish ruler, he was unable to hold it against the alliance of Italian states that banded together to drive him out. In 1499 Charles' successor, Louis XII (1498–1515), invaded Italy to claim Milan. Again the French king was driven out by a temporary alliance. These invasions continued under Francis I (1515–1547) and were aggravated by counter-invasions led by the Spanish king and Holy Roman Emperor, Charles of the Hapsburg dynasty. With each invasion, Italy was progressively devastated, and in 1527 the Hapsburg forces sacked Rome out of frustration after their pay had been long delayed.

Machiavelli. The chaos into which Italy was plunged by waves of invasion led some statesmen to urge its political unification. The most vocal of these was Niccolò Machiavelli (1469–1527), who wrote *The Prince* (1513) as an appeal to the Medici to provide a leader that all Italians could rally around. Machiavelli's *Prince* depicts the ideal ruler as an unscrupulous despot who uses any means to attain his ends. It presents historical examples to support the contention that human beings are unreliable and that successful rulers must be flexible and ignore the teachings of Christianity that would limit their range of strategy. Machiavelli blamed the papacy for preventing the unification of Italy, and he blamed the use of mercenaries for its endemic chaos; he recommended and organized militias of citizen-soldiers, reasoning that the most reliable troops were those who were defending their homes and families rather than serving for pay. *The Prince* can be seen as a desperate appeal for drastic action to correct an intolerable situation, for Machiavelli's historical study of ancient Rome, *The Discourses* (1531), identifies representative government as the ideal rather than despotism. Machievelli wrote both works in exile, after having served Florence as a diplomat, and he drew upon his experiences in politics as well as his humanistic study of history for his arguments.

ART AND ARCHITECTURE

Despite this political chaos, Italian art and architecture flourished, reviving the classical ideals of harmony and proportion.

Architecture. Italian architects revived the use of the dome, which had been neglected in the Middle Ages (although Muslim architects did make frequent use of this Roman design in their mosques). The earliest Renaissance dome was built for the cathedral of Florence between 1420 and 1436 according to the design by the Florentine architect Brunelleschi. In Rome, St. Peter's Basilica received a magnificent dome designed by Michelangelo and begun in 1546. Renaissance architects also showed a renewed sensitivity to the use of classical columns.

Sculpture. Italian sculpture, following classical models, revived the use of the nude figure and equestrian statues, both of which were pioneered by Donatello, whose bronze statue of *David* (c. 1430–1435) marks the first nude, and whose bronze sculpture of the mercenary general *Gattamelata* (1447–1450) marks the first equestrian statue. Statuary of the later Renaissance was dominated by Michelangelo Buonarroti, whose *Pietà* (1497–1500) powerfully elicits emotions of tenderness in its depiction of the Mother of Christ holding her dead son in her arms, and whose *David* (1501–1504) presents a monumental 17-foot-tall male nude with such realistic detail as the slight bulging of veins on the figure's hands. Michelangelo could not satisfy all the commissions that were requested of him. He sculpted his *David* for Florence, but most of his work was commissioned by the papacy. These masterpieces included the *Pietà* on display in the Vatican, the paintings on the ceiling of the Sistine Chapel (1508–1512), and the tomb of Pope Julius II, for which Michelangelo sculpted a statue of Moses with "horns of light" on his head to symbolize the wisdom he received from God (1515).

Painting. Renaissance painting developed out of Giotto's late medieval frescoes, which were marked by their naturalism, their humanistic focus, and the use of light and shadow (*chiaroscuro*) to indicate a sense of depth. Masaccio (1401–1428) improved upon Giotto's efforts by applying linear perspective for an accurate illusion of three-dimensionality, whose rules were scientifically studied by Brunelleschi, and later formulated by Leon Battista Alberti in his highly influential treatise *On Painting* (1436). Preeminent among the later masters were Michelangelo, Raphael, and Leonardo da Vinci. Renaissance painters often used their talents at naturalistic representation to include images of their patrons in a corner of their artwork, and portraiture became common.

Renaissance Men. Leonardo da Vinci (1452–1519) mastered not only painting, sculpture, and architecture, but was also renowned as an engineer, scientist, inventor, and musician. His most famous paintings are the *Last Supper* (c. 1495–1497) and the *Mona Lisa* (1503–1506), but he also designed cannons and canal-locks, and he had the imagination to theorize about flying machines centuries before the technology existed to make flight possible. Like Leonardo, Michelangelo (1475–1564) mastered painting, sculpture, and architecture; he also wrote poetry of a high quality. Perhaps his most significant contribution to Western civilization was the sheer force of his personality, whereby he defined the artist as a tormented genius whose inspiration leads him to test his powers to the limits. Da Vinci and Michelangelo are the most remarkable examples of "Renaissance men"—geniuses who mastered a broad range of talents in a display of individualistic virtuosity that defined Renaissance Humanism.

LITERATURE

The classic statement of the confidence in human reason and ability that epitomized Renaissance Humanism was the *Oration on the Dignity of Man* (1486) by Pico della Mirandola (1463–1494). Pico was a student of Marsilio Ficino and later set out on an ambitious program to develop a universal theory of human knowledge which was to include a Jewish form of mysticism known as the Cabbala as well as magic, but he fell under the influence of Savonarola and abandoned this grand design. Historical literature began to be written in the vernacular. In addition to Machiavelli's *Prince* and *Discourses*, there were the works of Francesco Guicciardini (1483–1540), whose *History of Italy* was based on a critical use of sources, and Giorgio Vasari (1511–1574), whose *Lives of the Artists* (1550) is an early history of art. *The Book of the Courtier* by Baldassare Castiglione (1478–1529) outlines the education and rules of etiquette which the well-rounded statesman should embody, and thus epitomizes the refined cultural ideals of Renaissance Humanism.

ECONOMIC INNOVATIONS

The artistic and scholarly endeavors of the Italian Renaissance would not have been possible without the wealth generated by new financial practices during the recovery from the Black Death. These practices included double-entry bookkeeping to record transactions accurately, bills of exchange (a prototype of the modern check), maritime insurance known as "sea loans" to minimize the effects of the loss of cargo, and the use of branch offices to establish international financial empires. Although the church still forbade usury, it allowed the exploitation of loopholes by which wealthy merchants could lend money in order to make profits from the charging of interest. The Medici were in fact bankers for the papacy. The Italians formed short-term partnerships known as *commenda* by which an investor would contribute capital while the recipient would conduct the actual commercial activity; this system allowed investors to diversify their commercial ventures to take advantage of changing circumstances in the market.

THE NORTHERN RENAISSANCE

Painting. Architecture and sculpture north of the Alps remained closely tied to the Gothic culture of the Middle Ages and lacked the revival of classicism that characterized the Italian Renaissance. The most innovative form of art was painting, and Flemish painters were leaders in the field. Their religious subject matter and style were developed from Gothic book illumination, but now images were more commonly painted on wooden panels, often as part of altar-pieces for the decoration of churches. Early Flemish masters, such as Jan van Eyck (c. 1390–1441) and Rogier van der Weyden (c. 1400–1464), shared with their Italian contemporaries a keen interest in naturalism, often expressed in minute detail (as seen in the folds of drapery, textures of surfaces, and background landscapes), but they lacked a fully developed linear perspective. They relied instead on aerial perspective, that is, the atmospheric effects of light and haze between foreground and background to express the illusion of distance. Northern art had extremely vibrant colors, largely due to the Flemish invention of oil-based paints, which allowed a wider range of technical possibilities. (Oil paints did not come into use in Italy until the time of Leonardo da Vinci, who was among the first to use the new medium.) Later northern artists were influenced by Italian art and excelled in realism, as seen in the portraits painted by two Germans—Albrecht Dürer (1471–1528) and Hans Holbein the Younger (1497–1543). Two prominent Dutch painters were Hieronymus Bosch (c. 1450–1516), who is famous for his allegorical works depicting fantastic scenes of devils tormenting people, and Pieter Bruegel the Elder (1525–1569), who was exceptional for his lively and intricate scenes of peasant life.

Printing. Around the year 1450, the printing press with movable metal type was invented. The invention is generally attributed to Johannes Gutenberg (c. 1400–1468) of Mainz in Germany. Gutenberg's books were not only intended to reduce the labor involved in producing literature, but were meant to be attractive as well. The printing press spread quickly, reaching Venice by 1469 and England by 1476. A prominent Venetian printer was Aldus Minutius (1450–1515), who replaced the Gothic-style black-letter casts of Gutenberg with more elegant letter-forms known as italics. The Italian humanist printers turned away from Gothic letters and revived Carolingian minuscule, thereby giving the modern world the typography it still uses.

Engraving. Another innovation of northern Europeans was the woodcut, which allowed the mass-production of identical images by impressing them onto paper (typically onto pages in books). Since woodcuts deteriorated with use, they were replaced in time by metal plates, which also allowed finer lines and thus more intricate engravings. A prominent northern artist who became skilled in this medium was Albrecht Dürer (1471–1528), who studied art in Italy and brought its styles back to Germany. By developing engravings which were reproduced in books, Dürer quickly disseminated the principles of Italian art north of the Alps.

Music. Northern Europeans also developed polyphony, or music consisting of several voices singing in harmony, from the twelfth century to the early fifteenth century. Until then music was predominantly monophonic, like Gregorian chant.

CHRISTIAN HUMANISM

Religious Fervor. Beginning in the fourteenth century, a religious movement developed among the laity in northern Europe that sought to bring the experience of God into daily life. The movement was inspired by the preaching of the German mystic, Meister Eckhart (1260–1327) and became known as the Modern Devotion, preached by a Dutch layman, Gerard Groote (1349–1384), whose followers founded the Brethren of the Common Life. Their ideals are expressed in *The Imitation of Christ* by Thomas à Kempis (c. 1380–1471). Many of them were also inspired by the revival of classicism that spread from Italy; in their schools they taught Latin and Greek.

Erasmus. Desiderius Erasmus of Rotterdam (c. 1466–1536) used his classical education to acquire a deeper understanding of early Christianity. He prepared a Greek edition of the New Testament and provided a commentary and a Latin translation that corrected errors in St. Jerome's Vulgate. Erasmus wanted to bring Christianity back to a simpler form based on a careful reading of the Bible, which he believed should be studied by all Christians, not just priests and theologians. He wrote his satirical *Praise of Folly* (1509) to demonstrate how far the religion of Christ had strayed from its roots. He was not, however, willing to oppose the papacy, but hoped to reform the church from within.

More. Erasmus traveled throughout Europe and corresponded with leading thinkers. One of these was Thomas More (1478–1535), an English statesman who criticized English society in his satirical essay, *Utopia* (1516), which describes an ideal society free from poverty and other social evils because the inhabitants have renounced money and private property.

Reuchlin. A German humanist, Johannes Reuchlin (1455–1522) advocated the study of languages for a better understanding of Scripture. Like Erasmus, he mastered Greek in order to read the New Testament. He then went on to master Hebrew as well in order to read the Old Testament. In 1506 he published a Hebrew grammar and in 1509 convinced the Holy Roman Emperor Maximilian I (1493–1519) to reject the Inquisition's call to burn the Talmud.

Erasmus, More, and Reuchlin were joined by the French theologian Jacques Lefèvre d'Étaples (c. 1450–1536) in the hope of reforming Christian society through humanistic education. They remained faithful to the Roman Catholic Church throughout their lives. Their works, however, inspired radical reformers who were less willing to compromise.

THE PROTESTANT REFORMATION

The Renaissance Papacy. The papacy during the Italian Renaissance became a worldly power and its character reverted back to the days of John XII (955–964) when the highest office in the Latin church became a trophy fought over by noble Italian families. Once in office, the popes behaved as secular despots and misused the papal treasury for their own luxuries. For example, when a member of the Medici family was elected Pope Leo X (1513–1521), he is reputed to have said, "God has given us the papacy— now let us enjoy it." The corruption of the papacy prevented it from dealing effectively with the crisis that suddenly faced it in 1517.

Sale of Indulgences. The extravagant spending of the Renaissance popes on military forces, patronage of the arts, and grandiose building programs led them to seek money by dubious means. A measure to which Leo X resorted was the sale of indulgences. Indulgences were pardons for sin, granted by the papacy, which were believed to shorten the time a person had to spend in Purgatory. Hoping to raise money for the building of St. Peter's Basilica, Leo X authorized a Dominican preacher, Johann Tetzel, to sell indulgences on a tour in Germany. When a theologian at the University of Wittenberg named Martin Luther (1483–1546) learned of Tetzel's mission, he responded by publishing in 1517 a collection of propositions opposing the sale of indulgences known as the "Ninety-Five Theses."

Martin Luther. Many shared Luther's objections, and soon a movement began that transformed an invitation for theological debate into a schism that altered the character of Western Christianity. Luther was excommunicated for his continuing opposition in 1521. He refused to recant at the Diet of Worms, responding, "Here I stand. I cannot do otherwise."

Citing Scripture and individual conscience as the only sources of religious authority, he denied the right of the papacy or councils to govern the church. Luther might have been burned at Worms as a heretic, but was instead protected by a sympathetic secular prince, Frederick, the Elector of Saxony. Soon other German princes in the northern part of the Empire sided with Luther as he appealed to their nationalistic pride against sending money to Italy to fund the artistic projects of corrupt popes. Since the Holy Roman Emperor, Charles V, was preoccupied with wars against the French and the Turks, he was unable to intervene militarily. Luther and the German reformers used the new technology of the printing press to disseminate their message quickly.

Luther's Theology. As a young man, Luther was obsessed with sin and guilt and feared for his own salvation. He joined the Augustinian friars and practiced good works, but was unable to acquire inner peace until his reading of the letters of St. Paul led him to conclude that salvation is achieved only by the gift of God's grace on those who make a sincere profession of faith. Thus, he rejected the efficacy of good works (as well as indulgences) and relied on justification by faith alone. Luther also rejected the exalted role of the priesthood and taught that the Church is a "priesthood of all believers." In rejecting the Mass (which could only be performed by a priest), Luther also rejected the doctrine of transubstantiation, which he replaced with *consubstantiation*—the doctrine that although the bread and wine do not become the actual substance of Christ's body and blood, he is present in them nonetheless. Rejecting celibacy as a morally superior way of life, Luther married a former nun, with whom he raised a family. Luther wrote numerous works, most notably *On Christian Liberty* (1519), and the *Small Catechism* (1529), which outlined the Lutheran creed. He also prepared the first German translation of the Bible (1534).

The Peasants' Revolt and the Jews. In 1525 the German peasants staged an uprising to better their economic situation and cited Luther's works in support of their cause. Luther thought they misunderstood his message (he was interested in religious, not economic, reform), but he sympathized with their plight and tried to reach a compromise between them and their lords. When the peasants resorted to violence, however, he sided firmly with the lords and urged forceful suppression of the revolt. A similar pattern is seen in Luther's treatment of the Jews. At first he was tolerant, hoping that they would convert to his reformed version of Christianity; but by 1537, when it was clear that the Jews were not interested in becoming Lutherans, he wrote bitter polemics against them.

Religious Fighting. In 1526 the princes of the Empire met at the Diet of Speyer and established a compromise which allowed Lutheran princes freedom to worship as they chose. When a second Diet of Speyer in 1529 repealed this agreement, the Lutheran princes rose in protest and thus became known as the "Protestants." In 1530 a Lutheran creed known as the Augsburg Confession was drawn up by the reformer Melanchthon as a conciliatory gesture, and in 1531 the Lutheran princes organized themselves into a defensive alliance known as the Schmalkaldic League. It was not until 1546 that the Emperor Charles V became free of international wars, and then struck the Schmalkaldic League. Although he was initially victorious, he could not achieve complete victory and the war ended in a draw. The Peace of Augsburg (1555) allowed each ruler of the approximately 300 states within the Holy Roman Empire to choose whether his state would be Catholic or Lutheran. About half the population of Germany thus became Lutheran, mostly in the north (as did their Scandinavian neighbors). A shortcoming of the Peace of Augsburg is that it made no provision for groups of Protestants other than the Lutherans.

DIVERSIFICATION OF PROTESTANTISM

Zwingli. By 1555, Lutherans were no longer the only Protestants. Luther's opposition to the sale of indulgences won the support of a Swiss reformer, Ulrich Zwingli (1484–1531). From the beginning, Swiss reformers wanted to promote religious change through political activism. Zwingli persuaded the town council of Zürich to reject the authority of the pope and to abolish many Catholic practices, such as fasting, monasticism, clerical celibacy, processions, the use of music in religious services, the adoration of saints through images, and the veneration of saintly relics. The Mass was simplified and the doctrine of transubstantiation was rejected. Zwingli disagreed with Luther over the Eucharist. Rejecting Luther's doctrine of *consubstantiation*, he believed that the ritual of the Lord's Supper was merely commemorative or symbolic and did not imply the special presence of divinity. The two men met in 1529, but were unable to resolve their differences. Zwingli turned his efforts to conversion beyond Zürich and won over half the Swiss Cantons; the others (known as the "Forest Cantons") remained Catholic and went to war with Zwingli's followers. Serving as chaplain for the Protestant forces, Zwingli was killed in the Battle of Kappel (1531).

Anabaptists. The call to individual conscience inspired many small sects which did not align themselves with either Luther or Zwingli but pursued their own interpretation of Scripture. Many of these groups required their converts to receive baptism a second time, and thus were called Anabaptists (*ana* means "again" in Greek). The Anabaptists were despised by Catholics, Lutherans, and Zwinglians alike. While many of the Anabaptists were peaceful, some of them had participated in the Peasant Revolt of 1525, and one group, led by John of Leiden, later seized the town of Münster, where in 1534 they established a theocracy ("New Zion") which practiced polygamy (after the model of the Old Testament) and communal ownership of property (after the model of the New Testament, as found in the Acts of the Apostles). The city was soon recaptured and John of Leiden was executed in 1536.

Calvin. After the generation of Luther and Zwingli, the Protestant movement was dominated by the French theologian John Calvin (1509–1564), who established a theocracy in Geneva, Switzerland. Like other reformers, Calvin was intolerant of those who opposed his position. He supported the execution of Michael Servetus (1511–1553) for denying the existence of the Trinity. Calvin established the Reformed tradition of Protestantism. His systematic theology, *Institutes of the Christian Religion* (1536–1559), stressed the sovereignty of God and the utter dependence of human beings on God's mercy. To emphasize that neither good works nor faith but only the power of God alone can guarantee salvation, Calvin taught the doctrine of double predestination—that God has determined in advance not only that some will be saved, but also that others will be damned. Calvinism was centered primarily in Switzerland, but there were Calvinist minorities throughout Europe. Those in France were called Huguenots. The Scottish reformer, John Knox (1513–1572), established Calvinism in Scotland, founding its Presbyterian Church. Calvin's Genevan Academy, which was designed to train preachers, was instrumental in the spread of his reform movement.

The Reformation in England. Unlike the movements on the Continent, the Reformation in England resulted not from theological differences with Rome, but from a conflict between the English monarchy and the papacy. Henry VIII (1491–1547) requested an annulment of his marriage to Catherine of Aragon because she did not produce a male heir, but Pope Clement VII (1523–1534) denied it. Clement was a virtual prisoner of the Emperor Charles V, the nephew of Catherine, and thus could not have granted Henry's request even if he was so inclined. Henry played up popular discontent with the extremely wealthy Catholic Church and in 1532 received support for his break with Rome from Parliament, which passed laws that shifted authority over the Church of England from the pope to the king. In addition to divorcing Catherine and marrying Anne Boleyn (Henry married six times in all), he took possession of church property, closed monasteries, and required his subjects to take an oath of supremacy recognizing his religious authority. Prominent individuals who refused were executed, including the former chancellor, the humanist Thomas More (1478–1535). Yet Henry VIII was conservative about religious doctrine, as his Six Articles (1539) outlining the theology of the Anglican Church demonstrate. Religious doctrine did not significantly change until the reigns of Henry's successors, his son Edward VI (1547–1553) and his daughter Elizabeth I (1558–1603).

THE CATHOLIC REFORMATION

Council of Trent. The Catholic Church was slow to respond to the Protestant challenge because it did not have an effective leader until Pope Paul III (1534–1549), but the experience ultimately revived the papacy as an effective institution for spiritual leadership. Paul III's most important action was to initiate the Council of Trent, which met three times between 1545 and 1563, establishing a thorough reform of the Roman Catholic Church and defining its dogmatic theological position in response to the issues raised by the Protestants. Although the Catholic Reformation is also known as the Counter Reformation, it was not merely a response to Protestantism; it also channeled energetic initiatives that were born of genuine faith and piety among the Catholic faithful.

New Religious Orders. One of the most important features of the Catholic Reformation was the foundation of new religious orders, of which the most prominent was the Society of Jesus, or Jesuits, founded in 1534 by St. Ignatius of Loyola (1491–1556) and approved by Paul III in 1540. Ignatius had been a soldier who turned to the religious life during hospitalization for a battlefield injury in 1521. He wrote a manual for meditation known as the *Spiritual Exercises* and soon attracted followers. The Jesuits specialized in education, founding schools of high quality for the education of Catholics and dedicating themselves to the conversion of Protestants through well-informed preaching. Missionary activity throughout the world was a major part of their work. In the 1540s, the Jesuit St. Francis Xavier (1506–1552) preached in the Far East, including India, Southeast Asia, and Japan. (He died on his way to China.) The Jesuits acquired a reputation for fanatical devotion to the papacy. Other new religious orders which served Catholicism in various ways included the Theatines, Ursulines, and Capuchins (a revival of the Franciscans). The Carmelite order was rejuvenated by the mystic St. Teresa of Avila (1515–1582) and her disciple St. John of the Cross (1542–1591).

Inquisition and Index. Another measure taken by Paul III to revive Catholicism was the Roman Inquisition (also known as the Holy Office), founded in 1542. This organization was not directly related to the medieval

Inquisition, and it was also distinct from the Spanish Inquisition, which was established in 1478. The Roman Inquisition was concerned primarily with monitoring newly published books for evidence of heretical theology, and thus focused its attention on the intellectual elite, which included men like Martin Luther and John Calvin. It was responsible for publishing an *Index of Prohibited Books*, of which the first appeared in 1559. The purpose of the index was to identify books that were considered dangerous to the Roman Catholic faith. As a form of censorship, it threatened to excommunicate any Catholic who read or distributed books on the index without special dispensation.

THE NEW MONARCHIES

The centralizing tendencies of the late Middle Ages became more pronounced during the Renaissance and Reformation in England and France. Spain quickly joined them as one of the most powerful nations in Europe. The weakness of Italy and the Holy Roman Empire stood in stark contrast to the rise of the New Monarchies.

Ottoman Turkish Empire. A cataclysmic event that altered the character of the European political configuration by reviving a powerful Mulism presence in Europe was the fall of Constantinople to the Ottoman Turks in 1453. The Ottomans were a Turkish dynasty established around 1300 in western Anatolia. For a time the Ottomans served as mercenaries to the Byzantines, but by about 1350 they established a base in the Balkans and set about expanding their domains. European crusades against them in the early 1400s were ineffective, and the capture of Constantinople by Mehmet (Muhammad) II the Conqueror (1451–1481) firmly established their control over the southeastern corner of Europe. The greatest of Ottoman rulers was Suleiman the Magnificent (1520–1566), whose forces captured Serbia and later Hungary (Battle of Mohacs, 1526). In 1529 the Ottomans lay siege to Vienna. Although they never took the city, they were a constant threat to central Europe well into modern times.

France. After the Hundred Years' War, the rise of France was challenged by the Duchy of Burgundy, which extended along the eastern border of the French domains from Switzerland to Flanders and threatened to become a powerful centralized state in itself. This threat was finally eliminated in 1477, when Louis XI (1461–1483) hired Swiss mercenaries to defeat the Burgundian duke, Charles the Bold. With France secure and administered by an effective bureaucracy, the Valois kings set out on ambitious campaigns to dominate their Italian neighbors, beginning with Charles VIII (1483–1498), who seized the Kingdom of Naples in 1495, and Louis XII (1498–1515), who seized Milan in 1499.

Francis I. The French campaigns in Italy were ultimately disastrous. Their claims entangled them with the Hapsburgs, and Francis I (1515–1547) fought four wars against Charles V, known as the Valois-Hapsburg Wars. Francis was captured in 1525 and had to surrender his claims to Burgundy and Italy. Although Francis and Charles signed the Treaty of Cambrai (1529) to end hostilities, the wars soon resumed and Charles invaded southern France (1530–1538). In a desperate bid to save the country, Francis made an alliance with the Ottoman sultan Suleiman the Magnificent, who relieved the pressure on France by striking at the Holy Roman Empire from the east and forcing Charles V to turn his attention to the defense of his own domains. The alliance between Catholic France and Muslim Turkey was scandalous from a religious point of view, but reflected the secular pragmatism of the new style of European statecraft, which conformed to the Machiavellian model outlined in *The Prince*. The French reaped considerable commercial benefits from their alliance with the Ottomans and were given control of the sacred sites in the Holy Land. The struggle between the Valois and the Hapsburgs for control of Italy was ended in 1559 by the Treaty of Cateau-Cambrésis, which required France to admit defeat.

England. The English emerged from the Hundred Years' War badly shaken, and England descended into a period of civil strife known as the Wars of the Roses (1455–1485) as two noble houses—Lancaster and York—fought over control of the kingdom. In the end it was neither of these dynasties, but the House of Tudor, that emerged triumphant. Established on the throne by his victory at Bosworth Field against Richard III of York (1483–1485), Henry VII (1485–1509) established England as a new monarchy. Henry continued to work with Parliament, streamlined the administration, and acquired lucrative commercial contracts for English merchants in Italy. He enhanced royal power by establishing the Court of the Star Chamber, which was designed to weaken the power of troublesome nobles by trying them without the benefit of a jury and allowing torture to exact confessions.

Henry VIII. The reign of Henry VIII (1509–1547) is marked primarily by his break with Rome, but he strengthened his monarchy in many other ways. He used the lands he seized from the church to build up a new class of loyal nobles who were dependent on his dynasty for their position, and he boosted national sentiment by working closely with Parliament to give his subjects a sense that the government was a partnership between the monarchy and the people. Henry was assisted by able administrators like Cardinal Wolsey and Thomas Cromwell. He built up the English fleet and fought limited wars on the Continent to maintain the balance of power.

Spain. By the fifteenth century, most of the Iberian peninsula had been won back from the Muslims. Long divided even among its Christian rulers, Spain began to coalesce into a strong centralized monarchy with the marriage of Ferdinand of Aragon (d. 1516) and Isabella of Castile (d. 1504) in 1469. They were able to dominate the *cortes* (parliamentary assemblies), reduce the power of the nobles, and streamline the bureaucracy. As both were devout Catholics, they received papal approval for the Spanish Inquisition in 1478, controlling it as an arm of the state in order to establish religious unity and to control dissidents. The first grand inquisitor was a Dominican friar, the dreaded Tomas de Torquemada (1420–1498). The Spanish Inquisition concentrated its attention at first on the Marranos (Jews who had converted to Christianity but were suspected of continuing to practice Judaism secretly) and later the Moriscos (Muslim converts). It later prevented Protestantism from establishing itself in Spain. Among its positive effects was the reform of the Catholic Church in Spain, a task that was guided by Cardinal Ximenes. In 1492, Ferdinand and Isabella expelled the Jews from Spain and completed the *Reconquista* with the invasion of Granada.

Charles I. In 1516, the kingdoms of Castile and Aragon passed to Ferdinand's grandson, who is known as Charles I (1516–1556) of Spain; later elected Holy Roman Emperor, he is also known as Charles V (1519–1558). In these two roles Charles inherited a collection of far-flung lands whose total expanse surpassed that of Charlemagne. It included the Netherlands, Sicily, and southern Italy. Although Charles was the first king of a unified Spain, he spent little time there. His early rule set off a revolt, but it was brought under control in 1521 and thereafter Charles made compromises that maintained peace in the realm. Charles relied on Spanish soldiers for his wars against the French, the Ottomans, the Protestants, and the Italians. At last weary of the endless wars, Charles divided his empire, giving Spain and the Netherlands to his son, Philip II (1556–1598), and arranging for his brother, Ferdinand I (1558–1564), to receive the imperial title. Charles then retired to a monastery in Spain, where he soon died.

CHAPTER 6
Early Modern Europe

Chapter 6

EARLY MODERN EUROPE

THE AGE OF EXPLORATION

During the Renaissance and Reformation, Europeans were embarking upon naval expeditions that looked beyond the confines of their world. The leaders in these voyages of discovery were the Portuguese and Spanish, who sometimes hired Italian captains.

Prince Henry the Navigator. A Portuguese prince known as Henry the Navigator (1394–1460) gave the first major impetus to exploration by funding voyages of discovery and establishing a school for navigation at Sagres, which included an observatory. He also made improvements in shipbuilding, and the caravel was adopted as the favored vessel for exploration. Henry's motives reflected military, religious, and economic concerns. His patronage of exploration began after he participated in the 1415 capture of Ceuta, a Muslim stronghold in North Africa across from the Strait of Gibraltar. He hoped that a more precise knowledge of African geography would help Christian forces to outflank the Muslims and thus gain a strategic advantage over them. He also hoped to make contact with a legendary figure named Prester John, who was rumored to rule a Christian kingdom in distant lands (possibly Ethiopia). More realistically, Henry thought to discover and convert pagans who lived on the edge of Muslim territories, thereby combining religious with military motives. Finally, Henry hoped to find deposits of gold and to generate wealth for Portugal by establishing a trade route to the Indies that could bypass the Mediterranean, which was dominated by the Italians and Turks.

Portuguese Exploration. With the support of Prince Henry, Portuguese explorers discovered the Azores, Canary, and Cape Verde Islands in the Atlantic Ocean and followed the African coast as far as Sierra Leone near the equator. They established a lucrative trade in gold, ivory, and slaves. In 1488 Bartholomew Diaz crossed the equator, sailed to the southern tip of Africa, and rounded the Cape of Good Hope. In 1497–1499 Vasco da Gama sailed to India and back, opening a trade route for spices and other luxury goods. In 1509–1515 Alfonso de Albuquerque established Portuguese trading posts along the west coast of India, the islands of Indonesia, and at the mouth of the Persian Gulf, thereby laying the foundations of the Portuguese Empire in the east, which was linked back to the capital of Lisbon through trading posts that dotted the African coast. In 1500, Pedro Cabral claimed Brazil—the only Portuguese territory in the New World.

Early Spanish Exploration. After the early successes of Portugal, the Spanish realized the potential for wealth that exploration could generate and became anxious to prevent their Iberian rival from dominating this trade. In 1492, Ferdinand and Isabella decided to fund a voyage by the Genoese mariner Christopher Columbus (1451–1504), who claimed that he could find a direct western route to the Far East without having to sail around Africa. Columbus had miscalculated the circumference of the earth and had no idea that massive continents barred the way, so that when he discovered the Caribbean islands (West Indies) and Central America, he thought he had reached Asia. Columbus established contact with the natives in four voyages, the last ending in 1504.

Treaty of Tordesillas (1494). Soon after Columbus's first voyage, Spain and Portugal decided to prevent imperialistic rivalry by dividing the world between them. In the Treaty of Tordesillas (1494) they agreed upon a longitude of demarcation that ran from pole to pole at an arbitrary distance in the Atlantic Ocean; Portugal could claim any land east of this line, whereas Spain could have any land west of it. Because of the terms of this treaty, the Spanish Empire was based mainly in the New World and the Philippines, while the Portuguese Empire focused on Africa, India, Indonesia, and Brazil (which lay east of the Tordesillas line as it bisects South America).

Conquistadors. Soon Spain sent adventurers known as *conquistadors*, or "conquerors," to explore the New World and claim it in the name of the Spanish monarchy. In Central and South America they came up against great empires and overthrew them by using the superior technology of firearms. The natives were also felled by diseases that Europeans brought with them, against which they had no immunity. Hernando Cortez conquered the Aztec Empire in Mexico (1519–1521), and Francisco Pizarro conquered the Inca Empire in Peru (1532–1533). The conquistadors seized the gold and silver of these empires and sent it back to Spain. Later (around 1550), silver was mined in Mexico and especially Bolivia (at Potosi).

Later Spanish Exploration. As the New World began to be economically exploited by Spain, exploration continued. Balboa crossed the Isthmus of Panama in 1513 and discovered the Pacific Ocean. A voyage commanded by Ferdinand Magellan (a Portuguese mariner employed by Spain) circumnavigated the world by rounding South America (1520–1522). Magellan himself did not complete the voyage, but was killed in a fight with natives in the Philippines (1521). Hernando De Soto explored Florida and the coast of the Gulf of Mexico, where he died in 1542.

Colonization. Spanish colonists soon began to settle the Caribbean islands in small numbers in order to establish plantations (mostly sugar cane) for the sake of making profits. They forced the native populations to work for them on estates granted by the Spanish king known as *encomiendas*. The *encomienda* system, which transplanted the model of the medieval manor into the New World, was so brutal that one of the colonizers, Bartolomé de Las Casas (1474–1566), campaigned against the harsh treatment of natives. He wrote numerous pamphlets and a history of Spanish colonization in the New World.

Naming the New World. The new continents were named by the German cartographer Martin Waldseemüller, who in 1516 published a map that labeled the new land masses "America"—a Latin adaptation of the first name of Amerigo Vespucci (1454–1512), a Florentine explorer who recognized that new continents had been discovered.

Exploration by Other European Nations. England, France, and the Netherlands followed Portugal and Spain in exploring the New World. They concentrated on North America, which had not yet been claimed and was not as wealthy as the more southerly regions. To extract wealth from the natural resources of North America, these countries put more emphasis on settlement.

England. In 1497, Henry VIII hired an Italian mariner, John Cabot, to seek a direct route to Asia in the northern hemisphere. However, no English expedition circumnavigated the globe until 1577–1580, when Sir Francis Drake landed on the west coast of North America and claimed it for Queen Elizabeth. Drake brought back a cargo of spices and treasure he had raided from Spanish shipping; upon his return he was knighted aboard his flagship, the *Golden Hind*. He later served as governor of English colonies in North America and as a member of Parliament. Sir Walter Raleigh launched two failed attempts at colonization at Roanoke Island, North Carolina (1585, 1587). The first permanent English settlement was Jamestown in Virginia (1607). Plymouth Colony was established in 1620, after which colonization gained momentum.

France. The leading French explorer was Jacques Cartier (1491–1557), who, like John Cabot, sought a northwest passage to the Far East. He explored the St. Lawrence River valley, which France later colonized. Samuel de Champlain founded a trading post in 1608 which later became Quebec City. Colonization in New France did not gain momentum until about 1650.

The Netherlands. The Dutch were the last to sponsor voyages of exploration. Their most famous explorer was an Englishman named Henry Hudson, after whom the Hudson River is named in commemoration of his voyage there in 1609. Dutch colonists founded New Amsterdam in 1624 (which later became New York City) and settled the Hudson Valley. This colonization was organized by the Dutch West India Company, a joint-stock company that reflected the new forms of financial organization that arose in the aftermath of the age of discovery.

THE COMMERCIAL REVOLUTION

The exploitation of the New World accelerated the evolution of economic life in Europe, resulting in dramatic changes that culminated in the rise of capitalism. Around 1500 the principal financial centers were Venice, Lisbon, and Madrid; Venice had long been the leader of commerce, whereas Lisbon and Madrid rose to prominence suddenly on the strength of their overseas imperialism. By the year 1600, however, the centers of finance had shifted to London, Paris, and Amsterdam as England, France, and the Netherlands developed new methods of economic organization to exploit the trade stimulated by overseas discoveries.

Inflation. As gold and silver poured into Europe via Portugal and Spain, the vast increase in quantities of precious metals caused runaway inflation, quadrupling prices between 1500 and 1600. Since wages did not rise equally, poverty became widespread and many people became vagrants. Nobles also suffered, since their income was based on fixed rents, which lost value as prices rose.

The Entrepreneurial Class. Wealth from the new commercial ventures tended to be concentrated in the hands of a relatively small group of people, the entrepreneurs—individuals who risked capital in order to turn a profit. The most successful entrepreneurs diversified their investments once they established themselves and commanded financial empires with branch offices in major cities throughout Europe. They often founded dynasties that established themselves as part of a new aristocracy of wealth. The Medici, for example, married into the French royal family and were made grand dukes of Tuscany in the sixteenth century. A French merchant and banker named Jacques Coeur (c. 1395–1456) was ennobled by King Charles VI and received a position of great influence in the government of Charles VII; he was prevented from founding a dynasty, however, when envious courtiers plotted his downfall. The most successful of the entrepreneurial families were the Fuggers of Augsburg, who began as cloth merchants and came to dominate mining in central Europe. They served as bankers for the Hapsburgs and thus wielded great political influence.

Changing Markets. The flexibility of the entrepreneurs was a key ingredient of their success. They were able to discern where money could be made and invested heavily in an industry for which there was high demand. In addition to overseas imports, these included shipbuilding, printing, mining, and metallurgy (to satisfy the demand for cannons). Once profit was made in one of these industries, it could be invested in another industry as capital for a diversified financial empire. The entrepreneurial spirit of taking advantage of supply and demand in order to maximize profits also affected agriculture, accelerating the specialization of production (a development that had already begun in the Middle Ages). In sixteenth-century England, lands that were once shared by peasants for common use were bought up by rich men and converted into pastures, a process known as the "enclosure movement," since the pastures were fenced off, or "enclosed," to prevent their use by peasants and promote specialization.

Decline of the Guilds. The transformation of economics, with the new emphasis on the private ownership of the means of production, sounded a death knell for the guilds. Craftsmen using traditional techniques of production could not supply the volume of goods that were demanded by the sixteenth-century economy. Entrepreneurs worked around the guilds using two methods, known as the "putting-out system" and the "gathering-in system." Although these changes in the means of production made entrepreneurs extremely wealthy and met demands for certain products, they had negative consequences in the dislocation of workers and disintegration of social norms.

The Putting-Out System. The use of unskilled labor, controlled by entrepreneurs, had already appeared toward the end of the Middle Ages in the textile industry. Entrepreneurs would buy wool and hire peasants to specialize in various stages of its manufacture into cloth: spinning the wool into thread, weaving the thread into cloth, and finally dyeing the cloth; the entrepreneur would then transport the thread to the weavers and the cloth to the dyers before selling the finished product on the market.

The Gathering-In System. This early form of the factory system was used in the boom industries of shipbuilding, printing, and iron-founding (for the manufacture of cannons). Entrepreneurs would gather workers to a single place where specialized tools for production were located and supervise them, thereby decreasing the cost of transportation and controlling quality.

Joint-Stock Companies. To finance the risky ventures of long-distance commerce, investors began to organize in associations known as "joint-stock companies." These evolved from "regulated companies," which were associations of professional traders. Both regulated companies and joint-stock companies were supported by governments, which granted monopolies in specific areas of commerce. Unlike regulated companies, joint-stock companies were associations of investors who bought shares in a business but entrusted the business itself to professionals. By pooling their financial resources, investors protected themselves against losses that could easily ruin them if they operated independently, and they were guaranteed a share of any profits. Although at first joint-stock companies focused on trade, they were later also used in industry. An early joint-stock company, known as the Russia Company, was sponsored by England in 1553. Other English joint-stock companies included the East India Company and Bank of England. The Netherlands sponsored the highly lucrative Dutch East India Company (1602) for trade in Asia and the Dutch West India Company (1621) for trade in the New World and Africa.

Mercantilism. Kings recognized that the strength of their state depended on the strength of their economy, so they often intervened in the activity of the entrepreneurs. State intervention in economics is known as mercantilism. Its central principle was the belief that the wealth of a nation is defined by the quantity of precious metals located within its borders. To keep as much gold and silver as possible within the nation, kings sought to maintain a favorable balance of trade (more exports than imports of commodities). Therefore they raised tariffs to discourage the purchase of foreign goods. They also sought to reduce internal trade barriers, such as tolls, in order to encourage trade within the nation's borders. An important feature of mercantilism was the exploitation of overseas empires through colonies, which served as sources of cheap raw materials and favorable markets for exported products.

Commodities. Spices were the most common import during the earlier phase of colonialism. By 1650, however, the European market was glutted with spices, decreasing the profits. Traders responded by diversifying imports to include more cotton fabrics, silk, coffee, and tea. Slaves were also imported from Africa, beginning around 1450. The slave trade to Europe was relatively modest. Although Portugal and Spain imported African slaves for agricultural labor, most European nations had little need of such help. Entrepreneurs did, however, purchase slaves for use in the colonies of the New World.

NATION-STATES AND WARS OF RELIGION

Nationalism and Religion. Politics in early modern Europe was dominated by the increasing power of centralized monarchies, which led to nationalism, dynastic struggles, and conflict over religious differences. These forces interacted in complex ways, for although Catholics and Protestants often fought one another, national interest also induced some of them to cooperate against a common political enemy and thus make alliances against co-religionists.

Cannons. The centralization of power was aided by new technologies, such as the cannon, which greatly shortened the length of sieges and led to major changes in military strategies and tactics. The Ottoman Turks were able to beat down the walls of Constantinople for the first time using cannons in 1453, and European monarchs used cannons against rebellious nobles, who could no longer hide within their castles. Cannons were also a vital ingredient of naval power, which made possible the rise and defense of vast overseas empires.

FRANCE

Religious War. Under Francis I (1515–1547), the French monarchy acquired control over the Gallican (French) church through the Concordat of 1516, whereby the papacy allowed French kings to appoint their own bishops. The spread of Calvinism in France, whose adherents were known as Huguenots, was seen as a threat to this national church. Persecution became systematic during the reign of Henry II (1547–1559), by which time a sizable minority of French nobles had become Huguenots. After Henry II's death, his widow, Catherine de' Medici (de Médicis), dominated her three sons who inherited the throne. Intermittent civil war over religion began in 1562, and in 1572 Catherine was involved in a purge of several thousand Huguenots known as the St. Bartholemew's Day Massacre. The wars continued until Henry of Navarre, the Huguenot leader, inherited the throne by right of succession and thus established the Bourbons as a royal dynasty. As Henry IV (1589–1610), he converted to Catholicism in order to placate his Catholic subjects (remarking "Paris is worth a Mass"), but he protected his Calvinist subjects through the Edict of Nantes (1598), which granted them freedom of worship.

Cardinal Richelieu. The political terms of the Edict of Nantes were revoked in 1628 by the chief minister of Louis XIII (1610–1643), Cardinal Richelieu (d. 1642), who subdued the Huguenot bastion of La Rochelle in order to eliminate their independent military and political power. However, he allowed them religious freedom as long as they agreed to serve the French monarchy. Richelieu was devoted to the cause of royal absolutism in France, and by 1630 was its virtual ruler. To make the monarchy more powerful, Richelieu curbed the power of the nobility and increased military spending. He was willing to make alliances with Protestant rulers in order to weaken the Hapsburgs, the chief rivals of the French kings.

SPAIN

Philip II. Charles V entrusted the crown of Spain to his son, Philip II (1556–1598), who had already received from him control of Milan (1540), the Kingdom of Naples and Sicily (1554), and the Netherlands (1555). Unlike his father, who had neglected the affairs of Spain, Philip II used his other lands for the good of his Spanish kingdom. Deeply opposed to Protestantism, Philip introduced the Inquisition into the Netherlands, which prompted a revolt that began in 1566. Although Philip sent the Duke of Alba to suppress the rebellion, his brutal tyranny only intensified opposition, which in 1572 rallied around William the Silent, Prince of Orange. The movement for independence was to last about 80 years. In the meantime Philip's suppression of religious dissidents extended to the former Muslim population of Spain, known as Moriscos (Muslim converts to Christianity who were suspected of secretly practicing Islam); nearly all of them were exiled in 1571. In the same year Philip sent a fleet commanded by his brother, John of Austria, to lead the Holy League (which included Spain, Venice, and the Papacy) against the Turks at Lepanto off the coast of Greece. John's victory did not result in any territorial gains against the Muslims, but it did free thousands of Christian galley slaves and proved that the Turks were not invincible. Philip annexed Portugal in 1580, but his attempted conquest of England ended in failure in 1588. Philip's last years were spent aiding the forces of the French Catholics in their war against Henry of Navarre.

ENGLAND

Elizabeth I. After a brief attempt by Mary I Tudor (1553–1558) to forcibly restore Catholicism, England became more fully Protestant. In 1559, Parliament passed the Act of Uniformity, which established the ceremonies of the Anglican Church and the Book of Common Prayer. In 1563, it passed the Thirty-Nine Articles, which outlined the nation's theological stance. Elizabeth I (1558–1603) tried to establish a moderate religious position, but faced severe challenges to her religious reforms. In 1569 she repressed a Catholic uprising, and in 1587 executed her cousin Mary, the exiled Queen of Scots, for her involvement in a Catholic plot. Yet Elizabeth also opposed the Puritans, religious extremists who wanted to eliminate all vestiges of Catholicism. Her moderate position is summed up in her refusal "to make windows into men's souls," by which she meant that she respected private dissent as long as it did not express itself in open opposition.

The Spanish Armada. When Elizabeth came to power in 1558, she was forced to abandon the city of Calais, last of England's holdings on the Continent, following Mary I's disastrous war against France. Elizabeth's foreign policy was dominated by her efforts to aid Protestants against their Catholic monarchs, including Scotland, France, and the Netherlands. Her aid for the Dutch rebellion against Spain (1585–1587) provoked Philip II to send the Spanish Armada against England in 1588, but this grand fleet was destroyed by a storm (called the "Protestant wind") and the formidable English fleet, whose vessels were smaller but more maneuverable and could fire cannonballs faster than the larger but slower Spanish galleons. The victory over the Spanish Armada boosted English nationalism and made possible the rise of the British empire.

The Stuarts. Elizabeth I strengthened the English monarchy by cooperating with Parliament and tactfully establishing their respective spheres of power. However, she never married, and her failure to produce an heir ended the Tudor dynasty. The rules of succession gave the crown of England to the Stuart dynasty of Scotland, whose tactless treatment of Parliament led to the English Civil War (1642–1649). Both James I (1603–1625) and his son, Charles I (1625–1649) maintained the doctrine of the divine right of kings, by which they claimed their power came directly from God rather than from the people. James used his supreme authority in matters of religion to persecute Catholics (provoking Guy Fawkes's failed Gunpowder Plot of 1605) and to authorize the translation of the Bible known as the King James Version (1611). Charles, on the other hand, was suspected of Catholic sympathies, having married the Catholic princess of France, Henrietta Maria, as part of an alliance against Spain. Both James and Charles suffered from budgetary difficulties, for Parliament expressed its opposition to their reigns by approving less money than they required to meet expenses. In response, they both tried to raise funds without parliamentary approval. Although Parliament challenged James's right to raise customs duties, the courts upheld his authority to do so and thus cleared the way for Charles to raise money by various means, including income from royal property, the sale of monopolies, the levying of ship money, and forced loans. In 1628 Parliament protested the forced loans through the Petition of Right, to which Charles responded by dismissing Parliament and ruling without them for eleven years (1629–1640). His measures to raise money were sufficient to meet expenses as long as there was no war, but when Scotland invaded northern England to protest the use of the Anglican Book of Common Prayer, Charles called Parliament to approve funds for the defense of the realm.

Civil War (1642–1649). The Long Parliament (1640–1653) immediately instituted a series of reforms that weakened the monarchy. It passed an act requiring the king to summon Parliament at least every three years, outlawed all forms of taxation without parliamentary approval, and abolished special courts, such as the Court of the Star Chamber. Soon the Puritans tried to push through their radical agenda of church reform, published the Great Remonstrance detailing grievances against Charles, and demanded control of the army. Charles became impatient and entered the House of Commons with an armed escort in order to arrest five men for treason. Later he refused the radical measures demanded in Parliament's Nineteen Propositions (1642). The country drifted into civil war, with Roundheads supporting Parliament and Cavaliers supporting the king. After initial royal victories, the parliamentarians under Oliver Cromwell captured the king and abolished the monarchy. Charles was beheaded.

DUTCH INDEPENDENCE

The Dutch revolt that began in 1566, and was led by William the Silent between 1572 and 1584, continued for about 80 years before the independence of the Netherlands was recognized. In 1579 the northern Dutch provinces formed the Union of Utrecht, which formally declared independence in 1581 and became the core of the Dutch Republic of the United Provinces. Spanish troops were expelled by 1600, and a truce halted fighting between 1609 and 1621. After a revival of the conflict, Spain finally recognized Dutch sovereignty in 1648 through the Treaty of Westphalia. In the meantime, the Dutch had become a world power and commanded a fleet greater than the fleets of all the other European nations. They took advantage of Philip II's conquest of Portugal (1580) to seize Portuguese colonies in the Far East and take over the spice trade, on which they exercised a near monopoly. This eastern commerce was controlled by the Dutch East India Company, a joint-stock company formed in 1602 and run by the United Provinces. It was later joined by the Dutch West India Company, which was active in North America, where in 1624 it founded New Amsterdam at the mouth of the Hudson (later New York City).

THE THIRTY YEARS' WAR

Origins. The last of the religious wars occurred in the birthplace of Protestantism. The Peace of Augsburg (1555) had resolved the initial religious war by allowing the ruler of each state within the Holy Roman Empire to determine its religion, but this caused problems because antagonism persisted between neighbors of the rival faiths and because it did not take into account the religious inclination of the majority of citizens in each state. The Empire became divided into two rival camps: the Evangelical Union (1608) and the Catholic League (1609). This powderkeg was then set off when the people of Bohemia, who were mostly Protestant, revolted in 1618 against their Catholic Hapsburg ruler and threw two imperial ministers out of a window in an act known as the Defenestration of Prague. The conflict that ensued came to be known as the Thirty Years' War (1618–1648), which occurred in four major phases.

Conduct of the War. In the Bohemian phase (1618–1625), Catholic forces succeeded in suppressing the rebellion within the Empire. The period of foreign intervention that followed is known as the Danish phase (1625–1629), when Christian IV of Denmark alone fought the Catholics, who were led by the ambitious mercenary Count Wallenstein. Denmark was defeated in 1629 and the Holy Roman Emperor, Ferdinand II (1619–1637), issued the Edict of Restitution, which transferred lands that the Protestants had seized from the Catholic Church. The Hapsburg victory prompted another round of foreign intervention—by Protestants who wished to reverse the Edict of Restitution and by Catholic France, which was encircled by the Hapsburgs and alarmed by their increased strength. Hoping to restore the balance of power, Cardinal Richelieu (d. 1642) of France agreed to provide financial support to the Protestants if they agreed to respect the religious freedom of Catholics in the territories they conquered. A Swedish phase (1630–1635) began when the Lutheran king of Sweden, Gustavus Adolphus (1611–1632), liberated northern Germany from Hapsburg occupation and seized Catholic lands in southern Germany. Gustavus Adolphus died in 1632, and the Protestant cause was carried on by his chancellor, Oxenstierna. However, Ferdinand II managed to roll back their victories (without Wallenstein, who was assassinated in 1634). In 1635 the Swedes and the Hapsburgs came to an agreement known as the Peace of Prague, which ended the religious aspects of the war by modifying the Edict of Restitution and settling territorial issues between Catholics and Lutherans. At this point Cardinal Richelieu intervened openly, initiating the French phase (1635–1648) by declaring war on Hapsburg Spain and sending French troops into the Holy Roman Empire. Thus, the last phase was a purely dynastic struggle in which the Catholic Bourbons of France were allied with Protestant (mostly Swedish) forces. As the fighting dragged on, Germany was devastated; it lost about a third of its population to war, famine, and plague.

Treaty of Westphalia. After several years of negotiation, the belligerents ended the war through the Treaty of Westphalia (1648). Furthermore, the treaty granted Alsace to France and certain Baltic regions to Sweden. It recognized the Swiss Confederacy and the Dutch Republic of the United Provinces as sovereign nations independent of Hapsburg control. It also recognized the sovereignty of the approximately 300 constituent states of the Holy Roman Empire, which effectively eliminated the Empire as a meaningful political entity. Among the German states was the new duchy of Prussia, which was formed from the lands of the Teutonic Knights when its last grand master, Albrecht von Hohenzollern, converted to Lutheranism in 1525. With regard to religion, the Treaty of Westphalia accepted the status quo. Although it reaffirmed the principle that the ruler of each state should determine its faith, it also stipulated that any prince who should change his faith in the future would forfeit his rule (thereby halting the spread of Protestantism). It improved on the Peace of Augsburg (1555) by extending recognition to Calvinism as well as to Lutheranism. Thus, the Treaty of Westphalia redefined the religious and political map of Europe. The division between Protestants and Catholics was recognized as a permanent schism, and France became the most powerful state on the Continent.

A REVOLUTION IN WORLD VIEW

The religious and political transformations of the sixteenth and seventeenth centuries coincided with perhaps even more momentous changes in its thought and culture. The most far-reaching development is known as the Scientific Revolution, but even as this statement of supreme confidence in the powers of human reason got under way, Europeans gave old superstitions new legitmacy in the charged atmosphere of the religious conflicts.

The Witch Craze. Belief in magic was common during Greco-Roman antiquity and persisted throughout the Middle Ages, but large-scale persecutions of witches were uncommon until the late fifteenth century, following the publication of a manual for witch-hunting known as the *Hammer of Witches* (1486), written by two Dominican Inquisitors. During the heightened tensions of the religious wars, Catholics and Protestants alike used this book as a guide for the detection, trial, and execution of witches, mostly targeting elderly women who lived alone. The persecutions did not end until about the year 1700, when the Scientific Revolution inspired an era of skepticism known as the Age of Enlightenment.

Astronomy. Although the Hellenistic astronomer Aristarchus (c. 310–250 B.C.E.) had first maintained that the earth orbits the sun, this heliocentric theory was largely ignored until the sixteenth century, when the geocentric, or earth-centered, theory advocated by Ptolemy was finally challenged by the Polish astronomer Nicholas Copernicus (1473–1543). His book *On the Revolutions of the Celestial Orbs* (1543) applied the principle of logical economy ("Ockham's Razor") to simplify the cosmic model: Copernicus concluded that the heliocentric theory better explained the observed motions of the planets than did the geocentric model, which required a complicated system of imaginary epicycles. Yet Copernicus's theory of circular orbits was not correct either, and problems with the heliocentric model were not resolved until Johannes Kepler (1571–1630) discovered, on the basis of the precise observations collected by Tycho Brahe (1546–1601), that planetary orbits are not circular but elliptical. This refined heliocentric theory was then popularized by Galileo Galilei (1564–1642). By writing in Italian rather than Latin, Galileo transferred the discussion from the tiny circle of a few specialists to a general audience. He was put under house arrest for his headstrong popularization of this controversial theory, which undermined confidence in ancient authority.

Bacon. The advances in astronomy could not have been made without precise observations and a revival of mathematics. These two elements, which are central to modern science, were promoted by the English scientific popularizer and theorist Francis Bacon (1561–1626). Although not a scientist but a statesman, Bacon's theoretical writings advanced the cause of science by downplaying the traditional deductive method of reasoning (which begins with general premises and draws conclusions about particulars), and advocating the inductive method (which begins with particulars and draws general conclusions). The inductive method became the basic procedure of the new science. Bacon also advocated the empirical method, which emphasized the importance of conducting experiments in order to provide accurate data for induction.

Descartes. Bacon's empirical method was challenged by thinkers known as rationalists, who held that accurate knowledge about the world could be attained by the faculty of human reason alone. The leading proponent of this method was the French philosopher René Descartes (1596–1650), who proved the validity of his position by making contributions to mathematics that remain in use to this day. Cartesian coordinates (the graphic depiction of algebraic equations as geometric lines on a two-dimensional grid) are named after him. Descartes was not wholly opposed to induction, and made contributions to science, but he is most famous for his achievements in philosophy which employ deductive reasoning, particularly his use of the axiom, "I think, therefore I am" (in Latin, *Cogito, ergo sum*), to serve as the foundation of his skeptical system of philosophy. Descartes used this proof of his own existence to construct arguments for the existence of God that were not based on authority or experimentation but on reason alone.

Pascal. The new arguments over the relative merits of induction and deduction were criticized by Descartes' countryman, Blaise Pascal (1623–1662). Despite making important contributions to mathematics (especially probability theory and conic sections in geometry) and science (such as observations of atmospheric pressure), Pascal found the relative absence of God in the new world view a troubling development. He turned for spiritual renewal to the Catholic reform movement known as Jansenism, which emphasized faith over reason and insisted on the human need for God's grace.

Medicine. The new confidence in human reason, which turned away from old authorities to study the world anew, transformed nearly all disciplines, including medicine. The Belgian physician Andreas Vesalius (1514–1564) conducted dissections of animals and human cadavers in order to dispute the ancient authority Galen (c. 129–199). He shared his discoveries in his book *On the Structure of the Human Body* (1543). An important contribution toward the study of the pulmonary circulatory system was made by the Spanish physician Michael Servetus (who was executed for heresy by the Calvinists in 1553). Later, the English physician William Harvey (1578–1657) published his discovery of the role of the heart in the circulatory system in his book *On the Motion of the Heart* (1628). The alchemist Paracelsus (c. 1493–1541) made an important contribution to medicine by arguing that diseases arise from the presence of foreign bodies; he recommended the use of minerals to neutralize these foreign bodies.

Literature. In literature as well, authors began to criticize the old world view. French literature was represented by the satires of François Rabelais (c. 1494–1553), who ridiculed European society in his often bawdy tales about two giants named Gargantua and Pantagruel, and by Michel de Montaigne (1533–1592), who established the essay as a literary form and used it in his skeptical enterprise of questioning dogmatic opinions that lack rational foundation. The finest Spanish response to the crisis presented by the clash of world views was the satirical novel *Don Quixote* by Miguel de Cervantes (1547–1616), which depicts an idealistic nobleman who finds that chivalry is useless in the modern world. Cervantes's own life in some ways mirrored that of his protagonist. Motivated by idealistic impulses, he fought at the naval Battle of Lepanto (1571) but found that crusading was no longer truly appreciated in his society, which had become mercilessly pragmatic. The finest English spokesman for the new attitudes was William Shakespeare (1564–1616), whose collection of plays and sonnets constitutes a kind of secular Bible for the early modern humanistic attitude.

Baroque Art and Architecture. The form of art and architecture of the early seventeenth century is known as Baroque, which is generally characterized by its dramatic, often flamboyant, qualities. Baroque architecture emphasizes grandiose designs with rich ornamentation, and its sculpture has a passionate, even histrionic, quality, as demonstrated in the *Ecstasy of St. Teresa* by Bernini (1598–1680). The path to Baroque painting, as represented by Velazquez (1599–1660), was blazed by the school known as Mannerism, whose dramatic qualities are demonstrated by El Greco (1541–1614). The Dutch masters of Baroque painting were Rubens (1577–1640) and Rembrandt (1606–1669); their works have a sensuous quality that exploits light and shadow for rich, emotional effects. The theatricality of Baroque art was represented in music by the new form known as opera.

Political Theory. The rise of the centralized monarchies and the wars they waged inspired political thinkers to explore new theories of power. Although many defended absolute monarchy with the doctrine of the divine right of kings, non-religious arguments for absolutism were put forward by the French philosopher Jean Bodin (1530–1596) and the English philosopher Thomas Hobbes (1588–1679). Bodin argued in his *Republic* (1576) that the king of each nation should have to answer to no one—whether the Holy Roman Emperor, the Pope, or his own people—and that he should not be bound by laws, although he should govern in accordance with natural law. Hobbes argued in the *Leviathan* (1651) that human life in the "state of nature" is "solitary, poor, nasty, brutish, and short," and that the only hope for establishing order is to obey an absolute monarch, who serves as the head of the body politic. Hobbes's attitude reflects the chaos that arose during the English Civil War. Another philosopher who wrote in response to the chaos of his age was Hugo Grotius (1583–1645), who used natural law to outline principles for international relations (including a theory of the just war) in his book *On the Law of War and Peace* (1625).

MODERNITY

By the middle of the seventeenth century, Europe had undergone crucial changes in a wide range of fields that dramatically altered its character and accelerated the pace of change. After the rise of centralized monarchies, experiments in parliamentary democracy, new ways of organizing society and its wealth, new ways of thinking about the universe, and new technologies, Europeans were prepared to dominate the rest of the world. As the rival states of Europe vied with one another to establish empires, they spread features of Western civilization around the globe and ushered in the modern age.

PRACTICE
TEST 1

CLEP WESTERN CIVILIZATION I

PRACTICE TEST 1

(Answer sheets appear in the back of this book.)

TIME: 90 Minutes
120 Questions

> **DIRECTIONS:** Each of the questions or incomplete statements below is followed by five possible answers or completions. Select the best choice in each case and fill in the corresponding oval on the answer sheet.

1. Sargon of Akkad (c. 2371–2316 B.C.E.) is best known for

   (A) establishing the art of writing among the Sumerians.

   (B) spreading monotheism in Egypt.

   (C) unifying Mesopotamia by conquering the Sumerian city-states and creating a vast empire.

   (D) bringing peace to the ancient Near East by sponsoring a treaty between the Babylonians and the Kassites.

   (E) freeing the Hebrews from exile in the Babylonian Empire.

2. All of the following are true of the Minoans EXCEPT

   (A) They dominated trade in the eastern Mediterreanean.

   (B) Their settlement on the Aegean island of Thera was destroyed by a volcanic eruption.

   (C) They built magnificent palaces adorned with frescoes that depicted women leading ritual events and athletes jumping over bulls.

   (D) They invented the first alphabet.

   (E) Their civilization on the isle of Crete was eventually invaded by the Mycenaeans.

3. The pyramids in Egypt provide evidence of all of the following EXCEPT

   (A) ancient techniques of harnessing the flooding of the Nile for agriculture.

   (B) belief in an afterlife among the ancient Egyptians.

   (C) the sophistication of ancient Egyptian engineering.

   (D) the great power of Egyptian kings to mobilize laborers in the service of the royal family.

   (E) the exceptional size and splendor of the building projects organized by the Fourth Dynasty.

4. The *Iliad* of Homer is an epic poem based on

   (A) the Dorian invasion of Greece.

   (B) a tragic play by Aeschylus.

   (C) the war against Troy waged by the Mycenaeans.

   (D) the wars between Athens and Sparta.

   (E) the wars between Greece and Persia.

5. The Greek *polis*, or city-state, was all of the following EXCEPT

   (A) the basic unit of social, economic, and political organization in ancient Greece.

   (B) a force for unity on the local level.

   (C) a cause of endemic warfare among the Greeks.

   (D) a source of inspiration for the establishment of a classless society.

   (E) an institution that prevented unity among the Greeks as a whole.

6.

The building shown above is the

(A) Parthenon in Athens.

(D) royal tomb in Mycenae.

(B) Pantheon in Rome.

(E) palace of Knossos in Crete.

(C) theater of Epidauros.

7. "Unhappiness is not caused by external events in themselves, but rather by our opinions about external events. It is within our power to change our thoughts about an event, and we can free ourselves from unhappiness by freeing ourselves from desire. Thus, if we no longer desire events to turn out one way or another, we will never be disappointed by them, and we can live a tranquil life, free from worry and unhappiness."

The outlook on life described above represents the teaching of which Greek school of philosophy?

(A) Epicureanism.

(D) Aristotelianism.

(B) Platonism.

(E) Stoicism.

(C) Skepticism.

8. During the Middle Ages, Constantinople was attacked by all of the following EXCEPT

(A) Arabs.

(D) Vikings.

(B) Mongols.

(E) Christians.

(C) Turks.

9. Medieval Europeans were indebted to the Muslims for all of the following EXCEPT

   (A) astrolabes.   (D) the numeral zero.

   (B) paper.   (E) the moldboard plow.

   (C) algebra.

10. The Frankish barbarians converted to Catholic Christianity during the reign of the Merovingian king named

   (A) Pepin the Short.

   (B) Clovis.

   (C) Charles Martel.

   (D) Merovech.

   (E) Gregory of Tours.

11. Which of the following did Pope Gregory I (590–604) NOT do?

   (A) Acknowledge the spiritual primacy of the patriarch of Constantinople.

   (B) Send missionaries to England.

   (C) Defend Rome from barbarians through diplomacy.

   (D) Promote Benedictine monasticism.

   (E) Feed the poor of Rome.

12. Philip IV (the Fair) of France did all of the following to increase his revenue EXCEPT

   (A) exile Jews and seize their wealth.

   (B) destroy the Order of Knights Templar and seize their wealth.

   (C) debase the coinage.

   (D) summon the Estates-General.

   (E) tax the clergy.

13. An artist of the northern Renaissance whose paintings show a preoccupation with grotesque and fantastic subjects in nightmarish scenes of great complexity was

   (A) Robert Campin.

   (B) Albrecht Dürer.

   (C) Hieronymus Bosch.

   (D) Jan van Eyck.

   (E) Hans Holbein.

14. All of the following were features of the Counter Reformation EXCEPT

   (A) the convocation of a church council to clarify doctrine.

   (B) the publication of an index of prohibited books.

   (C) the establishment of a new inquisition.

   (D) the founding of new religious orders.

   (E) the weakening of the pope's spiritual authority within the Roman Catholic Church.

15. The first international peace treaty that brought stability to the ancient Near East was negotiated between the Hittites and the

   (A) Sea Peoples.

   (B) Sumerians.

   (C) Neo-Babylonians.

   (D) Persians.

   (E) Egyptians.

16. The *ziggurat* was

   (A) a kind of royal palace.

   (B) a kind of Mesopotamian temple.

   (C) a particularly effective Assyrian siege engine.

   (D) a swift Phoenician cargo ship.

   (E) an administrative district in Egypt.

17. The table below shows the number of households that were taxed in a district of France in a given year (at ten-year intervals).

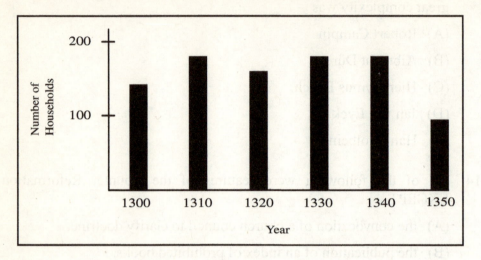

The table supports the thesis that

(A) European population grew steadily until the Black Death struck.

(B) the greatest population decline in Europe during the thirteenth century was due to famines caused by widespread crop failures.

(C) European agriculture had reached the limits of its ability to support its population during the thirteenth century.

(D) European population declined or was stagnating before the Black Death struck.

(E) tax-records do not correspond to events described in historical narratives from the period.

18. During the period of the late Merovingians, the most powerful office in the Frankish realm was that of the

(A) seneschal.

(B) constable.

(C) mayor of the palace.

(D) emperor.

(E) king.

19. The cause of ecclesiastical reform in western Europe before the twelfth century was led by the

    (A) Cluniacs.

    (B) Jesuits.

    (C) Franciscans.

    (D) Dominicans.

    (E) Merovingians.

20. Which of the following was NOT one of the achievements of Charlemagne?

    (A) He conquered the Saxons and forced them to convert to Christianity.

    (B) He seized territory in Spain from the Muslims.

    (C) He crowned himself emperor.

    (D) He defeated the Lombards in Italy and made their kingdom his own.

    (E) He gathered scholars from all over Latin Christendom to make his court an international center of learning.

21. "At first an unremarkable pastoral society, the people of this city-state expelled their kings early in their history and established a form of government consisting of elected public offices. Its domination by a few wealthy families led to tumultuous periods of class struggle. The society's favorable geographical position, in combination with the development of an innovative form of military organization and a tough-minded refusal to be discouraged by setbacks, enabled it to take a dominant role in international politics."

    The society described above was that of the

    (A) Carthaginians.

    (B) Athenians.

    (C) Etruscans.

    (D) Romans.

    (E) Gauls.

22. Which is true of Richard I the Lion-Hearted (1189–1199) during the Third Crusade?

 (A) He captured the coastal city of Acre and executed Muslim prisoners of war.

 (B) He was the first king to lead a crusade.

 (C) He invaded Egypt.

 (D) He founded the crusader kingdom of Jerusalem.

 (E) He persuaded Venetian forces to seize Constantinople.

23. "He was renowned as a charismatic teacher, and his decision to lecture on theology in Paris added to its reputation as a center of learning. He agreed to tutor a young woman of keen intelligence; they had a love affair with disastrous consequences, and in repentance he became a monk. Other monks considered his theology heretical, and he died shortly after a condemnation of his teaching."

 The passage above describes the career of

 (A) Anselm of Canterbury.

 (B) Peter Abelard.

 (C) Thomas Aquinas.

 (D) Nicholas of Cusa.

 (E) Bernard of Clairvaux.

24. Which of the following had the fewest theological differences with the Roman Catholic Church?

 (A) John Calvin

 (B) Ulrich Zwingli

 (C) Martin Luther

 (D) John Knox

 (E) Henry VIII

25. Italian politics during the Renaissance (c. 1400–c. 1600) was dominated at one time or another by all of the following EXCEPT

    (A) The Valois kings of France.

    (B) The Hapsburg Holy Roman Emperor.

    (C) The Republic of Florence.

    (D) The Duchy of Milan.

    (E) The Lombard League.

26. In the map of the western Mediterranean below, the shaded areas indicate

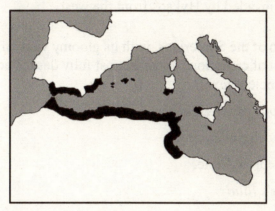

    (A) regions colonized by the Greeks.

    (B) areas devastated during the Peloponnesian War.

    (C) regions held by the Romans during the First Punic War.

    (D) areas seized by Augustus Caesar from the Carthaginians.

    (E) areas colonized by the Phoenicians.

27. The Old Babylonian kingdom of the Amorites in Mesopotamia disintegrated around 1600 B.C.E. because

    (A) increasingly oppressive taxes and repeated crop failures led to long-term economic depression.

    (B) the nobility and the priesthood conspired against the king, leading to political fragmentation.

    (C) a series of slave revolts destabilized government and undercut the economic foundations of the region.

    (D) it was invaded by Hittites from the north and Kassites from the east.

    (E) it was invaded by Hyksos from the west.

28. The religion of the Sumerians, with its gloomy view of the afterlife and its pantheon of capricious gods, is most fully described in which of the following ancient texts?

    (A) *The Book of the Dead*

    (B) *The Epic of Gilgamesh*

    (C) The Hebrew Bible

    (D) Homer's *Iliad*

    (E) The Letters of Akhenaton

29. Which of the following was true of ancient Greek tyranny?

    (A) It was never tolerated by any of the citizens of a polis.

    (B) It was synonymous with cruelty and oppression.

    (C) It was the form of government in Sparta.

    (D) It sometimes benefited a polis by preventing anarchy.

    (E) The philosopher Aristotle considered it an acceptable form of government.

30. All of the following are true of the Athenian political reformer Solon EXCEPT

    (A) He divided citizens into four classes based on their wealth.

    (B) He wrote poetry.

    (C) He canceled the debts of impoverished citizens.

    (D) He established a Council of 500 members.

    (E) He restored freedom to citizens who had been sold into slavery.

31. The military innovation devised by the Romans that enabled them to conquer the Mediterranean region was the

    (A) phalanx.

    (B) horse-drawn chariot.

    (C) war elephant.

    (D) legion.

    (E) trireme.

32. Ostracism was originally a practice in the ancient world by which

    (A) the Spartans forced their young men to leave their mothers and live a harsh life of military training in barracks.

    (B) criminals were sent to penal colonies.

    (C) the Romans executed individuals who tried to overthrow the Republic.

    (D) the Athenians temporarily exiled individuals whom they regarded as a threat to democracy.

    (E) the Phoenicians decided on members of the community to send out for the purpose of establishing colonies.

33. The Social War (90–88 B.C.E.)
    (A) was the civil war between Marius and Sulla.
    (B) began as an uprising led by Mithridates, the king of Pontus.
    (C) was fought between Athens and its allies in the Delian League.
    (D) was fought over the extension of Roman citizenship.
    (E) is the name of legislation giving greater freedom to Roman women in the late Republic.

34. Which of the following eastern European peoples were finally converted from paganism to Christianity in the fourteenth century, when their leader strengthened his realm by marrying the Catholic queen of a neighboring state?

    (A) Czechs

    (B) Poles

    (C) Lithuanians

    (D) Slovaks

    (E) Russians

35.

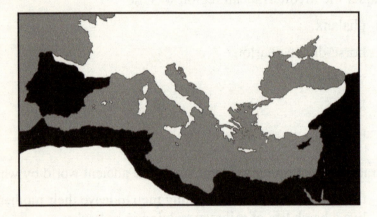

The areas shaded black on the map above represent territories controlled in the eighth century C.E. by the

    (A) Franks.

    (B) Magyars.

    (C) Ostrogoths.

    (D) Byzantines.

    (E) Muslims.

36. All of the following Greek philosophers are known as Pre-Socratics EXCEPT

    (A) Plato.
    (B) Pythagoras.
    (C) Heraclitus.
    (D) Empedocles.
    (E) Thales of Miletus.

37. Which of the following statements is NOT true of Pericles (c. 495–429 B.C.E.)?

    (A) He was frequently elected general by the people.

    (B) He led the imperialistic expansion of Athens.

    (C) He was an aristocrat who tried to restore oligarchy.

    (D) He hired the sculptor Phidias for his building program of the Acropolis.

    (E) He used tribute from the Delian League to fund artistic endeavors in Athens.

38. Which of the following was NOT a consequence of the Fourth Crusade?

    (A) Feudal states were established in Greece.

    (B) The patriarch of Constantinople attended the Fourth Lateran Council.

    (C) Works of Byzantine art were sent to Italy.

    (D) A legacy of ill-will was engendered between Muslims and Christians.

    (E) The Venetians acquired a monopoly on Byzantine trade.

39. Which of the following occupations did NOT fit into the medieval conception of society described by the phrase "those who fight, those who pray, those who work"?

    (A) knights

    (B) monks

    (C) merchants

    (D) priests

    (E) serfs

40. "Moreover, I think Carthage must be destroyed."

   This remark, frequently repeated at the end of his speeches in the Senate, was said by

   (A) Julius Caesar, to win support for his war against the Gauls.

   (B) Augustus Caesar, to win support for his war against the Germans.

   (C) Marius, to win support for the Jugurthine war.

   (D) Cato the Elder, to win support for the Third Punic War.

   (E) Scipio the Elder, to win support for the Second Punic War.

41. The Athenian political reformer, Cleisthenes, invented which political unit to serve as the basis of the new government espoused by the Athenians in 508 B.C.E.?

   (A) *phalanx.*

   (B) *phratry.*

   (C) *thetes.*

   (D) *boule.*

   (E) *deme.*

42. All of the following were Greek poets EXCEPT

   (A) Archilochus.

   (B) Pindar.

   (C) Ovid.

   (D) Hesiod.

   (E) Sappho of Lesbos.

43. The strongest monarchy during the twelfth century was

   (A) Germany.

   (B) Italy.

   (C) Spain.

   (D) England.

   (E) France.

44.

The structure shown above is

(A) the entrance to a Minoan palace.

(B) the entrance to an Etruscan temple.

(C) the Ishtar Gate of the Neo-Babylonians.

(D) the Parthenon of Athens.

(E) the Lion Gate of ancient Mycenae.

45. Martin Luther's outspoken opposition to the Roman Catholic Church was an immediate response to

(A) the sale of indulgences to fund the building of St. Peter's Basilica in Rome.

(B) his visit to Rome, where he saw the worldliness of the papacy.

(C) the call of several German princes for a national church independent of Rome.

(D) the execution of the religious reformer John Huss.

(E) the theological works of John Calvin.

46. The secular German state of Prussia was founded during the Reformation by

    (A) Gustavus Adolphus, King of Sweden.

    (B) Charles V, Holy Roman Emperor.

    (C) Count Philip of Hesse.

    (D) Frederick the Wise, Elector of Saxony.

    (E) Albrecht von Hohenzollern, Grand Master of the Teutonic Knights.

47. All of the following explorers and colonialists were sponsored by Spain EXCEPT

    (A) Ferdinand Magellan.

    (B) Hernando de Soto.

    (C) Vasco da Gama.

    (D) Hernando Cortez.

    (E) Francisco Pizarro.

48. Which of the following is true of Cardinal Richelieu?

    (A) He helped the Hapsburgs restore Catholicism to the Holy Roman Empire.

    (B) He confirmed the traditional privileges of the French nobles in order to prevent civil war in France.

    (C) He decreased military spending in order to balance the budget.

    (D) He used the Inquisition to convert the Huguenots to Catholicism.

    (E) He increased the power of the French monarchy.

49. The Peloponnesian League was

    (A) an alliance of Greek city-states led by Athens whose transformation into the Athenian Empire precipitated the Peloponnesian War.

    (B) an alliance of Greek city-states during the Hellenistic period.

    (C) an alliance of Greek city-states led by Sparta.

    (D) a commercial consortium of Greek city-states organized to promote overseas colonization.

    (E) a commercial consortium of Phoenician city-states organized to promote overseas colonization.

50. The fresco shown below, depicting an athlete somersaulting over the back of a charging bull, was produced by which of the following ancient cultures?

    (A) Egyptian
    (B) Greek
    (C) Roman
    (D) Sumerian
    (E) Minoan

51. "His father had wanted him to become a lawyer, but he eventually abandoned the study of law and turned to classical literature. Though he wrote extensively in Latin, which he sought to restore to its classical style, his more popular literary achievements consisted of his vernacular poetry."

Who was the individual described above?

(A) Francesco Petrarch

(B) Peter Abelard

(C) Paracelsus

(D) Baldassare Castiglione

(E) Marsilius of Padua

52. The ancient Greeks living around the year 500 B.C.E. honored all of the following gods in public festivals EXCEPT

(A) Dionysos.

(B) Mithras.

(C) Zeus.

(D) Athena.

(E) Apollo.

53. Which of the following Athenians wrote comedies that were critical of the Peloponnesian War (431–404 B.C.E.)?

(A) Aeschylus

(B) Sophocles

(C) Euripides

(D) Thucydides

(E) Aristophanes

54. Spread across three continents, the Hellenistic realms that emerged after a long period of civil war following the death of Alexander the Great were known as

    (A) the Achaean League and the Aetolian League.

    (B) the Peloponnesian League and the Delian League.

    (C) the kingdoms of Pergamum, Bithynia, and Cilicia.

    (D) Magna Graecia ("Great Greece").

    (E) the Antigonid, Ptolemaic, and Seleucid kingdoms.

55. All of the following features of civilization were present in the Fertile Crescent around the year 3000 B.C.E. EXCEPT

    (A) bronze-working.

    (B) irrigation.

    (C) writing.

    (D) the alphabet.

    (E) the wheel.

56. "Led by ruthless warrior-kings, their empire was known for its brutality. They completely destroyed rebellious cities and deported unruly subjects, such as the Hebrews of the kingdom of Israel, and they depicted scenes of violence in their art in order to discourage rebellion. Their military machine was so effective that they even briefly subjugated Egypt and were thus the first people to control both of the two great river-valleys of the ancient Near East, the Tigris-Euphrates and the Nile."

    The people described above are known as the

    (A) Babylonians.

    (B) Medes.

    (C) Romans.

    (D) Hittites.

    (E) Assyrians.

57.

The central, domed structure shown above was built by the

(A) Turks.

(B) Byzantines.

(C) Arabs.

(D) Mongols.

(E) Ostrogoths.

58. The most widely read philosopher in the medieval universities was

(A) Plotinus.

(B) Maimonides.

(C) Averroes.

(D) Aristotle.

(E) Plato.

59. "Paris is worth a Mass."

The statement above was made by

(A) Catherine de' Medici.

(B) Cardinal Richelieu.

(C) Henry of Navarre.

(D) Nicole Oresme.

(E) Philip the Fair.

60. Which of the following is NOT true of the Carolingian Renaissance?

   (A) It brought scholars from all over Western Europe to study at the court of Charlemagne.

   (B) It founded schools to train clerics.

   (C) It promoted a simplified script, which forms the basis of the modern printed alphabet.

   (D) It promoted Greek as the common language of the Frankish empire.

   (E) It preserved much of the classical literature of the pagans through the copying of manuscripts.

61. The Dominican friar Bartolomé de Las Casas was

   (A) the leader of the Spanish Inquisition during the reign of Queen Isabella.

   (B) the founder of the Dominican Order.

   (C) an early leader of the *Reconquista*.

   (D) an early critic of Spanish imperialism in the New World.

   (E) a humanist who wrote an *Oration on the Dignity of Man*.

62.

The areas shaded black on the map above represent the

(A) Macedonian kingdom of Philip II.

(B) Greek states that formed an alliance to fight the Persians led by Xerxes.

(C) territories of the Peloponnesian League led by Sparta.

(D) territories of the Athenian Empire on the eve of the Peloponnesian War.

(E) colonies founded by the Phoenicians before the Greeks settled the region.

63. "His father had been the governor of Britain. From his base there, he defeated his rivals in battle until finally his claim to the imperial throne was undisputed. Although he had worshiped the Persian god Mithras in his youth, he converted to Christianity and was baptized on his death-bed. He founded a new city in the east to serve as the capital of the Roman Empire."

Who was the emperor described above?

(A) Diocletian

(B) Decius

(C) Marcus Aurelius

(D) Constantine

(E) Claudius

64. The western half of the Roman Empire came to an end in 476 C.E. when the last emperor in the West was deposed by

    (A) Theodoric, king of the Ostrogoths.

    (B) Alaric, king of the Visigoths.

    (C) Odoacer, a Gothic chieftain.

    (D) Attila the Hun.

    (E) Gaiseric, king of the Vandals.

65. The written body of Jewish civil and religious law, compiled after the destruction of the Temple in 70 C.E., is known as the

    (A) Septuagint.

    (B) Torah.

    (C) Pentateuch.

    (D) Tanach.

    (E) Talmud.

66. The Gracchi attempted to reform the Roman Republic through all of the following measures EXCEPT

    (A) the extension of Roman citizenship to the Italian allies.

    (B) the reform of the legions.

    (C) the sale of state-subsidized grain to the poor.

    (D) land redistribution.

    (E) the transfer of jury duty from the senators to members of the equestrian class.

67. Spain was established as a centralized monarchy in the fifteenth century

    (A) when the Spanish princes decided to band together against the common threat of Islam.

    (B) through the marriage of the rulers who governed the two largest states in the Iberian peninsula.

    (C) as a result of a border war against France.

    (D) at the command of the Holy Roman Emperor.

    (E) by papal decree.

68. Which of the following beliefs is NOT consistent with the economic policy known as mercantilism, which was prevalent in early modern Europe?

    (A) A nation's wealth is defined primarily by its possession of precious metals.

    (B) Tolls should be used within a nation to raise government revenue.

    (C) Tariffs should be used to limit imports.

    (D) Colonies should be founded as a source of precious metals and raw materials.

    (E) Government regulation of commerce is good for a nation.

69. "As a young man he served in the military during the Thirty Years' War. However, mathematics was his passion, and his contribution to geometry endures to this day. He is most famous, however, for three Latin words that serve as the foundation for his philosophical system: *Cogito, ergo sum.*"

    The thinker described above is

    (A) Miguel de Cervantes.

    (B) Tycho Brahe.

    (C) Blaise Pascal.

    (D) René Descartes.

    (E) Francis Bacon.

70. All of the following were influenced by the artistic legacy of the Renaissance EXCEPT

    (A) Giotto.

    (B) El Greco.

    (C) Velazquez.

    (D) Rembrandt.

    (E) Rubens.

71. The sculpture presented below is characteristic of what kind of art?

    (A) Hellenistic

    (B) Classical Greek

    (C) Classical Roman

    (D) Renaissance Italian

    (E) Etruscan

72. The text that best demonstrates the influence of the Latin classics on the European imagination before the Renaissance is

    (A) *Lancelot*, by Chretien de Troyes.

    (B) *Parzival*, by Wolfram von Eschenbach.

    (C) *The Inferno*, by Dante Alighieri.

    (D) *The Romance of the Rose*, by Guillaume de Lorris.

    (E) *Tristan and Isolt*, by Gottfried von Strassburg.

73. Which of the following could NOT have written poetry praising the reign of Augustus Caesar?

   (A) Horace

   (B) Virgil

   (C) Juvenal

   (D) Ovid

   (E) Lucretius

74. Which of the following is NOT true of Roman Law?

   (A) It was influenced by Stoic philosophy.

   (B) It was influenced by the concept of natural law.

   (C) It was formulated in authoritative manuals toward the end of the *Pax Romana*, from the second to the early third century C.E.

   (D) It first received a written form during the reign of Augustus Caesar (27 B.C.E.–14 C.E.).

   (E) The emperor Justinian (527–565 C.E.) commissioned the codification of earlier law codes in an immense work known as the *Corpus Juris Civilis*.

75. The entire Greek world was conquered, and thus unified, for the first time by

   (A) Rome.

   (B) Macedon.

   (C) Persia.

   (D) Athens.

   (E) Phoenicia.

76. The system of writing developed in Greece after the Dark Age (c. 1100–800 B.C.E.), was based directly on

    (A) a Minoan syllabary.

    (B) the Roman alphabet.

    (C) the Etruscan alphabet.

    (D) the Phoenician alphabet.

    (E) Sumerian cuneiform.

77. Which of the following authors wrote satirical works during the French Renaissance which were notorious for their coarse and earthy sense of humor?

    (A) François Rabelais

    (B) Jean Bodin

    (C) Baldassare Castiglione

    (D) Michel de Montaigne

    (E) Catherine de' Medici

78. The Treaty of Tordesillas (1494)

    (A) founded the nation of Portugal.

    (B) ended the War of Spanish Succession.

    (C) introduced the Inquisition into Spain.

    (D) divided the New World between Spain and Portugual.

    (E) gave the Hapsburgs control of Spain.

79. "His rise to fame and fortune was based on his service as a privateer. He claimed part of the American west coast for his native land and was hailed as the first of his countrymen to circumnavigate the globe. In return for his service, he was knighted by his monarch aboard his flagship."

    Who is the individual described above?

    (A) Ferdinand Magellan

    (B) Francis Drake

    (C) Henry Hudson

    (D) John Cabot

    (E) John Hawkins

80.

The artistic piece shown above is

    (A) an Islamic wall-hanging.

    (B) a Gothic miniature.

    (C) a Celtic illumination.

    (D) a Persian rug.

    (E) a Turkish tapestry.

81. The city of Rome was attacked by all of the following groups EXCEPT

    (A) Gauls.

    (B) Huns.

    (C) Saracens.

    (D) Vandals.

    (E) Visigoths.

82. The principal textbook for the study of Roman law in the twelfth century was

    (A) Thomas Aquinas's *Summa Theologica.*

    (B) Peter Lombard's *Sententiae.*

    (C) Galen's *Tegni.*

    (D) Gratian's *Decretum.*

    (E) Justinian's *Corpus Juris Civilis.*

83. William the Silent was

    (A) a leader in the English struggle against the Stuart kings.

    (B) a leader in the Dutch struggle for independence.

    (C) a crusader against the Ottoman Turks.

    (D) a Holy Roman Emperor who opposed the Protestant Reformation.

    (E) the founder of a new monastic order during the Catholic Reformation.

84. Which of the following territories was NOT part of the Angevin Empire under Henry II Plantagenet (1154–1189)?

    (A) County of Anjou

    (B) Duchy of Normandy

    (C) Duchy of Saxony

    (D) Duchy of Aquitaine

    (E) Kingdom of England

85. The main purpose of the Magna Carta, signed by King John of England in 1215, was to

   (A) establish a parliamentary form of government.

   (B) extend freedom to all Englishmen by abolishing serfdom.

   (C) raise taxes for war against France.

   (D) establish a centralized judicial system for the entire realm.

   (E) safeguard the existing feudal privileges of the barons.

86. The College of Cardinals was established in 1059 for the purpose of

   (A) ending the "Babylonian Captivity" (Avignonese papacy).

   (B) ending the Great Schism in the Latin church.

   (C) providing accommodations for poor students at the university of Paris.

   (D) electing the pope.

   (E) training canon lawyers.

87. The traditional date for the schism between the Greek and Latin churches is

   (A) 395.

   (B) 1054.

   (C) 1204.

   (D) 1378.

   (E) 1417.

88. The sculpture shown below represents

(A) a Hittite emperor and his concubine.

(B) a Hebrew king and his queen.

(C) an Egyptian pharaoh and his queen.

(D) Alexander the Great and his Persian wife.

(E) Nebuchadnezzar and his Median wife.

89. All of the following were Renaissance humanists EXCEPT

(A) Marsilio Ficino.

(B) Coluccio Salutati.

(C) Girolamo Savonarola.

(D) Lorenzo Valla.

(E) Giovanni Pico della Mirandola.

90. The most intense period of the persecution of witches in Europe occurred during which of the following centuries (c.e.)?

(A) Fourth

(B) Seventh

(C) Tenth

(D) Thirteenth

(E) Sixteenth

91. All of the following were involved in the Hundred Years' War (1337–1453) EXCEPT

    (A) Henry V of England.

    (B) Philip the Good of Burgundy.

    (C) Otto III of Germany.

    (D) Charles VII of France.

    (E) Joan of Arc.

92. The largest of the empires of the ancient Near East, which was conquered by Alexander the Great (336–323 B.C.E.), was ruled by the

    (A) Assyrians.

    (B) Hittites.

    (C) Persians.

    (D) Neo-Babylonians.

    (E) Sumerians.

93. The English statesman Francis Bacon (1561–1626) aided the rise of modern science

    (A) by establishing a laboratory in which he conducted sophisticated experiments.

    (B) by arguing that the natural world is best studied using the deductive method of reasoning.

    (C) by encouraging the inductive method for the study of nature.

    (D) by rejecting the empirical method.

    (E) by winning Parliament's support for the foundation of the Royal Society.

94.

The triumphal arch shown above was built by which of the following ancient peoples?

(A) Romans

(B) Persians

(C) Macedonians

(D) Minoans

(E) Greeks

95. "He was an architect, a sculptor, a painter, and a poet. The favored subject of his art was the muscular male nude. Tormented by his own genius, he left many works unfinished. Perhaps his most influential legacy was the force of his personality, whose temperamental, brooding character defined the image of the new artist for later generations."

The individual described above is

(A) Lorenzo de' Medici.

(B) Thomas à Kempis.

(C) Michelangelo Buonarroti.

(D) Johann Reuchlin.

(E) Leonardo Bruni.

96. Who was the author of a book entitled *Utopia* (1516) about an ideal society?

    (A) Thomas More

    (B) Miguel de Cervantes

    (C) Desiderius Erasmus

    (D) Martin Luther

    (E) Andreas Vesalius

97. Which of the following was responsible for the execution of the Spanish religious dissident, Michael Servetus (1511–1553)?

    (A) Ignatius of Loyola

    (B) Tomas de Torquemada

    (C) John Calvin

    (D) Martin Luther

    (E) Ulrich Zwingli

98. All of the following contributed to the fall of the Roman Republic during the first century B.C.E. EXCEPT

    (A) invasions by tribes of Germanic barbarians.

    (B) the desire of wealthy citizens to expand their own power at the expense of the government.

    (C) the institution of clientage.

    (D) the unwillingness of the Senate to enact political reforms.

    (E) the professionalization of the army.

99. All of the following help explain the leading role taken by the Dutch in seventeenth-century trade EXCEPT

    (A) the innovative design of their merchant vessels.

    (B) their use of the joint-stock company.

    (C) the dominant position of merchants in the government of the United Provinces.

    (D) their geographic position.

    (E) their leading role in the earliest voyages of discovery.

100. The Renaissance philosopher Jean Bodin (1530–1596) strongly supported

    (A) the Holy Roman Empire.

    (B) royal absolutism.

    (C) the economic policies of the physiocrats.

    (D) the idea of democracy.

    (E) the papacy's right to exercise broad temporal powers over kings.

101. Philip II (1556–1598) assembled the Spanish Armada for all of the following reasons EXCEPT

    (A) to invade England.

    (B) to challenge Dutch naval superiority.

    (C) to punish England for aiding the Dutch.

    (D) to restore Catholicism in England.

    (E) to depose Elizabeth I.

102.

The sarcophagus shown above was produced by which of the following ancient peoples?

(A) Greeks

(B) Assyrians

(C) Celts

(D) Etruscans

(E) Romans

103. All of the following measures were tried by ancient Athens to prevent violent revolution within the *polis* EXCEPT

(A) constitutional reform.

(B) the cancellation of debts.

(C) the redistribution of land.

(D) colonization.

(E) tyranny.

104. What effect did the discovery of the New World have on the European economy in the sixteenth century?

    (A) It caused high unemployment because slaves from the New World became abundant throughout Europe.

    (B) It caused inflation due to the increased amount of precious metals in Europe.

    (C) It strengthened the craft guilds by stimulating trade.

    (D) It discouraged governments from interfering with the ventures of entrepreneurs.

    (E) It had no noticeable economic effect.

105. Which of the following statements is NOT true of feudalism?

    (A) It functioned according to a contractual agreement of a personal nature between two individuals.

    (B) As a system of political organization, it was characterized by weak central authority.

    (C) It involved a lord granting a fief to a vassal, who agreed to perform military or other service.

    (D) It reached the height of its development during the twelfth and thirteenth centuries in northern France and the Low Countries.

    (E) It describes the relationship between a lord and the serfs who worked his fief.

106. Socrates (469–399 B.C.E.) and Jesus of Nazareth (c. 4 B.C.E.–30 C.E.) shared all of the following in common EXCEPT

    (A) they did not write any books.

    (B) they urged their listeners to lead moral lives and embrace the cause of justice.

    (C) they tried to reform morals by providing a detailed outline of the ideal government.

    (D) they were executed at the command of the governments under which they lived.

    (E) they believed in the immortality of the soul.

107. Which is true of the Treaty of Westphalia (1648)?

    (A) It recognized the Dutch Netherlands and Switzerland as sovereign states.

    (B) It formally ended the Thirty Years' War.

    (C) It allowed each of the German principalities within the Holy Roman Empire to conduct its own foreign policy.

    (D) It reaffirmed the principle that the ruler of a German principality should decide the religious alignment of his state.

    (E) All of the above.

108. Queen Elizabeth I (1558–1603) was able to strengthen the power of the English monarchy by

    (A) declaring that monarchs owed their authority to God alone.

    (B) producing an heir who was able to prevent civil war.

    (C) rooting out all vestiges of Catholicism in England.

    (D) cooperating with Parliament.

    (E) maintaining peace with Spain.

109. All of the following were motivations for Prince Henry the Navigator (1394–1460) to sponsor voyages of discovery EXCEPT

    (A) to acquire accurate geographical information about Africa.

    (B) to find the kingdom of a legendary Christian ally, Prester John.

    (C) to outflank the Muslims by converting lands they had not yet reached.

    (D) to find gold and stimulate trade.

    (E) to prevent the Portuguese from dominating newly discovered lands.

110. Which of the following Roman emperors did NOT persecute Christians?

    (A) Decius

    (B) Tiberius

    (C) Diocletian

    (D) Marcus Aurelius

    (E) Nero

111.

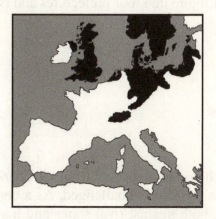

In the map of Europe shown above, the black areas indicate

    (A) all the states that signed the Treaty of Westphalia.

    (B) lands controlled by the Hapsburgs.

    (C) lands that suffered the greatest loss of population during the Black Death.

    (D) lands controlled by Protestants during the sixteenth century.

    (E) lands which pioneered the discovery of the New World.

112. The First Triumvirate is the name given to an informal alliance in Late Republican Rome between Pompey, Crassus, and

    (A) Lepidus.

    (B) Mark Antony.

    (C) Julius Caesar.

    (D) Octavian.

    (E) Sulla.

113. The emperor who tried to restore Roman stability after the *Pax Romana* by dividing the Empire into four prefectures and twelve dioceses was

    (A) Diocletian.

    (B) Claudius.

    (C) Decius.

    (D) Constantine.

    (E) Hadrian.

114. "The territories he ruled surpassed those of Charlemagne, but his control of them was frequently challenged. As a consequence, he fought numerous wars, both against rival states and his own subjects. In the end he abdicated and retired to a monastery, where he soon died."

    The individual described above is

    (A) Pope Julius II.

    (B) the Holy Roman Emperor, Charles V.

    (C) the Holy Roman Emperor, Frederick II.

    (D) the King of France, Francis I.

    (E) the King of England, Henry VIII.

115.

The cathedral shown above was built in the city of

(A) London.

(B) Rome.

(C) Constantinople.

(D) Florence.

(E) Paris.

116. Protestants established a lasting presence during the sixteenth century in all of the following EXCEPT

(A) the Holy Roman Empire.

(B) the Netherlands.

(C) Spain.

(D) France.

(E) England.

117. The *Rule* of St. Benedict (480–547) was an exceptional document in the history of monasticism because

(A) it required vows of poverty, chastity, and obedience.

(B) it was the only monastic rule available in Europe.

(C) it prohibited corporal punishment as a method of discipline.

(D) it outlined an ideal balance between prayer, study, and work.

(E) it focused on the individual monk rather than the community.

118. Which of the following best explains why the capital of the Roman Empire was eventually moved to the east?

    (A) The crowding and high unemployment in Rome caused so much instability that the emperors were constantly in fear of revolution.

    (B) The sack of Rome by the Gauls convinced the Romans that the city could not serve as an effective center of a great empire.

    (C) The increasingly frequent threats to the northern and eastern borders, as well as the greater wealth of the eastern provinces, made the east attractive as a more effective administrative location.

    (D) The sack of Rome by the Visigoths proved that the original capital was no longer defensible.

    (E) The spread of *latifundia*, which were worked by slaves captured in the wars of conquest, sparked a series of revolts that made Rome too unstable to serve as the capital any longer.

119. The mendicant friars founded in the thirteenth century received their name from their practice of

    (A) inquisitorial interrogation.

    (B) converting heretics.

    (C) frequent travel.

    (D) begging for food.

    (E) preaching on street corners.

120. The Punic Wars were fought between

    (A) Greece and Phoenicia over the colonization of the Mediterranean shores.

    (B) Greece and Persia over the freedom of the Ionians.

    (C) Rome and Macedon over control of Greece.

    (D) Tyre and Sidon over trading rights in the Mediterranean.

    (E) Rome and Carthage over their conflicting imperial ambitions.

CLEP WESTERN CIVILIZATION I
PRACTICE TEST I

ANSWER KEY

1. (C)	31. (D)	61. (D)	91. (C)
2. (D)	32. (D)	62. (D)	92. (C)
3. (A)	33. (D)	63. (D)	93. (C)
4. (C)	34. (C)	64. (C)	94. (A)
5. (D)	35. (E)	65. (E)	95. (C)
6. (A)	36. (A)	66. (B)	96. (A)
7. (E)	37. (C)	67. (B)	97. (C)
8. (B)	38. (D)	68. (B)	98. (A)
9. (E)	39. (C)	69. (D)	99. (E)
10. (B)	40. (D)	70. (A)	100. (B)
11. (A)	41. (E)	71. (A)	101. (B)
12. (D)	42. (C)	72. (C)	102. (D)
13. (C)	43. (D)	73. (E)	103. (C)
14. (E)	44. (E)	74. (D)	104. (B)
15. (E)	45. (A)	75. (B)	105. (E)
16. (B)	46. (E)	76. (D)	106. (C)
17. (D)	47. (C)	77. (A)	107. (E)
18. (C)	48. (E)	78. (D)	108. (D)
19. (A)	49. (C)	79. (B)	109. (E)
20. (C)	50. (E)	80. (C)	110. (B)
21. (D)	51. (A)	81. (B)	111. (D)
22. (A)	52. (B)	82. (E)	112. (C)
23. (B)	53. (E)	83. (B)	113. (A)
24. (E)	54. (E)	84. (C)	114. (B)
25. (E)	55. (D)	85. (E)	115. (D)
26. (E)	56. (E)	86. (D)	116. (C)
27. (D)	57. (B)	87. (B)	117. (D)
28. (B)	58. (D)	88. (C)	118. (C)
29. (D)	59. (B)	89. (C)	119. (D)
30. (D)	60. (D)	90. (E)	120. (E)

DETAILED EXPLANATIONS OF ANSWERS

PRACTICE TEST 1

1. **(C)** Sargon led the Akkadians, a Semitic people, in the conquest of the Sumerian city-states. His empire included and extended beyond the region of the Tigris and Euphrates rivers, as far as Lebanon in the west. The art of writing (A) was already known among the Sumerians whom Sargon conquered. The Kassites (D) were a later people, who overthrew the Old Babylonian dynasty around 1600 B.C.E. The Hebrews in exile in Babylonia (E) were freed by the Persian king Cyrus after he conquered the Neo-Babylonian dynasty in 539 B.C.E. An early form of monotheism (B) was promulgated in Egypt by the pharaoh Akhenaton (c. 1375–1358 B.C.E.), although his religious revolution was suppressed after his death; the Akkadians and Sumerians were polytheists.

2. **(D)** The first alphabet was devised by the scribes of Ugarit (in the Levant), probably during the fourteenth century B.C.E.—about 200 years after the end of Minoan civilization. (This alphabet was later adapted by the Phoenicians, and then, via the Phoenicians, by the Greeks.) The Minoans, in contrast, used a syllabary—their written symbols represented syllables rather than individual letters. Minoan writing is known as "Linear Script A" and has never been deciphered; another Minoan script, known as "Linear B," has been identified as an early form of Greek. Both scripts were found in ruins on the isle of Crete, where the Minoans lived. Since Linear B seems to have been used only toward the end of Minoan history, scholars have concluded that the Greek-speaking Mycenaeans invaded Crete perhaps around 1550 B.C.E. and tried to impose their rule there (E). It is not known when the Minoans first arrived on Crete, but their civilization flourished from about 2000 B.C.E.; among its finest achievements were a number of magnificent palaces, which were adorned with artwork characterized by the prominence of female figures and athletes (C). The prosperity that enabled the Minoans to build on such a grand scale was due to their control of maritime trade in

the eastern Mediterranean (A). Yet even during the time of their prosperity, the Minoans periodically endured terrible setbacks, such as earthquakes which destroyed many of their palaces (c. 1800 B.C.E.) and an exceptionally violent volcanic eruption around 1627 B.C.E. that devastated the Minoan colony on the island of Thera in the Aegean Sea (B).

3.   **(A)**   The pyramids had nothing to do with controlling the Nile River. The Egyptians used irrigation ditches to take advantage of its annual flooding. The pyramids were royal tombs, in which the bodies of the pharaohs and their dependents were mummified, demonstrating a belief in the afterlife (B) and the power of the pharaohs to organize laborers to work for them (D). Moreover, the massive scale of the construction, the architectural harmony of the buildings, and their endurance for about 4,000 years to the present testifies to the sophistication of Egyptian engineering (C). The most impressive of the pyramids, built by the Fourth Dynasty at Giza, mark a high point in the power of the pharaohs (E).

4.   **(C)**   Homer's *Iliad* is a legendary account of the Trojan War based on the actual war against Troy waged by the Mycenaean Greeks around 1200 B.C.E. The *Iliad* was composed at the end of Dark Age of ancient Greece (between about 850 and 700 B.C.E.) which began when the Dorian Greeks invaded the Balkan peninsula (A), but it does not mention that event. The Persian Wars (E) and the Peloponnesian War between Athens and Sparta (D) happened in the fifth century B.C.E., long after the age of Homer. Likewise, the tragedian Aeschylus (B) lived around 525–456 B.C.E., long after the *Iliad* was composed.

5.   **(D)**   The *polis* did not do away with class distinctions, and even democracies like Athens were divided into clearly-defined social groups, which often resulted in tension among the classes. The Greek *polis* was a small-scale unit which served as the nexus for social, economic, and political life (A), encouraging local unity (B); yet loyalty to a local center caused fierce regionalism that resulted in endemic warfare among the Greeks (C), preventing them from becoming unified (E).

6.   **(A)**   The structure is the Athenian Parthenon, which is characterized by the Doric columns, arranged in a colonnade, as well as the damaged pediment lacking its adornments, which were removed to the British Museum in the nineteenth century and are known as the Elgin Marbles. The photograph reveals one of the narrower ends of the building's rectangular layout. The structure cannot be the Pantheon (B), which is a domed struc-

ture, nor the theater of Epidauros (C), which is an open-air circular platform at the bottom of an immense semi-circle of stone seats. It cannot be the royal tomb in Mycenae (D), since that is a subterranean structure, nor the palace of Knossos in Crete (E), since Doric temples did not exist during the age of the Minoans.

7. **(E)** Stoicism suspected all emotions as a threat to tranquility and recommended a form of enlightened apathy as the cure for unhappiness (*apatheia* in Greek means "freedom from pain"). In contrast, Epicureanism (A) taught that the way to deal with anxiety was to pursue pleasure. Aristotelianism (D) was less concerned about overcoming negative psychological states than about developing moral virtue through the pursuit of the golden mean, avoiding any excessive behavior. Platonism (B) sought to develop moral perfection by training one's mind to perceive the Idea of the Good and make one's life conform to it. Skepticism (C), in contrast to all of the above schools of philosophy, tried to demonstrate that one cannot attain certainty in matters of philosophy.

8. **(B)** Of the groups listed, only the Mongols never threatened Constantinople. The city was attacked by Arabs (A) as early as 672 and eventually conquered by Turks (C) in 1453. The appearance of the Turks in the eleventh century prompted the Byzantine emperors to seek aid from the western Christians, who responded by launching a series of Crusades. There was simmering hostility between the forces of the Latin and Greek Christians, however, and the Fourth Crusade was diverted against Constantinople, which was thus sacked by Christians in 1204 (E). This surprise attack unseated the Byzantine emperors, who ruled in exile until 1261, when they were able to regain control. Vikings (D) from Sweden mounted a series of attacks between 860 and 1043.

9. **(E)** The moldboard plow was designed to turn over the damp, heavy soils of northern Europe. Its inspiration would not have come from the Muslims, who occupied Mediterranean lands where soil was lighter and drier. Although the moldboard plow may seem a humble invention, its boost to agricultural productivity was vital for the dramatic growth of population in Europe following the year 1000. Astrolabes (A), or instruments for the measurement of celestial bodies, were invented in the ancient world, acquired by the Arabs during the seventh or eighth centuries, and became known to medieval Europeans around the twelfth century. Paper (B) was invented in ancient China and acquired by the Arabs in the eighth century. Around 950 it was being produced in Muslim Spain; it was not until the fourteenth and

fifteenth centuries that Europeans were producing significant quantities of paper. Algebra (C), the branch of mathematics that uses letters to represent numbers, was studied by cultures before that of the Muslims, but the word itself is derived from Arabic—clearly indicating the culture from which Europeans acquired the study. Their principal source was a translation of a mathematical text by the Muslim scholar Al-Khwarizmi (from whose name "algorithm" is derived), which was produced in the twelfth century. Arabic numerals, including the numeral zero (D), also entered Europe during the Middle Ages via Islamic culture; the Romans had no numeral to represent zero.

10. **(B)** The Frankish king Clovis (481–511) married a Catholic Burgundian princess. After experiencing a battlefield conversion (like that of the Emperor Constantine), he required all his subjects to accept Catholicism rather than Arian Christianity. The Merovingian dynasty was named after Clovis's grandfather, Merovech (D). Charles Martel (C) was not a member of the Merovingian dynasty but the founder of the Carolingian dynasty: *Carolus* is the Latin form of "Charles," and "Martel" means "hammer," designating his prowess in battle, particularly his victory over the Muslims at the Battle of Tours in 732. Charles's son Pepin the Short (A) deposed the last Merovingian in 751 and was crowned king of the Franks in 754 by Pope Stephen II, who thus legitimized the transfer of power from the old dynasty to the new one. Gregory of Tours (538–594) (E) was not a king but a bishop who wrote a history of the Merovingians.

11. **(A)** Pope Gregory I asserted the spiritual primacy of the papacy, and thus claimed papal supremacy over the patriarch of Constantinople. During his pontificate Rome was nominally still part of the Byzantine Empire, but the emperor in Constantinople was unable to offer protection or other aid, and Gregory found it necessary to perform many of the functions that had formerly been the duty of the imperial government. Thus, he used the papal estates to feed the poor of Rome (E), and he conducted negotiations with the barbarians known as the Lombards (C), whose attacks he prevented by paying a tribute. In 597 he sent St. Augustine of Canterbury to England to convert the Anglo-Saxons (B). Gregory is known as a doctor of the Latin church for his massive literary output, including a biography of St. Benedict of Nursia, the founder of western monasticism. Gregory himself was a Benedictine and the first monk to become pope (D).

12. **(D)** The reign of Philip IV of France (1285–1314), called the Fair, was bedeviled by cash shortages due to his expensive wars with England

and Flanders. To remedy the problem, Philip tried various measures, but the summoning of the Estates-General in 1302 was not directly motivated by his desire to raise revenue. Philip knew that the Estates-General, as a new body of clerics, knights, and burghers who represented French society, lacked the prestige to serve as a centralized assembly for the gathering of taxes in a nation which respected long-established tradition and where loyalties were primarily regional, so he turned to his growing bureaucracy of lawyers and sent royal ministers to the various provinces of France to negotiate tax arrangements based on the manipulation of feudal law. His reason for summoning the Estates-General was, rather, to muster popular support for his opposition to the pope. In 1294, Philip began taxing the clergy (E), only to be forbidden in 1296 by the Pope, Boniface VIII (1294–1303). Philip responded by forbidding French clergy to send tithes to Rome, and by 1298 the pope finally conceded. Hostility between king and pope flared up again, however, when Philip arrested a French bishop in 1301. The pope criticized him, but Philip summoned the Estates-General, which supported him in a display of early nationalistic fervor. After the pope condemned Philip in 1302 with the bull *Unam sanctam*, which declared papal supremacy, the king's henchmen went to Italy and apprehended Boniface, to bring him to France for trial. Although the elderly pope escaped from his captors, he soon died from the rough treatment he had received. In 1305 a French pope, Clement V (1305–1314), was elected. He soon moved the papal curia to Avignon, a city technically within the Holy Roman Empire, but on the border of France. Thus began the Avignonese Papacy (1309–1378), known as the "Babylonian Captivity," when the popes were all French and avoided conflict with the French monarchy.

Philip's other measures to increase his revenue included debasing the currency (C) and persecuting wealthy and unpopular minority groups. In 1306 Philip arrested the Jews, seized their property, and expelled them from his kingdom (A). In 1307 he took advantage of rumors of immoral and heretical practices among the Knights Templar, a military monastic order, to begin proceedings against them (B). The Templars were Crusading warriors who took vows of poverty, chastity, and obedience. Although their primary purpose was to fight the Muslims, they had also developed a sophisticated system of international banking in order to fund their military campaigns. Philip urged Clement V to suppress them as heretics in 1312 and then seized their wealth.

13. **(C)** The paintings of Hieronymus Bosch (1450–1516) often depict wild scenes in which human beings are tormented by demons. His paintings include such titles as *Ship of Fools*, the *Earthly Paradise*, the *Seven Deadly Sins*, and the *Temptation of St. Anthony*. The almost "surreal" quality of

Bosch's paintings is not typical of the northern Renaissance, but his choice of non-classical themes reflects a characteristic difference between art of the northern Renaissance and art of the Italian Renaissance.

14. **(E)** The Counter (or Catholic) Reformation strengthened, not weakened, the spiritual authority of the papacy within the Roman Catholic Church. Pope Paul III (1534–1549) took a leading role in organizing Catholic reform in response to the Protestant Reformation. He approved the foundation of new religious orders (D), such as the Capuchins, Theatines, and especially the Jesuits, who were fanatically loyal to the papacy in their mission to win back Christians who had become Protestants. He established the Roman Inquisition in 1542, also known as the Holy Office, which was not directly related to the medieval Inquisition that had been established in the thirteenth century (C). The new Inquisition was more concerned with detecting doctrinal errors in works by theologians than with punishing heresy on the popular level. Finally, Paul III convoked the Council of Trent, which met three times between 1545 and 1563 in order to clarify doctrine (A). This important council continued after the pontificate of Pope Paul IV (1555–1559), who in 1559 published the first Index of Prohibited Books (B)—a list of books that Catholics were forbidden to read because their theological content opposed doctrines approved by the Roman Catholic Church.

15. **(E)** The Hittites and Egyptians ended two centuries of warfare in the Levant by signing a treaty after the indecisive battle of Kadesh in northern Syria in 1274 B.C.E. The two empires thereby agreed to share power in the region of Syria and Palestine, which marked their mutual border. This era of peaceful coexistence along the shores of the eastern Mediterranean was ended by the Sea Peoples (A), whose invasions around 1250–1150 B.C.E. destabilized the region. The Hittites could not have signed a treaty of coexistence with the Neo-Babylonians (C) or the Persians (D) because these two empires did not exist until many centuries after the Hittite empire had vanished, nor with the Sumerians (B) because the Sumerians had vanished before the Hittite empire arose.

16. **(B)** Ziggurats were distinctive, multi-tiered temples found in Mesopotamia. An administrative district in Egypt (E) was the *nome*. The other answers (A, C, D) point to characteristic features of ancient Near Eastern cultures, but have nothing to do with ziggurats.

17. **(D)** The graph provides evidence that the population of Europe declined or was stagnating before the Black Death struck. This thesis is

generally accepted among historians, although a lack of definite population records prevents agreement on points of detail—for example, it is uncertain whether European population as a whole actually declined because of the famine of 1315–1317, but it is clear that the population in some regions did. Since medieval governments did not keep a census, historians must rely on documents such as taxrolls, which count households rather than individuals, in order to estimate population. Research indicates that tax records do in general correspond to descriptions of famines and plague (E), even though there are regional variations that do not always fit the overall trends; the data provided in the present graph, however, does support chronicle accounts which mention famines between 1310 and 1320 and the onset of the plague between 1340 and 1350. Choices (B) and (C) can be eliminated, because the graph shows data mainly for the fourteenth century (the years 1301–1400 constitute the fourteenth century; the thirteenth century comprises the years 1201–1300). The data does suggest, however, that European agriculture had reached the limits of its ability to support its population during the *fourteenth* century, since the number of households was no longer growing but had leveled off, as a comparison of the columns for 1310, 1330, and 1340 indicates. Choice (A) can be eliminated on this basis, or simply because the column for 1320 shows a lower number of households than does the column for 1310.

18. **(C)** The Mayor of the Palace was the most powerful official in the Frankish realm during the period of the late Merovingian dynasty, whose last representatives were known as the "do-nothing" kings (E) because they entrusted all important affairs to their Mayor. All higher offices among the Franks, including seneschal and constable (A, B), were based on household duties, and that of the Mayor of the Palace was to oversee all the others. In time the office became hereditary and was held by the Carolingian dynasty, named after Charles Martel, who defeated Muslim raiders at Tours in 732. His son, Pepin the Short, asked Pope Stephen II (752–757) whether the man with the most power should not also be king, and the pope's positive reply emboldened him to claim the title. The pope consecrated Pepin king in 754. Pope Leo III (795–816) revived the office of emperor (D) by crowning Charlemagne with this title on Christmas Day of the year 800.

19. **(A)** The Cluniacs were monks who belonged to a consortium of Benedictine monasteries led by the abbey of Cluny in eastern France, founded in the tenth century. The Cluniacs cooperated with the papacy to reform ecclesiastical discipline. In the eleventh century, especially under the leadership of Pope Gregory VII (1073–1085), they strove to free the church from control by powerful members of the laity, who often appointed bishops and

abbots for political reasons rather than spiritual ones. The Jesuits, Franciscans, and Dominicans (B, C, D) were all religious orders founded after the twelfth century. The Merovingians (E) were Frankish kings during the fifth to eighth centuries under whom ecclesiastical discipline had become so lax that their successors, the Carolingians, had to institute reforms. The Cluniac monks continued the work that the Carolingian kings had undertaken.

20. **(C)** Although it is true that Charlemagne became emperor of a revived western Roman Empire, he did not crown himself (as Napoleon Bonaparte was to do centuries later). He was, rather, crowned by Pope Leo III (795– 816)—a fact which was to have crucial implications for the future of church and state relations. The coronation, which took place on Christmas Day of the year 800, was apparently not Charlemagne's idea, but that of Leo III, who hoped to increase the prestige of the papacy by claiming the right to make emperors. When Charlemagne later had his son crowned emperor, he excluded the pope from the ceremony, as if to challenge papal presumption. Charlemagne's claim to the title of emperor was based on the fact that he ruled the largest kingdom since the imperial succession had ended in the West (476 C.E.), comprising territories along the Rhine and all of Gaul (renamed France after the Franks), to which Charlemagne added Saxony (A), a part of Spain (B), and the kingdom of the Lombards in Italy (D). Although Charlemagne's reputation was based on his prowess as a warrior and defender of the papacy (which had been threatened by the Lombards), he was also a pious Christian who wanted to raise the quality of religion in his realm—a task which required educational reform. He therefore invited to his court scholars from all parts of the Latin world, including lands outside his own realm (E). Foremost of these outsiders was the Anglo-Saxon scholar Alcuin of York, who was instrumental in the revival of learning.

21. **(D)** Key features of Roman society and culture include: their rejection of monarchy, their representative form of government (the Republic), the domination of this government by the patrician class that constituted the Senate, the turmoil caused by the attempt of the plebeians to resist the self-serving policies of the patricians, the virtues of toughness and uncompromising tenacity, and the innovative military formation known as the legion, which was superior to the phalanx used by most ancient Mediterranean societies and enabled Rome to dominate its neighbors. The kings expelled by the early Romans were Etruscan (C), whose culture was eventually absorbed by the Romans. The Gauls (E) were Celts who conquered Rome in 390 B.C.E. but were later conquered by them. The Carthaginians (A) were Rome's greatest rivals, with whom they fought three conflicts known as the

Punic Wars to determine who would dominate the Mediterranean region. The Athenians (B) also governed an empire, albeit a smaller one and only briefly, but unlike the Romans, they managed to break the power of the wealthy families and institute a direct democracy.

22. **(A)** Richard I of England (1189–1199), known as the Lion-Hearted, was one of three kings to lead the Third Crusade. In 1191 he captured the city of Acre on the coast (now part of Israel) and ordered the execution of over two thousand Muslim prisoners of war. The Third Crusade failed to retake Jerusalem, which had been established as one of four states during the First Crusade (D) but subsequently captured by the Muslim warrior Saladin. European kings (Louis VII of France and Conrad III of Germany) led armies in the Holy Land during the Second Crusade (B). Venetian merchants persuaded the crusaders to seize Constantinople during the Fourth Crusade (E). Egypt was invaded by the armies of the Fifth Crusade (C).

23. **(B)** Peter Abelard (1079–1142) was an important figure in the rise of scholastic theology, which used logic to study the mysteries of revelation. Abelard's preference for Paris helped build momentum for the rise of the university there in the course of the twelfth century. While lecturing on theology in Paris, he agreed to tutor a young woman named Heloise, with whom he fell in love and had an affair. They married secretly, but when the uncle of Heloise found out, he had Abelard castrated. In disgrace, Abelard became a monk and Heloise became a nun. Abelard continued to lecture on theology, but was attacked for teaching heretical doctrines by some Cistercian monks, most notably Bernard of Clairvaux (E), who was opposed to the scholastic enterprise. Abelard died before his trial was resolved. Anselm of Canterbury (A) was a Benedictine monk of the late eleventh century who approved of the use of logic in the study of theology and served as the archbishop of Canterbury. Thomas Aquinas (C) taught theology at the university of Paris during the thirteenth century. Nicholas of Cusa (D) was a Neoplatonist of the fifteenth century.

24. **(E)** The English Reformation, as initiated by Henry VIII (1491–1547), was more political than theological in nature. In 1529 Henry petitioned Pope Clement VII for a marriage annulment, thinking that his wife, Catherine of Aragon, was responsible for the failure to produce a male heir. However, the pope was a virtual prisoner of Catherine's powerful nephew, the Holy Roman Emperor Charles V, and Henry's request was denied. In 1532 Henry divorced Catherine without the pope's permission and was excommunicated, whereupon Henry made himself the head of the Church of England and reorganized its administration. Apart from his unwillingness to accept a subordinate role

to the pope, Henry VIII remained theologically conservative even after his break with Rome. It was not until after Henry's reign that England became more typically Protestant in a theological sense.

25. **(E)** The Lombard League was an alliance of northern Italian city-states which banded together in the twelfth and thirteenth centuries to resist control by the German emperors, who claimed Italy as part of the Holy Roman Empire. The League won a victory against Frederick I (1152–1190) at Legnano in 1176 and later resisted his grandson, Frederick II (1215–1250) in protracted wars. During the Renaissance, Italy was dominated by five states: the Duchy of Milan (D), the Republic of Florence (C), the Republic of Venice, the Papal States, and Naples. The Treaty of Lodi (1454) brought Milan, Florence, and Venice into an alliance that established a balance of power against Naples and the Papal States. In 1494 French troops invaded Italy under Charles VIII (1483–1498) of the Valois dynasty (A). The Hapsburg Holy Roman Emperor, Charles V (1519–1558), later also led armies into Italy (B), where he fought the Valois for control of the country.

26. **(E)** The shaded areas indicate colonies established by the Phoenicians, mostly from about 900 to 750 B.C.E. The Greeks (A) also established colonies around the Mediterranean, but did so a little later (mainly from about 750 to 550 B.C.E.), and more extensively, including southern Italy and the shores of the Black Sea. The most important of the Phoenician colonies was Carthage, on the North African coast closest to Italy (modern Tunisia); it became an independent power when Phoenicia itself (located on the eastern shores of the Mediterranean) was conquered in the eighth century B.C.E. by the Assyrians. Rome fought three wars with Carthage for mastery of the Mediterranean, from the third to the second centuries B.C.E., which are known as the Punic Wars. The First Punic War (264–241 B.C.E.) was mainly fought in and around Sicily, but not in North Africa or Spain, so that answer (C) is incorrect. North Africa and Spain were battlegrounds during the Second Punic War (218–201 B.C.E.), and Carthage itself was destroyed during the Third Punic War (149–146 B.C.E.). Augustus Caesar (27 B.C.E.–14 C.E.) lived long after the Punic wars ended (D), when the areas shaded on the map were firmly under the control of the Romans. The Peloponnesian War (B) was fought from 431 to 404 B.C.E. between Athens and Sparta and their allies in Greece and Sicily, not in the region of Carthage or Spain.

27. **(D)** Around 1600 B.C.E. Mesopotamia was invaded by Hittites from Asia Minor (Anatolia) and Kassites from what is now Iran. Although the Hittites merely raided the Old Babylonian kingdom and returned home with

the spoils of war, the Kassites overthrew the Babylonian kings and ruled in their place for five centuries. Thus, the demise of the Old Babylonian kingdom was due to external pressures. Although the irregular and violent flooding of the Tigris and Euphrates rivers did not make agriculture easy, the use of irrigation and canals minimized the damage and kept the economy viable (A). Slaves existed, but were not so numerous as to pose a threat to stability, and often their status was temporary, so that widespread slave revolts did not trouble the kingdom (C). Nobles and priests generally supported the institution of kingship (B), perhaps because Mesopotamian kings for the most part claimed to be representatives of the gods rather than gods themselves. It was in Egypt, by contrast, that the kings (i.e., pharaohs) claimed to be gods and exercised absolute power during certain periods, especially during the Old Kingdom (c. 2700–c. 2200 B.C.E.). Similarly, the Hyksos (E) troubled Egypt rather than Old Babylonia, invading the Nile region, somewhat before the Hittite and Kassite invasions of Mesopotamia.

28. **(B)** *The Epic of Gilgamesh* describes the quest of the Sumerian king of Uruk who strove against the temperamental gods as he searched for immortality after the death of his friend Enkidu. In contrast, *The Book of the Dead* (A) and the letters of Akhenaton (E) found at Amarna are Egyptian rather than Sumerian and suggest an optimistic view of the afterlife. The Hebrew Bible (C) contains passages that suggest certain Mesopotamian influences, but it is concerned with the Hebrew commitment to monotheism. Finally, although Homer's *Iliad* (D) depicts the gods as capricious beings, they are not identified as members of the Sumerian pantheon, but are thought to dwell on Mt. Olympus in Greece.

29. **(D)** Tyranny in ancient Greece was sometimes used as a measure to prevent anarchy resulting from social strife between economic classes. Although it might be resisted by some of the citizens, it was seen as a good thing by others (usually citizens from the lower classes), who hoped to benefit from the arrangement (A). Thus, tyranny could actually be a relatively mild form of government that benefited the majority of citizens (B). Aristotle did not approve of tyranny, which was his term for unjust rule by one man (E); he approved of rule by one man if that man were moral and acted for the good of the community, a form of government which he called monarchy. Aristotle did not consider Sparta a tyranny (C) but thought it might be considered a balanced constitution which included elements of rule by the one, the few, and the many.

30. **(D)** Solon established a Council of 400, which drew 100 members from each of the four traditional tribes of Athens. The Council of 500

was established by a later reformer, Cleisthenes, who sought to break the power of the nobles, who dominated the four tribes, by establishing ten tribes based on new political units called *demes*; each of these ten new tribes supplied 50 members to the Council of 500. All the rest is true of Solon: he canceled the debts of impoverished citizens (C), restored freedom to citizens who had been sold into slavery (E), divided citizens into four classes based on their wealth (A), and wrote poetry, in which he described his political experiment (B).

31. **(D)** The legion was a military formation devised by the Romans that consisted of about 5,000 men organized into smaller units called *maniples*, which could act independently of one another. It could, thus, easily out-maneuver the phalanx (A), a formation of about 8,000 men who acted as a single unit and could not conduct complicated maneuvers but relied on brute force to overwhelm the opposition. The Romans were able to conquer the Mediterranean with the legion because their opponents relied on the more cumbersome phalanx. War elephants (C) were used by Rome's great-est enemy, Carthage. Triremes (E) were warships powered by three banks of oars, used by the Greeks. The horse-drawn chariot (B) was introduced into Egypt during the seventeenth century B.C.E. by the Hyksos.

32. **(D)** Ostracism derives from the Greek word *ostraka*, which was a piece of broken pottery on which the Athenians would write the name of an individual (usually a wealthy aristocrat) whom they considered a danger to their democracy. The individual had to go into exile for a period of ten years, but his property was not seized and his family was not harmed. The threat of ostracism was intended to deter wealthy and influential men from trying to dominate political life.

33. **(D)** The Social War (90–88 B.C.E.) was precipitated by the assassi-nation of the Roman tribune Marcus Drusus, who sought to extend Roman citizenship to Rome's Italian allies; the Senate opposed the measure because it threatened to dilute its own political power. In response, the Italian allies seceded from Rome, initiating a war that is named after the Latin word *socii*, which means "allies." The war ended in the allies' favor when Rome was suddenly threatened by a massive uprising in its eastern provinces led by Mithridates, the king of Pontus (B). Although the rivals Marius and Sulla both fought in the Social War (A), they did so as Roman generals; their con-flict arose over which of them would be given command of the expedition against Mithridates. While Roman women did acquire an increased measure of freedom in the late Republic (E), this development did not arise out of

the passage of legislation. Answer (C) cannot be correct because the Delian League ceased to exist in the fifth century B.C.E., when Athens lost the Peloponnesian War to Sparta.

34. **(C)** The Lithuanians were the last Europeans to accept Christianity. Their chieftain, Mindaugas, converted to Catholicism in 1251, but the people remained pagan when he was assassinated in 1263. It was not until 1386, when Jagiello, the grand duke of Lithuania, married Jadwiga, the queen of Poland, that the Lithuanians finally accepted Christianity from the Latin church. The Poles (B) had converted to Roman Catholicism in the tenth century. The Czechs and Slovaks (A, D) were converted initially by the Byzantine missionaries Cyril and Methodius in the ninth century, but they adopted Roman Catholicism in the tenth. The Russians (E) of Kiev accepted Greek Orthodoxy in the tenth century and remained within the religious orbit of Constantinople.

35. **(E)** The map shows areas controlled by the Muslims around the year 750 C.E. It represents approximately one hundred years of conquests that transformed a relatively small nation of desert nomads into an imperial power whose culture exercized major influences on Western civilization. It is possible to eliminate all the other choices. In the eighth century the Byzantines (D) controlled Greece and western Anatolia, whereas the Franks (A) controlled the region of modern France, neither of which is shaded on the map. The Ostrogoths (C) no longer existed in the eighth century, but had controlled Italy in the fifth and sixth centuries. The Magyars (B) appeared in Europe in the ninth century and settled the region which is now Hungary.

36. **(A)** Plato (c. 427–347 B.C.E.) was a student of Socrates (469–399 B.C.E.). After the death of Socrates, Plato wrote his philosophical *Dialogues*, in which Socrates is the principal speaker. All of the other Greek thinkers listed made their philosophical contributions before Socrates revolutionized philosophy by turning primarily to questions of ethics. The Pre-Socratics, by contrast, were best known for their interest in physics and mathematics. Thales of Miletus (c. 600 B.C.E.) speculated that the basic substance, from which all things are formed, is water (E). Heraclitus (c. 540–480 B.C.E.) believed it was fire (C). The theory proposed by Empedocles (c. 490–430 B.C.E.) that all things consist of four elements (earth, air, fire, and water) became the accepted answer and was the dominant scientific paradigm until modern times (D). Pythagoras (c. 580–500 B.C.E.) was famous for his studies in mathematics and his theory of musical harmony (B).

37. **(C)** Although Pericles (c. 495–429 B.C.E.) was an Athenian aristocrat, he championed the cause of democracy and actively opposed oligarchy ("government of the few") by transferring traditional powers of the aristocratic council of the Areopagus to the democratic Council of 500, and by introducing payment for public service so that even poor citizens could afford to participate in government. In pursuing these policies, Pericles was motivated by practical concerns, for he regarded democracy as the most effective form of government, which would make Athens powerful by motivating the entire population to strive for the community's welfare. Thus, under his leadership, Athens embarked upon an energetic program of imperialist expansion (B). This aggressive foreign policy brought wealth into the city, especially after Athens began to dominate the Delian League, a defensive alliance of Greek naval powers that had formed after the wars with Persia in order to protect against future invasions. Once Athens asserted its hegemony of the League, Pericles used the tribute of its members to fund an elaborate building program in Athens (E); under the guidance of the sculptor Phidias, whose masterpiece was the statue of Athena in the Parthenon, the Acropolis assumed the classical dimensions for which Athens is renowned (D). The people of Athens showed their gratitude to Pericles by frequently electing him a general (A).

38. **(D)** The Fourth Crusade never reached the Muslims but was instead diverted against the Christian city of Constantinople, which was sacked in 1204. Thus, the Fourth Crusade did not contribute to the legacy of ill-will between Muslims and Christians, as the other Crusades did, but instead poisoned relations between the Latin and Greek Christians, who had already been estranged since 1054. The Venetians were the masterminds behind the coup d'etat, and they used their constitutional influence in the new government to monopolize Byzantine trade (E) and to export works of Byzantine art, such as the guilded bronze horses of the Hippodrome, which were put on display at St. Mark's cathedral in Venice (C). The Venetians also dominated the office of the patriarch of Constantinople, and this Latin patriarch attended the Fourth Lateran Council convened by Pope Innocent III in the year 1215 (B). After seizing Constantinople, the Latin crusaders conquered the surrounding territory and set up feudal states throughout the region of Greece (A). This Latin Empire, however, was short-lived. In 1261 the Byzantine emperors, who had maintained a government-in-exile at Nicaea, succeeded in recapturing Constantinople.

39. **(C)** The concept of the three orders—those who fight, those who pray, those who work—reflected the society of the early Middle Ages, which was politically unstable, intellectually preoccupied with the supernatural, and economically based on agriculture rather than commerce. This was a world in which mer-

chants played a negligible role; indeed, they did not arise as a distinct class until the eleventh and twelfth centuries, when political stability made possible the revival of trade and the growth of towns, which are the centers of commerce. The three orders were viewed as complementary parts of an organic whole, in which members of each social class were satisfied with their place (as in the ideal society described in Plato's *Republic*). Thus, fighters, who were represented by knights (A), were needed to protect agricultural laborers called serfs (E) as well as men of prayer—such as priests (D) who administered the sacraments and monks (B) who prayed for the souls of the dead. Merchants, however, were a dynamic group who strove to increase their wealth and influence. Their preoccupation with making money was considered suspect by the Church, which condemned the charging of interest as usury and tried to curb the profit motive by substituting the "just price" for the principle of supply and demand.

40. **(D)** Cato the Elder (234–149 B.C.E.) was a Roman senator who led the war-party during the second century B.C.E. He ended all the speeches he gave in the Senate, regardless of the subject, with a call to renew the war against Carthage. Although Carthage posed no serious threat to Rome, which had already conquered its rival twice, the party led by Cato wanted it utterly destroyed so that Rome could have a free hand in subduing the rest of the Mediterranean. Cato eventually succeeded in convincing the Senate to begin the Third Punic War against Carthage, but did not live to see Scipio the Younger raze the city in 146 B.C.E.

41. **(E)** Cleisthenes's revolutionary new political unit was the *deme*, which was based on the word *demos* ("people") and inspired the word "democracy" (*demokratia*). The *demes* replaced the *phratries* (B), or "brotherhoods," subunits of the four traditional tribes, which were dominated by the aristocracy. Cleisthenes used the new *demes* to form ten new tribes, each of which contributed 50 members to a Council of 500, known as the *boule* (D). Cleisthenes did not invent the *boule*, but reformed the one that had been founded by Solon in 594 B.C.E., which included 400 members (100 individuals drawn from each of the four traditional tribes). The *phalanx* (A) was a military rather than a political unit, although its existence had extended political power to the hoplites, Greek infantrymen drawn from the middle class. Likewise, the *thetes* (C) were not a political unit but the lower class, which gained political power in Periclean Athens as a reward for their service as rowers during the Persian Wars.

42. **(C)** Ovid (c. 43 B.C.E.–17 C.E.) was a Latin poet who wrote during the time of the first Roman emperor, Augustus. Hesiod (D) was second only to Homer and wrote the *Theogony*, which describes the legends of the gods,

and *Works and Days*, which describes life on a Greek farm. The other poets, Archilochus, Pindar, and Sappho (A, B, E) wrote lyric poetry.

43. **(D)** The kingdom of England was the most unified monarchy in Europe during the twelfth century. The Anglo-Saxons had united all of England under one king by the eleventh century, and William the Conqueror introduced the highly organized feudal government of Normandy there after his victory at Hastings in 1066. His successors, especially Henry II (1154–1189), continued to strengthen the central authority of the monarchy and established an empire that controlled large portions of France. At this time, France (E) was highly divided and its kings were generally weak, but a few exceptional monarchs, most notably Philip II Augustus (1180–1223), took the first steps toward unifying the nation. Germany (A), by contrast, was progressively disintegrating. The nobles of the Holy Roman Empire had taken advantage of the emperor's struggle against the pope during the Investiture Controversy to strengthen their own control. Italy (B) was technically part of the Holy Roman Empire, but its independent towns, called communes, likewise made gains at the emperor's expense and resisted his claim to their lands. Spain (C) was made up of a collection of Christian and Muslim states frequently at war with one another.

44. **(E)** The structure is the Lion Gate at Mycenae, named so because the sculptures on either side of the column set above the doorway represent lions. The doorway is set within Cyclopean walls, made up of huge stone slabs instead of bricks and named after the race of mythical one-eyed giants known as the Cyclops that supposedly built the walls.

45. **(A)** Luther's Ninety-Five Theses, which initiated his outspoken opposition to the Roman Catholic Church, were published in 1517 to dispute the idea that indulgences are effective in the forgiveness of sins. Luther was reacting specifically to the sale of indulgences, as practiced by a Dominican monk named Tetzel who was traveling through Germany in an effort to raise money for the construction of St. Peter's Basilica in Rome. Luther had visited Rome, where he was scandalized by the worldliness of the clergy (B), but that was in 1510, some seven years earlier, and it did not excite an outspoken reaction. Luther was also influenced by the theology of John Huss, but Huss had been executed about 100 years earlier, at the Council of Constance in 1415 (D). Luther was not inspired to speak out by John Calvin, who was only eight years old in 1517 and who published the first edition of his *Institutes of the Christian Religion* in 1536 (E). The German princes did not call for a national church before Luther took his stand (C), but several of them came to his support afterwards.

46. **(E)** The Hohenzollern dynasty ruled Prussia throughout its history as an independent secular state. The state was founded in 1525 during the Reformation when Albrecht (Albert) von Hohenzollern, the last Grand Master of the Teutonic Knights, became a Lutheran and secularized the lands of the religious order.

47. **(C)** Vasco da Gama was employed by Portugal when he sailed for India in 1497. Although Magellan (A) was Portuguese, he was employed by Spain during the first circumnavigation of the globe for which his expedition is famous (although he himself died while crossing the Pacific Ocean, in 1521). Among the Spanish conquistadors, Cortez (D) overthrew the Aztecs in what is now Mexico, and Pizarro (E) overthrew the Incas in what is now Peru. De Soto (B) participated in Pizarro's campaigns against the Incas; he later explored Florida and the coast along the Gulf of Mexico.

48. **(E)** Richelieu's central policy was to increase the power of the French monarchy. All of his other policies were but means to this end, and his religious affiliation did not affect his political calculations. Thus, although the Hapsburgs were fellow Catholics, Richelieu sided with the Protestants in the Thirty Years' War because the presence of Protestantism in the Holy Roman Empire weakened the Hapsburgs and allowed France to emerge as the most powerful state in Europe (A). Richelieu was also willing to tolerate Protestantism in France. Although he attacked the Huguenot bastion of La Rochelle to eliminate their military and political power, he allowed them freedom of religion afterwards, as long as they agreed to serve the French monarchy (D). Richelieu increased military spending (C) and took measures to curb the power of the French nobility (B), since both of these policies strengthened the French monarchy.

49. **(C)** The Peloponnesian League was organized and led by Sparta as a mutual defense organization composed of most of the city-states on the peninsula in southern Greece known as the Peloponnesus. It lent its name to the Peloponnesian War (431–404 B.C.E.) because Sparta led it in its assault on Athens. The Athenian system of alliances, which had become the basis of its empire, was the Delian League (A). A system of alliances during the Hellenistic period was the Achaean League (B). Finally, although the Greeks and Phoenicians engaged in overseas colonization, their city-states did so on an individual basis rather than within commercial organizations (D, E).

50. **(E)** The image of an athlete somersaulting over a charging bull is distinctively Minoan, and may represent some sort of religious ritual, since

bulls seem to have been an important symbol of Minoan religion (as suggested by the Greek myth of the Minotaur, the half-man, half-bull inhabiting the labyrinth on Crete).

51. **(A)** Francesco Petrarch (1304–1374) abandoned his legal studies at the University of Bologna when his father died, for he preferred the contemplative life of letters to the active life of practicing law. He wrote an epic poem in Latin on the Roman hero Scipio Africanus, as well as numerous works in prose, but his sonnets in the Tuscan dialect of the Italian vernacular earned him the most praise. Peter Abelard (B) was a twelfth-century theologian whose best-known work is the *Sic et Non*, which notes contradictions among the Church Fathers in order to develop a method to resolve their differences; he thus tried to demonstrate that arguments from authority were not enough, but that logical proofs were necessary as well. Marsilius of Padua (ca. 1275–1342) (E) was a Franciscan friar who wrote an important work of political theory, entitled *The Defender of the Peace*, in which he argued that the authority of a government derives from the body of its citizens, not from divine favor supposedly bestowed on an individual, whether a pope, emperor, or king; he asserted that popes have no right to claim temporal power. Castiglione (1478–1529) (D) wrote an influential work of etiquette, *The Book of the Courtier* (1528). Paracelsus (1493–1541) (C) was a physician who developed a form of medical alchemy that in some aspects prefigured modern medicine; he theorized that diseases are caused by foreign agents rather than an imbalance of bodily humors, and that sick patients could be cured by treating them with chemical compounds that would neutralize the foreign agents.

52. **(B)** Greeks alive in the year 500 B.C.E. did not engage in public worship of Mithras, a Persian god whose cult did not become popular in the Greek world until after Alexander the Great's conquest of the Persian empire (334–323 B.C.E.), when the *polis* was in decline and the demoralized Greeks turned away from the public worship of their traditional patron deities to private worship in mystery cults. Dionysos (A), the god of wine, was publicly honored by the Greeks, especially the Athenians, who dedicated to him a drama competition at a festival instituted by Peisistratus in 534 B.C.E. Zeus, Athena, and Apollo (C, D, E) were all gods of Olympus, worshiped by the Greeks since the age of the Mycenaeans.

53. **(E)** Aristophanes (c. 450–385 B.C.E.) was renowned for his comedies, some of which criticized the Peloponnesian War (such as *The Acharnians* and *Lysistrata*). Thucydides (D) was a general who wrote a history of the war. Aeschylus, Sophocles, and Euripides (A, B, C) were renowned for their tragedies.

54. **(E)** The three Hellenistic kingdoms that emerged from the civil war following the death of Alexander the Great were the Antigonid, Ptolemaic, and Seleucid kingdoms, named after the generals who founded these realms in Europe, Africa, and Asia. Magna Graecia (D) was the Latin name for the region of southern Italy colonized by the Greeks. The kingdoms of Pergamum, Bithynia, and Cilicia (C) were all located in Asia Minor. The Achaean League and the Aetolian League (A) arose within the Antigonid kingdom as alliances to fight for their independence. The Peloponnesian League and the Delian League (B) were led by Sparta and Athens, respectively, and fought the Peloponnesian War.

55. **(D)** When the earliest civilizations appeared in the river valleys of the Fertile Crescent, they were already making use of the wheel (E), irrigation (B), bronze-working (A), and writing (C). However, the alphabet was not developed until about 1400 B.C.E., when the Syrian city-state of Ugarit adapted the cuneiform writing that was used in 3000 B.C.E. (which represented syllables and entire words), in order to represent individual sounds, which is the hallmark of an alphabet. The Phoenicians replaced the cumbersome cuneiform letters of the Ugaritic alphabet with simpler symbols, and these were eventually imitated by the Hebrews, Greeks, and Romans to form the alphabets that bear their name.

56. **(E)** The Assyrians were renowned for their effectiveness in war and their harsh methods of controlling their empire. They conquered the Near East during the eighth and seventh centuries B.C.E., including Egypt. However, in 612 B.C.E. they themselves were finally conquered by a Neo-Babylonian dynasty (A), with help from the Medes (B). Although the Romans (C) eventually deported Hebrew people from Judea, there was no kingdom of Israel during their reign. The Hittites (D) fought several wars with Egypt, but they never took control of the Nile valley.

57. **(B)** The photograph shows the exterior of the Hagia Sophia in Constantinople, built in 532–537 at the command of the emperor Justinian (527–565). It is the most impressive example of Byzantine architecture, demonstrating its characteristic design of a dome over a square base. Note that the towers, known as minarets, were built later by the Turks (A), who captured the city in 1453 and converted the Christian church into a mosque (it is now a museum). Minarets were originally an Arab design (C).

58. **(D)** Aristotle was so important in the medieval universities that he was often referred to simply as "the Philosopher." His works were initially read through the commentaries of the twelfth-century Muslim philosopher

Averroes (C), but later Scholastics preferred to separate the two and focus on Aristotle himself, especially when his texts became available in new translations based on the original Greek text. The twelfth-century Jewish philosopher Maimonides (B) was also highly regarded by some prominent Christian Scholastics (such as Thomas Aquinas), but his works never occupied the preeminent position in the curriculum of the medieval university. Aristotle's teacher, Plato (E), had been regarded as the foremost philosopher before the rise of the universities. However, the influx of Aristotelian translations in the twelfth century (when the universities were coming into being) led to a loss of interest in Plato. Plotinus (A), the third-century Neoplatonist, was hardly known in the Latin-reading world.

59. **(C)** Henry of Navarre (1553–1610), of the Bourbon dynasty, was the leader of the Huguenots (Protestants) in the French wars of religion. When the last Valois king of France, Henry III, died in 1589 without an heir, the rules of succession made Henry of Navarre the first Bourbon king of France, as Henry IV (1589–1610). Most of the French people, however, who were Catholic, refused to accept a Protestant as their king and resisted Henry IV's attempts to enter Paris. In order to win the acceptance of his people, Henry IV converted to Catholicism in 1593, on which occasion he reputedly uttered the phrase, "Paris is worth a Mass," indicating his willingness to accept Catholic practices (such as the ritual of the Mass), which he had rejected as a Protestant, for the sake of political expediency. Although the Huguenots were initially dismayed at the conversion of their defender, Henry did not forsake them but used his power as a Catholic king of France to issue the Edict of Nantes (1598), which granted religious toleration to the French Protestants and ended the wars of religion in France.

60. **(D)** Only a few Carolingian scholars (especially those from Ireland) could read Greek. Charlemagne promoted Latin as the common language of his empire. While the group of scholars at Charlemagne's court (A), led by Alcuin of York (735–804), was the intellectual jewel in the Frankish crown, ordinary cathedral schools were the mainstay of the Carolingian Renaissance, for they trained clerics to perform their ecclesiastical duties (B). The education provided by the schools was based on the liberal arts, which included the reading of classical literature written by the ancient pagans. Charlemagne's instructions to preserve these classical works through the copying of manuscripts (E) saved many of them from oblivion—virtually all the Latin literature that survives today was preserved by the Carolingians. In order to make the texts as legible as possible, Charlemagne charged Alcuin to create a new script. The result, which is known as Carolingian (or Caroline) minuscule, was so clear and useful that the humanists of the

Italian Renaissance (in the fifteenth and sixteenth centuries) chose it to serve as the model for printed books. Caroline minuscule thus forms the basis of modern typography (C).

61. **(D)**   Bartolomé de Las Casas (1474–1566) was a Spanish missionary in the New World who was appalled at the brutal enslavement of native peoples and campaigned for their humane treatment. He wrote a history of early Spanish colonialism as well as political pamphlets. The *Oration* was written by the Italian humanist, Pico della Mirandola (E). Isabella's Grand Inquisitor was Torquemada (A). The founder of the Dominican Order was Domingo de Guzman, better known as St. Dominic (B). The most famous early leader of the *Reconquista*, or "reconquest" of Spain from the Muslims, was Rodrigo Diaz de Vivar (1043–1099), better known as El Cid (C).

62. **(D)**   The shaded areas on the map represent the Athenian Empire during the Peloponnesian War (431–404 B.C.E.). This empire included the region of Attica where Athens was situated, as well as the city-states of the Delian League which Athens controlled. Note that all the territories are located along the coasts or on islands, for the Athenians relied on their navy to control their empire. They did have a few minor footholds on the Peloponnesus (the large peninsula at the southern end of Greece), but the rest of the peninsula was controlled by Sparta and its allies, known as the Peloponnesian League (C). The other answers can be rejected by a process of elimination. Answer (B) cannot be correct because the shaded area does not include Sparta, which allied with Athens in 480 B.C.E. to fight off the Persians; it also includes many northern territories that remained neutral, as well as the Ionian cities (in Asia Minor), which were under the control of Persia. Answer (E) cannot be correct because the Phoenicians did not become a major maritime power until after the Greeks arrived in the Aegean (around 2300 B.C.E.). Answer (A) cannot be correct because the Macedonian kingdom of Philip II lay toward the northern end of the map and mostly inland.

63. **(D)**   The paragraph describes the career of Constantine the Great (306–337 C.E.), who in 330 C.E. founded a city near the site of ancient Byzantium which he called New Rome, but which was later renamed Constantinople in his honor. He was not the first to transfer the seat of power to the east; Diocletian (A) had temporarily made the city of Nicomedia in Asia Minor his capital. However, unlike Constantine, who legalized Christianity, Diocletian persecuted the Christians, as did the emperors Decius (B) and Marcus Aurelius (C). Britain was added to the Empire in 43 C.E. during the reign of Claudius (E).

64. **(C)** The last Roman emperor in the West, Romulus Augustulus (475–476) was deposed by Odoacer, a Gothic chieftain, who ruled Italy as his personal kingdom with the permission (though not necessarily the approval) of the eastern Roman emperor, Zeno. Since the western emperor was never replaced, the Empire in the West is traditionally said to have come to an end in 476. Odoacer was himself deposed in 493, by Theodoric, king of the Ostrogoths (A). Alaric, king of the Visigoths (B), sacked Rome in 410, but this event did not involve the overthrow of the western emperor, Honorius (395–423), whose capital was Ravenna (a more defensible city, on the coast of the Adriatic Sea). Attila the Hun (D) was on the verge of sacking Rome in 452, but Pope Leo I dissuaded him. Three years later, in 455, however, Rome was sacked by the Vandals of King Gaiseric (E).

65. **(E)** The Talmud is the written body of Jewish civil and religious law, which provides a framework for the practice of rabbinic Judaism. It consists of two basic parts, the Mishnah, or codification of the laws, and the Gemara, a commentary on the Mishnah. The Mishnah was established toward the end of the second century C.E., and two parallel traditions of Gemara developed thereafter, one compiled by rabbis in Palestine and the other by the rabbinic academies in Babylonia. The Babylonian compilation became the authoritative version. The Talmud includes commentaries on the Torah (B), or five books of Moses, which is also known by the Greek name, Pentateuch (C). The Tanach (D) is the complete Hebrew Bible, corresponding to the Old Testament, as it is called by Christians. The Septuagint (A) is the ancient Greek translation of the Tanach.

66. **(B)** The Gracchi were the brothers Tiberius and Gaius Gracchus, who served as People's Tribunes and were murdered in political riots in 133 and 121 B.C.E., respectively. Tiberius tried to help the plight of small farmers who had lost their property during the rise of the *latifundia* (large estates) by proposing a policy of land redistribution (D), whereby public lands held illegally by wealthy patricians would be divided up into small plots and given to the dispossessed citizens. Although Tiberius won popular support with this proposal, he was murdered in a riot incited by the Senate before he could enact the necessary legislation. His brother, Gaius, attempted a yet more ambitious program of reform, in which he appealed to a broader base of support, including members of the equestrian class, whom he strove to place on juries, which had been dominated by the Senate (E). Gaius also tried to extend Roman citizenship to the allies (A). His most successful reform was the sale of state-subsidized grain to the poor (C), which was retained in the imperial policy known as "bread and circuses." Although the

Gracchi were aware of a crisis of manpower in the military, which relied on citizens who owned land for its recruits, their solution was to revive the small farm, and thereby raise recruit levels, rather than suggest military reforms (B). Decades later, when it was clear that the Senate would never allow land redistribution, the consul Marius resolved the manpower shortage by reforming the military, in effect professionalizing what had previously been a militia, by allowing landless men to serve in the military for pay.

67. **(B)**   The marriage between Ferdinand of Aragon and Isabella of Castile in 1469 established a single large state in the Iberian peninsula, in which the rulers took dynamic measures to strengthen the power of the monarchy. Until that time, the divided states in Spain had frequently fought among themselves even during the *Reconquista*, as the crusade against the Muslims is known (A). Ferdinand and Isabella agreed that religious homogeneity was essential for unity. To this end they instituted the Spanish Inquisition in 1478, then in 1492 expelled the Jews and drove the Muslims out of Granada through conquest. Thus, Ferdinand and Isabella used Catholicism to centralize their monarchy, but the monarchy did not depend on the pope for its authority (E). The border with France was secured by means of a treaty in 1493 (C). The grandson of Ferdinand and Isabella, Charles I (1516–1556), was elected Holy Roman Emperor in 1519, by which time the centralized monarchy was already firmly established (D).

68. **(B)**   Mercantilism was opposed to internal trade barriers, such as tolls. Mercantilists believed that governments should regulate commerce (E) by eliminating internal trade barriers and by using tariffs to limit imports (C). It was believed this combination of economic policies would encourage exchange within the national market and reduce the export of precious metals, which defined the wealth of a nation (A). The government also promoted colonies as a source of precious metals and raw materials (D), as well as a market for the sale of products manufactured by the nation.

69. **(D)**   Descartes (1596–1650) sought a military career in his twenties and served during the early phase of the Thirty Years' War (1618–1648). Soon, however, his preoccupation with mathematics and philosophy led him to devote his life to the study of truth. He established a connection between algebra and geometry that is expressed in the system of Cartesian coordinates, which graphically depicts algebraic equations on a two-dimensional grid. Descartes also made contributions to science, but his most famous achievement was in philosophy. His axiom "*Cogito, ergo sum,*" which means "I think, therefore I am," was a skeptical reaction to scholasticism, which had used authority as the starting point of its conclusions. Des-

cartes, in contrast, considered the relationship between thinking and being as the essential starting point for a logically consistent system of knowledge. Although his point of departure was skeptical in nature, he constructed logical arguments from this foundation to prove the existence of God.

70. **(A)** Giotto (c. 1267–1337) was a medieval painter whose innovative naturalistic art inspired the Italian Renaissance. All the others painted within the naturalistic tradition established during the Renaissance, of which Giotto was a precursor. El Greco (1541–1614) (B) is considered a Mannerist, whereas Velazquez (1599–1660) (C) represents baroque painting. Rembrandt (1606–1669) (D) and Rubens (1577–1640) (E) were both baroque Dutch artists.

71. **(A)** The sculpture is known as the Laocoön Group, which dates from the first century B.C.E. and depicts a scene from the legend of Troy in which a Trojan priest and his sons were attacked by sea serpents. The high degree of naturalistic detail, as well as the theatricality of the poses which heighten the emotional impact of the scene, are characteristic of Hellenistic sculpture.

72. **(C)** Dante's *Inferno* is the first part of *The Divine Comedy*, which describes the poet's dream-like journey through hell, purgatory, and heaven. In the *Inferno* Dante's guide is the Roman poet Vergil, whose own *Aeneid* describes a visit to the underworld by the Trojan hero Aeneas. The other works look to non-classical sources of inspiration. Those by Chretien de Troyes and Wolfram von Eschenbach (A, B) are named after knights of King Arthur, a legendary British leader during the decline of the Roman Empire. The Arthurian cycle became very popular during the twelfth century with the rise of courtly love literature. The legend of the tragic lovers Tristan and Isolt was recounted by many poets of courtly love, including Gottfried von Strassburg (E), and is of Celtic inspiration. The *Romance of the Rose* (D), an immensely popular thirteenth-century work, was begun by Guillaume de Lorris and later expanded by Jean de Meun. It is a pre-eminent example of medieval allegory, whose characters are personified abstractions, such as Idleness, Nature, and the Rose itself.

73. **(E)** Lucretius (96–55 B.C.E.) was active during the late Republic, before the reign of Augustus Caesar (27 B.C.E.–14 C.E.). Lucretius wrote a philosophical poem *On the Nature of Things*, which championed Epicurean philosophy and presented the theory that the world is made up of atoms. Horace, Virgil, and Ovid (A, B, D) were the chief poets of the Golden Age of Latin literature during the reign of Augustus. Juvenal (C) was a satirist during the Silver Age who criticized the decline of morals during the early Empire.

74. **(D)** Roman Law received its first written form around 450 B.C.E. with the promulgation of the Twelve Tables. It evolved over the centuries as the Romans conquered the Mediterranean and had to administer law to diverse peoples, each with their own law code. This need to provide justice to diverse groups inspired Roman leaders to devise a single law code for the whole empire, which was influenced by the concept of natural law (B), a feature of Stoic philosophy (A), which was popular among the ruling class. Toward the end of the *Pax Romana*, when the Empire was at the height of its prosperity, Roman jurists made the most important formulations of Roman Law (C), publishing authoritative textbooks from the second to the third century C.E. In the sixth century C.E., the emperor Justinian sponsored a codification of these jurists' authoritative teachings (E).

75. **(B)** King Philip II (359–336 B.C.E.) led Macedon in the unification of Greece by conquering the allied forces of Thebes and Athens at the Battle of Chaeronea in 338 B.C.E. The Greeks later regained their independence but were eventually conquered by Rome (A) and made part of the empire in 146 B.C.E. Persia (C) made two failed attempts to conquer Greece, in 490 and 480 B.C.E. Although Athens (D) under the leadership of Pericles (from 461 to 429 B.C.E.) dominated much of Greece, its hegemony was challenged by Sparta. The Phoenicians (E) never exerted much political power over Greece, even though their cultural influence was strong and the colonies of the two groups fought one another throughout the Mediterranean.

76. **(D)** The Greek alphabet was based on the Phoenician alphabet, but differed from it by using some of the symbols to represent vowels (Phoenician letters represented consonants only). The Etruscan alphabet (C) was based on the Greek alphabet, whereas the Roman alphabet (B) was based on the Etruscan. The Mycenaean form of writing, which ceased to be used around 1100 B.C.E., was based on a Minoan syllabary (A).

77. **(A)** Rabelais (c. 1494–1553) wrote satires describing the adventures of two giants named Gargantua and Pantagruel. His works, which were notorious for their bawdy humor and iconoclastic views of European society, were admired by King Francis I (1515–1547), a great patron of the Renaissance in France. Catherine de' Medici (E) was the queen of Francis's successor, Henry II (1547–1559), but she represented refined etiquette, as did Castiglione (C), who was an Italian writer famous for his work, *The Book of the Courtier* (1528). Montaigne (D) was famous as an essayist, and Bodin (B) as a political theorist.

78. **(D)** The Treaty of Tordesillas revised a settlement that Spain and Portugal had conducted in 1493 with Pope Alexander VI, who had divided

the Atlantic along a longitude one hundred leagues west of the Azores, giving all lands west of that line to Spain, and all lands east of it to Portugal. The new line was established 370 leagues west of the Cape Verde Islands, which gave the easternmost part of South America to Portugal. Because of the Treaty of Tordesillas, Brazil became part of the Portuguese empire. The independence of Portugal was recognized in 1179 (A). The Inquisition was introduced into Spain in 1478 (C). The Hapsburgs acquired Spain through a marriage alliance (E). The War of Spanish Succession took place in 1701–1714 (B).

79. **(B)**   Francis Drake began his career as a raider of Spanish shipping. He claimed a portion of the American west coast for England in 1579 and returned to England in 1580 by circumnavigating the globe. Queen Elizabeth I (1558–1603) knighted him aboard the *Golden Hind*. Magellan (A) was born in Portugal but served Spain; although his crew completed the first voyage around the world in 1522, he died while crossing the Pacific Ocean. Hawkins (E) was a privateer at the time of Francis Drake and was knighted by the queen, but he was not celebrated as the first Englishman to circumnavigate the world, nor was Hudson (C). Cabot (D) sailed for the English, but was Italian by birth.

80. **(C)**   The artwork is taken from a page of the *Lindisfarne Gospels*, a manuscript book on parchment produced around 700 C.E. at the monastery of Lindisfarne, England; it shows Irish (Celtic) influence. Artwork in medieval books is called "illumination," and such intricate pen-and-ink designs are characteristic of Celtic art. Although Islamic, Persian, and Turkish art (A, D, E) had a similar geometric quality, the stylized outline of a cross in the midst of the designs should intimate the Christian character of the piece. It is not a Gothic miniature (B) because the Gothic style, which appeared in the twelfth century, was not influenced by Celtic art and was not characterized by such complexity of interwoven patterns. Note that "miniature" is another name for an illumination; it is sometimes so named because the pigment was made from *minium*, the Latin word for red lead.

81. **(B)**   Although the Huns threatened to sack Rome in 452 C.E., they turned back after Pope Leo I spoke with their leader, Attila, and dissuaded him. This event was of considerable significance, for it suggested the future role that the papacy would play in filling the power vacuum left by the gradual disintegration of the Roman imperial administration in the West. One should be careful to distinguish between the fall of the city of Rome and the fall of the Roman Empire; the former occurred several times, while the latter was actually a slow process of diminishing power rather than a sudden

collapse. The Celtic tribes known as the Gauls (A) sacked Rome for the first time in 390 B.C.E., and they threatened the Romans for centuries after. Their continuing menace motivated Julius Caesar to conquer their homeland in a series of campaigns from 58 to 50 B.C.E.; Caesar's political standing was thus greatly enhanced by defeating a dangerous traditional enemy. There after, the city of Rome was not seriously threatened by foreign invaders until the fifth century C.E., when it was sacked twice: in 410, by the Visigoths (E); and in 455, by the Vandals (D). The city of Rome was attacked again during the Middle Ages, in 846, this time by the Saracens (the name that medieval Christians gave to the Muslims), who had gained control of North Africa, Spain, and the islands in the Mediterranean Sea (C).

82. **(E)** The *Corpus Juris Civilis*, which the Emperor Justinian (527–565) commissioned in the sixth century, became the principal textbook for the study of Roman law, which scholars at Bologna revived in the eleventh century. Their method was to "gloss" this basic text, that is, to write comments on passages that required elaboration. The three other major fields of advanced study at medieval universities—canon law, medicine, and theology—proceeded by similar methods. Gratian's *Decretum* (D) was the textbook for the study of canon law, or church law, which was based on the pronouncements of councils and popes. Galen's works (C) were taken as a standard in medicine. Lombard's *Sententiae* (B) was the textbook for theology. Aquinas' *Summa* (A) became the basic text of Catholic doctrine in the later Middle Ages, but it was not written until the thirteenth century.

83. **(B)** William the Silent, or William I, prince of Orange (1533–1584), opposed the regime of the Spanish king Philip II, who controlled the Netherlands and established the Inquisition to persecute Dutch Protestants. William aided a rebellion against Spanish rule. He carried on the struggle as the leader of the Union of Utrecht, an alliance of Dutch provinces against Spain formed in 1579. Although William was assassinated five years later and the struggle for independence continued into the seventeenth century, the Union of Utrecht served as the foundation for the Dutch state.

84. **(C)** Henry II Plantagenet never ruled the duchy of Saxony, which was part of the Holy Roman Empire (Germany) until 1180, when the Emperor Frederick I (1152–1190) dissolved it as a political unit to punish its rebellious duke, Henry the Lion (the duchy was later reconstituted). Henry II was a member of the House of Anjou, a noble dynasty in northwestern France, and thus inherited the county of Anjou (A) and the duchy of Normandy (B) from his father, Geoffrey Plantagenet (who died in 1151). Through his marriage to Eleanor of Aquitaine in 1152, Henry II acquired the western half of France, including

the duchy of Aquitaine (D). In 1154 he inherited the kingdom of England (E) through his mother Matilda (Maud), the daughter of King Henry I of England (1100–1135). Although Matilda had been designated the rightful heiress by her father, she was deprived of her inheritance by her cousin, Stephen of Blois (reigned 1135–1154), whom Henry II had to fight in order to be recognized as the rightful heir to the throne. Henry II later invaded Ireland and forced Wales and Scotland to recognize him as overlord, but much of his empire was established through peaceful means. The rise of the Angevin Empire demonstrates how marriage in medieval Europe could be a powerful political tool.

85. **(E)** The Magna Carta was concerned primarily with the protection of feudal privileges traditionally held by the English barons against royal attempts to expand the powers of the monarchy. This document was precipitated by King John's effort to raise money for his ongoing war against France by demanding new taxes (C) without first consulting his barons, as he was bound to do by feudal law and custom. There was no need to establish a centralized judicial system for the entire realm (D), for King John's father, Henry II (1154–1189), had already achieved that. The Magna Carta, as a document produced by the barons for the protection of their existing feudal privileges, was certainly not concerned with abolishing serfdom (B). Political reform for the sake of establishing parliamentary government (A) was not attempted until 1258, when a committee of barons, known as the Oxford Parliament, forced Henry III (1216–1272) to share power with them. Despite the Magna Carta's narrow focus, the document was cited centuries later as an early milestone in the gradual process of extending freedom to all inhabitants of England, and thus a key moment in the evolution of western democracy.

86. **(D)** The purpose of the College of Cardinals, founded in 1059, was (and is) to elect the pope. By founding an electoral college restricted to members of the church hierarchy, reformers hoped to keep laymen, such as emperors, kings, or the Roman nobility, from installing their own candidates for political ends. The Babylonian Captivity took place from 1309 to 1377 (A), followed by the Great Schism from 1378 to 1417 (B), which was ended by the Council of Constance. The university of Paris did not appear until the twelfth century (C), and canon lawyers were trained in universities such as Bologna, which revived the study of law in the eleventh century (E).

87. **(B)** Greek and Latin Christians, having become estranged over theological and political issues, excommunicated one another in the year 1054, the traditional date marking the Great Schism beween the eastern and western churches. The main theological point of contention was the Latin

church's use of the *filioque* clause in the Nicene Creed, whereby the Latins said that the Holy Spirit (the third person of the Trinity) proceeds from the Father "*and* the Son." The Greek church, by contrast, maintained the older formula, that the Holy Spirit proceeds from the Father only. This difference in theology caused friction since the ninth century, when Photius, the patriarch of Constantinople, critized the Latin church's unilateral alteration of the Nicene Creed. The two churches did not go their separate ways, however, until many years of tense relations were aggravated by political events. When Pope Leo IX (1048–1054) tried to extend the jurisdiction of the papacy by interfering in the affairs of the Greek church in southern Italy, the patriarch of Constantinople, Michael Caerularius (1043–1058), responded by closing down Latin churches in Constantinople. When a papal delegation arrived in 1054 to remonstrate, Caerularius refused to accept the papal claim to supremacy, and the two churches declared one another heretical, using the *filioque* clause as a theological justification for their division.

In 395 (A) the Roman Empire was divided into two halves for administrative purposes. This division did not imply a distinction of ecclesiastical jurisdiction but roughly corresponded to a linguistic division between Latin-speaking and Greek-speaking parts of the Empire, on which the later ecclesiastical division was based. In 1204 (C), the Latin Christians of the Fourth Crusade sacked Constantinople instead of proceeding to the Holy Land and established a short-lived Latin Empire that ruined any hope of reconciling the sundered churches. In 1378 (D), the Great Schism within the Latin church began, and in 1417 (E) it ended. During the intervening period the Latin church was divided at first between two, and later three, popes.

88. **(C)** The sculpture represents the Egyptian pharaoh Mycerinus and his queen; it was crafted around 2500 B.C.E., during the period of the Old Kingdom. The royal head-dress (*nemes*) worn by the male figure is characteristically Egyptian.

89. **(C)** Girolamo Savonarola (1452–1498) was a Dominican friar who lived in Florence at the height of the Italian Renaissance, but he urged asceticism and repentance of sins rather than the humanistic studies that the others advocated as a path to moral improvement. Denouncing the wealthy Medici family who supported humanism, Savonarola succeeded in having them temporarily exiled, but he ultimately failed to reform Florence into the ideal Christian government that he hoped; his attempt ended in his execution as a heretical fanatic. Coluccio Salutati (1331–1406) (B) was a Florentine statesman who developed an ideology of civic humanism. Lorenzo Valla (1407–1457) (D) recommended the study of Greek in order to renew

Christian theology by a careful re-reading of the New Testament according to the principles of historical linguistics. Marsilio Ficino (1433–1499) (A), who was supported by the Medici family, advocated the study of Plato's dialogues as an aid to Christian theology, and he translated Platonic and Neoplatonic texts into Latin in order to make them available to readers who did not know Greek. Giovanni Pico della Mirandola (1463–1494) (E), who studied with Ficino, issued a kind of humanistic manifesto in his *Oration on the Dignity of Man*; however, he was influenced by Savonarola's preaching toward the end of his life.

90. **(E)** Witches were not persecuted as intensively in the Middle Ages as they were in early modern times. Medieval accusations of witchcraft tended to be isolated incidents, whereas those during the sixteenth century tended to result in numerous convictions. While the medieval Inquisition of the thirteenth century established an environment of suspicion, and the manual known as *The Hammer of Witches* (published in 1486 by two Dominican inquisitors) systematized the process of trying suspects, it was the environment of the religious wars that fanned the flames of persecution. Both Catholics and Protestants tried and executed thousands of witches. The Enlightenment finally put an end to the witch-craze.

91. **(C)** The Hundred Years' War (1337–1453) was fought between France and England, with Burgundy aiding the English for a time. Otto III of Germany, the Holy Roman Emperor from 980 to 1002, died long before the event took place. Actually lasting some 116 years, the Hundred Years' War did not consist of continuous fighting but was frequently interrupted with truces. All of the individuals mentioned were involved in the last phase of the fighting, which began with the invasion of France by Henry V (1413–1422) (A). Philip the Good, the duke of Burgundy (B), initially aided England. In 1430 he captured Joan of Arc (E) and delivered her to the English, who executed her as a heretic. Joan had rallied the French, however, and in 1435 Philip abandoned the English to become the ally of the French king, Charles VII (1422–1461) (D), who saw the conflict end at last in victory for France.

92. **(C)** The Persians ruled the largest empire of the ancient Near East until the time of the Macedonian king Alexander the Great (336–323 B.C.E.), whose empire included not only the former holdings of the Persians, but also Egypt and Greece. The Persians had conquered the Neo-Babylonians (D), who had conquered the Assyrians (A). The empires of the Sumerians (E) and Hittites (B) had ceased to exist many centuries before Alexander the Great was born and were considerably smaller than the empires of the Assyrians, Neo-Bablyonians, and Persians.

93. **(C)** Francis Bacon (1561–1626) recommended *induction* as the best method for the advance of scientific knowledge. Inductive reasoning begins with particular instances and draws general conclusions. It is contrary to *deduction*, which proceeds from the general to the particular (B)—in other words, deduction begins with general principles and uses them to derive conclusions about specific instances. Bacon supported the empirical method, which emphasized that knowledge is derived from experience (D). Thus, Bacon believed that science should conduct experiments and use its observations (empiricism) to draw general conclusions formulated as natural laws (induction). Although Bacon theorized about science, he himself was not a practicing scientist (A). Bacon saw scientific progress as a collaborative effort that could benefit from the foundation of scientific academies, but he did not suggest the foundation of the Royal Society to Parliament (E). This scientific association was founded in 1660 and received a royal charter in 1662, long after Bacon's death.

94. **(A)** The triumphal arch was a characteristically Roman architectural design, built by the emperors as monuments to commemorate military victories, and thus to display imperial power. The structure shown in the photograph is the Arch of Titus, which was erected in 81 C.E. by the emperor Domitian (81–96 C.E.) to commemorate the conquest of Judea by his brother Titus in 70 C.E.; Titus had just died, having ruled as emperor from 79 to 81 C.E.

95. **(C)** Michelangelo Buonarroti (1472–1564) was, with Leonardo da Vinci and Raphael, one of the three great artists of the later Italian Renaissance. He finished the design of St. Peter's Basilica in the Vatican, sculpted the larger-than-life statue of *David* in Florence, painted the Sistine ceiling, and wrote memorable verse as well. The dramatic poses of Michelangelo's figures gave rise to Mannerism, and his volatile personality defined the modern image of the artist as a tormented genius.

96. **(A)** Thomas More (1478–1535) was an English humanist and statesman who hoped to reform Christian society. His *Utopia* depicted an imaginary island with a government founded upon Christian principles, where property was held communally, the individual worked for the good of his or her neighbors rather than private gain, and tolerance was a basic principle. More worked toward his vision of such a society by participating in English government and in 1529 became King Henry VIII's lord chancellor. However, his support of Rome in the dispute between the king and the pope resulted in his imprisonment and execution.

97. **(C)** Michael Servetus was executed in Geneva as a heretic at the recommendation of John Calvin (1509–1564). Thus, the reformers were often no

more tolerant of dissenting opinions than were the Catholics. Servetus's principal heresy, offensive to Catholics and Protestants alike, was his denial of the Trinity.

98. **(A)** Germanic barbarians were not a serious threat to the Roman Republic but to the Empire. During the age of the Republic, the only threat posed by Germanic tribes was that of the Cimbri and Teutones, who were defeated in southern Gaul by the general Marius in 102–101 B.C.E. The fall of the Roman Republic was due to internal factors, including the prominence of the institution of clientage (C), whereby Romans looked to a wealthy patron for their security rather than directly to the state, and the professionalization of the army (E), which made soldiers loyal to their general, who supplied them with pay and pensions, rather than the Republic, which did not. These two institutions—the system of clientage and the professionalized army—were used by wealthy citizens (B), such as Marius, Sulla, and the six members of the First and Second Triumvirates, to establish a base of political power which could be used to oppose the Senate. The Senate itself was responsible for much of the weakening of the Republic, since its selfish reluctance to share effective political power with the Roman people and their allies precipitated most of the crises that eventually brought about their own collapse (D). There was nothing foreordained in the fall of the Republic. Even though it was a form of government that was best suited to meet the needs of a small city-state and ill-equipped to administer an immense empire, its constitution was also adaptable, and it could arguably have been modified for effective administration had the Senate turned aside from its stubborn conservatism and enacted timely reforms.

99. **(E)** The Dutch did not take a leading role in the earliest voyages of discovery, which were headed by the Portuguese and Spanish, but they were better equipped than most European powers to take advantage of economic possibilities once the discoveries were made. The Dutch did not engage in overseas exploration until 1600. When they did, the government of the Dutch Republic of the United Provinces, which was dominated by businessmen (C), took a very proactive role in encouraging commerce. It sponsored the Dutch East India Company, a highly successful joint-stock company for long-distance commercial voyages (B). The Dutch also enjoyed advantages in ship design and geography. Their merchant vessels, known as "flyships," were specially designed to maximize cargo space (A), and their position on the North Sea enabled them to act as middlemen between the Baltic Sea and the Iberian peninsula, which was the port of entry for New World commodities transported by Spain and Portugal (D).

100. **(B)** Jean Bodin supported royal absolutism. He argued that kings should not be restrained by laws but should enjoy supreme power over their subjects (however, he also believed that monarchs should follow natural law and custom in exercising their authority). Thus, he opposed the claims of emperors (A), popes (E), and ordinary citizens (D) over the authority of kings. Bodin died long before the eighteenth-century thinkers known as physiocrats (C) put forward their economic theories.

101. **(B)** The Spanish Armada was not intended to challenge Dutch naval superiority because the Dutch had not yet achieved independence from Spain and therefore did not yet control a powerful fleet of their own. The Dutch rebelled against Spain in 1566 and were aided by England between 1585 and 1587. Philip II realized that he could not suppress the Dutch insurgency unless England was neutralized, so he assembled an armada of 130 ships to punish the English intervention (C) by invading England (A). He also hoped to restore Catholicism in England (D) by deposing the Protestant Queen, Elizabeth I (E). However, Philip's armada was destroyed by storms and the English navy.

102. **(D)** Sculptures set upon sarcophagi (coffins) depicting a husband and wife in a cheerful attitude were characteristically Etruscan. The angular features of the figures, especially their sharp, exaggerated smiles and almond-shaped eyes, are also typical of Etruscan statues.

103. **(C)** Despite the threat of violent revolution, the Athenians did not tamper with property ownership. The city-states of Greece tried to relieve socio-economic tensions primarily through colonization (D), which reduced pressure on scarce resources by removing part of the population overseas, and tyranny (E), whereby a dictator stood above the law and settled disputes. Most city-states ended up reforming their political constitutions (A), as nobles who dominated the community conceded a share of power to the lower classes. In Athens, the constitutional reformer Solon (c. 594 B.C.E.) cancelled the debts owed by poor citizens to wealthy citizens (B), but he refused to seize the property of the wealthy in order to redistribute their land to the poor (C).

104. **(B)** The discovery of the New World led to conquests of native peoples from whom large amounts of gold and silver were taken and sent to Europe. With more money in circulation, the value of the currency declined: between 1500 and 1600, the prices of most commodities rose about 300 percent. Although the slave trade was an important part of the new economy, demand for slaves was highest in the colonies, where they were needed to work on plantations; relatively few were brought to Europe (A), and these came from Africa rather than the New World. The stimulation of trade did

not strengthen craft guilds, which were unable to keep up with the increased volume of trade (C). Their inability to meet heightened demand gave capitalist entrepreneurs an opportunity to reorganize manufacturing, resulting in the putting-out and gathering-in systems of labor organization, which bypassed the guilds. The dramatic rise in entrepreneurial commerce prompted governments to interfere in various ways, resulting in a system of economic management known as mercantilism (D).

105. **(E)** Feudalism does not describe the relationship between a lord and his serfs (which is called manorialism), but rather the relationship between one member of the nobility and another. It takes its name from the Latin word *feudum*, which means "fief"—a grant of land that a high-ranking noble, called a *lord*, made to a lower-ranking noble, called a *vassal*, in exchange for military and other service, such as duty at the lord's court of law (C). If the fief received was large enough, the vassal could grant portions of it to yet lower-ranking nobles and thus become a lord in relation to his own vassals (a practice called *subinfeudation*). The exchange of land for service made the relationship contractual, and the swearing of loyalty oaths ("fealty") made it personal as well (A). Since this form of political organization depended on personal relationships and distributed power in a highly fragmented form that emphasized government at the local level, it was characterized by weak central authority (B). In theory, the king was supreme, but in practice his nobles might be stronger and own more land than he—as in the example of Henry II of England (1154–1189), whose possession of territories in France made him a vassal of the French king, yet whose personal possessions and power dwarfed that of his feudal lord.

It should be noted that feudalism was not a single "system," for feudal practices varied considerably from one locality to another and changed over time as well; it is, rather, a historical term of convenience to describe certain broad similarities discernible between different regions. Feudalism reached its zenith during the twelfth and thirteenth centuries, and particularly in northern France, England, and the Low Countries (D); the feudal model does not describe medieval society as well in other times and places. For example, the Carolingian kings did grant plots of land to their soldiers, but their grants were only temporary (limited to the period of the vassal's service) and were called *benefices* rather than fiefs. In contrast, the adoption of the term *fief* around the year 1000 indicated a change of policy: the grant was no longer merely for the period of the vassal's service but became hereditary, so that the vassal's heir would receive the fief and owe service to the lord (or the lord's heir) just as his father had.

Feudalism was closely related to manorialism, which is named after the manor that the lord held as a fief, and focuses attention on the relationship between the serfs who worked on the manor and their lord. Manorialism is also called seignorialism, from the French word for lord (*seigneur*). Like feudalism, manorialism (or seignorialism) is a historical term of convenience, describing broad similarities among varying local forms of economic administration rather than a single universally consistent form of resource management.

106. **(C)**   Although both Socrates and Jesus urged moral reform, only Socrates outlined the political structure of an ideal government, as shown in Plato's *Republic*. Jesus took a more spiritual approach which insisted that a person can repent of sins and live a moral life under any external form of government, even that of the Roman Empire, which many Jews of his day considered intolerably evil. Although Jesus' insistence on living up to a moral code of social justice had political implications, he did not offer a blueprint for an ideal form of government, and he did not even present a clear structure for the organization of the Christian community. Thus, although he appointed St. Peter as the head of the Christian community, the institution of the papacy was not clearly enunciated until centuries later. Moreover, the organization of the early Church into dioceses, which imitated the structure of the Roman Empire, evolved as required by necessity. Neither Socrates nor Jesus wrote any books (A), but relied solely on oral instruction; their teachings were later preserved in writing by their followers—Plato recorded the teachings of Socrates in his *Dialogues*, and the teachings of Jesus were preserved in the four Gospels attributed to his disciples, Matthew, Mark, Luke, and John. Jesus and Socrates both focused on justice and the moral life (B). Both were executed by their governments (D)—the Athenian government condemned Socrates to death by drinking hemlock because they feared he was corrupting public morals with his philosophical approach to religion, and Jesus was crucified at the command of the Roman governor of Judea, Pontius Pilate, who feared that Jesus might start a revolt against the Empire. Neither Socrates nor Jesus tried to escape death, for both believed that the soul was immortal (E).

107. **(E)**   The Treaty of Westphalia, named after the German province in which the peace-talks occurred, formally ended the Thirty Years' War (B) and revised the political landscape of Europe. It recognized the sovereignty of two relatively new states—Switzerland and the United Provinces of the Netherlands (A)—and it effectively deprived the Holy Roman Emperor of any real power over the German principalities by granting each of them the right to make its own alliances and declare war (C). It also gave Sweden some of the Empire's Baltic territories, granted France a few fortress towns on the border, recognized France's claims in Alsace, and gave both Sweden and France the right to vote in the imperial diet. With regard to religion, the treaty largely restored the status quo at the beginning of the war. It reaffirmed the principle that the ruler of each of the German princi-

palities should decide the religious alignment of his state (D) and added that any prince who changes his denomination forfeits his right to rule—a clause intended to prevent the further spread of Protestantism within the Empire.

108. **(D)**   Elizabeth's reign was characterized by her judicious cooperation with Parliament. She knew when to enlist Parliament for support, when to compromise, and when to challenge parliamentary attempts to set royal policy. For example, she opposed calls by the Puritans to eliminate all Catholic traditions and strove instead for a religious compromise that was acceptable to moderate Catholics and Protestants (C). She was careful not to reveal her political ambitions too openly and did not express a belief in the divine right of kings, unlike her successor, James I (1603–1625), who actually weakened the monarchy by his frank assertions that he enjoyed his power from God alone (A). Elizabeth did not produce an heir. She never married, and was in fact known as the "Virgin Queen" (B). She did not maintain peace with Spain (E), but precipitated a major confrontation (the attack of the Spanish Armada in 1588) by supporting the movement for Dutch independence.

109. **(E)**   Henry the Navigator was Prince of Portugal, and therefore sought to promote Portuguese preeminence in voyages of discovery. In fact, the expeditions he promoted (although he himself did not participate in them) were the earliest, beginning after the Portuguese capture of Ceuta in North Africa in 1415. Prince Henry's motivations were scientific (A), military and religious (B, C), and economic (D).

110. **(B)**   Tiberius (14–37 C.E.) was the successor of Augustus, and it was during his reign that Jesus of Nazareth was crucified in Jerusalem by the regional governor, Pontius Pilate, without the emperor's knowledge. Subsequently, the Christians were too few in number for Tiberius to organize persecutions against them. Nero (54–68 C.E.) was the first Roman emperor to persecute the Christians, blaming them for a conflagration that destroyed much of Rome in 64 C.E. Most of the persecutions that Christians suffered during the first two centuries C.E. were not organized by the emperors but were the result of mob violence. Official imperial persecution of the Christians became fairly frequent when they had become numerous enough to be seen as a real threat to the imperial system because of their refusal to worship the emperor. Marcus Aurelius (161–180) saw them as a threat, as did Decius (249–251) and Diocletian (284–305), who organized persecutions to eradicate what they regarded as a danger to the welfare of the state.

111. **(D)**   The map represents areas controlled by Protestants during the sixteenth century. Scandinavia and the northern regions of the Continent

were dominated by Lutherans, England was dominated by Anglicans, and the southern area, Switzerland, was dominated by Calvinists.

112. **(C)**   The First Triumvirate was an informal alliance made in 60 B.C.E. between the generals Pompey, Crassus, and Julius Caesar, who joined ranks to oppose the power of the Senate and carve the Roman territories into personal spheres of interest. The First Triumvirate ended in 53 B.C.E. when Crassus died while campaigning in the Near East; the remaining two generals could not agree on redrawing their spheres of interest and led Rome into a civil war, in which Pompey was killed (48 B.C.E.). Lepidus, Mark Antony, and Octavian (later called Augustus Caesar) were members of the Second Triumvirate, founded in 43 B.C.E. (A, B, D). Sulla (E) was an earlier general, who defied Roman tradition by serving as dictator for more than the customary six months. He vied with his rival, Marius, for control of Rome and retired from politics in 80 B.C.E.

113. **(A)**   Diocletian (284–305 C.E.) took the step of dividing the Empire up into four prefectures and twelve dioceses in the hope of streamlining imperial administration to deal with external and internal threats. He hoped that the appointment of co-emperors in each of the four prefectures would enable a more efficient response to threats arising on the borders, since a single ruler could not deal with multiple simultaneous invasions at opposite ends of the Empire. He also hoped that the threat posed by provincial generals and governors, who sometimes used their positions to attempt a coup d'etat, could be eliminated by reducing the size and increasing the number of the provinces, thereby putting fewer resources in the hands of individual administrators; these numerous provinces were organized into twelve dioceses to ease their management. The system of four co-emperors is known as the Tetrarchy. Constantine (306–337 C.E.) abolished the Tetrarchy when it proved ineffective (D). Decius (249–251 C.E.) did not institute major reforms during his brief reign; he died defending the northern borders from Germanic barbarians (C). Answers (B) and (E) cannot be correct because Claudius and Hadrian were emperors during the *Pax Romana* (27 B.C.E.–180 C.E.).

114. **(B)**   Before his election as Holy Roman Emperor in 1519, Charles was king of Spain. Thus, he is known as Charles I of Spain (1516–1556) and Charles V, Holy Roman Emperor (1519–1558). By acquiring the title of emperor, Charles added the domains of the Empire to his Hapsburg possessions, which made him the most powerful man in Europe. However, much of his power was hollow, for his authority was challenged by the Protestant princes in Germany, and his wars against them resulted in a stalemate. He also fought the French and the Italians, as well as the Ottoman Turks, who besieged Vienna in 1529.

115. **(D)**   The dome of the cathedral in Florence was designed by Filippo Brunelleschi (1377–1446) and built between 1420 and 1436. It is the pre-eminent example of early Renaissance architecture.

116. **(C)**   The presence of a dynamic Inquisition in Spain prevented Protestantism from being tolerated there. Instituted in 1478 to bring uniformity to Spanish religion by persecuting the Moors and the Jews, the Inquisition was also a powerful deterrent against the rise of Protestant influences on the Iberian peninsula. Protestantism arose in the Holy Roman Empire (A) and retained its hold over the northern part of the realm. Although Philip II of Spain (1556–1598) tried to use the Inquisition to suppress Protestantism in the Netherlands (B), his efforts succeeded only in sparking an independence movement there. Protestants in France (D) were known as Huguenots, and a Huguenot even became the King of France, Henry IV (1589–1610). England (E) broke away from Rome at the decision of Henry VIII (1509–1547), and it became more fully Protestant in its theology during the reign of his son, Edward VI (1547–1553).

117. **(D)**   The Benedictine *Rule* was exceptional for its balance of three basic activities that defined the monastic regimen: prayer, study, and work. Thus, monks who lived according to the Benedictine *Rule* spent roughly equal amounts of time praying and chanting hymns, reading the Scriptures and works of theology, and engaging in manual labor (such as raising crops or copying books). It was not the only monastic rule available in Europe (B), most of which commonly required vows of poverty (the renunciation of personal possessions), chastity (acceptance of celibacy), and obedience (submission to the will of an abbot) (A). The *Rule* composed by St. Benedict focused on cooperation between monks living in a community rather than the development of exceptional individuals who could practice amazing acts of asceticism (E), and it was thus ideally suited to serve as a model for most people who felt a calling to the religious life. This broad appeal was a major factor for its success. Although the Benedictine *Rule* did not recommend harsh punishments for offenses, it did allow corporal punishment as a means of disciplining otherwise unmanageable individuals (C).

118. **(C)**   As Roman emperors found themselves forced to defend the borders against Germanic barbarians in the north and the Sassanians in the east, they moved the capital closer to the scene of battle in order to coordinate the defense more effectively. Roman emperors began to use Milan as their capital rather than Rome, and Diocletian (284–305 c.e.) temporarily transferred his capital to the eastern city of Nicomedia in Asia Minor. Constantine (306–337 c.e.) made the transfer permanent in 330 c.e. by founding a new capital near the site of ancient Byzantium, which was renamed Constantinople. Not only

was Constantinople closer to the embattled borders, but the wealthiest provinces were also in the east, which made the collection of taxes and the exercise of administration easier.

The spread of *latifundia* (large estates) worked by slaves did spark several menacing revolts (E), but this development occurred during the late Republic following the Third Punic War (149–146 B.C.E.), centuries before the capital was transferred to the east. High unemployment in Rome (A) was kept under control through a policy of "bread and circuses." Rome was sacked by the Gauls (B), but in 390 B.C.E.—long before it aspired to the status of a great empire. Finally, the sack of Rome by the Visigoths (D) occurred in 410 C.E.—long after the capital had been transferred to the east.

119. **(D)** "Mendicant" is derived from the Latin word *mendicare*, which means "to beg." The first of the mendicant orders was founded by St. Francis of Assisi (1181–1226), who reacted against the rising wealth and greed of thirteenth-century Italian society by embracing poverty as the ideal form of Christian life. His complete renunciation of private property required him to beg for his sustenance, and the life of Christian simplicity that he manifested so inspired others that they flocked to follow his example. Pope Innocent III (1198–1216) recognized his followers as the Order of Friars Minor, more commonly known as the Franciscans. Like the Benedictine monks, Franciscan friars had to renounce personal property; unlike the Benedictines, they did not live in monasteries but traveled among the people (C) on a mission of preaching and good works (E). Since they did not have monasteries to support themselves, they depended on the charity of Christian society for their support, and thus became known as mendicants, or beggars. Their contribution to society was so greatly appreciated that the Order soon became very wealthy through donations and established friaries (dormitories) all over western Europe. Among those inspired by St. Francis was St. Dominic (c. 1170–1221), who founded another mendicant brotherhood, the Order of Preachers, which specialized in the conversion of heretics (B). In time the Dominicans were put in charge of the Inquisition (A).

120. **(E)** Rome and Carthage fought the Punic Wars. The name is derived from the Latin word *Punicus*, which means "Phoenician," and refers to the descendents of the Phoenician settlers who founded Carthage. The Romans and Carthaginians fought three wars over the course of two centuries (from the third to the second B.C.E.) to determine which of them would control an empire dominating the shores of the Mediterranean Sea.

▼
PRACTICE
TEST 2

PRACTICE
TEST 2

CLEP WESTERN CIVILIZATION I

PRACTICE TEST 2

(Answer sheets appear in the back of this book.)

TIME: 90 Minutes
120 Questions

DIRECTIONS: Each of the questions or incomplete statements below is followed by five possible answers or completions. Select the best choice in each case and fill in the corresponding oval on the answer sheet.

1. Most of the earliest examples of cuneiform suggest that the Sumerians invented writing to

   (A) preserve epic poetry.

   (B) codify the laws.

   (C) record business transactions and keep inventories of goods.

   (D) demonstrate mathematical theorems.

   (E) cast magic spells that would control the flooding of the Tigris and Euphrates rivers.

2. The Code of Hammurabi was

   (A) a collection of laws in which justice was meted out by the king on behalf of the gods according to a principle of harsh punishments which corresponded to specific crimes.

   (B) an early experiment in democracy, by which the nobles of ancient Mesopotamia elected their kings on behalf of the people.

   (C) an ancient text used by modern scholars to decipher cuneiform writing for the first time.

   (D) a body of beliefs for conducting honorable warfare, which was espoused by ancient warriors.

   (E) a set of instructions to help the kings of Mesopotamia organize the economy of their people.

3. During the period of the Old Kingdom in Egypt (c. 2700–c. 2200 B.C.E.), the Egyptians regarded the pharaoh as

   (A) the chief high priest.

   (B) a representative of the gods.

   (C) a god.

   (D) a figurehead with merely symbolic power.

   (E) the foremost citizen of the republic.

4. All of the following are true of King Nebuchadnezzar II (605–562 B.C.E.) EXCEPT

   (A) He was a member of the Neo-Babylonian dynasty.

   (B) He ordered the deportation of the ten tribes of Israel.

   (C) He built the Hanging Gardens for his wife.

   (D) He conquered the kingdom of Judah.

   (E) He destroyed Jerusalem and deported Jews to Babylon.

5.   Which of the following is NOT true of Ulrich Zwingli (1484–1531)?

   (A) He taught that it is not necessary to fast during Lent.

   (B) He banned the use of religious images in churches.

   (C) He agreed with Martin Luther on the doctrine of the Lord's Supper.

   (D) He died at a battle between Catholic and Protestant forces.

   (E) He abolished monasteries.

6.   "Their level of culture was at first relatively primitive in comparison to the contemporary civilizations of the ancient Near East, but their contacts with the people of Crete while trading and raiding in the eastern Mediterranean inspired certain advances, most notably the acquisition of writing and the use of the palace as an administrative center. Nevertheless, they remained politically divided in their mountainous homeland, banding together at times for the purpose of war."

   The people described above are known as the

   (A) Sumerians.

   (B) Mycenaeans.

   (C) Minoans.

   (D) Egyptians.

   (E) Phoenicians.

7.

The structure shown above is the

(A) Hagia Sophia in Constantinople

(B) Pont du Gard, an aqueduct in southern France

(C) Roman Colosseum

(D) Roman Pantheon

(E) Parthenon in Athens

8. The geography of Greece

(A) favored the formation of large, unified empires.

(B) made sea-faring impractical.

(C) favored the formation of small, self-governing city-states.

(D) kept the Greeks safe from foreign invasion.

(E) made political unification of the Greeks impossible.

9. Hoplites were Greek soldiers who fought in formations known as

(A) phalanxes.

(B) legions.

(C) triremes.

(D) maniples.

(E) squadrons.

10. The Romans were indebted to the Etruscans for all of the following EXCEPT

    (A) their alphabet.

    (B) the legion.

    (C) the practice of divination.

    (D) the arch.

    (E) techniques for draining marshes and building sewers.

11. All of the following were achievements of Augustus Caesar EXCEPT

    (A) He established a calendar consisting of 365 days which added an extra day every four years to keep the year in step with the seasons.

    (B) He established Rome's first police department.

    (C) He established Rome's first fire department.

    (D) He organized a grand building program in Rome.

    (E) He ended almost a century of civil wars in Rome.

12. The philosopher Plotinus (c. 200–270 c.e.) founded which school of philosophy?

    (A) Neoplatonism

    (B) Stoicism

    (C) Epicureanism

    (D) Skepticism

    (E) Neopythagoreanism

13. "Among his achievements are counted a monumental codification of law, the beautification of the capital through an ambitious building program, and the recovery of lands that had originally constituted the very heart of the empire. Yet early in his reign he nearly abdicated because of a massive riot that broke out at the chariot races, until his wife, who had formerly been a dancing girl, prompted him to risk his life and restore order."

The emperor described in the passage above is

(A) Heraclius.

(B) Marcus Aurelius.

(C) Commodus.

(D) Constantine.

(E) Justinian.

14. The relief shown below is an example of art that is characteristic of which of the following ancient cultures?

(A) Celtic

(B) Minoan

(C) Assyrian

(D) Greek

(E) Roman

15. In the ninth and tenth centuries C.E., western Europe suffered invasions from

    (A) Ostrogoths, Visigoths, and Vandals.

    (B) Vikings, Visigoths, and Vandals.

    (C) Vikings, Huns, and Mongols.

    (D) Lombards, Magyars, and Mongols.

    (E) Saracens, Vikings, and Magyars.

16. Which of the following groups of barbarians were NOT despised and dreaded as heretics by Catholic Christians?

    (A) Vandals

    (B) Lombards

    (C) Franks

    (D) Visigoths

    (E) Ostrogoths

17. The *Domesday Book* is

    (A) a *chanson de geste* composed in southern France in the twelfth century.

    (B) an inventory of property in Norman England used to determine taxes.

    (C) a manual for hunting witches written in the fifteenth century.

    (D) John Wycliffe's fourteenth-century translation of the Bible.

    (E) a medieval commentary on the Apocalypse (Book of Revelation).

18. The Russian national hero, Alexander Nevsky (c. 1220–1263), is best remembered for his victory over the

    (A) Turks.

    (B) Mongols.

    (C) Poles.

    (D) Byzantines.

    (E) Teutonic Knights.

19. The architectural feature below is characteristic of which of the following cultures?

(A) Germanic

(B) Greek

(C) Persian

(D) Celtic

(E) Assyrian

20. The primary aim of merchant guilds in the eleventh century was

(A) to restrain competition among craftsmen.

(B) to raise joint-stock companies.

(C) to lend money to kings and nobles.

(D) to protect their own members and wares.

(E) to promote the economic policy known as mercantilism.

21. "The followers of this ancient religious visionary saw reality in terms of a great struggle between the forces of good, led by Ahura Mazda, and the forces of evil, led by Ahriman. Human beings had to choose which side to join. At the end of time there would be a final battle and a day of judgment, when Ahriman would be defeated and his followers would suffer eternal torment while the followers of Ahura Mazda would be rewarded with eternal life."

The religious leader who inspired the view of reality described above was

(A) Amos.

(B) Zoroaster.

(C) Hammurabi.

(D) Isaiah.

(E) Akhenaton.

22. "Their entire society was organized on a permanent war-footing. Males began to receive military training from the age of seven and had to live in barracks until the age of thirty. Women received physical training and were hardened to a lifestyle without comforts in order to promote a militaristic mind-set. The citizen-soldiers were vigilant against the possibility of slave revolt, for most of the region's inhabitants had been conquered in war and worked the land against their will for the conquerors."

The paragraph above describes the people of

(A) Rome.

(B) Carthage.

(C) Sparta.

(D) Corinth.

(E) Athens.

23. The Dark Age of ancient Greece (c. 1100–800 B.C.E.) was caused by

(A) the Persian invasion of the Balkan peninsula.

(B) the fall of Troy.

(C) the migration of the Dorians into Mycenaean centers of civilization.

(D) the conquest of Minoan Crete by the Mycenaeans.

(E) the Roman invasion of Greece.

24.

The structure shown above was most likely built by the

(A) Romans.

(B) Arabs.

(C) Greeks.

(D) Turks.

(E) Celts.

25. Which of the following works could not have been written before the Edict of Milan (313 C.E.) was promulgated by Constantine the Great?

(A) *On the Nature of Things*, Lucretius

(B) *City of God*, Augustine of Hippo

(C) *Aeneid*, Virgil

(D) *On Farming*, Cato the Elder

(E) *Philippics*, Cicero

26. Which of the following is true of the tyrant Peisistratus?

(A) He was assassinated in a violent uprising of the Athenians.

(B) He instituted the harsh laws that governed Spartan society.

(C) He led the Macedonians in the conquest of Greece.

(D) He abandoned the constitutional reforms instituted by Solon.

(E) He instituted the festival of Dionysos at Athens, where Greek drama flourished.

27. The Waldensians were

    (A) monks who led the reform of the Church in the eleventh century.

    (B) Christian reformers who denounced the accumulation of wealth and were declared heretics at the Fourth Lateran Council (1215).

    (C) a commercial league of Mediterranean coastal towns headquartered in Lyons (southern France) during the twelfth to fifteenth centuries.

    (D) a mystery cult of the third century.

    (E) a military religious order, founded in the twelfth century, who were charged with the defense of pilgrims in the Holy Land.

28.

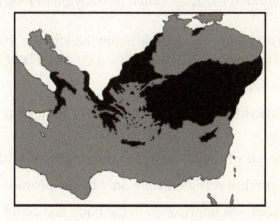

The areas shaded black on the map above represent territories controlled by

    (A) the Athenian Empire, around 450 B.C.E.

    (B) Alexander the Great, in 323 B.C.E.

    (C) Justinian the Great, in 565 C.E.

    (D) the Byzantine Empire, around 1000 C.E.

    (E) the Ottoman Turks, around 1400 C.E.

29. All of the following are true of the Persian king Cyrus the Great (559–530 B.C.E.) EXCEPT

    (A) He freed the Persians from domination under the Medes.

    (B) He established an empire that reached from the Indus valley to the shores of the Mediterreanean Sea.

    (C) He used respect and tolerance instead of cruelty and repression to gain the obedience of the subject peoples within his empire.

    (D) He abandoned the westward expansion of his empire after losing the battle of Salamis to the Greeks.

    (E) He allowed the Jews exiled in Babylon to return to Judah.

30. In contrast to Sumerian beliefs about the afterlife, the Egyptians of the Middle Kingdom (c. 2050–c. 1700 B.C.E.) and later believed that

    (A) there was no life after death.

    (B) the afterlife was a gloomy, shadowy form of existence, without joy.

    (C) all levels of society could enjoy a happy afterlife.

    (D) the afterlife was attainable only by the pharaoh.

    (E) the soul was imprisoned in the body and could be happy only when death released it.

31. "He was committed to the cause of reform. In order to free the Church from political manipulation, he challenged the emperor over the right to invest bishops. His claim that popes have the power to depose kings seemed proven when the emperor stood before him in the snow and begged for absolution. However, the emperor later forced him to flee Rome, and he died in exile. The struggle between popes and emperors over the appointment of bishops continued for a generation before it was resolved."

    The passage above describes the career of which of the following popes?

    (A) Pius II

    (B) Leo III

    (C) Innocent III

    (D) Gregory VII

    (E) Urban II

32. The Hanseatic League was

    (A) an organization of Italian communes for defense against the Holy Roman Empire.

    (B) a religious alliance of Swiss cantons for the promotion of Calvinism.

    (C) an opposition party against the Hapsburgs within the Holy Roman Empire.

    (D) a consortium of Danish and Swedish coastal cities for defense against English privateers.

    (E) a commercial association of northern German cities to promote trade in the Baltic Sea and the North Sea.

33. The most important geographical region for the exchange of ideas between Christian, Muslim, and Jewish scholars during the twelfth century was

    (A) Palestine.

    (B) Syria.

    (C) Spain.

    (D) Greece.

    (E) Italy.

34. The Greeks founded numerous colonies throughout the Mediterranean basin and the Black Sea from c. 700 to c. 550 B.C.E. primarily in order to

    (A) share Greek civilization with the barbarians.

    (B) found an empire uniting southern Europe, northern Africa, and the Near East.

    (C) relieve socio-economic tensions in mainland Greece.

    (D) counter the rising threat from the Roman Empire.

    (E) establish a network of commercial trading posts.

35. "If we win another battle against the Romans, we shall be utterly ruined."

    This remark was most likely said by which of the following leaders?

    (A) Scipio the Elder

    (B) Alexander the Great

    (C) Philip II of Macedon

    (D) Pyrrhus of Epirus

    (E) Xerxes

36. The appearance of the *latifundia* in the Roman Republic precipitated a severe political crisis because

    (A) this new magistracy had the power to veto the Senate, bringing Roman government to a standstill.

    (B) this new military formation made Rome so powerful that it could not assimilate its rapid conquests.

    (C) these desperate slaves from the newly-conquered provinces staged numerous large-scale revolts.

    (D) these private armies of wealthy patrician generals were obedient to their patrons rather than to the Senate.

    (E) these large estates drove small farmers out of business, causing high unemployment among the plebeians.

37. The democracy of Athens in the fifth century B.C.E. was revolutionary in the ancient world because

    (A) it extended the right to vote to women.

    (B) it outlawed slavery.

    (C) it gave *metics* (resident aliens) a voice in government.

    (D) all male citizens, not just those born into prominent or wealthy families, participated directly in the administration of government.

    (E) it united all of the Greek city-states in their fight against the Persians.

38. Which of the following Greek philosophers taught that virtue consists in choosing the golden mean and theorized that governments can be divided into three basic types (rule by the one, the few, and the many)?

    (A) Plato

    (B) Aristotle

    (C) Socrates

    (D) Pythagoras

    (E) Thales of Miletus

39. "Of the three great Athenian playwrights who are renowned for their tragedies, this one won fewer awards than his colleagues, yet his plays resonate more with modern audiences because of the psychological depth of his characters. His play *Medea* describes the gruesome murders committed by a sorceress who escaped punishment from the gods."

    Which of the following authors does the passage describe?

    (A) Aeschylus

    (B) Plato

    (C) Aristophanes

    (D) Sophocles

    (E) Euripides

40.

The standing sculpture shown above is known by art historians as a

(A) pediment.

(B) caryatid.

(C) Corinthian column.

(D) Doric column.

(E) frieze.

41. The decline of the *polis* in the Hellenistic period and the opening of the Near East to the Greeks after Alexander the Great's conquest of the Persian Empire led to the rise of a religion in the Mediterranean known as

(A) Epicureanism.

(B) Christianity.

(C) Mithraism.

(D) Stoicism.

(E) the Eleusinian Mysteries.

42. Machiavelli was critical of the Italian city-states for their

(A) opposition to the pope.

(B) use of violence to attain their goals.

(C) patronage of the arts.

(D) failure to honor treaties.

(E) dependency on mercenaries.

43. An artist whose use of copper engraving and woodcuts extended the principles of Renaissance art far beyond Italy was

    (A) Jan van Eyck.

    (B) Titian.

    (C) Sandro Botticelli.

    (D) Albrecht Dürer.

    (E) Donatello.

44. The Battle of Lepanto (1571) was a victory for

    (A) an alliance of Christian states against the Ottoman Turks.

    (B) the Ottoman Turks against the Holy Roman Empire.

    (C) the French against the Ottoman Turks.

    (D) the English against the Spanish.

    (E) the Venetians against the Spanish.

45. From the sixteenth to the seventeenth centuries, the Dutch fought a struggle for independence against

    (A) Burgundy.

    (B) France.

    (C) England.

    (D) Spain.

    (E) the Holy Roman Empire.

46. An important feature of Renaissance art that originated outside Italy was

    (A) the use of linear perspective.

    (B) the use of oil paint as a new medium.

    (C) the revival of nudes in sculpture.

    (D) the revival of classical themes.

    (E) the revival of the dome as an architectural feature.

47. An entrepreneur who had offices in many financial centers of Europe and served as banker to the Hapsburg family was

    (A) Jacques Coeur.

    (B) Jakob Fugger.

    (C) Wat Tyler.

    (D) Francesco Guicciardini.

    (E) Cesare Borgia.

48. The wife of Henry II of France (1547–1559), who as Queen Mother used her influence both to set policy in France and to introduce cultural features of the Italian Renaissance beyond the Alps, was

    (A) Christine de Pisan.

    (B) Catherine de' Medici.

    (C) Catherine of Aragon.

    (D) Henrietta Maria.

    (E) Eleanor of Aquitaine.

49. Which of the following is true of the joint-stock company of the sixteenth and seventeenth centuries?

    (A) It was made up exclusively of traders.

    (B) It was an innovative method of labor organization.

    (C) It revived the guilds.

    (D) It was an association of investors.

    (E) It was free of government interference.

50. The Society of Jesus was founded in the sixteenth century by

    (A) John Knox.

    (B) John Calvin.

    (C) Thomas Erastus.

    (D) Ulrich Zwingli.

    (E) Ignatius of Loyola.

51. All of the following made contributions to astronomy EXCEPT

    (A) Galileo Galilei.

    (B) Tycho Brahe.

    (C) Copernicus.

    (D) William Harvey.

    (E) Johannes Kepler.

52. Which of the following was the most commonly imported colonial commodity to Europe around 1600?

    (A) cotton fabrics

    (B) spices

    (C) coffee

    (D) tea

    (E) silk

53.

The building interior shown above is that of

    (A) the Hagia Sophia in Constantinople.

    (B) the Colosseum in Rome.

    (C) the Dome of the Rock Mosque in Jerusalem.

    (D) the Great Mosque at Cordoba.

    (E) Notre Dame in Paris.

54. Battles were fought at all of the following sites during the Persian Wars (490 and 480–479 B.C.E.) EXCEPT

    (A) Marathon.

    (B) Salamis.

    (C) Zama.

    (D) Plataea.

    (E) Thermopylae.

55. The Peloponnesian War (431–404 B.C.E.) was caused by

    (A) Xerxes's invasion of Greece.

    (B) a Roman invasion of Macedon.

    (C) an Athenian invasion of the Peloponnesus.

    (D) imperialistic conflict between Rome and Carthage.

    (E) Sparta's fear of Athenian imperialistic expansion.

56. Which of the following was NOT a reason for the rapid conquest of the Near East and North Africa by the Arabs during the seventh century?

    (A) resentment against Constantinople for the suppression of Monophysitism in the Byzantine provinces of the Near East

    (B) long wars of attrition between the Byzantine and Sassanian Empires

    (C) uninterrupted unity among the Arab tribes

    (D) the zeal of a new religion proclaimed by the prophet Muhammad

    (E) overpopulation in Arab lands

57. Lorenzo the Magnificent, the Florentine patron of arts, was a member of which influential dynasty?

    (A) Borgia

    (B) Hapsburg

    (C) Medici

    (D) Sforza

    (E) Visconti

58. A Dutch humanist who published an edition of the Greek New Testament was

    (A) Marsilio Ficino.

    (B) John Colet.

    (C) Johann Reuchlin.

    (D) Desiderius Erasmus.

    (E) Thomas More.

59. Which of the following threatened to interfere with the rise of the French nation during the fifteenth century by establishing itself as a powerful state on the frontier between France and the Holy Roman Empire?

    (A) Aquitaine

    (B) Aragon

    (C) Burgundy

    (D) Navarre

    (E) Granada

60. Martin Luther was NOT executed as a heretic because

    (A) he was able to escape to neutral Switzerland.

    (B) he won the support of the Holy Roman Emperor.

    (C) he won the support of many of the German princes.

    (D) he sided with the German peasants in their revolt.

    (E) the Roman Catholic Church no longer recommended capital punishment for religious dissidents.

61. Which of the following gave religious toleration to the Huguenots?

    (A) Treaty of Westphalia

    (B) Treaty of Tordesillas

    (C) Edict of Milan

    (D) Edict of Worms

    (E) Edict of Nantes

62. The city of Rome was sacked in 1527 by the forces of

    (A) the Venetian Republic.

    (B) the Ottoman Turkish Emperor, Suleiman the Magnificent.

    (C) the King of England, Henry VIII.

    (D) the Holy Roman Emperor, Charles V.

    (E) the King of France, Francis I.

63. A Dutch political theorist who used the concept of natural law to discuss the nature of just war was

    (A) John Colet.

    (B) Hugo Grotius.

    (C) Niccolo Machiavelli.

    (D) Nicole Oresme.

    (E) Ulrich Zwingli.

64. "Give me a lever long enough and a place to stand, and I will move the world."

    This declaration was made by

    (A) Aristotle.

    (B) Pythagoras.

    (C) Euclid.

    (D) Archimedes.

    (E) Socrates.

65. The following political figures all contributed to the evolution of Athenian government before the Peloponnesian War EXCEPT

    (A) Pericles.

    (B) Cleisthenes.

    (C) Draco.

    (D) Polybius.

    (E) Peisistratus.

66. Which Catholic ruler made an alliance with the Ottoman Turkish sultan, Suleiman the Magnificent?

    (A) Gustavus Adolphus, King of Sweden

    (B) Charles V, the Holy Roman Emperor

    (C) Francis I, King of France

    (D) Philip II, King of Spain

    (E) Henry VIII, King of England

67.

The equestrian statue shown above commemorates the achievements of

    (A) the Roman emperor Marcus Aurelius.

    (B) the Frankish emperor Charlemagne.

    (C) the Italian *condottiere* Gattamelata.

    (D) the Italian *condottiere* Bartolommeo Colleoni.

    (E) the Mongol emperor Genghis Khan.

68. Which of the following did NOT field large armies in the Thirty Years' War?

    (A) Denmark

    (B) England

    (C) Sweden

    (D) France

    (E) Bohemia

69. "Before he had reached the age of 33, he had conquered the Near East and founded several cities that bore his name, the most famous of which was in Egypt. He hoped to conquer India as well, but was prevented by the mutiny of his troops."

   The paragraph above describes which of the following?

   (A) Philip of Macedon

   (B) Cyrus the Great

   (C) Julius Caesar

   (D) Augustus Caesar

   (E) Alexander the Great

70. All of the following were titles of public offices in ancient Rome EXCEPT

   (A) consul.

   (B) tribune.

   (C) dictator.

   (D) archon.

   (E) censor.

71. The survival of the Roman Republic during the first century B.C.E. was most seriously threatened by which of the following?

   (A) slave revolts

   (B) wealthy citizens who commanded the armies of the Republic

   (C) religious leaders who converted Roman citizens to various eastern mystery cults

   (D) Carthaginian spies and saboteurs

   (E) hordes of northern barbarians

72. Each of the following was true of the *Pax Romana* EXCEPT

    (A) It was a time of unprecedented prosperity in the Mediterranean.

    (B) Roman legions were not used in war.

    (C) There was high unemployment and poverty in the city of Rome.

    (D) Christians were publicly executed.

    (E) The city of Rome reached a population of about one million.

73. "As an orator, he was unequalled in the Roman Republic and enjoyed a successful career as a senator and lawyer. Yet he was forced into retirement by Julius Caesar and passed the time by writing philosophical works. After the assassination of Caesar, he supported Octavian against Mark Antony, but when these two concluded an alliance among themselves, he was executed for his outspoken criticism."

    The individual described above was

    (A) Catullus.

    (B) Lucretius.

    (C) Cicero.

    (D) Cato.

    (E) Pompey.

74. In ancient Greece, *helots* were

    (A) traders in Sparta who had no political rights.

    (B) members of the enslaved population at Sparta.

    (C) the poorest class of Athenian citizens.

    (D) middle-class Athenians who fought as infantry in phalanxes.

    (E) pieces of broken pottery used by the Athenians to exile citizens who seemed to pose a threat to democracy.

75.

The building interior shown above is that of

(A) a mosque in Damascus from the eighth century.

(B) a church in Paris from the thirteenth century.

(C) a temple to Jupiter in Rome from the first century.

(D) a church in Ravenna from the sixth century.

(E) a synagogue in Jerusalem from the twelfth century.

76. Which of the following theologians is NOT considered one of the four Latin doctors of the Church?

(A) St. Gregory the Great

(B) St. Augustine of Hippo

(C) St. John Chrysostom

(D) St. Jerome

(E) St. Ambrose of Milan

77. In the system of medieval economics known as manorialism, the *demesne* was

(A) a plot of land granted by a lord to his vassal in exchange for feudal services.

(B) the land whose produce was reserved for the lord of the manor.

(C) woodland cleared for agricultural use.

(D) strips of land reserved for individual peasant families.

(E) a hedge that separated strips of land belonging to different peasant families.

78. Medieval colleges, such as the one founded by Robert de Sorbon in Paris during the thirteenth century, were originally

    (A) schools that were devoted entirely to the liberal arts.

    (B) schools that specialized in the study of law, medicine, or theology.

    (C) guild-like associations of teachers and students.

    (D) residence-halls for poor students enrolled in a university.

    (E) associations of churchmen who met periodically to elect a new pope.

79. All of the following inventions appeared in Europe before the fifteenth century EXCEPT

    (A) mechanical clocks.

    (B) the printing press with movable metal type.

    (C) magnetic compasses.

    (D) astrolabes.

    (E) eyeglasses.

80. Which of the following inspired the religious reformers John Huss and Martin Luther?

    (A) Thomas Aquinas

    (B) John Wycliffe

    (C) Francis of Assisi

    (D) Benedict of Nursia

    (E) Chretien de Troyes

81. The Golden Bull of 1356

    (A) ended the Investiture Controversy.

    (B) established a college of electors made up of seven German states which were responsible for choosing the Holy Roman Emperor.

    (C) ended the Hundred Years' War.

    (D) ended the Great Schism in the Latin church.

    (E) declared the doctrine of papal supremacy in relations between kings and emperors.

82.

The structure pictured above is

(A) the Athenian Parthenon.

(B) the Pantheon in Rome.

(C) the Greek theater at Epidauros.

(D) the Roman Colosseum.

(E) the Hagia Sophia of Constantinople.

83. The complete works of Plato first became available in western Europe due to the efforts of

(A) ancient Roman scholars.

(B) medieval scholastics.

(C) medieval monks.

(D) Italian humanists during the Renaissance.

(E) French humanists during the Renaissance.

84. Which of the following brought the Great Schism in the Latin church to an end?

(A) the election of Urban VI in 1378

(B) the election of a new pope in 1409

(C) the Council of Constance (1414–1418)

(D) the Council of Basel (1431–1449)

(E) the Council of Florence (1438–1445)

85. Which of the following was NOT an action of Pope Innocent III (1198–1216)?

    (A) He instructed the Fourth Crusade to sack Constantinople.

    (B) He presided over the Fourth Lateran Council.

    (C) He proclaimed a crusade against heretics in southern France.

    (D) He approved the foundation of the Franciscans and Dominicans.

    (E) He made England a papal fief.

86. The Peace of God was a movement led by the Latin Church during the Middle Ages to

    (A) end warfare with the Muslims in the Holy Land.

    (B) achieve reconciliation with the Greek Church.

    (C) protect non-combatants.

    (D) end feudal warfare.

    (E) restrict warfare to certain days of the year.

87. The members of the Second Triumvirate in Late Republican Rome were Octavian, Lepidus, and

    (A) Mark Antony.

    (B) Crassus.

    (C) Pompey.

    (D) Julius Caesar.

    (E) Augustus Caesar.

88. In the year 100 c.e., most converts to Christianity were

    (A) Greek philosophers.

    (B) wealthy Roman citizens.

    (C) slaves and the poor.

    (D) Pharisees.

    (E) Roman soldiers.

89. The Gospels, which form the core of the New Testament, are attributed to

(A) Matthew, Luke, James, and John.

(B) Matthew, Thomas, Luke, and John.

(C) Matthew, Thomas, James, and John.

(D) Matthew, Mark, Luke, and John.

(E) Matthew, Mark, Thomas, and James.

90. The Emperor Hadrian's decision to rebuild Jerusalem on the model of a Greco-Roman city

(A) ended the Diaspora.

(B) revived Jerusalem as the most important center of Christianity.

(C) was greeted by the Jews as a welcome gesture.

(D) triggered the Bar Kochba rebellion.

(E) led ultimately to the siege of Masada.

91.

The statue shown was crafted by

(A) Leonardo da Vinci.

(B) Donatello.

(C) Brunelleschi.

(D) Michelangelo.

(E) Raphael.

92. The Council of Nicaea, organized by the emperor Constantine in 325 C.E., condemned the heresy known as

    (A) Monophysitism.

    (B) Arianism.

    (C) Iconoclasm.

    (D) Gnosticism.

    (E) Catharism.

93. The papacy became a political power in addition to a religious authority during the Middle Ages because

    (A) the disintegration of imperial government in western Europe forced the bishops of Rome to assume diplomatic and administrative duties.

    (B) Jesus of Nazareth made no distinction between religious and political authority.

    (C) the Emperor Constantine entrusted the governance of Italy to the papacy when he moved his capital to the east.

    (D) popes were able to convince Christian society that secular rulers depended on the Church's hierarchy for their authority.

    (E) the barbarians that invaded the Empire were overawed by the popes.

94. Which of the following works of medieval literature was written in Old English?

    (A) *Song of Roland*

    (B) *Divine Comedy*

    (C) *Canterbury Tales*

    (D) *Edda*

    (E) *Beowulf*

95. Which of the following is a novel about the opposition between chivalric ideals and the realities of early modern society?

    (A) Pico della Mirandola's *Oration on the Dignity of Man*

    (B) Boccaccio's *Decameron*

    (C) Shakespeare's *Romeo and Juliet*

    (D) Machiavelli's *The Prince*

    (E) Cervantes's *Don Quixote*

96. "Although he was a vassal, he controlled more territory than his lord. When he himself became a king, he married his lord's former wife. Within his own kingdom, he expanded the royal authority by centralizing the system of justice. His energetic efforts to this end, however, brought him into conflict with the Church and led to the assassination of a man who had once been a close friend. Later his sons rebelled against him with the support of their mother."

    The paragraph above describes the life of

    (A) Louis VII of France.

    (B) Philip II Augustus of France.

    (C) Richard I of England.

    (D) Henry II of England.

    (E) Henry IV of Germany.

97. The areas shaded black on the map below indicate the territories controlled by Rome at which stage of its expansion?

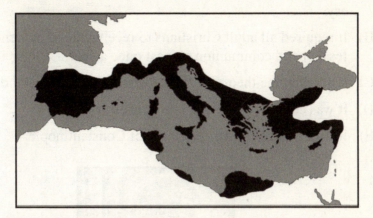

   (A) before the First Punic War

   (B) between the First and Second Punic Wars

   (C) after the Third Punic War but before the reign of Augustus Caesar

   (D) at the end of the reign of Augustus Caesar

   (E) at the end of the reign of Marcus Aurelius

98. In *The Defender of the Peace*, Marsilius of Padua argued that

   (A) kings rule by divine right.

   (B) popes have the right to depose emperors.

   (C) all political authority derives from the people.

   (D) the church should be governed by councils made up of bishops.

   (E) only a government dominated by nobles could guarantee peace.

99. People who opposed the emperors and supported the popes in the political
struggles of Italy from the twelfth to the fifteenth centuries were known as

   (A) Condottieri.

   (B) Janissaries.

   (C) Marranos.

   (D) Guelfs.

   (E) Ghibellines.

100. Which of the following is NOT true of the Fourth Lateran Council?

(A) It exonerated the Waldensians, who had been suspected of heresy.

(B) It required all adult Christians to receive the sacraments of confession and communion at least once a year.

(C) It adopted the theory of transubstantiation as official dogma.

(D) It was convened by Pope Innocent III in 1215.

(E) It was attended by the patriarch of Constantinople.

101.

The structure shown above displays the characteristics of what kind of architecture?

(A) Gothic

(B) Mycenaean

(C) Romanesque

(D) Minoan

(E) Baroque

102. Which of the following was a consequence of the Treaty of Verdun (843)?

    (A) The Frankish Empire was divided three ways between the sons of Charlemagne.

    (B) The foundations were laid for the evolution of France and Germany.

    (C) The Viking raids at last came to an end.

    (D) The Magyar raids at last came to an end.

    (E) The Muslims agreed to open the Mediterranean Sea to Frankish shipping.

103. Which of the following was the leading fourteenth-century thinker of the nominalist school, whose formulation of a principle of logical economy later influenced modern science?

    (A) Duns Scotus

    (B) Thomas Aquinas

    (C) Dante Alighieri

    (D) Roger Bacon

    (E) William of Ockham

104. The Hellenistic scientist Aristarchus (c. 250 B.C.E.) was exceptional in the history of science because he

    (A) first put forward the theory that the Earth revolves around the Sun.

    (B) designed a pump known as "Archimedes' screw."

    (C) wrote a geometry book known as the *Elements*.

    (D) invented the astrolabe.

    (E) accurately calculated the circumference of the Earth.

105. The *Odyssey* of Homer is a Greek epic that portrays

(A) the voyage of the hero Aeneas to found a new kingdom after the fall of Troy.

(B) the voyage of the Argonauts to seize the Golden Fleece.

(C) the war of the Mycenaeans against Troy.

(D) the return of the king of Ithaca to his homeland after the fall of Troy.

(E) the journey of Gilgamesh to the underworld in search of immortality.

106. The reconstruction of an ancient gateway shown below (originally constructed around 575 B.C.E.) represents the artistry of which of the following peoples?

(A) Greeks

(B) Minoans

(C) Neo-Babylonians

(D) Hittites

(E) Assyrians

107. In order to regulate spiritual practices in his realm, Charlemagne promoted which monastic order?

   (A) Augustinians

   (B) Benedictines

   (C) Jesuits

   (D) Dominicans

   (E) Franciscans

108. Which of the following was NOT an immediate consequence of the Black Death?

   (A) Businesses and banks collapsed.

   (B) Serfdom became more prevalent.

   (C) Peasant revolts became more common.

   (D) Wages increased.

   (E) The price of food decreased.

109. "God has given us the papacy. Now let us enjoy it."

   This remark was made by which pope?

   (A) Innocent III

   (B) Leo I

   (C) Leo X

   (D) Gregory I

   (E) Gregory VII

110. Dante Alighieri and Francesco Petrarch had all of the following in common EXCEPT

(A) they were both active in politics.

(B) they wrote poetry about women whom they adored.

(C) they wrote works in Latin, but their most memorable achievements were in the Italian vernacular.

(D) their families were Florentine, but they spent much of their lives outside Florence.

(E) their love for classical literature inspired them to espouse a form of humanism.

111. All of the following were part of the financial practices of Italian bankers during the Renaissance EXCEPT

(A) bills of exchange.

(B) maritime insurance.

(C) double-entry bookkeeping.

(D) the establishment of branch offices in cities across Europe.

(E) the *encomienda* system.

112. The geocentric theory of the universe was first opposed in the sixteenth century by the European astronomer

(A) Michel de Montaigne.

(B) François Rabelais.

(C) Johannes Kepler.

(D) Galileo Galilei.

(E) Nicholas Copernicus.

113. Which of the following was most deeply affected by the invention of the printing press?

    (A) the Gregorian Reform

    (B) the Hundred Years' War

    (C) the Reconquista

    (D) the Protestant Reformation

    (E) Conciliarism

114. All of the following explorers and colonialists were sponsored by Portugal EXCEPT

    (A) Vasco da Gama.

    (B) Alfonso de Albuquerque.

    (C) Bartholomew Diaz.

    (D) Hernando Cortez.

    (E) Pedro Cabral.

115.

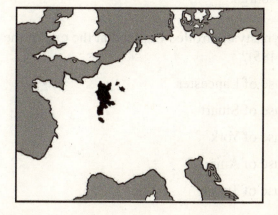

The areas shaded black on the map above represent the only territories directly controlled in 1180 by

    (A) the duke of Normandy.

    (B) the count of Anjou.

    (C) the duke of Aquitaine.

    (D) the king of England.

    (E) the king of France.

116. Which of the following is NOT true of the Peace of Augsburg (1555)?

    (A) It recognized the Augsburg Confession as a legitimate religious position.

    (B) It ended the war between Charles V and the Protestant princes.

    (C) It recognized the legitimacy of Lutheranism.

    (D) It extended toleration to the reformed churches of Calvin and Zwingli.

    (E) It established the principle that the religion of a state should be decided by its prince.

117. In 1529, the city of Vienna was besieged by the

    (A) Holy Roman Emperor.

    (B) Ottomans.

    (C) Seljuks.

    (D) Hohenzollerns.

    (E) Hapsburgs.

118. Which dynasty controlled England at the end of the Wars of the Roses (1454–1485)?

    (A) House of Lancaster

    (B) House of Stuart

    (C) House of York

    (D) House of Anjou

    (E) House of Tudor

119. The ancient Hebrew prophets taught all of the following EXCEPT

    (A) The Hebrews are a chosen nation.

    (B) Yahweh is the one true God.

    (C) The leader of the nation should be immune from criticism.

    (D) Amassing wealth is sinful if it exploits poor people.

    (E) Judah's exile was divine punishment for its sins.

120. Which of the following was a prominent Anabaptist who established a theocracy in the German town of Münster?

(A) Thomas More

(B) Ulrich Zwingli

(C) John of Leiden

(D) Martin Luther

(E) John Calvin

CLEP WESTERN CIVILIZATION I
PRACTICE TEST 2

ANSWER KEY

1. (C)	31. (D)	61. (E)	91. (D)
2. (A)	32. (E)	62. (D)	92. (B)
3. (C)	33. (C)	63. (B)	93. (A)
4. (B)	34. (C)	64. (D)	94. (E)
5. (C)	35. (D)	65. (D)	95. (E)
6. (B)	36. (E)	66. (C)	96. (D)
7. (B)	37. (D)	67. (A)	97. (C)
8. (C)	38. (B)	68. (B)	98. (C)
9. (A)	39. (E)	69. (E)	99. (D)
10. (B)	40. (B)	70. (D)	100. (A)
11. (A)	41. (C)	71. (B)	101. (C)
12. (A)	42. (E)	72. (B)	102. (B)
13. (E)	43. (D)	73. (C)	103. (E)
14. (C)	44. (A)	74. (B)	104. (A)
15. (E)	45. (D)	75. (D)	105. (D)
16. (C)	46. (B)	76. (C)	106. (C)
17. (B)	47. (B)	77. (B)	107. (B)
18. (E)	48. (B)	78. (D)	108. (B)
19. (B)	49. (D)	79. (B)	109. (C)
20. (D)	50. (E)	80. (B)	110. (A)
21. (B)	51. (D)	81. (B)	111. (E)
22. (C)	52. (B)	82. (D)	112. (E)
23. (C)	53. (A)	83. (D)	113. (D)
24. (A)	54. (C)	84. (C)	114. (D)
25. (B)	55. (E)	85. (A)	115. (E)
26. (E)	56. (C)	86. (C)	116. (D)
27. (B)	57. (C)	87. (A)	117. (B)
28. (D)	58. (D)	88. (C)	118. (E)
29. (D)	59. (C)	89. (D)	119. (C)
30. (C)	60. (C)	90. (D)	120. (C)

DETAILED EXPLANATIONS OF ANSWERS

PRACTICE TEST 2

1. **(C)** The earliest surviving examples of cuneiform (c. 3000 B.C.E.) are records of business transactions and inventories of goods and property, which suggest that writing was initially and primarily an aid to memory, intended to help keep track of economic matters, and thus a matter of practical concern for daily life. Cuneiform evolved beyond early pictographs (signs that represent physical objects, such as an asterisk indicating a star) to represent phonetic values (more abstract marks, representing the sounds of syllables rather than physical objects); thus, it could be used for any purpose, including poetry (A), such as the *Epic of Gilgamesh*, which was preserved on a dozen clay tablets. Although the Sumerians believed in magic and also suffered the effects of severe floods (E), the early use of cuneiform for economic purposes indicates that writing in and of itself was not thought to possess special magical properties. Cuneiform writing was used to preserve the laws (B), but this was a later use. Finally, while it is true that the Sumerians were mathematically sophisticated, their treatment of mathematics was more practical than theoretical (D).

2. **(A)** Hammurabi (c. 1792–1750 B.C.E.) was an Amorite king who organized, revised, and expanded earlier collections of laws. The principle of justice espoused in Hammurabi's Code is that of "an eye for an eye, a tooth for a tooth." The Code does not imply that the king is responsible to the people for his authority, but to the gods (B). Although ancient Mesopotamian kings planned the economy of their societies, Hammurabi's Code was not a set of instructions for this purpose (E). Even though the Code implies a model of correct moral behavior, it was not intended as a military code of conduct like the rules of chivalry during the Middle Ages or the Geneva Conventions in modern times (D). Finally, although the Code was written in cuneiform, it was not used by modern historians as a key for deciphering that ancient script (C)—the key text for unraveling cuneiform script was the Behistun inscription, engraved on a cliff-face

in Iran; it thus served a similar function to the Rosetta stone, which enabled modern linguists to decipher Egyptian hieroglyphics.

3. **(C)** During the earliest phase of Egyptian kingship, the pharaoh was looked upon not merely as a high priest (A) or a representative of the gods (B), but as a god. Since the people accepted the idea that he owned all the land of Egypt and that his word was law, he was no mere figurehead (D). The idea that the leader of an empire was simply the foremost citizen of a republic (E) was a propaganda ploy of the first Roman emperor, Augustus Caesar (27 B.C.E.–14 C.E.), who drew attention away from his seizure of power by claiming to restore the Roman Republic.

4. **(B)** Nebuchadnezzar had nothing to do with the Ten Lost Tribes of Israel, which had been deported by the Assyrians approximately a hundred years before the rise of the Neo-Babylonian dynasty, of which Nebuchadnezzar was a member (A). Nebuchadnezzar conquered the kingdom of Judah (D) in 598 B.C.E. and deported its people to Babylon (E) after destroying Jerusalem in 586 B.C.E. because of Hebrew unwillingness to acknowledge his rule. Nebuchadnezzar strove to outdo earlier kings in a display of power and cultural magnificence by sponsoring grand building projects in his capital city. The Hanging Gardens (probably a huge ziggurat covered with plants) was a particularly famous example of his building program, reportedly constructed as a gift for his Median queen (C).

5. **(C)** Zwingli was a Swiss reformer who served as the religious advisor of the city of Zürich. Although he was inspired by Luther's teaching, the two men disagreed on the subject of the Lord's Supper and were unable to reconcile their views during a meeting in 1529. Luther believed that Christ is present in the Eucharist, although he denied that the bread and wine is actually changed into the body and blood of Christ, as the Catholic doctrine of transubstantiation maintained. Luther's position is known as consubstantiation. Zwingli, however, denied that Christ is substantially present in the Eucharist, which he believed has merely a symbolic meaning. This theological disagreement prevented the German and Swiss Protestants from coordinating their efforts. As a Protestant reformer, Zwingli taught that the pope has no authority to lead the Christian people, and he rejected the Catholic tradition of fasting during the forty days before Easter known as Lent (A). He also rejected monasticism, and therefore closed down monasteries (E). For the sake of simplifying Christian worship, he banned both music and religious images (B). Zwingli converted several of the Swiss cantons besides Zürich, but a civil war broke out between the Protestant cantons and the cantons that remained Catholic. Serving as a chaplain, Zwingli was killed by the victorious Catholic forces following the Battle of Kappel in 1531 (D).

6.   **(B)**   The early Greeks are known as the Mycenaeans because they nominally recognized the king of Mycenae as their overlord. However, most of the time the rulers of the various Greek towns were proudly independent. This political fragmentation of the Greek mainland may have been largely due to geographical factors, for the mountains of the Balkan peninsula inhibited communication between political centers. When the Greek kings did unite under the leadership of Mycenae, it was for the sake of foreign conquest, such as the sacking of Troy, which inspired the Homeric poems, or the seizure of Crete from the Minoans (C). Although the Phoenicians (E) also traded in the eastern Mediterranean and were politically divided among themselves, they lived along a narrow strip of coastal territory rather than a mountainous hinterland and did not learn the art of writing from the inhabitants of Crete. The Sumerians (A) and Egyptians (D) were never primitive in comparison to other contemporary cultures, but were the most advanced societies of the ancient Near East from the very beginning of civilization.

7.   **(B)**   The aqueduct at Nîmes, known as the Pont du Gard, was built by the Romans in the province of Gaul (modern France) late in the first century B.C.E. or early in the first century C.E. It stands over the Gard River and is therefore known in French as the "Bridge of the Gard." Standing some 160 feet tall, it allowed fresh water to reach the city of Nîmes from a location some 30 miles away. In distinguishing this structure from the other choices, the viewer is aided by the presence of rounded arches, a feature not shared by the Athenians (E). Choices (A) and (D) can also be eliminated because the Hagia Sophia and Pantheon are domed buildings. Choice (C) can be eliminated because the Roman Colosseum is an open-air stadium with curved walls.

8.   **(C)**   The mountainous geography of Greece favored the formation of small, self-governing city-states (known as *poleis* in Greek). The topography of Greece, coupled with the proud independence of the little city-states, made the political unification of the Greeks difficult, but not impossible (E), because this feat was in fact achieved by Philip of Macedon and his son Alexander, and it was later repeated by the Roman Empire. Although determined foreign powers could control Greece, the geography was a hindrance rather than a help (A). Because the Balkan peninsula is surrounded on three sides by large bodies of water, sea-faring became an important feature of Greek civilization (B). Indeed, it was necessary to maintain fleets of warships to prevent foreign invasion, such as that of the Persians in 490 and 480 B.C.E., because the geography did not keep the Greeks safe by itself (D).

9. **(A)** Hoplites fought in phalanxes, which were units of about 8,000 men armed with spears who stood side by side several ranks deep. A frontal assault by cavalry was not much use against a phalanx. Thus, phalanxes revolutionized ancient Greek warfare, and they were also of political importance because the hoplites, who belonged to the class of small farmers, were able to demand a share of political rights from the nobility, who previously dominated the Greek city-states when their cavalry had been supreme. The extension of political rights on the basis of a social class's military importance later occurred again in Athens when the *thetes*—the lowest class of citizens, who rowed in the oared warships called triremes (C)—demanded more participation in the political process after the victory of the Athenian fleet at Salamis in 480 B.C.E. Because the hoplites were neither cavalry nor naval units but infantry, they were not organized into squadrons (E). The Greeks were not organized into legions (B) or maniples (D), which were Roman units.

10. **(B)** Of the items listed, the only one for which the Romans were not indebted to the Etruscans was the legion. The Etruscans had trained the Romans to fight in phalanxes, but Roman ingenuity devised a variation on the phalanx known as the legion—a formation that allowed greater flexibility and tactical sophistication and enabled the Romans to conquer the Mediterranean region.

11. **(A)** The calendar consisting of 365 days with an extra day added every leap year was an accomplishment of Julius Caesar, and for this reason is known as the Julian Calendar (which served as the basis for the Gregorian Calendar that is currently in use). Julius Caesar adopted Octavian, his grandnephew (later called Augustus Caesar), as his heir. All the other choices accurately reflect the achievements of Augustus.

12. **(A)** Plotinus was the founder of Neoplatonism, a philosophical movement which sought to revive the philosophy of Plato. Although Plotinus and later Neoplatonists (such as Porphyry, Iamblichus, and Proclus) insisted that they were merely giving a systematic form to the content of the Platonic *Dialogues*, they included many ideas drawn from schools of philosophy that arose after the career of Plato; the successors of Plotinus also included magical rituals. Neoplatonism vied with Christianity for intellectual leadership in the later Roman Empire. It was endorsed by the reactionary emperor Julian (361–363) but eventually suppressed by Justinian (527–565).

13. **(E)** The most influential achievement of the Emperor Justinian (527–565) was his codification of Roman Law, known as the *Corpus Juris Civilis*, which began in 528 under the guidance of the jurist Tribonian. Justinian engaged in an ambitious program of civic architecture, not only in Constantinople, where he built the Church of the Hagia Sophia (532–537), but also in provincial capitals throughout his empire. His most ambitious undertaking, but also his least enduring, was the conquest of Italy, North Africa, and part of Spain, which he recovered from the barbarians through long years of struggle (533–553). All these achievements, however, may never have occurred if not for the intervention of Justinian's wife, the empress Theodora, who had been a performer in her youth. During the Nika revolt, which broke out at the circus of Constantinople in 532 and quickly spread throughout the city, Justinian feared for his life and would have fled had Theodora not urged him to suppress the uprising, even at the risk of death. Theodora was an important advisor to Justinian, and became involved in a theological dispute known as the Monophysite controversy.

14. **(C)** This war-scene is characteristic of Assyrian art, which used stone carvings in relief to decorate palaces and to boast the military culture that maintained the Assyrian empire through a policy of terror. This image once adorned the Assyrian palace at Khorsabad.

15. **(E)** During the ninth and tenth centuries, western Europe suffered repeated invasions by Vikings from the north, Magyars from the east, and Saracens (a name often given to medieval Arabs or Muslims) from the south. The Vikings, who depended on hit-and-run tactics using their longships, mostly struck the coastlines and river valleys of England, Ireland, and France. The Magyars were horsemen from central Asia whose raids were finally ended by the German king Otto I (936–973) at the Battle of Lechfeld in 955; they settled central Europe and from them are descended the Hungarians. The Saracens, who were based in Spain, North Africa, and the Mediterranean islands, raided southern France and Italy.

16. **(C)** The Franks accepted Catholic Christianity under the Merovingian king Clovis around the year 500, and therefore easily received the support of the clergy and people in western Europe. They in fact gave their name to the land which they occupied, changing this geographic entity from Gaul to France. All the other Germanic tribes listed were despised and feared as heretics, for they had accepted the Arian form of Christianity (which taught that Christ became divine when adopted by God as his Son, rather than eternally divine as Catholic orthodoxy maintained).

17. **(B)** The *Domesday Book* is a systematic inventory of all feudal property in Norman England, prepared in 1086 at the command of William the Conqueror (1066–1087) for the sake of determining taxes. It was named after the Day of Judgment (Doomsday) because anything written in the book was to be considered as unchangeable as the final word of God.

18. **(E)** Alexander Nevsky, elected prince of Novgorod in 1236, is best remembered for his victory over the Teutonic Knights at Lake Peipus in 1242. His successful defense of Novgorod prevented the monastic military order that was expanding in the Baltic region from establishing a firm foothold within Russian lands. Nevsky did not fight the Mongols (B) but cooperated with them and thus increased his power over neighboring Russian princes. He did not have significant contact with the other groups listed.

19. **(B)** Of the cultures listed, only the Greeks developed round open-air theaters. The one in the photograph was built at Epidauros toward the end of the Classical Age (c. 350 B.C.E.).

20. **(D)** When trade revived in Europe during the eleventh century, it faced high risks. Merchants banded together in caravans and hired guards in order to defend themselves from brigands and the loss of their wares through highway robbery. They also agreed to help one another in legal disputes. These associations developed into merchant guilds that came to dominate commerce in the towns. The craftsmen who bought raw materials from the merchants soon banded together in craft guilds of their own, which had as their primary aim the regulation of their respective trades, including the restraint of competition (A). Merchants were not supposed to lend money for profit (C), a practice that the Church regarded as usury. Joint-stock companies (B) and mercantilism (E) were not factors in European economics before the sixteenth century.

21. **(B)** Zoroaster (also known as Zarathustra) was a Persian prophet who may have lived around 600 B.C.E. (although some scholars would put his career around 1000 B.C.E.) and preached that the cosmos was gripped in a great dualistic struggle between good and evil. His religious vision was eschatological (teaching that there would be an end of time) and soteriological (teaching that there would be a day of judgment when some people would be saved and others damned). Zoroastrianism became widespread in the parts of the ancient Near East ruled by the Persian Empire and influenced Judaism, Christianity, and Islam. Amos (A) and Isaiah (D) were Hebrew prophets, whereas Akhenaton (E) was a pharaoh who attempted to institute an early form of monotheistic religion. Hammurabi (C) was an Old Babylonian emperor who claimed to be a representative of the gods.

22. **(C)**   The Spartans had an unusual society that was entirely geared for war on a permanent basis. Although the Romans (A) and their rivals the Carthaginians (B) were also warlike, their societies followed the normal patterns found throughout the ancient Mediterranean, as in Athens (E) and Corinth (D).

23. **(C)**   The Dark Age of ancient Greece (c. 1100–800 B.C.E.) was caused by the migration of Dorian Greeks into the Balkan peninsula, where they overthrew the civilized centers of the Mycenaean Greeks. The Mycenaeans had conquered Minoan Crete around 1400 B.C.E., when civilization in the Balkan peninsula was at its height before the Dark Age (D), and they conquered Troy around 1200 B.C.E. (B). The Persians did not invade Greece until the fifth century B.C.E. (A), and the Romans did not invade Greece until the second century B.C.E. (E).

24. **(A)**   The Pantheon, or temple to all the gods, was built in Rome at the command of the emperor Hadrian between 118 and 128 C.E. Because it is made up of a classical porch surmounted by a dome—an architectural form that is characteristically Roman—one can eliminate the Greeks (C), who used columns but not domes. One can also eliminate choices (B) and (D), the Arabs and Turks, who used domes but not the classical porch made up of columns surmounted by a triangular pediment. The Celts (E) are not known for architectural achievements other than megalithic monuments like Stonehenge.

25. **(B)**   Since Constantine the Great's Edict of Milan legalized Christianity in 313 C.E., the only work listed that could not have been written before that event is Augustine of Hippo's *City of God*, which was produced as a response to the pagan argument that the legalization of Christianity was responsible for the sack of Rome in 410 C.E. The full title of Augustine's massive work is *The City of God against the Pagans*, and its 22 books were written between 413 and 426. All the other books were written before the founding of Christianity.

26. **(E)**   The tyrant Peisistratus sought to legitimate his seizure of political power in Athens by winning over the goodwill of the citizens through a building program and through the institution of religious holidays, including the festival of Dionysos. In order to assure Greek citizens that he was on their side, he preserved the constitution established by Solon (D), although he staffed it with his supporters. Peisistratus ruled Athens continuously from 546 B.C.E. until 527, when he died a peaceful death; his sons, however,

were later overthrown (A). The harsh laws that governed Spartan society were instituted by the legendary lawgiver, Lycurgus, and their government was not considered a tyranny but a balanced constitution, with kings, council of elders, and assembly (B). Philip of Macedon conquered Greece; he was considered a tyrant by some Greeks but was supported by others (C).

27. **(B)** The Waldensians were named after Peter Waldo, a rich merchant of Lyons who in the twelfth century experienced a religious conversion that inspired him to give his wealth to the poor and embrace a life of poverty. His followers traveled about Europe preaching a simple message based on their reading of the Bible and criticizing the Church for its accumulation of wealth. They were condemned as heretics at the Fourth Lateran Council (1215) and persecuted by the Inquisition.

28. **(D)** The map represents areas governed by the Byzantine Empire around 1000 C.E. The choices can be reduced by process of elimination. No part of Italy was ever controlled by the ancient Athenian Empire (A), the Ottoman Turks (E), or Alexander the Great (B). Justinian (C), who was the Byzantine emperor from 527 until 565 C.E., controlled not merely the southern portion of Italy, but the entire peninsula. He had regained this territory from the Ostrogoths after long years of fighting. He also controlled the Near East, Egypt, and North Africa, none of which are shaded black on the map.

29. **(D)** Although the Greeks did prevent the westward expansion of the Persian empire at the battle of Salamis, this event took place in 480 B.C.E., some 50 years after Cyrus had died. Having begun his career by successfully leading an uprising of the Persians against the Medes in 550 B.C.E. (A), Cyrus went on in 546 B.C.E. to conquer Greece's neighbor in Anatolia, the famously wealthy king Croesus of Lydia. However, once Cyrus had established his empire on the shores of the Mediterranean Sea, he returned his attention to the east, conquering the lands as far as the Indus valley (B). Cyrus was not only a military genius, but an exceptionally shrewd political thinker and an enlightened ruler as well, as he showed from the very beginning when he treated the overthrown Medes with leniency. Thus, departing from the infamous terror tactics of the Assyrians, Cyrus gained the obedience of the peoples he conquered by showing them tolerance (C). Cyrus's decision to allow the Jews exiled in Babylon to return to Judah (E) was one example of his policy of respect and tolerance toward subject peoples.

30. **(C)** Egyptians of the Middle Kingdom (c. 2050–c. 1700 B.C.E.) believed that the soul of every human being was immortal and could gain entry into the realm of the blessed if the correct funeral ritual was followed; because it was believed that the individual would be judged for misdeeds, it was also important that he or she should lead a moral life. Egyptians who lived during the Old Kingdom (c. 2700–c. 2200 B.C.E.) believed that only the pharaoh and his officials could attain immortality (D); for the rest, there was apparently no life after death (A). Thus, Egyptian attitudes toward the afterlife evolved over time. The Egyptians did not consider soul and body to be in conflict (E); the value they placed on the body inspired their practice of mummification. The Sumerians, in contrast to the Egyptians, did not share a sense of optimism about the possibility of a happy afterlife; while they did not think an individual's existence ended entirely, they regarded existence after death as a shadowy, gloomy condition (B).

31. **(D)** Gregory VII (1073–1085) was an energetic pope who led what has been called the Gregorian Reform, which sought to improve the quality of the clergy and establish the papacy as unquestioned leader of European society. Gregory opposed the practice of secular rulers who appointed bishops for political ends, claiming that laymen could not appoint clerics, not even if the layman were an emperor. His position brought him into conflict with the Holy Roman Emperor Henry IV (1056–1106) in a struggle between church and state known as the Investiture Controversy. Gregory initially had the better of the struggle. He excommunicated Henry in 1076, precipitating a revolt that forced the emperor to ask for absolution the following year at a place called Canossa. Eventually Henry and Gregory revived the struggle, but this time the emperor brought an army into Italy and the pope had to flee Rome. The Investiture Controversy was not resolved until the Concordat of Worms in 1122.

32. **(E)** The Hanseatic League, or Hansa, arose in the mid-twelfth century as a loose commercial association of northern German towns, most notably Lübeck, Hamburg, and Bremen, for the promotion of trade in the North and Baltic Seas. The coastal towns initially banded together to defend against piracy and to compete with Scandinavian shipping, then began to conclude formal alliances with one another in the thirteenth century, extending membership to inland cities along rivers, such as Cologne. The League was at its zenith in the fourteenth century, when it successfully went to war with Denmark over encroachments of its trading privileges in the Baltic. In the sixteenth century it was overshadowed by the rise of England and the Netherlands as major military and economic powers, and it was marginalized by the opening of Atlantic trade with the New World. It was finally dealt a death-blow by the Thirty Years' War (1618–1648).

33. **(C)** The region of Spain (the Iberian peninsula) was the most important area of cultural interaction between Christians, Muslims, and Jews during the twelfth century. Although cultural exchanges also took place in the Crusader states of Syria (B) and Palestine (A), it was in Spain that visiting scholars from Christian Europe read philosophical and scientific texts (especially of Aristotle) and translated them into Latin. Upon returning home, they shared these translations with scholars eager to revitalize European education.

34. **(C)** Greek colonization was motivated primarily by economic problems that caused social strife in the mother city-states. By removing part of the population to colonies outside Greece, it was hoped that the demand for scarce resources could be relieved and that social tensions would be decreased as the economic situation improved. Because the city-states were politically divided within Greece, the colonies they founded were not part of a single empire (B); indeed, they were usually politically independent of the founding city-state. Likewise, even though colonization was spurred on by pressing economic motives and did result in stimulating trade, the lack of concerted effort between the city-states in the founding of colonies indicates that their primary goal was not to establish a network of commercial trading posts (E). Finally, the Greeks, who considered all non-Greeks barbarians, did not care about sharing their culture with outsiders (A). The Romans were not a threat at the time (D); they were not free of Etruscan domination until 509 B.C.E., when most of the Greek colonies were already established.

35. **(D)** King Pyrrhus of Epirus, who fought the Romans in southern Italy in the 270s B.C.E., defeated them twice but at a very high rate of casualties to his own forces. Finding the Romans to be relentless fighters, Pyrrhus despaired of a final victory against them and abandoned the Greek city-states who had called upon him for help. Today, the term "Pyrrhic victory," named after Pyrrhus of Epirus, refers to a battle that is won at such great cost that the victorious side cannot afford to continue fighting.

36. **(E)** *Latifundia* were large estates which patricians assembled during the second century B.C.E. by buying up small farms that had become too costly for plebeians to maintain in the aftermath of the Punic Wars. The dispossessed farmers, who had been forced to sell their farms by economic necessity, migrated to the city of Rome, where they swelled the ranks of the unemployed and caused social unrest. The attempt of the Gracchi to resolve the crisis by enacting legislation that would reinstate the small farmers and expand the political rights of the plebeians initiated a period of turmoil that ended in the collapse of the Republic and its replacement by the Empire.

37. **(D)** Athenian democracy was exceptional in the ancient world because it enabled all male citizens to participate in government, not only members of wealthy and privileged families. It differed markedly from modern democracy in the degree of direct participation that was required of all male citizens, who did not merely vote for professional politicians to represent them in government office, but actually served from time to time as public officials themselves. Although Athenian democracy extended real political power to a much larger segment of society than anywhere else in the ancient world, freedom and equality existed only among the adult male citizens, who constituted about a quarter of the total population. Athenian democracy did not attempt to do away with slavery (B), which was considered an indispensable feature of the ancient economy. Slaves were, of course, excluded from government, as were all women (A) and "metics," that is, resident aliens (C). The metics, who were immigrants from other Greek city-states, could not become Athenian citizens and could not own land, yet they had to serve in the military and pay taxes. It is important to remember, also, that democracy was exceptional within the Greek world itself. Thus, while the wars with the Persians stimulated Athenian democracy (because the commoners who rowed the victorious ships demanded more political privileges after risking their lives for the community), democracy was not a force that united the Greek city-states (E). In fact, Sparta, the other major Greek power, feared the spread of democracy, which incited it to wage the Peloponnesian War (431–404 B.C.E.) against Athens.

38. **(B)** Aristotle taught the ethical doctrine of the golden mean, which recommended moderation in all behavior, as well as the political theory that government consists of three basic types: monarchy (rule by one man), aristocracy (rule by a few men), and "polity" (rule by the majority); he also presented three forms of misgovernment: tyranny (misrule by one man), oligarchy (misrule by a few men), and democracy (misrule by the majority) which he equated with mob rule or anarchy. Plato recorded Socrates' theory of ideal government in the *Republic*, where he divided society into three levels, in which workers at the bottom of the social pyramid were protected by guardians and governed by philosopher-kings (A, C). Pythagoras (c. 500 B.C.E.) coined the term "philosopher," which originally indicated someone who loves wisdom and the moral life, and he strove to understand the mysteries of harmony and numerical relationship in all aspects of reality (D). Thales of Miletus (c. 600 B.C.E.) was the earliest of the Greek Pre-Socratics, who believed that water was the universal substance from which all things are made (E).

39. **(E)**   The paragraph describes Euripides (c. 480–406 B.C.E.). His fellow tragedians were Aeschylus and Sophocles (A, D). Aristophanes (C) was famous as a writer of comedies. Although the youthful Plato (B) had ambitions as a playwright, the death of his teacher Socrates prompted him to devote his life to the writing of philosophical dialogues portraying Socrates as the principal speaker.

40. **(B)**   A caryatid is a column sculpted in the form of a maiden who supports the roof of a building with her head. Corinthian and Doric columns (C, D) are typically fluted (cut with grooves). A pediment (A) is the triangular area beneath the roof of a Greek temple, whereas a frieze (E) is the horizontal band that runs along the bottom of the roof; both of these architectural features were typically decorated with sculptures.

41. **(C)**   Mithraism, or the worship of Mithras, the ancient Persian god of light, spread to the Mediterranean after Alexander the Great's conquest of the Persian Empire (334–323 B.C.E.), when the Greeks began to turn away from the traditional civic deities of the *polis* and participate in mystery cults that promised immortality. The cult was especially popular later on in the Roman Empire and was a serious rival of Christianity (B), which of course did not arise until the first century C.E., that is, after the end of the Hellenistic period (323–30 B.C.E.). Although the Eleusinian Mysteries (E) were a kind of mystery cult (in honor of Demeter, at Eleusis, near Athens), they were known to the ancient Greeks long before the Hellenistic period. Finally, although Epicureanism and Stoicism (A, D) arose during the Hellenistic period and tried to give the Greeks something to organize their lives around other than the *polis*, they were not religions but schools of philosophy.

42. **(E)**   Machiavelli criticized the Italian city-states for their use of mercenary armies led by figures called *condottieri* because these soldiers-of-fortune were unwilling to take risks and were often unreliable. He recommended the use of citizen militia, because they would not be tempted to switch their loyalties and would be willing to risk their lives to save their families and property.

43. **(D)**   Albrecht Dürer (1471–1528) was a German artist who visited Italy and brought the principles of the Renaissance north of the Alps. His paintings and drawings are rich in detail, and their perspective and realism are enhanced by the use of light and shadow. Dürer also mastered the medium of engraving, so that his artwork could be mass-produced in books, and thus his examples of the new styles of the Renaissance reached a much larger audience than did the works of artists who restricted themselves to paintings or sculptures.

44. **(A)** The Battle of Lepanto was a naval engagement fought in 1571 between the Ottoman Turks and a coalition of Christian states known as the Holy League. Led by the pope, the Holy League included Spain, Venice, and Genoa. The battle was the first major victory by Europeans against the Ottomans and succeeded in freeing thousands of Christian slaves, even if nothing of long-term strategic value was attained.

45. **(D)** The Dutch rebelled against the rule of the Spanish king, Philip II (1556–1598), who inherited the Netherlands from his father, the Holy Roman Emperor Charles V (also Charles I of Spain). The movement for Dutch independence coincided with the spread of Protestantism. Rioting broke out in 1566 to protest Philip's use of the Inquisition to enforce obedience to the Roman Catholic Church. In 1579 the Union of Utrecht, led by William the Silent, prince of Orange, became the core of the independence movement. The struggle was not concluded until 1648, when Spain finally recognized the independence of the Dutch Republic of United Provinces.

46. **(B)** Oil paints were first developed in Flanders. This innovation gave paintings a brighter, more vivid quality and allowed the artist a wider range of technical possibilities. Among the earliest artists to use the new medium was the Flemish painter Jan van Eyck (1390–1441). All the other innovations originated in Italy.

47. **(B)** Jakob Fugger (1459–1525) was a member of an entrepreneurial family that began in the cloth industry and later invested in mining. The Fuggers' immense profits enabled them to offer loans to the Hapsburgs. Based in Augsburg, Jakob Fugger had offices in most financial centers of the day, including Antwerp (the financial capital of Europe in the early sixteenth century), Vienna, Rome, Madrid, and many others.

48. **(B)** Catherine de' Medici (1519–1589), the great-granddaughter of Lorenzo the Magnificent, is credited with introducing Italian etiquette to the French court and was renowned as a patron of the arts. Her influence in politics was felt during the regency and reign of her sons, especially Charles IX (1560–1574). Catherine was implicated in the St. Bartholomew's Day Massacre (1572), which touched off a round of fighting between Catholics and Huguenots when the former launched a bloody purge against the latter.

49. **(D)** The characteristic feature of the early modern joint-stock company was its status as an association of investors. In order to make the expensive and high-risk venture of overseas trade profitable, individuals would buy shares in

a company, thereby protecting themselves from heavy losses while earning a percentage of profits. They did not need to be professional traders, only have enough capital to buy shares in the business. Associations of traders, which preceded the joint-stock companies, were known as "regulated companies" (A). Governments sponsored joint-stock companies and used them in their system of national economic management known as mercantilism (E). The guilds were not revived by the new economic forms, but suffered decline as they became marginal to the economic life of Europe (C). The rise of innovative methods of labor organization, such as the putting-out system and the gathering-in system (B), which were managed by entrepreneurs, gave jobs to peasants in the countryside rather than to members of guilds based in the towns.

50. **(E)** Ignatius of Loyola (1491–1556) founded the Society of Jesus, or Order of Jesuits, which received papal approval in 1540. This new religious order was an important instrument of the Catholic Reformation. All the other choices are Protestant reformers.

51. **(D)** The English physician, William Harvey (1578–1657), published a ground-breaking study on the circulation of the blood in 1628. This study, based on the new experimental method, replaced Galen as the authority on the subject and laid the foundations of modern physiology.

52. **(B)** Spices were the staple import during the earlier phase of colonialism, but by about 1650 European markets were oversupplied with this commodity, resulting in decreased profits. Traders responded to the situation by diversifying imports.

53. **(A)** The interior shown is from the Hagia Sophia in Constantinople, which was converted into a mosque after the conquest of the city by the Turks in 1453 and is now a museum. The Hagia Sophia was built during the reign of Justinian (527–565) and represents the characteristics of Byzantine architecture, such as the placing of a dome atop a square base and the structure's massive scale.

54. **(C)** The Battle of Zama (202 b.c.e.) ended the Second Punic War between Rome and Carthage. The Athenian army defeated the Persians at Marathon in 490 b.c.e. (A), and their navy defeated the Persians at Salamis in 480 (B). The Spartans were defeated by the Persians at Thermopylae in 480 (E), but vanquished the Persians at Plataea the following year (D).

55. **(E)** Fear of the steady expansion of the Athenian Empire was the root cause of the Peloponnesian War (431–404 B.C.E.), which led Sparta to invade Attica in the hope of humbling Athenian power in a pitched land-battle. The Athenians did not start the conflict by invading the Peloponnesus (C); the war was named after the Peloponnesian League led by Sparta. The conflicts between Rome and Carthage are known as the Punic Wars (D), Xerxes's invasion of Greece was part of the Persian Wars (A), and the Roman invasions of Macedon are known as the Macedonian Wars (B).

56. **(C)** The Arabs began their invasion of the Near East in 634 and by 712 had invaded Spain in the west and reached India in the east. Within this period of rapid conquest, however, their initial unity was interrupted by a civil war, from 656 to 661, when they could not agree on the caliph. This civil war, and another in 680, transformed the history of Islam by creating a schism between Sunnites and Shiites. The Shiites, or "sectarians," insisted that Muhammad's successor be a member of his family; they supported Muhammad's son-in-law, Ali, and denied the legitimacy of the first three caliphs, who had not been closely related to Muhammad. The Sunnites, or "traditionalists," believed Muhammad's successor did not need to be related to him by close family ties. When Ali was assassinated in 661, the Muslims accepted as their next caliph Muawiyah, founder of the Umayyad dynasty. Ali's son, Hussein, challenged the heir of Muawiyah in 680, but died fighting at Karbala. Under Umayyad leadership, Arab expansion resumed, but the seeds of future dissent and instability were sown.

Islam, the religion proclaimed by the prophet Muhammad (D), gave the Arabs a religious justification for expansion as well as a point of focus for cooperation, but overpopulation (E) had already prompted some Arabs to leave their native lands and settle in the border territories of the Byzantine and Sassanian Empires. When the Muslim armies invaded these territories, they found little opposition, partly because the two empires had so greatly weakened each other in long wars of attrition that they could not mount effective resistance (B), and partly because the inhabitants in the Byzantine provinces, who had come to resent the rule of Constantinople because of the imperial suppression of Monophysite Christianity, were unwilling to fight the invaders (A). The Monophysite Christians preferred to live under Muslim rule, for it was religiously more tolerant than that of the Christian emperors of Constantinople.

57. **(C)** Lorenzo the Magnificent was the leader of the Medici family from 1469 to 1492. His father, Cosimo, made a fortune in banking, and the Medici used their wealth to dominate politics during the Renaissance—first in Florence, and later throughout Italy by influencing the papacy. Three members of the Medici became popes (Leo X, Clement VII, and Leo XI). The Medici also used their wealth to patronize artists and scholars of the Renaissance.

58. **(D)** Desiderius Erasmus (1466–1536), also known as Erasmus of Rotterdam, was a Dutch humanist who hoped to reform the Church by seeking inspiration from Christianity in its earliest stages. To this end he published in 1516 an edition of the original Greek text of the New Testament, including notes and a new Latin translation, which he hoped could be used to inspire spiritual renewal. He corresponded with religious reformers yet took a moderate position and never broke away from the Roman Catholic Church.

59. **(C)** The only choice on the frontier between France and the Holy Roman Empire is Burgundy. During the later phase of the Hundred Years' War (1337–1453), Philip the Good, the duke of Burgundy (1396–1467), fought against France, captured Joan of Arc, and handed her over to the English for execution. Philip was later reconciled with the French monarchy, but he also vied with it by assembling a collection of territories that constituted one of the most powerful European states of the fifteenth century, reaching as far north as the Netherlands. Philip commanded considerable wealth and his court was renowned for its cultural achievements. When Philip's son, Charles the Bold, inherited the duchy, he challenged the authority of King Louis XI of France (1461–1483) in an ambitious project of expansion. His efforts came to naught, however, when he died fighting in 1477. Thereafter Burgundy posed no threat to the rise of France.

60. **(C)** Luther's teachings were condemned in 1520 by Pope Leo X. He was subsequently excommunicated but refused to recant at the Diet of Worms in 1521, where the emperor, Charles V, condemned Luther (B). He was not put to death, however, because his patron, Frederick the Wise of Saxony, hid him in Wartburg Castle. Later more princes with grievances against Rome or the emperor joined the Protestant cause, and they successfully resisted imperial attempts to crush their rebellion. In the peasant revolt of 1524–1525, Luther sided with the nobles (D).

61. **(E)**   The Edict of Nantes, issued in 1598 by Henry IV of France (1589–1610), granted religious toleration to French Calvinists, known as Huguenots. The king, who was known as Henry of Navarre before his coronation, was himself a Calvinist and fought against the Catholics in the French wars of religion. In 1593 he converted to Catholicism in order to establish peace in his realm, since many refused to acknowledge a Protestant as king of France. Henry nevertheless continued to care for his Protestant subjects and sanctioned their form of worship with the Edict of Nantes, which remained in effect until revoked by Louis XIV in 1685.

62. **(D)**   The troops of Charles V, Hapsburg ruler of the Holy Roman Empire (1519–1558), sacked Rome while capturing Pope Clement VII (1523–1534) during one of the Valois-Hapsburg wars for control of Italy. The pope had allied himself with Francis I of France (1515–1547), and his imprisonment was intended as punishment for his opposition to imperial authority. The troops looted the city because they had not been paid.

63. **(B)**   The Dutch jurist Hugo Grotius (1583–1645) wrote a book *On the Law of War and Peace* (1625) in which he presented a model for the correct relations between sovereign states. He based his discussion on the concept of natural law. Although Grotius argued that war is a violation of natural law, he outlined a set of conditions in which war could justifiably be waged. Thus, he made an important contribution to the theory of the just war.

64. **(D)**   The Hellenistic scientist, Archimedes (287–212 B.C.E.), is famous for having made discoveries in the field of mechanics and for demonstrating the power of pulleys and levers. The quotation attributed to him illustrates his confidence in the power of science to control the environment. Pythagoras and Euclid (B, C) are famous for mathematical proofs, not mechanics. Aristotle (A) was renowned as a systematizer of knowledge, but his scientific strength was demonstrated predominantly in biology. Socrates (E), by contrast, neglected science in favor of ethics.

65. **(D)**   Polybius (c. 200–118 B.C.E.) was a Hellenistic historian who wrote about the Roman rise to dominance in the Mediterranean; because he lived long after the Peloponnesian War (431–404 B.C.E.), he could not have played a part in the early evolution of Athenian government. Draco gave the Athenians their first written law code in 621 B.C.E. (C). Peisistratus was a tyrant (died in 527 B.C.E.) whose contribution to Athenian political development was to preserve the constitution established by Solon in 594 B.C.E. (E). Cleisthenes led a democratic revolution in 508 B.C.E. which reformed

Solon's constitution (B). Pericles broadened the reforms of Cleisthenes in the 450s B.C.E. by initiating payment for public service, thereby making political action feasible for the poor (A).

66. **(C)** Francis I of France (1515–1547) made an alliance with the Ottoman sultan, Suleiman the Magnificent, in 1536 while the Holy Roman Emperor, Charles V, was conducting an invasion of southern France. The Turks aided their French ally by attacking Charles V's possessions in Hungary and the Mediterranean. The French also benefited from the alliance by receiving favorable trade status within the Ottoman Empire and a protectorate over sites of Christian worship in the Holy Land.

67. **(A)** The equestrian statue, which was made around 175 C.E., is a representation of the Roman emperor Marcus Aurelius (161–180 C.E.). It served as a source of inspiration for later equestrian statues, such as the Renaissance sculptures of two Italian *condottieri* (mercenary generals) named Gattamelata (C) and Bartolommeo Colleoni (D). However, the ancient Roman statue is easily distinguished from the later Renaissance examples by the fact that Marcus Aurelius is clothed in a simple Roman tunic, whereas the figures in the Renaissance sculptures are clad in heavy metal armor, which was not developed until long after the Roman period. There is also a famous ninth-century equestrian statue of the Frankish emperor Charlemagne (B), but it is also easily distinguishable from the statue of Marcus Aurelius because the figure wears a crown and holds an orb—symbols of power that were not used until the Middle Ages. The Mongol emperor Genghis Khan (E) was not honored by European sculptors with an equestrian statue.

68. **(B)** During the Thirty Years' War (1618–1648), England was preoccupied with an internal conflict between Parliament and the Stuart kings, James I (1603–1625) and Charles I (1625–1649), which prevented the island nation from becoming deeply involved in the Continental war. The tension between king and Parliament exploded into civil war between 1642 and 1649, ending in the execution of Charles I.

69. **(E)** When Alexander the Great (336–323 B.C.E.) died before his thirty-third birthday, he had conquered the entire Persian Empire as well as a few territories that the Persians had not controlled, including borderlands near India. His conquest of that region, however, was thwarted in 326 B.C.E. by the mutiny of his troops, who wanted to return home after long years of campaigning.

70. **(D)** An archon was a public official in ancient Greece; Solon had been elected archon of Athens in 594 B.C.E. in order to reform its constitution. A consul (A) was one of two annual chief magistrates in Rome elected by the assembly, which also elected tribunes (B) who defended the rights of the plebeians and could veto measures by the Senate. A dictator (C) was appointed by the Senate in times of crisis and given power for a period of six months. A censor (E) was an official in charge of drawing up the census and was chosen from the ranks of those who had once served as consul.

71. **(B)** The greatest danger to the survival of the Roman Republic in the first century B.C.E. came from its own ruling elite, which was riven with factionalism. These struggles began when the Gracchi (the brothers Tiberius and Gaius Gracchus) tried to address popular discontent by instituting reforms that challenged the virtual monopoly of political power enjoyed by the Senate. Later on, some wealthy citizens, who served as legionary commanders, used their position to gain an advantage over their rivals in the Senate. They adopted the practice of paying soldiers from their personal wealth (the state did not pay troops but required them to serve at their own expense), which shifted the loyalty of troops from the state to their commanders.

The Carthaginian threat (D) had been eliminated in the Third Punic War (149–146 B.C.E.). Although slave revolts (A) did become a serious problem due to the influx of captive laborers from the conquered territories, they were always successfully put down within a fairly short amount of time; the most serious was the revolt led by the gladiator Spartacus in 73–71 B.C.E. The Romans did not have much trouble with barbarians until after the Republic had come to an end (E). Although Rome had been sacked by Gauls in 390 B.C.E. and fought off the Teutones and Cimbri in 102–101 B.C.E., the city of Rome was not threatened again for centuries. Finally, eastern mystery cults (C) posed no threat to Roman political life, and the government (both republican and imperial) generally allowed these forms of worship to exist alongside the state religion.

72. **(B)** The *Pax Romana*, which means "Roman Peace," refers to about 200 years from the reign of Augustus Caesar (27 B.C.E.–14 C.E.) to the reign of Marcus Aurelius (161–180 C.E.), during which the Roman state enjoyed unprecedented stability. Although Rome was not wracked by civil wars of the kind that destroyed the Republic, its legions were frequently used on the frontiers of the Empire, either to extend the borders or to defend them against barbarian raids. During this time, the lands surrounding the Mediterranean

Sea enjoyed unprecedented prosperity as commerce flourished within a large and stable area unified and maintained by the Roman state (A). However, the profits from this trade were very unevenly distributed, so that there was high unemployment and poverty in the city of Rome itself (C), which reached a population of about one million (E). The impoverished were kept pacified with free bread and entertainment, which took the form of chariot races and gladiatorial fights. A taste for displays of bloodshed was also satisfied by the public execution of criminals, including the early Christians (D), whose crime was a refusal to worship the emperor.

73. **(C)** Marcus Tullius Cicero (106–43 B.C.E.) devoted his life to the service of the Roman Republic and gave his life defending it in its closing days. Catullus and Lucretius (A, B) were poets of the late Republic. Cato (D) was a senator who instigated the Third Punic War (149–146 B.C.E.), which brought the Republic to unchallenged supremacy in the Mediterranean and set the stage for the rise of the Empire. Pompey (E) was Caesar's rival, whom Cicero supported during the civil war that began in 49 B.C.E. Cicero's support for Pompey (who died in the course of the war) precipitated his forced retirement by Caesar.

74. **(B)** The *helots* were members of the enslaved population at Sparta, whom the *Spartiates*, or dominant class, used to work the land. The *helots* were descended from the Messenians, a neighboring people whom the Spartans had conquered, and they outnumbered the *Spartiates* approximately ten to one. The ever-present threat of revolt required the *Spartiates* to be on a permanent war-time footing, so the task of conducting trade for the necessities of life was left to a merchant class (A) known as the *perioikoi*, who had no political rights. The poorest class of Athenian citizens were the *thetes* (C). Middle-class Greeks who fought as infantry in phalanxes were *hoplites* (D). Pieces of broken pottery on which the Athenians wrote the names of citizens to be exiled were *ostraka*, from which the word "ostracism" is derived (E).

75. **(D)** The interior shown is from the church of *Saint Apollinare in Classe*, built during the sixth century (533–549) in Ravenna, Italy. The image of the cross should rule out the possibility of a temple to Jupiter (C), a mosque (A), or a synagogue (E). It cannot be a church in Paris from the thirteenth century (B) because the presence of a domed ceiling indicates that it is not in the Gothic style.

76. **(C)** John Chrysostom (347–407) is considered one of the four *Greek* doctors (that is, "teachers") of the Church; he served as patriarch of Constantinople from 397. The three other eastern fathers, who also spoke Greek, are: Athanasius (c. 296–373), who led the fight against Arianism; Basil the Great (c. 330–379), who wrote a monastic rule; and Gregory of Nazianzus (329–389), who taught the Latin doctor, St. Jerome (340–420) (D). Jerome used his ability to read Greek (and Hebrew) to translate the Bible into Latin. This translation, known as the Vulgate because it employed the language of the people (*vulgus*) rather than classical models, became the standard version of the Bible known in the west. The Latin doctor Ambrose of Milan (c. 340–397) (E) criticized and punished the Emperor Theodosius I (379–395) for a terrible massacre of Roman citizens during the suppression of a riot; he also baptized the Latin doctor, St. Augustine of Hippo (354–430) (B), who wrote a theological analysis of history known as *The City of God* as well as an introspective autobiography (*The Confessions*). Gregory the Great (c. 540–604) (A) was pope from 590 to 604, during which time he expanded the role of the papacy to meet the needs of the Latin church during the decline of the Roman Empire in the west. He also wrote a lengthy and influential commentary on the biblical Book of Job (known as the *Moralia*) and a collection of *Dialogues* which recount the life of St. Benedict of Nursia, the founder of western monasticism.

77. **(B)** The *demesne* was the portion of a manor reserved for the use of the lord and his family. Serfs were required to work this land for their lord, in addition to the strips assigned for the support of their own families (D). There were no hedges between strips of land belonging to different peasant families (E), but narrow margins of unplowed land between the strips were known as *balks*. The strips assigned to each family would be scattered in various fields in order to ensure that everyone had a share of the best and worst portions of the manor. Woodlands cleared for agricultural use (C) were known as *assarts*. A plot of land granted by a lord to his vassal in exchange for feudal services (A) was a *fief*—from which the word "feudalism" is derived. In Carolingian times, the land-grant was known as a *benefice*.

78. **(D)** The earliest colleges, such as the one founded by the philanthropist Robert de Sorbon in 1257, were initially residence-halls for the support of students enrolled in a university who could not afford to pay living expenses. Colleges were also founded at Oxford and Cambridge. They took their name from the Latin word *collegium*, which means "association." As a general term, this word was also applied to the College of Cardinals, founded in 1059 for the election of new popes (E); only later did colleges

acquire their academic meaning. The Latin word *universitas*, from which "university" is derived, similarly had a broad meaning which later acquired a strictly academic one. "University" originally meant any "corporation" or "guild." The medieval university was, in fact, a corporation of teachers and students (C). The universities commonly provided instruction in the liberal arts (A) and offered particular specialized studies as well (B).

79. **(B)** The printing press with movable metal type was invented in the middle of the fifteenth century, around 1450. It is generally accepted that Johannes Gutenberg of Mainz in Germany achieved the first effective model. Astrolabes (D), or instruments for measuring the position of celestial bodies, were acquired from the Arabs by the year 1100. Magnetic compasses (C) were in use around 1100. Lenses were used to correct vision (E) in the thirteenth century. Mechanical clocks (A) were assembled in Europe during the fourteenth century.

80. **(B)** John Wycliffe (c. 1330–1384) was an Oxford scholar who first declared many of the ideals espoused by later reformers, including John Huss (c. 1372–1415) and Martin Luther (1483–1546). Wycliffe opposed the privileged status of the clergy. He also translated the Bible into English in order to make it accessible not only to scholars who could read Latin, but also to Englishmen who knew only the vernacular. Huss and Luther would not have been inspired by Aquinas (A), who had formulated the Catholic theology which they opposed, nor Francis of Assisi (C), who had recognized the supremacy of the pope. Since they did not accept the idea of an elite form of Christian life, such as that represented by monks, they would not have been inspired by Benedict of Nursia (D), the founder of western monasticism. Chretien de Troyes (E) was a twelfth-century poet who wrote *chansons de geste*, and thus had nothing to offer to the cause of religious reform.

81. **(B)** The Golden Bull of 1356, issued by the Holy Roman Emperor Charles IV (1347–1378), formalized the procedure for electing emperors by establishing the rulers of seven German states as a college of electors: the archbishops of Cologne, Mainz, and Trier; and the secular rulers of Bohemia, Brandenburg, Saxony, and the Rhineland-Palatinate. The Investiture Controversy (A) was ended in 1122 by the Concordat of Worms. The doctrine of papal supremacy (E) was declared in 1302 in the bull *Unam sanctam*. The Great Schism (D) was ended in 1417 by the Council of Constance. The Hundred Years' War (C) ended in 1453 with the Battle of Castillon, which expelled the English from Aquitaine.

82. **(D)** Also known as the Flavian Amphitheater, the Colosseum in Rome was built from 72 to 80 C.E. by the emperors known as the Flavians as a sign of their power and care for their people as well as the magnificence of the empire they ruled. It was a stadium for gladiatorial games, with seating for 45,000 spectators. In distinguishing this structure from the other choices, the viewer is aided by the presence of rounded arches as well as columns that are built into the walls rather than free-standing, both of which are distinctively Roman features. Thus, one can eliminate choices (A) and (C), which are Greek. The Colosseum is an open-air structure and thus lacks a dome, which eliminates the domed temple known as the Pantheon (B) and the domed church known as the Hagia Sophia (E).

83. **(D)** Only a few works of Plato were known in Europe outside of Greece before the Italian Renaissance. The *Timaeus*, which describes the creation of the world, was the only work to be translated by ancient Roman scholars (A). The text was later preserved by medieval monks (C). It was not until the twelfth century that a few other dialogues—the *Meno* and the *Phaedo*—were translated into Latin. Even then, they did not circulate widely and did not make much of an impression. The most famous of Plato's dialogues, *The Republic*, could not be read in Europe until it was translated into Latin by the Italian humanists, who turned to Plato as part of their reaction against the favored position of Aristotle in the scholastic universities (B). The most prominent of the Italian Platonists was the Florentine philosopher, Marsilio Ficino, who translated the complete works of Plato into Latin under Medici patronage. From Italy, the works reached France, where the humanistic printer, Henri Estienne (c. 1528–1598) (E), established a famous edition.

84. **(C)** The Great Schism in the Latin church, which began in 1378, was ended in 1417 by the Council of Constance. This event signifies the high-water mark of the conciliar movement. The Council of Basel (D) set itself up as a rival to the pope, declaring that councils should hold supreme power in the Church at all times, not only in moments of crisis. In the end its intransigence merely discredited the conciliar movement. The Council of Florence (E), which was convened by the pope as a rival to the Council of Basel, tried to end the schism between the Latin and Greek churches. The election of Pope Urban VI (A) in 1378 *began* the schism within the Latin church, and the election of a new pope in 1409 (B) merely aggravated it, for then three rival popes each claimed sole authority over the Church.

85. **(A)** Innocent III did not plan the diversion of the Fourth Crusade but wanted to strike the Muslims in the Holy Land. Thus, he condemned the sack of Constantinople perpetrated by the crusaders in 1204. However, he later supported the Latin empire of Constantinople as a means of ending the schism with the eastern Church, not by effecting a true reconciliation with Greek Christians, but by replacing the Greek patriarchs with Latin patriarchs. These attended the Fourth Lateran Council, convened by Innocent III in 1215 (B), which proved a major milestone in the regulation of ecclesiastical life. Innocent III took energetic measures against heresy, not only at the council, but also by approving the foundation of the Franciscans and Dominicans (D) and by launching a crusade against the Albigensians, heretics who set up a rival church in southern France (C). Innocent III intervened in the political life of Europe as well, as evidenced by his dealings with England. When King John (1199–1216) refused to accept Stephen Langton as the next Archbishop of Canterbury, Innocent III threatened to support a French invasion of England planned by Philip II Augustus (1180–1223). It was only when King John surrendered and agreed to accept England as a papal fief (E) that Innocent III relented and forbade the French king from invading England.

86. **(C)** The Peace of God is the name of the movement organized by the Latin Church to protect non-combatants, who were often victimized by warfare between feudal lords. It began in northwestern Europe during the tenth century and urged rival warriors to spare churchmen and serfs in the lands of their enemies. It was initially resisted by feudal lords, but in the eleventh century was adopted by them to curb violence among their vassals. The Peace of God should not be confused with the Truce of God, which was a movement to ban combat on holy days, such as Sundays, Easter, and Christmas (E), not an attempt to end feudal warfare altogether (D). The Peace of God had nothing to do with the attempt to achieve reconciliation between the Latin and Greek Churches (B), which were separated by schism in 1054, nor did it have anything to do with attempts to establish peace between the Crusader states and Muslims in the Holy Land (A).

87. **(A)** The Second Triumvirate consisted of Octavian, Lepidus, and Mark Antony. It was founded in 43 B.C.E. to end the chaos following the assassination of Julius Caesar (106–44 B.C.E.). Crassus, Pompey, and Julius Caesar (B, C, D) were members of the First Triumvirate, which had set a precedent for how to maintain order in Rome when the Senate could not. Like the First Triumvirate, which eventually led to civil war, the Second Triumvirate also did not endure but ended in a struggle for supremacy between

Mark Antony and Octavian (the grandnephew and adopted heir of Julius Caesar). Answer (E) is incorrect because Augustus Caesar was in fact Octavian; moreover, he did not use the name Augustus Caesar during the Second Triumvirate but was later given the title *Augustus*, which means "revered one," by the Senate.

88. **(C)** The Christian message of an imminent end of the world followed by the reward of eternal life for virtuous believers appealed at first mostly to slaves and the urban poor, who had little else to hope for in the harsh realities of the early Roman Empire. The Pharisees (D) rejected Christianity, which began as a reform movement within Judaism. Early Christianity competed with mystery cults, which also offered the hope of life after death. Among the most popular of the mystery cults was Mithraism, which was favored among Roman soldiers (E). Yet Christianity had a broader appeal—unlike Mithraism, Christianity included women in its ceremonies. Eventually even wealthy Romans (B) would become Christians, usually beginning with the women in the household, who might learn of the new faith from their slaves. Greek philosophers (A) generally did not find the Christian faith logically rigorous enough for their tastes; schools of Neoplatonists, for example, persisted into the sixth century c.e., long after most Roman citizens had become Christian. However, the development of a Christian theology, which combined elements of Greek philosophy with the Christian message, attracted many highly educated men, such as Ambrose of Milan (c. 340–397) and Augustine of Hippo (354–430).

89. **(D)** The four canonical Gospels, which constitute the centerpiece of Christian Scripture, are attributed to the early disciples Matthew, Mark, Luke, and John. They were written between 70 and 100 c.e., within a generation of the destruction of the Temple in Jerusalem (70 c.e.). "Gospel" means "good news" and refers to a text that describes the ministry of Jesus of Nazareth. The first three Gospels are called "synoptic" because they show close similarities; the Gospel of John, however, which was the last to be written, is very different in its presentation of the events of Jesus' ministry. These four texts were not the only Gospels to be written. There were, in fact, many, but only four were accepted by the Church as "canonical," that is, "authoritative." The non-canonical texts, such as the Gospels of Thomas and James, focus on events not described in the authoritative books (such as the childhood of Jesus). Some of them were written by the Gnostics (followers of an early Christian heresy).

90. **(D)** The decision by Hadrian (117–138) to rebuild Jerusalem triggered a rebellion led by the Jewish warrior Simon Bar Kochba. The bloodshed lasted from 132 to 135. Since many Jews left the region, it intensified the Diaspora (A). A major cause of the fighting was Hadrian's decision to include a pagan temple, which the Jews regarded as blasphemous (C). The Bar Kochba rebellion was even more disastrous than the uprising against the Romans that began in 66 C.E., which ended in the destruction of the Temple of Jerusalem in 70 and the capture of the last fortress of Masada in 73 (E). By the time of Hadrian, Rome was becoming the most important center of Christianity (B).

91. **(D)** Michelangelo Buonarroti's *David*, depicting the ancient king of the Israelites, is one of the most famous works of art from the Renaissance. It was sculpted from marble between 1501 and 1504 and stands on display in Florence. Some 17 feet tall, this muscular male nude is characteristic of Michelangelo's monumental style.

92. **(B)** The Council of Nicaea organized by the emperor Constantine in 325 defined correct, or orthodox, teaching concerning the Trinity. It condemned the belief taught by the bishop Arius, and therefore known as Arianism, that Jesus Christ was created by God rather than begotten from the eternal divine substance, and that the Son is therefore of lesser dignity than the Father. The council was a victory for the bishop Athanasius (c. 293–373), one of the Greek doctors of the Church, who maintained that the Son was eternally begotten of the same divine substance rather than created, and therefore equal in dignity to the Father. The council concluded that Athanasius represented the correct teaching, or orthodoxy, which then became a feature of Catholic doctrine, encapsulated in the Nicene Creed. Although Arianism was formally condemned at this time, it persisted for several centuries before its final disappearance, in part because Constantine and his successors had second thoughts about the issue, and in part because the barbarians who had been converted by Arian missionaries refused to abandon the form of Christianity that they had initially accepted.

A second council at Nicaea, convened by the Byzantine empress Irene in 787 C.E., condemned Iconoclasm (C), that is, the destruction of religious images called *icons*. The heresy known as Monophysitism (A) contradicted the orthodox teaching that Jesus Christ had a dual nature (fully human and fully divine) and instead maintained that he had only one nature (*mono-* one, *physis* nature), in which the human aspect was overshadowed by the divine. Monophysitism was condemned at the Council of Chalcedon in 451. Gnosticism (D) was an early heresy that challenged Christian orthodoxy in the second and third centuries by rejecting the Old Testament and teaching that matter was created by an evil deity who trapped spirits in bodies. Although Gnosticism was suppressed, its basic dualism was revived during the twelfth and thirteenth centuries in the heresy of Catharism (E), also known as Albigensianism, after the southern French town of Albi in which the heresy was mainly centered.

93. **(A)** The inability of the western half of the Roman Empire to fulfill its duties after the fourth century resulted in the transfer of some government functions to the only other bureaucratic organization available, namely, the Church, which was led by the bishop of Rome known as the pope. Although Pope Leo the Great (440–461) demonstrated how the papacy began to assume diplomatic responsibilities when he persuaded Attila the Hun not to sack Rome in 452, he was unable to protect Rome against the Vandals in 455 (E). Similarly, Pope Gregory the Great (590–604) did not overawe the Lombards who threatened Rome, but managed to protect the city against them only by paying tribute. Later, Stephen II (752–757) turned to the Franks for protection. The Frankish king, Pepin the Short, defeated the Lombards and gave the pope some of their territories in central Italy to govern. This "Donation of Pepin," which established the Papal States, was the formal beginning of the papacy as a political entity. It inspired an eighth-century forgery known as the "Donation of Constantine," which claimed that Constantine the Great had appointed the popes as rulers in the west when he moved his capital to the east (C). Popes referred to this document to defend their right to rule until its falsity was proven in the fifteenth century. In general, popes had considerable difficulty convincing European society that they had political authority over kings (D). The Investiture Controversy of the eleventh and twelfth centuries demonstrates the level of resistance to this idea. Christianity did not initially combine political and religious authority, for it arose as an underground religion without political power, and its founder's words—"Render unto Caesar what is Caesar's, render unto God what is God's"—indicate a distinction between political and religious forms of authority (B).

94. **(E)** The Old English epic *Beowulf*, which survives in a manuscript written about the year 1000, describes the adventures of a hero who fights a series of monsters. This literary work is not attributed to any author. The Old English language is also called Anglo-Saxon. It flourished until the twelfth century, when the influence of the Normans, who invaded England in 1066, began to change the language into a distinctly different form known as Middle English, represented by Geoffrey Chaucer's *Canterbury Tales* (C), which were written in the fourteenth century. The *Edda* (D) was written

in Old Norse, or Old Icelandic. There are actually two texts of that name: the *Elder Edda* (also known as the *Poetic Edda*) is a collection of poems recounting stories of Scandinavian and Germanic mythology. The *Younger Edda* (also known as the *Prose Edda*), is a narrative on the same subject written down in the thirteenth century by the Icelandic author, Snorri Sturluson (1179–1241). The anonymous *Song of Roland* (A) was written in Old French during the eleventh or twelfth century. The *Divine Comedy* (B) was written in the Italian vernacular by Dante Alighieri (1265–1321).

95. **(E)** *Don Quixote* (written in two parts, in 1605 and 1615) is a novel about an idealistic Spanish nobleman who seeks adventure as a knight-errant but finds that chivalry is out of step with the modern world. Miguel de Cervantes (1547–1616) used the work as a vehicle to satirize early modern Spanish society. His own life reflects the misadventures of his novel's protagonist. Cervantes fought at the naval battle of Lepanto in 1571, was captured by pirates, and sold as a slave. He made several attempts to escape before family and friends were finally able to ransom him. Unable to secure employment, he took odd jobs and wrote novels and plays in order to support himself. Success eluded him until he wrote about the misadventures of Don Quixote, and even then pirated editions deprived him of much of the royalties he deserved.

96. **(D)** Henry II of England (1154–1189) was initially the vassal of Louis VII of France (A). When he became king of England, he married Eleanor of Aquitaine, whose marriage with Louis VII had just been annulled. Henry soon appointed his chancellor, Thomas Becket, as the archbishop of Canterbury, but Henry's attempts to put churchmen accused of crimes on trial in his own royal courts rather than in the ecclesiastical courts brought the two men into conflict. Their stand-off ended in 1170 with the murder of Becket by some of Henry's knights. Within a few years, Henry's sons, egged on by their mother, rebelled against him. Among these was Richard the Lion-Hearted, himself later king of England (C). Philip II Augustus (B), the son of Louis VII, participated with Richard in the Third Crusade. Henry IV of Germany (E), as the Holy Roman Emperor, was vassal to no one.

97. **(C)** The map represents areas controlled by Rome after the Third Punic War (which ended in 146 B.C.E.) but before the Second Triumvirate (which began in 43 B.C.E.); in fact, the map represents Roman territory around the year 60 B.C.E. It is possible to arrive at the answer by a process of elimination. Choice (A) cannot be right because Rome did not control Sicily until after the First Punic War (264–241 B.C.E.). Choice (B) is incorrect because Rome did not control Carthage (in North Africa) until after the Third Punic War.

Choices (D) and (E) can be eliminated because Rome controlled Gaul (the region of modern France) during the reigns of Augustus Caesar (27 B.C.E.–14 C.E.) and Marcus Aurelius (161–180 C.E.); in fact, Julius Caesar conquered Gaul between 58 and 50 B.C.E.—soon after the date depicted by the map.

98. **(C)** *The Defender of the Peace*, which Marsilius of Padua wrote in 1324, argued that political power derives from the people. Marsilius rejected the notion that the emperor receives his authority from God (A). He believed that the pope should have no political authority whatsoever (B) and should not even enjoy spiritual leadership of the Church, which should be governed by councils composed of lay people (D). His ideal form of government was not that of the nobles (E), but that of the Italian communes (city-states), whose rule was based on representation.

99. **(D)** The Guelfs were members of a political faction that opposed the authority of the Holy Roman Emperor in Italy and rallied around the pope for solidarity. Their counterparts—those who wanted Italy to remain part of the Holy Roman Empire, under the control of the emperor—were known as Ghibellines (E). Condottieri (A) were leaders of mercenary armies in Italy. Janissaries (B) were Ottoman soldiers, recruited as children from the Christian population and converted to Islam, who were trained to be loyal only to the sultan. Marranos (C) were Jews who converted to Christianity in order to escape torture by the Spanish Inquisition; they were suspected of divided loyalty and often persecuted.

100. **(A)** The Fourth Lateran Council, convened by Pope Innocent III in 1215 (D), did not exonerate the Waldensians but declared them heretics. The Waldensians were named after their leader, Peter Waldo, a wealthy merchant of Lyons who embraced a life of poverty and Christian simplicity around 1170. His followers criticized the hierarchy of the Church and denied that the sacraments were necessary for salvation. In condemning the Waldensians, the Fourth Lateran Council reaffirmed the necessity of receiving the sacraments for salvation, identified seven of them, and required all adult Christians to receive the sacraments of confession and communion at least once a year (B). With regard to communion (the Eucharist), it adopted as dogma the theory of transubstantiation, which maintained that the bread and wine used in the Mass are transformed into the substance of Christ's body and blood (C). The council was the most widely attended in the Middle Ages and even included the patriarch of Constantinople (E). Although the Latin and Greek churches were still estranged at this time, Constantinople was in the hands of Latin Christians who had conquered it during the Fourth Crusade.

101. **(C)** The interior shown is from the church of St.-Sernin in Toulouse, which was built 1080–1120 and is an example of Romanesque architecture. The characteristic that identifies this style of architecture is the rounded arch, which was a Roman feature used in medieval churches during the eleventh and twelfth centuries—hence "Romanesque," which means "Roman-like." It is not Gothic (A) because the Gothic style used a pointed arch, not a rounded one. Baroque architecture (E) was highly ornate, not sparse and simple as the Romanesque pictured here. There are no fully intact examples of Mycenaean or Minoan architecture, which rules out (B) and (D).

102. **(B)** When the Treaty of Verdun was concluded in 843, neither France nor Germany yet existed, but the treaty divided the Frankish Empire into a western kingdom that would evolve into France, an eastern kingdom that would evolve into Germany, and a middle kingdom that would be absorbed by its neighbors. The process of absorption generated tension between the westerners and easterners which, in the modern age, presented cause for war between France and Germany. The Treaty of Verdun was concluded between the grandsons of Charlemagne, not his sons (A). Charlemagne's son and heir was Louis the Pious (814–840). Louis' three sons fought among themselves before settling their differences with the Treaty of Verdun, whereby Charles the Bald received the western kingdom, Louis the German received the eastern kingdom, and Lothair received the middle kingdom. Even though France and Germany did not yet exist, there were already strong cultural differences between the eastern and western ends of the Frankish Empire, as seen in the Strasbourg Oaths, which established an alliance between Charles and Louis in 842; the text reveals that Charles swore the oath in a Latinate language recognizable as Old French, whereas Louis swore the oath in an archaic form of the German language.

Since the Treaty of Verdun was a measure intended to stop the civil wars that raged between Charlemagne's grandsons, it did nothing to stop the Viking raids (C), which only increased in intensity until 911, when a successor of Charles the Bald recognized the right of the Northmen to settle the lands along the lower Seine River (named Normandy after them). The Magyar raids (D) did not begin until about 900, and were ended in 955 at the Battle of Lechfeld by the German king Otto I (later Holy Roman Emperor), who ruled a successor state to that of Louis the German. The Muslims (E) lost control of the Mediterranean by the time of the Crusades.

103. **(E)**   Nominalism was a theory that ideas have no substantial reality of their own, but are merely verbal labels or "names" (in Latin, *nomina*) which human beings attach to the concepts that exist nowhere but in their own thoughts. William of Ockham is famous for formulating the principle of logical economy, which maintains that entities should not be multiplied without cause. In other words, if one cannot provide a logical justification for the existence of some abstract being, one cannot use its existence as a premise upon which to build a logical system, be it a system of natural philosophy or theology, as the scholastics before William of Ockham had done. This principle of logical economy is known as "Ockham's razor," whose function is to reduce any system to the smallest possible number of elements. Modern science proceeds according to this fundamental principle, in conjunction with experimentation and measurement; thus, if a supposed entity—whether the soul or God—cannot be measured or its existence proven logically in some way, the scientist should proceed under the assumption that it does not exist. While William of Ockham was a forerunner of modern science because of his reductionism, he did not reject the existence of the soul or God because he did not adhere to logic alone; he also accepted the evidence of divine revelation. His "razor" was not used against the Christian faith but against the elaborate systems of theology that were constructed on what he regarded as faulty premises. Thus, he was an opponent of the Thomists and Scotists, as the followers of Thomas Aquinas (B) and Duns Scotus (A) are known. Roger Bacon (D) made important contributions to the study of natural philosophy which helped pave the way for the rise of modern science, but he was active in the thirteenth century, not the fourteenth. Dante Alighieri (C) was a poet, whose *Divine Comedy* presents the various philosophical schools of thought, but he was not a leading thinker of the nominalist school. Nominalism was already debated in the twelfth century, when it was set in contrast to "realism," the philosophical position that ideas are not merely concepts but are real, having a substantial existence of their own outside the human mind (as Plato had taught with his Theory of Forms or Ideas).

104. **(A)**   Aristarchus argued that the Earth revolves around the Sun (known as the heliocentric theory) and that days and nights are caused by the rotation of the Earth. The astrolabe (a device for making observations of the sky) was invented by Hipparchus (D). The circumference of the Earth was accurately calculated by Eratosthenes (E). The geometry book known as the *Elements* was written by Euclid (C). The pump known as "Archimedes' screw" was, of course, invented by Archimedes (B).

105. **(D)**   Homer's *Odyssey* describes the homeward voyage of Odysseus, the king of Ithaca who designed the Trojan horse used by the Mycenaean

Greeks to enter and overthrow the city of Troy. Homer's *Iliad* describes the war of the Mycenaeans against Troy (C). The voyage of the Trojan prince, Aeneas, to found a new city (Rome) was a Latin epic written by Virgil, entitled the *Aeneid* (A). The voyage of the Argonauts is described in the *Argonautica*, written by the Hellenistic poet, Apollonius of Rhodes (c. 295–215 B.C.E.) (B). *Gilgamesh* (E) is not a Greek epic but a Sumerian epic.

106. **(C)** The photograph shows a reconstruction of the famous Neo-Babylonian *Ishtar Gate*, on display in Berlin. It is made of colorful glazed brick and is decorated with alternating images of bulls and dragons. It was commissioned by Nebuchadnezzar II as part of his project to rebuild Babylon.

107. **(B)** Charlemagne sought to promote uniformity of monastic practice within his realm by imposing the form of monasticism established by St. Benedict of Nursia (c. 480–547). Before Charlemagne's intervention, monasticism varied widely from one community to another. Some communities were marked by excessive austerity, others by laxness; but the *Rule* of St. Benedict effectively balanced prayer, study, and physical labor. There existed a *Rule* of St. Augustine (written in the fifth century), but it was a very brief document that required additional commentary before it could serve as an outline for a daily regimen, and it was not revived until the eleventh and twelfth centuries, when the canons regular (priests who live together in a community and follow a rule) adopted it as part of the reforms associated with Pope Gregory VII (1073–1085). An order of Augustinian friars later arose in the thirteenth century (A). These Augustinians (also known as Austin friars) were part of the same thirteenth-century spiritual revival that inspired St. Francis of Assisi to found the Franciscan friars (E) and St. Dominic de Guzman to found the Dominican friars (D). The Jesuits (C), or members of the Society of Jesus, did not appear until the sixteenth century; they were founded by St. Ignatius of Loyola as part of the Counter Reformation.

108. **(B)** The Black Death first struck western Europe between 1347 and 1351, killing one-third or more of the European population and causing the rapid collapse of financial institutions (A). Although everyone suffered from the disaster, serfs and workers in the towns were eventually able to improve their employment conditions as a delayed effect of this terrible loss of population. Before the Black Death, Europe suffered from overpopulation: the number of people had swelled to the point that not enough food could be raised to support everyone, and there was more manpower than opportunity for employment. After the Black Death, however, Europe was faced with a manpower shortage. Since laborers were now low in supply and high in

demand, they were able to demand wage increases (D); and since the existing fields could raise more than enough food for the survivors, the supply of food exceeded demand so that prices decreased (E). Not all the consequences were immediate. Lords initially tried to resist any drastic changes in their economic practices and refused to acknowledge the demands of the peasants, triggering widespread revolts (C). Although the uprisings were crushed by the upper classes, the laborers eventually were able to negotiate favorable terms of employment. Thus, laborers received higher pay and serfs were able to reduce their manorial obligations.

109. **(C)**   The remark is attributed to Pope Leo X (1513–1521), the second son of the Florentine banker and patron of the arts, Lorenzo de' Medici. This Renaissance pope squandered the papal treasury on luxuries and artistic endeavors; his attempt to replenish the coffers and fund his building programs in Rome by selling indulgences precipitated Martin Luther's rebellion against the Roman Catholic Church. The other popes listed were individuals of high ideals and strong leadership. Pope Leo I, known as Saint Leo the Great (440–461), established the primacy of the bishop of Rome and used his authority to dissuade Attila the Hun from sacking the city in 452 (B). Pope Gregory I (590–604), also known as Saint Gregory the Great, was a Benedictine monk, and in fact the first monk to become pope (D). Not only did Gregory I lead the Church spiritually, but he cared for the physical needs of the people of Rome during a time when the emperor in Constantinople had abandoned them to their fate among the warlike Lombards. Gregory introduced the motto that later popes adopted: "servant of the servants of God." An eleventh-century pontiff took the name Gregory VII (1073–1085) in memory of Gregory the Great as he set out upon his program of extensive ecclesiastical reform (E). Gregory VII's assertion that only the pope can appoint bishops brought him into conflict with the Holy Roman Emperor, Henry IV, in a struggle over the relationship between church and state known as the Investiture Controversy. Finally, the pontificate of Innocent III (1198–1216) has been regarded as the achievement of a "papal monarchy," in which the papacy attained power over matters both spiritual and temporal (A).

110. **(A)**   Although Dante (1265–1321) was active in Florentine politics, Petrarch (1304–1374) shunned politics in order to devote himself fully to a life of letters. Both wrote significant works in Latin, but they are best known for their Italian literature (C), which includes lyric poetry about their infatuation for women who did not return their love (B): Dante idealized Beatrice, and Petrarch idealized Laura. Dante spent much of his life in exile and died in Ravenna, where he is buried; although Petrarch was not exiled from Florence, his father had been, and he spent much of his life traveling

between France and Italy (D). Both poets drew heavily upon classical Latin literature for inspiration (E), as seen in Petrarch's avowed love for the writings of Cicero, and Dante's choice of Virgil as a guide through the Inferno in his vernacular epic, the *Divine Comedy*.

111. **(E)**   The *encomienda* system was used by the Spanish in their New World colonies. It forced native Americans to work on great plantations and was closer to the medieval manorial system than the new economic forms of nascent capitalism that the Italians were developing. The Spanish *encomienda* should not be confused with the Italian *commenda*, a temporary partnership which arose in the late Middle Ages whereby an investor contributed capital to a trader who then did all the work required to turn a profit; the profits were shared between the two. The *commenda* was a prototype of the joint-stock companies that arose during the Commercial Revolution of the sixteenth century.

Although during the Middle Ages the Church had condemned the charging of interest as usury and therefore denied banking as a legitimate profession for Christians, it was more flexible during the Renaissance in its definition of what constituted usury, which allowed wealthy merchants, like the Medici of Florence, to invest their profits in money-lending. In fact, the popes employed the Medici as their bankers until 1494 (when the Medici bank collapsed). The new apparatus of money-making involved an international network of branch offices (D) which provided a form of credit known as bills of exchange (A), as well as insurance policies for cargo known as "sea loans" (B). Double-entry bookkeeping (C) was developed to record the complex transactions that were now taking place.

112. **(E)**   The Polish astronomer Nicholas Copernicus (1473–1543) was the first European scholar to challenge the geocentric model of the Ptolemaic universe, which held that the earth is at the center and the sun travels around it. Copernicus made the case for a heliocentric, or sun-centered universe, in his book *On the Revolutions of the Celestial Orbs* (1543). He was later supported by Kepler and Galileo (C, D). Montaigne and Rabelais (A, B) were not astronomers but writers; Montaigne was renowned for his essays, and Rabelais for his satires.

113. **(D)**   The Protestant Reformation greatly benefited from the printing press as a means for the rapid dissemination of information—especially theological works and political pamphlets. The power of printing was acknowledged by the papacy in its publication of an Index of Prohibited

Books in 1559, which sought to limit the spread of Protestantism through censorship. Both the Hundred Years' War, which ended in 1453 (B), and the Reconquista (the Christian reconquest of Spain from the Muslims), which ended in 1492 (C), were drawing to a close when printing appeared around 1450. Likewise, conciliarism (E), or the primacy of councils in the governance of the Church, was largely over by the time printing appeared; the height of conciliarism was the Council of Constance, from 1414 to 1418. The renovation of the church known as the Gregorian Reform (A) occurred in the eleventh century, long before the invention of printing.

114. **(D)**   Cortez was a Spanish conquistador who overthrew the Aztec Empire. Bartholomew Diaz (C) rounded the Cape of Good Hope in 1488. Da Gama (A) reached India in 1497. Pedro Cabral (E) crossed the Atlantic and claimed Brazil for Portugal in 1500. Albuquerque (B) effectively laid the foundations for the Portuguese empire in the east by establishing a string of trading posts along the coast of India; he served as governor from 1509 to 1515.

115. **(E)**   The area shaded on the map represents the only territories controlled by the king of France, Philip II Augustus (1180–1223), at the time of his accession. It constituted the region surrounding Paris and is known as the Île de France, or "island of France." All the other titles listed were held in 1180 by one man—Henry II, the king of England (1154–1189) (D), who was nominally a vassal to Philip II inasmuch as Henry was duke of Normandy (A), duke of Aquitaine (C), and count of Anjou (B). His entire realm, which included half of France, is known as the Angevin Empire (after the Latin form of his dynastic name, Anjou). Philip II earned the title "Augustus" because of his energetic efforts to extend the royal domain, mostly at the expense of Henry II's sons. At the time of Philip's death, the royal territory was roughly equal in size to the regions under English control.

116. **(D)**   The Peace of Augsburg did not recognize Calvin's or Zwingli's religious reforms. It ended a civil war within the Holy Roman Empire which began in 1546 when Charles V (1519–1558) attacked the Schmalkaldic League, a defensive alliance of Protestant princes (B), and established the principle that the prince of a sovereign state should decide the religious alignment of his state (E). The only religious alternative to Catholicism it recognized was Lutheranism (C), as outlined in the Augsburg Confession drawn up by Luther's discipline, Melanchthon (A).

117. **(B)** Vienna was besieged in 1529 by the Turks of the Ottoman sultan, Suleiman the Magnificent (1520–1566). However, the Hapsburgs (E), led by the Holy Roman Emperor (A), Charles V (1519–1558), were able to defend it. The Seljuks (C) were an earlier Turkish dynasty. The Hohenzollerns (D) founded Prussia during the Reformation.

118. **(E)** The Tudor dynasty came to power in England when Henry Tudor, earl of Richmond, defeated Richard III (1483–1485) at the Battle of Bosworth Field in 1485. This engagement concluded the dynastic struggle known as the Wars of the Roses, an English civil war in which the House of York (C) challenged the House of Lancaster (A). Richard III was the last representative of the House of York. The Tudors reigned until the death of Elizabeth I (1558–1603), after which the Stuarts (B) inherited the crown. The House of Anjou (D) preceded the House of Lancaster.

119. **(C)** The prophets did not refrain from criticizing their kings when their kings acted unjustly. Thus, the prophet Elijah denounced Ahab, king of Israel (871–852 B.C.E.), for executing one of his subjects on false charges so that he could seize his property. Since the prophets dared to challenge the authority even of the head of state, they can be seen as ancient proponents of civil disobedience. They also served as the conscience of the Hebrews. The prophets frequently criticized the Hebrew people for continuing to worship many gods (especially in the form of idols). They declared that Yahweh was the one true God (B) and the Hebrews were specially chosen by Yahweh to worship him alone (A). When Hebrew society shifted from a pastoral economy to a town-based economy, the prophet Amos denounced the poverty caused by exploitative businessmen (D). The prophets commonly taught that misfortunes afflicting the Hebrew people (both those of the kingdom of Judah and the kingdom of Israel) were divine punishments for sin, intended by God to bring the wayward people back to their senses (E).

120. **(C)** John of Leiden led a takeover of the German town of Münster in 1534 and declared himself the king of a New Zion, which permitted polygamy on the model of the ancient patriarchs of the Old Testament and established the communal possession of property on the model of the early Christians in the New Testament. The city was besieged and captured, and John of Leiden was executed in 1536. None of the other choices fit the profile. Thomas More (A) was an English Catholic and saint who wrote a book about an ideal state (*Utopia*, 1516). John Calvin (E) was active primarily in Geneva. Zwingli and Luther (B, D) both opposed Anabaptism, which took its name from its practice of re-baptizing Christians who joined the sect.

BIBLIOGRAPHY

The following are a few Western Civilization textbooks currently in print that are often assigned in introductory college courses. You may find them helpful in preparing for the CLEP examination, especially if you want to give more attention to maps or artwork. While the editions are current at the time of this writing, be aware that such textbooks are updated every few years (at which time they may also change publishers).

Kagan, Donald; Steven Ozment; Frank Turner, *The Western Heritage*, 8th ed. (Prentice Hall, 2004).

McKay, John P.; Bennett D. Hill; John Buckler, *A History of Western Society*, 8th ed. (Houghton Mifflin Co., 2005).

Noble, Thomas F.X.; Barry Strauss; Duane J. Osheim; Kristen B. Neuschel; William B. Cohen; David D. Roberts, *Western Civilization: The Continuing Experiment*, 4th ed. (Houghton Mifflin Co., 2005).

Perry, Marvin; Myrrna Chase; James R. Jacob; Margaret C. Jacob; Theodore H. Von Laue; George W. Bock, *Western Civilization: Ideas, Politics, and Society*, 7th ed. (Houghton Mifflin Co., 2004).

Spielvogel, Jackson J., *Western Civilization*, 6th ed. (Wadsworth Publishing Co., 2005).

CLEP WESTERN CIVILIZATION I—TEST 1

1. Ⓐ Ⓑ Ⓒ Ⓓ Ⓔ	41. Ⓐ Ⓑ Ⓒ Ⓓ Ⓔ	81. Ⓐ Ⓑ Ⓒ Ⓓ Ⓔ
2. Ⓐ Ⓑ Ⓒ Ⓓ Ⓔ	42. Ⓐ Ⓑ Ⓒ Ⓓ Ⓔ	82. Ⓐ Ⓑ Ⓒ Ⓓ Ⓔ
3. Ⓐ Ⓑ Ⓒ Ⓓ Ⓔ	43. Ⓐ Ⓑ Ⓒ Ⓓ Ⓔ	83. Ⓐ Ⓑ Ⓒ Ⓓ Ⓔ
4. Ⓐ Ⓑ Ⓒ Ⓓ Ⓔ	44. Ⓐ Ⓑ Ⓒ Ⓓ Ⓔ	84. Ⓐ Ⓑ Ⓒ Ⓓ Ⓔ
5. Ⓐ Ⓑ Ⓒ Ⓓ Ⓔ	45. Ⓐ Ⓑ Ⓒ Ⓓ Ⓔ	85. Ⓐ Ⓑ Ⓒ Ⓓ Ⓔ
6. Ⓐ Ⓑ Ⓒ Ⓓ Ⓔ	46. Ⓐ Ⓑ Ⓒ Ⓓ Ⓔ	86. Ⓐ Ⓑ Ⓒ Ⓓ Ⓔ
7. Ⓐ Ⓑ Ⓒ Ⓓ Ⓔ	47. Ⓐ Ⓑ Ⓒ Ⓓ Ⓔ	87. Ⓐ Ⓑ Ⓒ Ⓓ Ⓔ
8. Ⓐ Ⓑ Ⓒ Ⓓ Ⓔ	48. Ⓐ Ⓑ Ⓒ Ⓓ Ⓔ	88. Ⓐ Ⓑ Ⓒ Ⓓ Ⓔ
9. Ⓐ Ⓑ Ⓒ Ⓓ Ⓔ	49. Ⓐ Ⓑ Ⓒ Ⓓ Ⓔ	89. Ⓐ Ⓑ Ⓒ Ⓓ Ⓔ
10. Ⓐ Ⓑ Ⓒ Ⓓ Ⓔ	50. Ⓐ Ⓑ Ⓒ Ⓓ Ⓔ	90. Ⓐ Ⓑ Ⓒ Ⓓ Ⓔ
11. Ⓐ Ⓑ Ⓒ Ⓓ Ⓔ	51. Ⓐ Ⓑ Ⓒ Ⓓ Ⓔ	91. Ⓐ Ⓑ Ⓒ Ⓓ Ⓔ
12. Ⓐ Ⓑ Ⓒ Ⓓ Ⓔ	52. Ⓐ Ⓑ Ⓒ Ⓓ Ⓔ	92. Ⓐ Ⓑ Ⓒ Ⓓ Ⓔ
13. Ⓐ Ⓑ Ⓒ Ⓓ Ⓔ	53. Ⓐ Ⓑ Ⓒ Ⓓ Ⓔ	93. Ⓐ Ⓑ Ⓒ Ⓓ Ⓔ
14. Ⓐ Ⓑ Ⓒ Ⓓ Ⓔ	54. Ⓐ Ⓑ Ⓒ Ⓓ Ⓔ	94. Ⓐ Ⓑ Ⓒ Ⓓ Ⓔ
15. Ⓐ Ⓑ Ⓒ Ⓓ Ⓔ	55. Ⓐ Ⓑ Ⓒ Ⓓ Ⓔ	95. Ⓐ Ⓑ Ⓒ Ⓓ Ⓔ
16. Ⓐ Ⓑ Ⓒ Ⓓ Ⓔ	56. Ⓐ Ⓑ Ⓒ Ⓓ Ⓔ	96. Ⓐ Ⓑ Ⓒ Ⓓ Ⓔ
17. Ⓐ Ⓑ Ⓒ Ⓓ Ⓔ	57. Ⓐ Ⓑ Ⓒ Ⓓ Ⓔ	97. Ⓐ Ⓑ Ⓒ Ⓓ Ⓔ
18. Ⓐ Ⓑ Ⓒ Ⓓ Ⓔ	58. Ⓐ Ⓑ Ⓒ Ⓓ Ⓔ	98. Ⓐ Ⓑ Ⓒ Ⓓ Ⓔ
19. Ⓐ Ⓑ Ⓒ Ⓓ Ⓔ	59. Ⓐ Ⓑ Ⓒ Ⓓ Ⓔ	99. Ⓐ Ⓑ Ⓒ Ⓓ Ⓔ
20. Ⓐ Ⓑ Ⓒ Ⓓ Ⓔ	60. Ⓐ Ⓑ Ⓒ Ⓓ Ⓔ	100. Ⓐ Ⓑ Ⓒ Ⓓ Ⓔ
21. Ⓐ Ⓑ Ⓒ Ⓓ Ⓔ	61. Ⓐ Ⓑ Ⓒ Ⓓ Ⓔ	101. Ⓐ Ⓑ Ⓒ Ⓓ Ⓔ
22. Ⓐ Ⓑ Ⓒ Ⓓ Ⓔ	62. Ⓐ Ⓑ Ⓒ Ⓓ Ⓔ	102. Ⓐ Ⓑ Ⓒ Ⓓ Ⓔ
23. Ⓐ Ⓑ Ⓒ Ⓓ Ⓔ	63. Ⓐ Ⓑ Ⓒ Ⓓ Ⓔ	103. Ⓐ Ⓑ Ⓒ Ⓓ Ⓔ
24. Ⓐ Ⓑ Ⓒ Ⓓ Ⓔ	64. Ⓐ Ⓑ Ⓒ Ⓓ Ⓔ	104. Ⓐ Ⓑ Ⓒ Ⓓ Ⓔ
25. Ⓐ Ⓑ Ⓒ Ⓓ Ⓔ	65. Ⓐ Ⓑ Ⓒ Ⓓ Ⓔ	105. Ⓐ Ⓑ Ⓒ Ⓓ Ⓔ
26. Ⓐ Ⓑ Ⓒ Ⓓ Ⓔ	66. Ⓐ Ⓑ Ⓒ Ⓓ Ⓔ	106. Ⓐ Ⓑ Ⓒ Ⓓ Ⓔ
27. Ⓐ Ⓑ Ⓒ Ⓓ Ⓔ	67. Ⓐ Ⓑ Ⓒ Ⓓ Ⓔ	107. Ⓐ Ⓑ Ⓒ Ⓓ Ⓔ
28. Ⓐ Ⓑ Ⓒ Ⓓ Ⓔ	68. Ⓐ Ⓑ Ⓒ Ⓓ Ⓔ	108. Ⓐ Ⓑ Ⓒ Ⓓ Ⓔ
29. Ⓐ Ⓑ Ⓒ Ⓓ Ⓔ	69. Ⓐ Ⓑ Ⓒ Ⓓ Ⓔ	109. Ⓐ Ⓑ Ⓒ Ⓓ Ⓔ
30. Ⓐ Ⓑ Ⓒ Ⓓ Ⓔ	70. Ⓐ Ⓑ Ⓒ Ⓓ Ⓔ	110. Ⓐ Ⓑ Ⓒ Ⓓ Ⓔ
31. Ⓐ Ⓑ Ⓒ Ⓓ Ⓔ	71. Ⓐ Ⓑ Ⓒ Ⓓ Ⓔ	111. Ⓐ Ⓑ Ⓒ Ⓓ Ⓔ
32. Ⓐ Ⓑ Ⓒ Ⓓ Ⓔ	72. Ⓐ Ⓑ Ⓒ Ⓓ Ⓔ	112. Ⓐ Ⓑ Ⓒ Ⓓ Ⓔ
33. Ⓐ Ⓑ Ⓒ Ⓓ Ⓔ	73. Ⓐ Ⓑ Ⓒ Ⓓ Ⓔ	113. Ⓐ Ⓑ Ⓒ Ⓓ Ⓔ
34. Ⓐ Ⓑ Ⓒ Ⓓ Ⓔ	74. Ⓐ Ⓑ Ⓒ Ⓓ Ⓔ	114. Ⓐ Ⓑ Ⓒ Ⓓ Ⓔ
35. Ⓐ Ⓑ Ⓒ Ⓓ Ⓔ	75. Ⓐ Ⓑ Ⓒ Ⓓ Ⓔ	115. Ⓐ Ⓑ Ⓒ Ⓓ Ⓔ
36. Ⓐ Ⓑ Ⓒ Ⓓ Ⓔ	76. Ⓐ Ⓑ Ⓒ Ⓓ Ⓔ	116. Ⓐ Ⓑ Ⓒ Ⓓ Ⓔ
37. Ⓐ Ⓑ Ⓒ Ⓓ Ⓔ	77. Ⓐ Ⓑ Ⓒ Ⓓ Ⓔ	117. Ⓐ Ⓑ Ⓒ Ⓓ Ⓔ
38. Ⓐ Ⓑ Ⓒ Ⓓ Ⓔ	78. Ⓐ Ⓑ Ⓒ Ⓓ Ⓔ	118. Ⓐ Ⓑ Ⓒ Ⓓ Ⓔ
39. Ⓐ Ⓑ Ⓒ Ⓓ Ⓔ	79. Ⓐ Ⓑ Ⓒ Ⓓ Ⓔ	119. Ⓐ Ⓑ Ⓒ Ⓓ Ⓔ
40. Ⓐ Ⓑ Ⓒ Ⓓ Ⓔ	80. Ⓐ Ⓑ Ⓒ Ⓓ Ⓔ	120. Ⓐ Ⓑ Ⓒ Ⓓ Ⓔ

CLEP WESTERN CIVILIZATION I—TEST 2

1. Ⓐ Ⓑ Ⓒ Ⓓ Ⓔ	41. Ⓐ Ⓑ Ⓒ Ⓓ Ⓔ	81. Ⓐ Ⓑ Ⓒ Ⓓ Ⓔ
2. Ⓐ Ⓑ Ⓒ Ⓓ Ⓔ	42. Ⓐ Ⓑ Ⓒ Ⓓ Ⓔ	82. Ⓐ Ⓑ Ⓒ Ⓓ Ⓔ
3. Ⓐ Ⓑ Ⓒ Ⓓ Ⓔ	43. Ⓐ Ⓑ Ⓒ Ⓓ Ⓔ	83. Ⓐ Ⓑ Ⓒ Ⓓ Ⓔ
4. Ⓐ Ⓑ Ⓒ Ⓓ Ⓔ	44. Ⓐ Ⓑ Ⓒ Ⓓ Ⓔ	84. Ⓐ Ⓑ Ⓒ Ⓓ Ⓔ
5. Ⓐ Ⓑ Ⓒ Ⓓ Ⓔ	45. Ⓐ Ⓑ Ⓒ Ⓓ Ⓔ	85. Ⓐ Ⓑ Ⓒ Ⓓ Ⓔ
6. Ⓐ Ⓑ Ⓒ Ⓓ Ⓔ	46. Ⓐ Ⓑ Ⓒ Ⓓ Ⓔ	86. Ⓐ Ⓑ Ⓒ Ⓓ Ⓔ
7. Ⓐ Ⓑ Ⓒ Ⓓ Ⓔ	47. Ⓐ Ⓑ Ⓒ Ⓓ Ⓔ	87. Ⓐ Ⓑ Ⓒ Ⓓ Ⓔ
8. Ⓐ Ⓑ Ⓒ Ⓓ Ⓔ	48. Ⓐ Ⓑ Ⓒ Ⓓ Ⓔ	88. Ⓐ Ⓑ Ⓒ Ⓓ Ⓔ
9. Ⓐ Ⓑ Ⓒ Ⓓ Ⓔ	49. Ⓐ Ⓑ Ⓒ Ⓓ Ⓔ	89. Ⓐ Ⓑ Ⓒ Ⓓ Ⓔ
10. Ⓐ Ⓑ Ⓒ Ⓓ Ⓔ	50. Ⓐ Ⓑ Ⓒ Ⓓ Ⓔ	90. Ⓐ Ⓑ Ⓒ Ⓓ Ⓔ
11. Ⓐ Ⓑ Ⓒ Ⓓ Ⓔ	51. Ⓐ Ⓑ Ⓒ Ⓓ Ⓔ	91. Ⓐ Ⓑ Ⓒ Ⓓ Ⓔ
12. Ⓐ Ⓑ Ⓒ Ⓓ Ⓔ	52. Ⓐ Ⓑ Ⓒ Ⓓ Ⓔ	92. Ⓐ Ⓑ Ⓒ Ⓓ Ⓔ
13. Ⓐ Ⓑ Ⓒ Ⓓ Ⓔ	53. Ⓐ Ⓑ Ⓒ Ⓓ Ⓔ	93. Ⓐ Ⓑ Ⓒ Ⓓ Ⓔ
14. Ⓐ Ⓑ Ⓒ Ⓓ Ⓔ	54. Ⓐ Ⓑ Ⓒ Ⓓ Ⓔ	94. Ⓐ Ⓑ Ⓒ Ⓓ Ⓔ
15. Ⓐ Ⓑ Ⓒ Ⓓ Ⓔ	55. Ⓐ Ⓑ Ⓒ Ⓓ Ⓔ	95. Ⓐ Ⓑ Ⓒ Ⓓ Ⓔ
16. Ⓐ Ⓑ Ⓒ Ⓓ Ⓔ	56. Ⓐ Ⓑ Ⓒ Ⓓ Ⓔ	96. Ⓐ Ⓑ Ⓒ Ⓓ Ⓔ
17. Ⓐ Ⓑ Ⓒ Ⓓ Ⓔ	57. Ⓐ Ⓑ Ⓒ Ⓓ Ⓔ	97. Ⓐ Ⓑ Ⓒ Ⓓ Ⓔ
18. Ⓐ Ⓑ Ⓒ Ⓓ Ⓔ	58. Ⓐ Ⓑ Ⓒ Ⓓ Ⓔ	98. Ⓐ Ⓑ Ⓒ Ⓓ Ⓔ
19. Ⓐ Ⓑ Ⓒ Ⓓ Ⓔ	59. Ⓐ Ⓑ Ⓒ Ⓓ Ⓔ	99. Ⓐ Ⓑ Ⓒ Ⓓ Ⓔ
20. Ⓐ Ⓑ Ⓒ Ⓓ Ⓔ	60. Ⓐ Ⓑ Ⓒ Ⓓ Ⓔ	100. Ⓐ Ⓑ Ⓒ Ⓓ Ⓔ
21. Ⓐ Ⓑ Ⓒ Ⓓ Ⓔ	61. Ⓐ Ⓑ Ⓒ Ⓓ Ⓔ	101. Ⓐ Ⓑ Ⓒ Ⓓ Ⓔ
22. Ⓐ Ⓑ Ⓒ Ⓓ Ⓔ	62. Ⓐ Ⓑ Ⓒ Ⓓ Ⓔ	102. Ⓐ Ⓑ Ⓒ Ⓓ Ⓔ
23. Ⓐ Ⓑ Ⓒ Ⓓ Ⓔ	63. Ⓐ Ⓑ Ⓒ Ⓓ Ⓔ	103. Ⓐ Ⓑ Ⓒ Ⓓ Ⓔ
24. Ⓐ Ⓑ Ⓒ Ⓓ Ⓔ	64. Ⓐ Ⓑ Ⓒ Ⓓ Ⓔ	104. Ⓐ Ⓑ Ⓒ Ⓓ Ⓔ
25. Ⓐ Ⓑ Ⓒ Ⓓ Ⓔ	65. Ⓐ Ⓑ Ⓒ Ⓓ Ⓔ	105. Ⓐ Ⓑ Ⓒ Ⓓ Ⓔ
26. Ⓐ Ⓑ Ⓒ Ⓓ Ⓔ	66. Ⓐ Ⓑ Ⓒ Ⓓ Ⓔ	106. Ⓐ Ⓑ Ⓒ Ⓓ Ⓔ
27. Ⓐ Ⓑ Ⓒ Ⓓ Ⓔ	67. Ⓐ Ⓑ Ⓒ Ⓓ Ⓔ	107. Ⓐ Ⓑ Ⓒ Ⓓ Ⓔ
28. Ⓐ Ⓑ Ⓒ Ⓓ Ⓔ	68. Ⓐ Ⓑ Ⓒ Ⓓ Ⓔ	108. Ⓐ Ⓑ Ⓒ Ⓓ Ⓔ
29. Ⓐ Ⓑ Ⓒ Ⓓ Ⓔ	69. Ⓐ Ⓑ Ⓒ Ⓓ Ⓔ	109. Ⓐ Ⓑ Ⓒ Ⓓ Ⓔ
30. Ⓐ Ⓑ Ⓒ Ⓓ Ⓔ	70. Ⓐ Ⓑ Ⓒ Ⓓ Ⓔ	110. Ⓐ Ⓑ Ⓒ Ⓓ Ⓔ
31. Ⓐ Ⓑ Ⓒ Ⓓ Ⓔ	71. Ⓐ Ⓑ Ⓒ Ⓓ Ⓔ	111. Ⓐ Ⓑ Ⓒ Ⓓ Ⓔ
32. Ⓐ Ⓑ Ⓒ Ⓓ Ⓔ	72. Ⓐ Ⓑ Ⓒ Ⓓ Ⓔ	112. Ⓐ Ⓑ Ⓒ Ⓓ Ⓔ
33. Ⓐ Ⓑ Ⓒ Ⓓ Ⓔ	73. Ⓐ Ⓑ Ⓒ Ⓓ Ⓔ	113. Ⓐ Ⓑ Ⓒ Ⓓ Ⓔ
34. Ⓐ Ⓑ Ⓒ Ⓓ Ⓔ	74. Ⓐ Ⓑ Ⓒ Ⓓ Ⓔ	114. Ⓐ Ⓑ Ⓒ Ⓓ Ⓔ
35. Ⓐ Ⓑ Ⓒ Ⓓ Ⓔ	75. Ⓐ Ⓑ Ⓒ Ⓓ Ⓔ	115. Ⓐ Ⓑ Ⓒ Ⓓ Ⓔ
36. Ⓐ Ⓑ Ⓒ Ⓓ Ⓔ	76. Ⓐ Ⓑ Ⓒ Ⓓ Ⓔ	116. Ⓐ Ⓑ Ⓒ Ⓓ Ⓔ
37. Ⓐ Ⓑ Ⓒ Ⓓ Ⓔ	77. Ⓐ Ⓑ Ⓒ Ⓓ Ⓔ	117. Ⓐ Ⓑ Ⓒ Ⓓ Ⓔ
38. Ⓐ Ⓑ Ⓒ Ⓓ Ⓔ	78. Ⓐ Ⓑ Ⓒ Ⓓ Ⓔ	118. Ⓐ Ⓑ Ⓒ Ⓓ Ⓔ
39. Ⓐ Ⓑ Ⓒ Ⓓ Ⓔ	79. Ⓐ Ⓑ Ⓒ Ⓓ Ⓔ	119. Ⓐ Ⓑ Ⓒ Ⓓ Ⓔ
40. Ⓐ Ⓑ Ⓒ Ⓓ Ⓔ	80. Ⓐ Ⓑ Ⓒ Ⓓ Ⓔ	120. Ⓐ Ⓑ Ⓒ Ⓓ Ⓔ

Index

A

Abbasids, 76
Abelard, Peter, 108
Abu Bakr, 76
Acropolis, 32, 41
Adolphus, Gustavus, 145
Aenid, 54
Aeschylus, 36, 37
Afterlife, 8, 10, 11
Agriculture, 4, 86, 139
  irrigation, importance of, 4
  medieval improvements in, 86
  surpluses, and rise of cities, 4
Ahura Mazda, 19
Akkadians, 5–6
Alberti, Leon Battista, 121
Albigensian crusade, 100, 102
Albuquerque, Alfonso de, 135
Alcibiades, 33
Alexander the Great, 18, 41, 42
Alfarabi, 107
Alphabet, 7, 15, 35
Ambrose, 68
Amorites, 6
Anabaptists, 127–128
Ancestor worship, 57
Ancient Greece
  Acropolis, 32, 41
  Alexander the Great, 18, 41, 42
  Archaic Period, 26–27
  architecture, 41, 44
  Aristotle, 40, 43
  art, 40–41, 44
  Athens, 28–30, 32
  citizenship, 33
  classical culture, 34
  colonization by, 26
  cults, 35, 44
  Dark Age, 25–26, 35
  Delian League, 31–32
  democracy, limitations of, 33
  drama, 36–37
  fall to Rome, 49
  geography and the *polis*, 26
  the Hellenistic Age, 22, 41–44
    literature, 35–40
    medicine, 38
    military in, 27
    Parthenon, 32, 41
    Peloponnesian League, 28, 31
    Peloponnesian War, 33–34
    Pericles, 32–33
    Persian wars, 30–31
    Philip of Macedon, 41, 42
    philosophy, 38, 39–40
    Plato, 39–40
    political fragmentation in, 28
    pre-Socratics, 38
    religion, 34–35, 44
    revolution, 26–27
    science and technology, 43
    Socrates, 39
    Sophists, 38
    Sparta, 27–28
    tyrants in, 27
Ancient Near East
  Assyrians, 15, 16–17, 21
  Egypt and the Nile, 8–12
  Fertile Crescent, 3–5
  Hittites, 6, 10, 12, 16
  Jews, 19–22
  Mesopotamia, 5–8
  Minoans, 13–14, 25
  Mycenaeans, 14–15, 25
  Neo-Babylonians, 17, 21–22
  Persians, 17–19
  Phoenicians, 15–16, 35
  Sea Peoples, 13, 15, 20, 25
Ancient Rome
  architecture, 56, 68–69
  art, 55–56
  Augustus Caesar, 52, 54, 64
  "bread and circuses" policy, 53
  Burgundians, 66
  Christianity in, 59–63
  citizenship, 51, 53
  civil war, 51
  classics, imitation and preservation of, 68
  class struggle, 50
  conquests, 49–40

Ancient Rome (continued)
Constantine the Great, 61, 64
Diocletian, 61, 63–64
"Doctors of the Church," 68
emperors, 52–53
the Empire, 52–53, 63–64, 67–68
engineering, 56
Etruscans, rule by, 47
expansion, 48–49
fall of, 69
first triumvirate, 51–52
geography, 47
Germanic invasions, 64–67
the Gracchi, 50
Jews in, 58–59
Julius Caesar, 51–52, 54, 57, 64
law, 55
literature, 53–55
Marius, 50, 51, 64
Pax Romana, 53, 69
public office, 48
Punic Wars, 49
religion, 56–57
the Republic, 47–48
second triumvirate, 52
third century, crisis of, 63
unrest, 50
Angles, 66
Anthropomorphic gods, 7
Antony, Marc, 52, 54
Apostolic succession, 63, 81
Apuleius, 55
Aqueducts, 56
Archilochus, 36
Archimedes, 43
Architecture
in ancient Greece, 41, 44
in ancient Rome, 56, 68–69
baroque, 149
in the Byzantine Empire, 74
and Christianity, 68–69
in Egypt, 11–12
gothic, 114
Italian Renaissance, 121
Romanesque, 113
Arianism, 62
Aristarchus, 43, 146
Aristophanes, 37
Aristotle, 40, 43, 106
Armageddon, 10

Art
in ancient Greece, 40–41, 44
in ancient Rome, 55–56
baroque, 149
in the Byzantine Empire, 74
classicism in, 117
Estruscan, 55–56
medieval, 114
naturalism, 123
oil paints, invention of, 123
Renaissance, 120–122, 123
Assyrians, 15, 16–17, 21
Astrolabes, 109
Astrology, 17
Astronomy, 17, 55, 109, 146–147
Athens
constitutional reforms in, 29
defeat of, 33–34
democratic reforms of Cleisthenes, 30
Draco, 29
empire, 32
origins and early evolution of, 28
ostracism, 30
Solon, 29
tyranny of Peisistratus, 30
Augsburg Confession, 127
Augustine of Hippo, 67–68, 118
Augustus Caesar, 52, 54, 64
Averroes, 106
Avicenna, 107

B

Babylonian Captivity, 17, 21–22
Bacon, Francis, 147
Bacon, Roger, 110
Balance of trade, 140
Balboa, Vasco Núñez de, 136
Bar-Kochba, 58
Benedictine Rule, 79, 83, 89
Beowulf, 110
Bernini, Giovanni, 149
Bible
German translation of, 126
King James Version, 143
origin of the word *Bible*, 16
Vulgate, 68, 79, 104, 124
Black Death, 112–113
Boccaccio, Giovanni, 112
Bodin, Jean, 149
Boethius, 105

"Bonfire of the vanities," 119
Book of the Dead, 11
Bosch, Hieronymus, 123
Botticelli, Sandro, 119
Brahe, Tycho, 147
Brethren of the Common Life, 124
Bronze Age, 4
Brunelleschi, Filippo, 121
Bruni, Leonardo, 118
Burgundians, 66
Buridan, Jean, 110
Byzantine Empire, 73–74

C

Cabot, John, 137
Cabral, Pedro, 136
Caesaropapism, 63
Calendar, in Egypt, 12
Caligula, 53
Calvin, John, 128, 130
Canaanites, 19, 20
Cannons, 141
The Canterbury Tales, 110
Capuchin order, 129
Carmelite order, 129
Carolingians, 78, 79
Carthage, 16, 49
Cartier, Jacques, 137
Cassian, John, 61
Cassiodorus, 106
Castiglione, Baldassare, 122
Cathars, 101
Cathedral schools, 107
Catholic League, 145
Catholic Reformation, 129–130
Cato the Elder, 54
Catullus, 54
Censorship, 130
Cervantes, Miguel de, 148
Chaldeans. *See* Neo-Babylonians
Champlain, Samuel de, 137–138
Charlemagne, 78–79
Chaucer, Geoffrey, 110
Christian humanism, 124–125
Christianity
    Ambrose, 68
    appeal of, 60
    architecture and, 68–69
    Augustine of Hippo, 67–68
    church leadership, 62–63
    conversion of Britain, 79–80
    Crusades, 99–100
    "Doctors of the Church," 68, 82
    early preaching, 59
    Eastern European conversion to, 97
    Edict of Milan, 61
    heresy and orthodoxy, 61–62
    Jerome, 68
    Jesus of Nazareth, 59
    medieval church, 81–84
    monasticism, 61, 83–84
    New Testament, 60
    persecutions, 60
    Stoicism, influence of, 44
    toleration and official status of, 61
Cicero, Marcus Tullius, 54
Cities, rise of, 4
The City of God, 67
Civil humanism, 118
Civilization, 3, 12
Cleisthenes, 30, 32
Cleopatra, 52
Clovis, 77
Cluniacs, 89
Coeur, Jacques, 138
Colonization, 16, 26, 137
Columbus, Christopher, 136
Commerce
    balance of trade, 140
    changing markets, 139
    commodities, 140
    entrepreneurial class, 138–139
    gathering-in system, 139
    guilds, decline of, 139
    inflation, 138
    joint-stock companies, 140
    maritime trade, 13, 88, 122
    mercantilism, 140
    and New World exploration, 138
    by Phoenicians, 15–16
    putting-out system, 139
    regulated companies, 140
Concordat of Worms, 90, 91
The Confessions, 68, 118
Conquistadors, 136
Constantine the Great, 61, 64
Constantinople, founding of, 64, 73
Consubstantiation, doctrine of, 126, 127
Copernicus, Nicholas, 147
Corpus Juris Civilis, 55, 74, 108

Cortez, Hernando, 136
Council of Basel, 105
Council of Chalcedon, 62
Council of Clermont, 99
Council of Constance, 104, 105
Council of Ephesus, 62
Council of Ferrara-Florence, 105
Council of Nicaea, 62
Council of Trent, 129
Counter Reformation. *See* Catholic Reformation
Creation story, 8
Cromwell, Oliver, 144
Cromwell, Thomas, 132
Crusades, 99–100
Cults
    ancient Greece, 35, 44
    of the emperor, ancient Rome, 53, 64
    mystery, ancient Rome, 57
Cuneiform system, 7, 12, 15
Cyrus the Great, 17–18, 22, 31

D

Dante Alighieri, 111
Darius, 18, 31
Decameron, 112
Decius, 61
Deductive reasoning, 147
Defender of the Peace, 109
Defenestration of Prague, 145
Delian League, 31–32
Democritus, 38
Deportation (of Jews), 16, 17
Descartes, René, 147–148
Desert Fathers, 61
De Soto, Hernando, 137
D'Etaples, Jacques Lefevre, 125
Dialogues, 39
Diaspora (Jews), 21, 58–59
Diaz, Bartholomew, 135
Diet of Speyer, 127
Diet of Worms, 125
Diocletian, 61, 63–64
The Divine Comedy, 111
Divine right of kings, 149
"Doctors of the Church," 68
Domesday Book, 93
Dominican order, 103
Donation of Constantine, 82, 118
Donation of Pepin, 78
Don Quixote, 148

Dorians, 25
Double-entry bookkeeping, invention of, 122
Draco, 29
Drake, Sir Francis, 137
Drought, 4
Dürer, Albrecht, 123, 124
Dutch East India/Dutch West India Companies, 140, 144

E

Early modern Europe
    commercial revolutions, 138–140
    Dutch independence, 144
    England, 142–144
    exploration, 135–138
    France, 141–142
    modernity, 149
    nation-states and wars of religion, 141
    Spain, 142
    Thirty Years' War, 144–146
    world-view, 146–149
Earthquakes, 14
Eastern Europe, 97–98
    conversion to Christianity, 97
    the Mongols, 98
    Russia, 98
    Teutonic Knights, 97–98
East India Company (England), 40
Eckhart, Meister, 124
Edict of Milan, 61
Edict of Nantes, 141
Edict of Restitution, 145
Egypt
    afterlife, 8, 10, 11
    Amarna Period, 11
    Archaic period, 8, 9
    architecture in, 11–12
    Assyrian invasion, 17
    calendar in, 12
    dynasties, 8–10
    fall to Rome, 50
    hieroglyphics, 12
    mummification, 9, 10
    Nile River, influence of, 8
    pharaoh in, 9
    pyramids, 9, 11
    religion in, 10–11
    Tutankhamen (King Tut), 11
    writing in, 12
El Cid, 97, 111

Elder Edda, 111
Eleusinian Mysteries, 35
Elgin Marbles, 41
El Greco, 149
Empedocles, 38
Empirical method,147
"Enclosure movement," 139
Encomienda system, 137
Engineering, 7, 56. *See also* Architecture
England
    Angevin Empire, 93
    Anglo-Saxons in, 80, 92
    Civil War, 143, 144, 149
    conversion of to Christianity, 79–80
    Edward III, 95
    Elizabeth I, 129, 142–143
    "enclosure movement," 139
    exploration by, 137
    Germanic invasion of, 80
    Henry II, 93
    Henry VIII, 128–129, 131–132, 137
    Hundred Years' War, 95–96
    literature, 110
    Magna Carta, 93–94
    Norman rule in, 92–93
    Parliament, 94
    Protestant Reformation in, 128–129, 142
    Spanish Armada, defeat of, 143
    the Stuarts, 143–144
    War of the Roses, 131
Engraving, 124
Enlightenment, Age of, 34, 146
Ennius, 53
Entrepreneurial class, growth of, 138
Enuma Elish, 8
Epicureanism, 44
Epicurus, 44
Erasmus, 124
Eratosthenes, 43
Essenes, 58
Etruscans, 47, 55–56
Eucharist, 59, 60, 102, 127
Euclid, 43
Euripides, 37
Europe. *See* Early modern Europe; Eastern
    Europe
Evangelical Union, 145
Exploration, age of
    colonization, 137
    England in, 137

France in, 137–138
Henry the Navigator, 135
naming the New World, 137
the Netherlands in, 137, 138
Portugal in, 135–136
Spain in, 136–137
Eyck, Jan van, 123

F

Fairs, 87
Fall of Rome, 69
Famine, 4, 9, 13, 113, 145
Fawkes, Guy, 143
Fertile Crescent, 3–5
Feudalism, 84–85
Ficino, Marsilio, 119
Filioque controversy, 82–83
Florence, 118–119, 122
Fourth Lateran Council, 102
France
    campaigns in Italy, 131
    Cardinal Richelieu, 141–142
    Edict of Nantes, 141
    exploration by, 137–138
    following the Treaty of Westphalia, 146
    Francis I, 131
    Hugenots, 128, 141
    Hundred Years' War, 95–96
    literature, 110–111
    Louis IX, 95
    Philip II Augustus, 94–95
    Philip IV the Fair, 95
    religious wars, 141
    Renaissance, 130–131
Franciscan order, 103
Franks, 66, 77

G

Galen, 55, 148
Galileo Galilei, 147
Gama, Vasco da, 135
Gathering-in system, 139
Genghis Khan, 98
Gentiles, 22, 59
Geocentric theory, 147
Gerbert of Aurillac, 106, 109, 110
Germanic kingdoms, 77–81
    Anglo-Saxon England, 80
    Carolingians, 78, 79
    Charlemagne, 78–79

Germanic kingdoms (continued)
    Magyars, 80–81
    Merovingians, 77–78
    Saracens, 80
    Vikings, 80
    Visigothic Spain, 77
Germany, 91, 111
Ghibellines, 91
Gilgamesh, 8
Giotto, 114, 121
Gnosticism, 57
The Golden Ass, 55
Golden Bull, 92
Gracchi brothers, (Tiberius and Gaius) 50
Great Interregnum, 91
Great Schism, 103–104
Greek architecture, 41
Greek literature. *See also* Roman Literature
    drama, 36–37
    history, 37–38
    literacy, 35
    philosophy, 38
    poetry, 35, 36
    prose, 37
Gregorian chant, 124
Gregory the Great, 81–82
Groote, Gerard, 124
Grosseteste, Robert, 110
Grotius, Hugo, 149
Guelfs, 91
Guicciardini, Francesco, 122
Guide for the Perplexed, 107
Guilds, 87, 88, 139
Gunpowder Plot, 143
Gutenberg, Johannes, 123

H

Hadrian, 54, 55
Haggia Sophia, 74
Hammer of Witches, 146
Hammurabi's Code, 6
Hanging Gardens, 17
Hannibal, 49
Hanseatic League (Hansa), 88
Hans Holbein the Younger, 123
Hapsburgs, 91–92, 145
Harvey, William, 148
Hebrews. *See* Jews
Heliocentric theory, 146–147
Hellenistic Age, 22, 41–44

Henry the Navigator, 135
Heraclitus, 38
Heresy, 61–62
Heretical movements, 101
Herod, 58
Herodotus, 37
Hesiod, 36
Hieroglyphics, 12
Hipparchus, 43
Hippocrates, 38
Hippocratic Oath, 38
Hittites, 6, 10, 12, 16
Hobbes, Thomas, 149
Hohenstaufen dynasty, 91
Hohenzollern, Albrecht von, 146
Holy Roman Empire, 91–92
Homer, 35–36, 54
Homosexuality, 36
Horace, 54
Hospitallers, 100, 101
Hubris, 36
Hudson, Henry, 138
Hugenots, 128, 141
Humanism, 117–118, 124–125
Hundred Years' War, 95–96, 113
Huns, 66
Hurrians, 6
Hussite Wars, 105
Huss, John, 104–105
Hyksos, 9–10

I

Icelandic literature, 111
Iconoclasm, 82
Ideograms, 7
Iliad, 14, 35–36
Index of Prohibited Books, 130
Inductive reasoning, 147
Inflation, 138
Inquisition, 102, 129–130, 132
Intellectual tradition
    Abelard, Peter, 108
    cathedral schools, 107
    classical scholarship, 118
    colleges and universities, 107–108
    curriculum and specialized studies, 108
    European philosophy, Arabic and Jewish
    influences on, 106–107
    nominalism, 108
    political theory, 108

St. Thomas Aquinas, 108–109
scholasticism, 108
science and technology, 108–109
Twelfth-Century Renaissance, 107
Iron Age, 16
Irrigation, 4
Ishtar Gate, 17
Isidore of Seville, 106
Islam, 74–77
    Abbasids, 76
    conquest, 75
    division of the Muslim world, 76–77
    five pillars of, 75
    Hajj, 75
    Hegira, 75
    Muhammad, 74–75
    Muslim influences on European philosophy,
        106–107
    Sunnites and Shiites, 75–76
    Umayyads, 76
Italy
    architecture, 121
    art, 120–122
    city-states, wars between, 119
    civic humanism, 118
    classical scholarship, 118
    economic innovations, 122–123
    Florence, 118–119
    in the Holy Roman Empire, 91
    humanism, 117–118
    invasions, 120
    Kingdom of Naples, 119
    literature, 111–112, 122
    Papal States, 78, 81, 119
    Renaissance in, 117–123
    Roman conquest of, 119
    Treaty of Lodi, 119–120

J

Jacobite Church, 62
Jacquerie, 113
Jansenism, 148
Jerome, 68
Jesuits (Society of Jesus), 129
Jesus of Nazareth, 59
Jews
    in ancient Rome, 58–59
    Assyrian deportation of, 16, 21
    Babylonian exile of, 17, 21–22
    Diaspora, 22, 58–59

influence of on European philosophy,
    106–107
    kingdoms of Judah and Israel, 19–20
    Luther's treatment of, 126
    monotheism, 20
    patriarchs, 19
    prophets, 20–21
    rebellions by, 58
    return of to Jerusalem, 22
    under Roman rule, 58–59
    social justice, 21
John of Leiden, 128
John of Salisbury, 109
Joint-stock companies, 140
Jugurthine War, 50
Julian, 61
Julius Caesar, 51–52, 54, 57, 64
Justinian, 55, 67, 73
Justinian's Code, 74
Jutes, 66
Juvenal, 55

K

Kassites, 6
Kepler, Johannes, 147
Knox, John, 128

L

Las Casas, Bartolomé de, 137
Law
    Draconian code, 29
    Hammurabi's Code, 6
    Justinian's Code, 74
    Lycurgan code, 27
    Mishnah, 58–59
    Roman contributions to, 55
    Talmud, 59
    Theodosian Code, 55
    Twelve Tables, 48, 55
Leonardo Da Vinci, 121–122
Liberal arts, 105–106
Literature, 148
    ancient Greek, 35–40
    ancient Rome, 53–55
    early modern Europe, 148
    English, 110
    French, 110–111
    German, 111
    Icelandic, 111
    Italian, 111–112, 122

Literature (continued)
  Mesopotamian, 8
  Renaissance, 122
  Spanish, 111
Livy, 54
Lollards, 104
Lombard, Peter, 108
Lombard League, 91
Lorris, Guillaume de, 111
Lucan, 54
Lucretius, 54
Luther, Martin, 125–126, 130
Lycurgan code, 127

M

Maccabees, 58
Machiavelli, Nicolò, 120, 122, 131
Macrobius, 55
Magellan, Ferdinand, 136–137
Magna Carta, 93–94
Magna Graecia, 26
Magyars, 80–81
Maimonides, 107
Manichaeism, 57, 68
Mannerism, 149
Manorialism, 85, 86
Marcus Aurelius, 53, 55, 56, 61, 63, 65, 119
Maritime insurance, 122
Maritime trade, 13, 88
Marius, 50, 51, 64
Marsilius of Padua, 109
Martel, Charles, 78
Martianus Capella, 55, 106
Masada, 58
Massaccio, 121
Mathematics, 7, 38
Mecca, 75
Medes, 17–18
Medici family, 118–119, 122
Medicine, 38, 148
Medieval church, 81–84
  Albigensian crusade, 100, 102
  Avignon papacy, 103
  Benedictine Rule, 83–84
  canons regular, 90
  Cluniacs, 89
  College of Cardinals, 89
  conciliar movement, 104, 105
  conflicts with the Greeks, 82

Council of Clermont, 99
  the Crusades, 99–100
  decline of the papacy, 103
  Diocesan structure, 81
  Donation of Constantine, 82
  filioque controversy, 82–83
  Fourth Lateran Council, 102–103
  Great Schism, 103–104
  Greek philosophy in, 34
  Gregorian reforms, 90
  Gregory the Great, 81–82
  heretical movements, 101, 104–105
  iconoclasm, 82
  Inquisition, 102
  investiture controversy, 90
  monasticism, 83–84
  papacy, 81, 89, 98–99, 102
  peace movements, 84
  religious orders, 100–101, 103
  renewal of, 88–89
Megiddon, 10
Mendicant orders, 103
Mercantilism, 140
Merchant guilds, 87
Merovingians, 77–78
Mesopotamia, 5–8
  Akkadians, 5–6
  Amorites, 6
  cuneiform system in, 7, 12
  engineering in, 7
  Hittites, 6
  Hurrians, 6
  Kassites, 6
  literature in, 8
  mathematics in, 7
  religion in, 7–8
  slavery in, 6
  Sumer, 5
  Ur, Third Dynasty of, 6
Metamorphoses, 54
Michelangelo Buonarroti, 119, 121, 122
Middle ages
  agricultural improvements, 86
  architecture, 113–114
  art, 114
  Black Death, 112–113
  Byzantine Empire, 73–74, 77
  centralized monarchies, rise of, 90–91
  church in, 81–84, 88–90, 98–105

Crusades, 99–100
cultural tradition, 105–106
Eastern Europe, 97–98
England, 92–94
feudalism and manorialism, 84–86
France, 94–95
Germanic kingdoms, 77–81
Holy Roman Empire, 91–92
Hundred Years' War, 95–96
intellectual tradition, 106–110
Islam in, 74–77
literature, 110–112
Plato and Aristotle in, 106
population growth, 86–87
social opportunities, 86–87
Spain, 96–97
trade and towns, 87–88
vernacular tradition, 110–112
Military religious orders, 100
Minoans, 13–14, 25
Minutius, Aldus, 123
Missionaries, 129
Mithraism, 44, 57, 60
Modern Devotion, 124
Monasticism, 61, 83–84
Money lending, 122
Monfort, Simon de, 94
Mongols, 98
Monophysitism, 62, 73, 75
Monotheism, 11, 20, 29
Montaigne, Michel de, 148
More, Thomas, 124, 129
Moriscos, 132, 142
Movable type, invention of, 123
Muhammad, 74, 75
Mummification, 9, 10
Mycenaeans, 14–15, 25
Mystery cults, 57

N

Naples, Kingdom of, 119–120
Nationalism, rise of, 140
Naturalism, 123
Near East. *See* Ancient Near East
Nebuchadnezzar II, 17
Neo-Babylonians, 17, 21–22
Neolithic Age, 4
Neoplatonism, 57–58, 61, 68, 105
Nero, 53, 60, 62

Nestorianism, 62
Netherlands
    exploration by, 137, 138
    independence from Spain, 142, 144
New Rome, 64
New Testament, 60
Nicene Creed, 62, 82
Nile River, influence of on Egypt, 8
Nomadism, 4
Nomarchs, 9
Nominalism, 108, 109

O

Ockham's Razor, 109, 147
Octavian, 52
Odoacer, 66
Odyssey, 35–36
Old Babylonian Dynasty. *See* Amorites
Old Testament, 60
On Christian Liberty, 126
Oresme, Nicole, 110
Orthodoxy, 61–62
Ostracism, 30
Ostrogoths, 66
Ottoman Empire, 130
Ovid, 54

P

Paganism, 22
Paleolithic Age, 4
Palestine, 20
Pantheon, 56
Papacy
    apostolic succession and, 62
    in Avignon, 103
    College of Cardinals, 89
    decline of, 103
    Great Schism, 103–104
    Gregorian reforms, 90
    indulgences, sale of, 125
    Innocent III, 102
    investiture controversy, 90
    Medici influence on, 119, 122, 125
    papal monarchy, 98–99
    reform of, 89
Papal States
    creation of, 78
    rise of, 81
    Treaty of Lodi, 119

Paper, invention of, 110
Papyrus, 12
Paracelsus, Philippus, 148
Parthenon, 41
Parzifal, 111
Pascal, Blaine, 148
Patriarchs, 19
Pax Romana, 53, 69
Peace of Augsburg, 127, 144, 146
Peasant Revolt (1525), 126, 128
Peisistratus, 30
Peloponnesian League, 28, 31
Peloponnesian War, 33–34
"People of the Book," 75
Pericles, 32–33
Persian Empire, 17–19
   conquest by Alexander the Great, 18
   conquest of the Medes by, 18
   under Cyrus the Great, 17–18, 22, 31
   under Darius, 18, 31
   expansion, 18
   religion in, 18, 19
   wars with Greece, 30–31
   under Xerxes, 18, 31
   Zoroastrianism, 19
Persius, 55
Petrarch, Francesco, 117–118
Petronius, 55
Pharaoh, defined, 9
Pharisees, 58
Philip of Macedon, 41, 42
Philistines, 20
Philosophy, ancient Greece, 38, 39–40
Phoenicians, 15–16, 35
Phonetic symbols, 7
Pico della Mirandola, 122
Pictographs, 7, 12
Pieter Bruegel the Elder, 123
Pindar, 36
Pizarro, Francisco, 136
Plague. *See* Black Death
Plato, 39–40, 106
Plautus, 54
Poetry
   in ancient Greece, 35, 36
   in ancient Rome, 53–54
Polo, Marco, 112
Polygamy, 128
Polytheism
   in ancient Greece, 34

   in ancient Rome, 56
   in Egypt, 10
   in Persia, 19
Pompey, 51, 58
Pontifex Maximus, 57
Porphyry, 57
Portugal, exploration by, 135–136
Predestination, doctrine of, 128
Prehistory, 5
Pre-Socratics, 38
The Prince, 120
Printing press, invention of, 123
Probability theory, 148
Proclus, 57
Procopius, 74
Prophets, 20–21
Protestant Reformation
   Diet of Speyer, 127
   diversification of Protestantism, 127–129
   in England, 128–129
   Martin Luther, 125–126
   Ninety-Five Theses, 125
   Peasant Revolt (a525), 126
   religious fighting, 127
   Renaissance papacy, 125
   sale of indulgences, 125
Protestants, origin of the term, 127
Ptolemy, 55, 147
Punic Wars, 49
Putting-out system, 139
Pyramids, 9, 11
Pythagoras, 38

Q

Quran, 75

R

Rabelais, Francois, 148
Raleigh, Sir Walter, 137
Raphael, 121
Rationalism, 147
Realism, 109
Reformation. *See* Catholic Reformation; Protestant Reformation
Regulated companies, 140
Religion. *See also* Christianity; Islam
   ancient Greece, 34–35, 44
   ancient Rome, 56–57
   in the Byzantine Empire, 73–74
   cannons, 141

in Egypt, 10–11
Jews, 20
in Mesopotamia, 7–8
nationalism and, 141
in Persia, 18, 19
wars of in early modern Europe, 141
witch craze, 146
Zoroastrianism, 19
Rembrandt, 149
Renaissance
Carolingian, 79, 107
Catholic Reformation, 129–130
Christian humanism, 124–125
defined, 117
Greek culture, celebration of, 34
in Italy, 117–123
new monarchies, 130–132
in northern Europe, 123–124
papacy during, 11, 125
Protestant Reformation, 125–129
Twelfth Century, 107
"Renaissance Man," 122
Republic, 39
Reuchlin, Johannes, 125
Richelieu, Cardinal, 141–142, 145
The Romance of the Rose, 111
Roman Inquisition, 129–130
Roman literature. *See also* Ancient Rome;
Greek Literature
early poetry and drama, 53–54
Golden Age, 54
prose, 54
Silver Age, 54–55
Romulus Augustulus, 67
Rubens, Peter Paul, 149
Rule of St. Augustine, 90
Russia, 98

S

Sacrifice, 8
Sadduccees, 58
St. Bartholomew's Day Massacre, 141
St. Benedict, 83–84
St. Dominic Guzman, 103
St. Francis of Assisi, 103
St. Patrick, 80
St. Paul, 59, 60
St. Peter, 62
St. Thomas Aquinas, 108–109
Saladin, 99

Salutati, Coluccio, 118
Sappho of Lesbos, 36
Saracens, 80
Sargon, 5–6, 8
Savonarola, Girolamo, 119
Saxons, 66
Schmalkaldic League, 127
Scholasticism, 108
Scientific Revolution, 146
Script, 114
Sea Peoples, 13, 15, 20, 25
Seneca, 54
Servetus, Michael, 128, 148
Sforza, Francesco, 119
Shakespeare, William, 148
Silk Road, 112
Skepticism, 44
Slaves
in ancient Greece, 26
as a commodity, 140
Jews in Egypt, 19
in Mesopotamia, 6
revolt of led by Spartacus, 50
Small Catechism, 126
Socrates, 39
Solon, 29
The Song of Roland, 110
Sophists, 38
Sophocles, 36–37
Spain
Armada, defeat of, 143
Charles I, 132
colonization by, 137
exploration by, 136–137
Ferdinand and Isabella, 132, 136
literature, 111
Phillip II, 132, 142
Reconquista, 96–97, 111
Renaissance in, 132
Spanish Inquisition, 130, 132
Sparta, 27–28
government, 28
Peloponnesian League, 28, 31
society, 27–28
Sphinxes, 11
Stoicism, 44, 54, 57
Strassburg, Gottfried von, 111
Sturluson, Snorri, 111
Subinfeudation, 85
Sumer, 5

Summa Theologiae, 108
Syllabary, 7, 13
Syncretism, 10, 56

T

Tacitus, 54
Talmud, 59
Tariffs, 140
Templars, 100–101
Ten Commandments, 20–21
Ten Lost Tribes of Israel, 16, 20, 21
Terence, 54
Terrorism, 16
Tetzel, Johann, 125
Teutonic knights, 97–98, 101
Thales of Miletus, 38
Theatines, 129
Themistocles, 31
Theocracy, 9
Theodora, 73
Theodosian Code, 55
Theodosius, 68
Theodosius II, 55
Thirty-Nine Articles (England), 142
Thirty Years' War, 144–146
Thomas à Kempis, 124
Thomism, 109
Thucydides, 37–38
Tiberius, 54, 59
Tidal waves, 14
Timaeus, 40
Towns, rise of, 87
Transubstantiation, doctrine of, 109, 126, 127
Treaty of Lodi, 119–120
Treaty of Mersen, 79
Treaty of Tordesillas, 136
Treaty of Verdun, 79
Treaty of Westphalia, 144, 146
Tristan and Isolt, 111
Twelfth-Century Renaissance, 107
Twelve Tables code of laws, 48
Tyler, Wat, 113
Tyrants, 27, 30

U

Umayyads, 76
Unemployment, Middle Ages, 113
Universities, Middle Ages, 107–108
Ur, 6
Ursuline order, 129

V

Valla, Lorenzo, 82, 118
Vandals, 66
Vasari, Giorgio, 122
Velazquez, Diego de, 149
Venerable Bede, 80
Vesalius, Andreas, 148
Vespucci, Amerigo, 137
Vikings, 80
Virgil, 54, 112
Visigoths, 65–66, 77
Volcanoes, 14
Vulgate, 68, 79, 104, 124

W

Waldensians, 101
Waldseemüller, Martin, 137
Weyden, Rogier van der, 123
Witch Craze, 146
Wolfram von Eschenbach, 111
Wolsey, Cardinal Thomas, 131–132
Women
    in ancient Greece, 33
    Christianity and, 60
    homosexuality, 36
    in Sparta, 27–28
Writing, 4, 5, 12
Wycliffe, John, 104

X

Xerxes, 18, 31

Y

Yahweh, 19, 20, 22
Younger Edda, 111

Z

Zealots, 58
Ziggurats, 7
Zoroastrianism, 19
Zwingli, Ulrich, 127